Kershaw's Brigade
Volume 2

Kershaw's Brigade
Volume 2

South Carolina's Regiments in the American Civil War:
at the Wilderness, Cold Harbor, Petersburg, the Shenandoah Valley & Cedar Creek

D. Augustus Dickert

Kershaw's Brigade Volume 2: South Carolina's Regiments
in the American Civil War—at the Wilderness, Cold Harbor,
Petersburg, the Shenandoah Valley & Cedar Creek
by D. Augustus Dickert

Originally published under the title
The History of Kershaw's Brigade

Published by Leonaur Ltd

Material original to this edition and its publication in this form
copyright © 2006 Leonaur Ltd

ISBN (10 digit): 1-84677-110-2 (hardcover)
ISBN (13 digit): 978-1-84677-110-1 (hardcover)

ISBN (10 digit): 1-84677-108-0 (softcover)
ISBN (13 digit): 978-1-84677-108-8 (softcover)

http://www.leonaur.com

Note to the 2006 Edition

We would ask readers to remember that this book necessarily reflects the attitudes of a sector of American society at the time in which it was written. We in no way endorse the views of the author when he expresses his beliefs regarding the nature and status of African Americans and in re-publishing this book we had to decide whether to amend such references to make them more palatable to modern readers. After much consideration our final decision was that historical accuracy would be best served by leaving them as originally published. We hope this decision does not cause offence.

Contents

In Winter Quarters 7
In Camp on the Holston 14
Battle of the Wilderness 21
To North Anna 33
From North Anna to Cold Harbor 42
From Cold Harbor to Petersburg 53
In the Trenches Around Petersburg 64
Leaving the Shenandoah Valley 95
Reminiscences of the Valley 103
The Second Valley Campaign 114
Battle of Cedar Creek or Fisher's Hill 121
Leaving the Valley for the Last Time 145
Peace Conference 162
The Return Home 169
On the Saltkahatchie 181
March Through South Carolina 187
The Surrender 199
Retrospect 205
Appendices 209

CHAPTER 27

In Winter Quarters

Christmas came as usual to the soldiers as to the rest of the world, and if Longstreet's men did not have as "merry and happy" a Christmas as those at home, and in the armies outside, they had at least a cheerful one. Hid away in the dark and mysterious recesses of the houses of many old Unionists, was yet a plentitude of "moon-shine," and this the soldiers drew out, either by stealth or the eloquent pleadings of a faded Confederate bill. Poultry abounded in the far away sections of the country, not yet ravaged by either army, which it was a pleasure to those fixtures of the army called "foragers" to hunt up. The brotherhood of "foragers" was a peculiar institute, and some men take as naturally to it as the duck to water. They have an eye to business, as well as pleasure, and the life of a "forager" becomes almost an art. They have a peculiar talent, developed by long practice of nosing out, hunting up, and running to quarry anything in the way of "eatables or drinkables." During the most stringent times in a country that had been over-run for years by both armies, some men could find provisions and delicacies, and were never known to be without "one drink left" in their canteens for a needy comrade, who had the proper credentials, the Confederate "shin-plaster." These foragers had the instinct (or acquired it) and the gifts of a "knight of the road" of worming out of the good housewife little dainties, cold meats, and stale bread, and if there was one drop of the "oh be joyful" in the house, these men of peculiar intellect would be sure to get it. So with such an acquisition to the army, and in such a country as East Tennessee, the soldiers did not suffer on that cold Christmas day. Bright and cheerful fires burned before every tent, over which hung a turkey, a chicken, or a choice slice of Tennessee pork, or, perhaps, better still, a big, fat sausage, with which the smoke-houses along the valleys of the French Broad were filled.

It was my misfortune, or rather good fortune, to be doing picket duty on the Holston on that day. Here I had an adventure rather out of the regular order in a soldier's life, one more suited to the character of Don Quixote. I, as commandant of the post, had strict orders not to allow anyone to cross the river, as "beyond the Alps lie Italy," beyond the Holston lay the enemy. But soldiers, like other men, have their trials. While on duty here a buxom, bouncing, rosy cheeked mountain lass came up, with a sack of corn on her shoulder, and demanded the boat in order that she might cross over to a mill and exchange her corn for meal. This, of course, I had to reluctantly deny, however gallantly disposed I might otherwise have been. The lass asked me, with some feeling of scorn, "Is the boat yours?" to which I was forced to answer in the negative. She protested that she would not go back and get a permit or pass from anyone on earth; that the boat was not mine, and she had as much right to its use as anyone, and that no one should prevent her from getting bread for her family, and that "you have no business here at best," arguments that were hard to controvert in the face of a firey young "diamond in the rough." So to compromise matters and allow chivalry to take, for the time being, the place of duty, I agreed to ferry her over myself. She placed her corn in the middle of the little boat, planting herself erect in the prow; I took the stern. The weather was freezing cold, the wind strong, and the waves rolled high, the little boat rocking to and fro, while I battled with the strong current of the river. Once or twice she cast disdainful glances at my feeble and emaciated form, but at last, in a melting tone, she said: "If you can't put the boat over, get up and give me the oar." This taunt made me strong, and the buxom mountain girl was soon at the mill. While awaiting the coming of the old miller, I concluded to take a stroll over the hill in search of further adventure. There I found, at a nice old-fashioned farm house, a bevy of the prettiest young ladies it had been my pleasure to meet in a long while—buoyant, vivacious, cultured, and loyal to the core. They did not wait very long to tell me that they were "Rebels to the bone." They invited me and any of my friends that I chose to come over the next day and take dinner with them, an invitation I was not loath nor slow to accept. My mountain acquaintance was rowed back over the Holston in due season, without any of the parting scenes that fiction delight in, and the next day, armed with passports, my friends and myself were at the old farm house early. My companions were Colonel Rutherford, Dr. James Evans, Lieutenant Hugh Farley, Captains Nance, Cary, and Watts, with Adjutant Pope as our chaperone.

Words fail me here in giving a description of the dinner, as well as of the handsome young ladies that our young hostess had invited from the surrounding country to help us celebrate.

Now will any reader of this question the fact that Longstreet's men suffered any great hardships, isolated as they were from the outside world? This is but a sample of our sufferings. We had night parties at the houses of the high and the low, dinners in season and out of season, and not an enemy outside of the walls of Knoxville. Did we feel the cold? Did the frozen ground cut our feet through our raw-hide moccasins? Did any of the soldiers long for home or the opening of the next campaign? Bah!

It was during our stay in winter quarters, March, 1864, that the term of our second enlistment expired. The troops had volunteered for twelve months at the commencement of the war; this expiring just before the seven days' battle around Richmond, a re-enlistment and reorganization was ordered in the spring of 1862 for two more years, making the term of Kershaw's Brigade equal with other troops that had enlisted for "three years or the war." By an Act of Congress, in 1862, all men between the ages of eighteen and thirty-five years were compelled to bear arms. This had been extended first to forty and then to forty-five and during Grant's memorable campaign against Richmond, the ages ran from sixteen to fifty-five, though those between sixteen and eighteen and those between fifty and fifty-five were to be used only in State service. This brought out the expression of Grant to the authorities in Washington, that "Lee had robbed the cradle and the grave." Our re-enlistment was only a form, no change in officers or organization. Some few failed to voluntarily re-enlist, not with any view to quit the army, but some had grown weary of the hard marches of the infantry service and wished to join the cavalry. However, when the morning came for re-enlistment the troops were called out in line of regiments and a call made by the Colonel to all who were willing to enlist for the war to step two paces to the front. All, with the very fewest exceptions, stepped proudly to the front. Of course, none were permitted to leave his company for the cavalry, as that branch of the service was yet filled to its full quota, its ranks had in no discernable degree been depleted by the casualties of war. It seemed that fortune favored our troopers, for battle as they would, none were scarcely ever wounded, and a less number killed. Infantry soldiers were furloughed, through wounds, by the thousands, and artillerymen by the hundreds, after every great battle, but the cavalryman was denied this luxury, and his only hope in a furlough was a short leave of absence to replace a wornout horse that had fallen by the wayside. Their ranks of furloughed men in this line were usually quite full.

As for returning to their homes, no soldier, however humble his station, either in the army or socially at home, would have dared to leave the service had a discharge been offered him. A man in good health and with stout limbs preferred facing bullets and even death, rather than bracing the scorn and contempt the women of the South had for the man who failed his country when his services were needed. No man, however brave, would have had the hardihood to meet his wife or mother unless "with his shield or on it" in this hour of his country's need. There were some few exemptions in the conscript law; one particularly was where all the men in a neighborhood had gone or was ordered to the front, one old man to five plantations, on which were slaves, was exempted to look after said farms, manage the negroes, and collect the government taxes or tithes. These tithes were one-tenth of all that was raised on a plantation—cotton, corn, oats, peas, wheat, potatoes, sorghum, etc.—to be delivered to a government agent, generally a disabled soldier, and by him forwarded to the army.

During the winter most of the vacancies in company and field officers were filled by promotion, according to rank. In most cases, the office of Third Lieutenant was left to the choice of the men, in pursuance to the old Democratic principle, "government by the will of the people." Non-commissioned officers usually went up by seniority, where competent, the same as the commissioned officers.

All these vacancies were occasioned by the casualties of war during the Pennsylvania, Chickamauga, and Knoxville campaigns. The Seventh, Fifteenth, and Third Battalion were without field officers. Captain Huggins was placed in command of the Seventh, and Captain Whiter, the Third Battalion. No promotions could be made in the latter, as Major Miller and Colonel Rice had not resigned, although both were disabled for active service in consequence of wounds.

There was considerable wrangling in the Fifteenth over the promotion to the Colonelcy. Captain F.S. Lewie, of Lexington, claimed it by seniority of rank, being senior Captain in the regiment. Captain J.B. Davis, of Fairfield, claimed it under an Act of the Confederate Congress in regard to the rank of old United States officers entering the Confederate service—that the officers of the old army should hold their grade and rank in the Confederate Army, the same as before their joining the South, irrespective of the date of these commissions issued by the war department. Or, in other words, a Lieutenant in the United States Army should not be given a commission over a Captain, or a Captain, over a Major, Lieutenant Colonel, or Colonel, etc., in the Southern Army. As all the old army officers entering the service of the South at different periods, and all wanted a Generalship, so this mode of ranking was adopted, as promising greater harmony and better results. Captain Davis had been a Captain in the State service, having commanded a company in Gregg's six months' troops around Charleston. And, furthermore, Davis was a West Pointer—a good disciplinarian, brave, resolute, and an all round good officer. Still Lewie was his peer in every respect, with the exception of early military training. Both were graduates of medical colleges—well educated, cultured, and both high-toned gentlemen of the "Old School." But Lewie was subject to serious attacks of a certain disease, which frequently incapacitated him for duty, and on marches he was often unable to walk, and had to be hauled for days in the ambulance. Then Lewie's patriotism was greater than his ambition, and he was willing to serve in any position for the good of the service and for the sake of harmony. Captain Lewie thus voluntarily yielded his just claims to the Colonelcy to Captain Davis, and accepted the position of Lieutenant Colonel, places both filled to the end.

Colonel J. B. Davis

Colonel J.B. Davis was born in Fairfield County, of Scotch-Irish decent, about the year 1835. He received his early education in the schools of the country, at Mount Zion Academy, at Winnsboro, in same county. Afterwards he was admitted to the United States Military School, at West Point, but after remaining for two years, resigned and commenced the study of medicine. He graduated some years before the war, and entered upon the practice of his profession in the western part of the county. He was elected Captain of the first company raised in Fairfield, and served in Gregg's first six mouths' volunteers in Charleston. After the fall of Sumter, his company, with several others, disbanded.

Returning home, he organized a company for the Confederate service, was elected Captain, and joined the Fifteenth Regiment, then forming in Columbia under Colonel DeSaussure. He was in all the battles of the Maryland campaign, in the brigade under General Drayton, and in all the great battles with Kershaw's Brigade. In the winter of 1863 he was made Colonel of the Fifteenth, and served with his regiment until the surrender. On several occasions he was in command of the brigade, as senior Colonel present. He was in command at Cold Harbor after the death of Colonel Keitt. Colonel Davis was one among the best tacticians in the command; had a soldierly appearance—tall, well-developed, a commanding voice, and an all round good officer.

He returned home after the war and began the practice of medicine, and continues it to the present.

Colonel F. S. Lewie

Colonel F.S. Lewie was born in Lexington County, in 1830, and received his early training there. He attended the High School at Monticello, in Fairfield County. He taught school for awhile, then began the study of medicine. He attended the "College of Physicians and Surgeons" in Paris, France, for two years, returning a short while before the breaking out of hostilities between the North and South.

At the outbreak of the war he joined Captain Gibbs' Company, and was made Orderly Sergeant. He served with that company, under Colonel Gregg, in the campaign against Sumter. His company did not disband when the fort fell, but followed Gregg to Virginia. At the expiration of their term of enlistment he returned to Lexington County, raised a company, and joined the Fifteenth. He was in most of the battles in which that regiment was engaged. Was promoted to Lieutenant Colonel, and in 1864 was elected to the State Senate from Lexington. He refused to leave his regiment, and did not accept the honor conferred upon him by the people of his county. While with his regiment in South Carolina, early in the spring of 1865, he was granted a few days' furlough to visit his home, at which smallpox had broken out, but was captured by Sherman's raiders before reaching home. He was parolled in North Carolina.

He was elected to the Legislature in 1866, serving until reconstruction. He died in 1877.

There was never a Major appointed afterwards in the Fifteenth.

About the last of January we had another little battle scare, but it failed to materialize. General Longstreet had ordered a pontoon bridge from Richmond, and had determined upon a descent upon Knoxville. But the authorities at Washington having learned of our preparation to make another advance, ordered General Thomas to reinforce General Foster with his corps, take command in person, and to drive Longstreet "beyond the confines of East Tennessee." The enemy's cavalry was thrown forward, and part of Longstreet's command having been ordered East, the movement was abandoned; the inclemency of the weather, if no other cause, was sufficient to delay operations. Foster being greatly reinforced, and Longstreet's forces reduced by a part of his cavalry going to join Johnston in Georgia, and a brigade of infantry ordered to reinforce Lee, the commanding General determined to retire higher up the Holston, behind a mountain chain, near Bull's Gap.

On the 22nd of February we quit our winter quarters, and took up our march towards Bull's Gap, and after a few days of severe marching we were again snugly encamped behind a spur of the mountain, jutting out from the Holston and on to the Nolachucky River. A vote of thanks from the Confederate States Congress was here read to the troops:

"Thanking Lieutenant General James Longstreet and the officers and men of his command for their patriotic services and brilliant achievements in the present war, sharing as they have the arduous fatigues and privations of many campaigns in Virginia, Maryland, Pennsylvania, Georgia, and Tennessee," etc.

CHAPTER 28

In Camp on the Holston

While Longstreet's Corps had done some of the most stubborn fighting, and the results, as far as victories in battle were concerned, were all that could be expected, still it seemed, from some faults of the Generals commanding departments, or the war department in Richmond, that the fruits of such victories were not what the country or General Longstreet expected. To merely hold our own, in the face of such overwhelming numbers, while great armies were springing up all over the North, was not the true policy of the South, as General Longstreet saw and felt it. We should go forward and gain every inch of ground lost in the last campaign, make all that was possible out of our partial successes, drive the enemy out of our country wherever he had a foot-hold, otherwise the South would slowly but surely crumble away. So much had been expected of Longstreet's Corps in East Tennessee, and so little lasting advantage gained, that bickering among the officers began. Brigadier Generals were jealous of Major Generals, and even some became jealous or dissatisfied with General Longstreet himself. Crimination and recrimination were indulged in, censures and charges were made and denied, and on the whole the army began to be in rather a bad plight for the campaign just commencing. Had it not been for the unparalleled patriotism and devotion to their cause, the undaunted courage of the rank and file of the army, little results could have been expected. But as soon as the war cry was heard and the officers and men had sniffed the fumes of the coming battle, all jealousies and animosities were thrown aside, and each and every one vied with the other as to who could show the greatest prowess in battle, could withstand the greatest endurance on marches and in the camp.

General Law, who commanded an Alabama Brigade, had been arrested and courtmartialed for failing to support General Jenkins at a critical moment, when Burnside was about to be entrapped, just before reaching Knoxville. It was claimed by his superiors that had Law closed up the gaps, as he had been ordered, a great victory would have been gained, but it was rumored that Law said "he knew this well enough, and could have routed the enemy, but Jenkins would have had the credit," so that he sacrificed his men, endangered the army, and lost an opportunity for brilliant achievements through jealousy of a brother officer. Much correspondence ensued between General Longstreet and President Davis, and as usual with the latter, he interfered, and had not the Wilderness campaign commenced so soon, serious trouble would have been the result between General Lee and General Longstreet on one side, and President Davis and the war department on the other. But General Law never returned to our army, and left with any but an ennobling reputation.

General Robertson, commanding Hood's old Texas Brigade, was arrested for indulging in mutinous conversation with his subaltern officers, claiming, it was said, that should General Longstreet give him certain orders (while in camp around Lookout Mountain), he would not recognize them, unless written, and then only under protest. He was relieved by General Gregg.

General McLaws was relieved of his command from a want of confidence in General Longstreet, and more especially for his inactivity and tardiness at the assaults on Fort Sanders, at Knoxville. On ordinary occasions, General McLaws was active and vigilant enough—his courage could not be doubted. He and the troops under him had added largely to the name and fame of the Army of Northern Virginia. He had officers and men under him who were the "flower of chivalry" of the South, and were really the "Old Guard" of Lee's Army. McLaws was a graduate of West Point, and had seen service in Mexico and on the plains of the West. But General McLaws was not the man for the times—not the man to command such troops as he had—was not the officer to lead in an active, vigorous campaign, where all depended on alertness and dash. He was too cautious, and as such, too slow. The two Georgia brigades, a Mississippi brigade, and a South Carolina brigade, composed mostly of the first volunteers from their respective States, needed as a commander a hotspur like our own J.B. Kershaw. While the army watched with sorrow and regret the departure of our old and faithful General, one who had been with us through so many scenes of trials, hardships, and bloodshed, whose name had been so identified with that of our own as to be almost a part of it, still none could deny that the change was better for the service and the Confederacy.

One great trouble with the organization of our army was that too many old and incompetent officers of the old regular army commanded it. And the one idea that seemed to haunt the President was that none but those who had passed through the great corridors and halls of West Point could command armies or men—that civilians without military training were unfit for the work at hand—furthermore, he had favorites, that no failures or want of confidence by the men could shake his faith in as to ability and Generalship. What the army needed was young blood—no old army fossils to command the hot-blooded, dashing, enthusiastic volunteers, who could do more in their impetuosity with the bayonet in a few moments than in days and months of manoeuvering, planning, and fighting battles by rules or conducting campaigns by following the precedent of great commanders, but now obsolete.

When the gallant Joe Kershaw took the command and began to feel his way for his Major General's spurs, the division took on new life. While the brigade was loath to give him up, still they were proud of their little "Brigadier," who had yet to carve out a name for himself on the pillars of fame, and write his achievements high up on the pages of history in the campaign that was soon to begin.

It seems from contemporaneous history that President Davis was baiting between two opinions, either to have Longstreet retire by way of the mountains and relieve the pressure against Johnston, now in command of Bragg's Army, or to unite with Lee and defend the approaches to Richmond.

A counsel of war was held in Richmond between the President, General Bragg as the military advisor of his Excellency, General Lee, and General Longstreet, to form some plan by which Grant might be checked or foiled in the general grand advance he was preparing to make along the whole line. The Federal armies of Mississippi and Alabama had concentrated in front of General Johnston and were gradually pressing him back into Georgia.

Grant had been made commander in chief of all the armies of the North, with headquarters with General Meade, in front of Lee, and he was bending all his energies, his strategies, and boldness in his preparations to strike Lee a fatal blow.

At this juncture Longstreet came forward with a plan—bold in its conception; still bolder in its execution, had it been adopted—that might have changed the face, if not the fate, of the Confederacy. It was to strip all the forts and garrisons in South Carolina and Georgia, form an army of twenty-five thousand men, place them under Beauregard at Charleston, board the train for Greenville, S.C.; then by the overland route through the mountain passes of North Carolina, and by way of Aberdeen, Va.; then to make his way for Kentucky; Longstreet to follow in Beauregard's wake or between him and the Federal Army, and by a shorter line, join Beauregard at some convenient point in Kentucky; Johnston to flank Sherman and march by way of Middle Tennessee, the whole to avoid battle until a grand junction was formed by all the armies, somewhere near the Ohio River; then along the Louisville Railroad, the sole route of transportation of supplies for the Federal Army, fight a great battle, and, if victorious, penetrate into Ohio, thereby withdrawing Sherman from his intended "march to the sea," relieving Lee by weakening Grant, as that General would be forced to succor the armies forming to meet Beauregard.

This, to an observer at this late hour, seems to have been the only practical plan by which the downfall of the Confederacy could have been averted. However, the President and his cabinet decided to continue the old tactics of dodging from place to place, meeting the hard, stubborn blows of the enemy, only waiting the time, when the South, by mere attrition, would wear itself out.

About the 10th of April, 1864, we were ordered to strike tents and prepare to move on Bristol, from thence to be transported to Virginia. All felt as if we were returning to our old home, to the brothers we had left after the bloody Gettysburg campaign, to fight our way back by way of Chickamauga and East Tennessee. We stopped for several days at Charlottesville, and here had the pleasure of visiting the home of the great Jefferson. From thence, down to near Gordonsville.

The 29th of April, 1864, was a gala day for the troops of Longstreet's Corps, at camp near Gordonsville. They were to be reviewed and inspected by their old and beloved commander, General R.E. Lee. Everything possible that could add to our looks and appearances was done to make an acceptable display before our commander in chief. Guns were burnished and rubbed up, cartridge boxes and belts polished, and the brass buttons and buckles made to look as bright as new. Our clothes were patched and brushed up, so far as was in our power, boots and shoes greased, the tattered and torn old hats were given here and there "a lick and a promise," and on the whole I must say we presented not a bad-looking body of soldiers. Out a mile or two was a very large old field, of perhaps one hundred acres or more, in which we formed in double columns. The artillery stationed on the flank fired thirteen guns, the salute to the commander in chief, and as the old warrior rode out into the opening, shouts went up that fairly shook the earth. Hats and caps flew high in the air, flags dipped and waved to and fro, while the drums and fifes struck up "Hail to the Chief." General Lee lifted his hat modestly from his head in recognition of the honor done him, and we know the old commander's heart swelled with emotion at this outburst of enthusiasm by his old troops on his appearance. If he had had any doubts before as to the loyalty of his troops, this old "Rebel yell" must have soon dispelled them. After taking his position near the centre of the columns, the command was broken in columns of companies and marched by him, each giving a salute as it passed. It took several hours to pass in review, Kershaw leading with his division, Jenkins following. The line was again formed, when General Lee and staff, with Longstreet and his staff, rode around the troops and gave them critical inspection. No doubt Lee was then thinking of the bloody day that was soon to come, and how well these brave, battle-scarred veterans would sustain the proud prestige they had won.

Returning to our camp, we were put under regular discipline—drilling, surgeon's call-guards, etc. We were being put in active fighting trim and the troops closely kept in camp. All were now expecting every moment the summons to the battlefield. None doubted the purpose for which we were brought back to Virginia, and how well Longstreet's Corps sustained its name and reputation the Wilderness and Spottsylvania soon showed. Our ranks had been largely recruited by the return of furloughed men, and young men attaining eighteen years of age. After several months of comparative rest in our quarters in East Tennessee, nothing but one week of strict camp discipline was required to put us in the best of fighting order. We had arrived at our present camp about the last week of April, having rested several days at Charlottesville.

General Lee's Army was a day's, or more, march to the north and east of us, on the west bank of the Rapidan River. It was composed of the Second Corps, under Lieutenant General Ewell, with seventeen thousand and ninety-three men; Third Corps, under Lieutenant General A.P. Hill, with twenty-two thousand one hundred and ninety-nine; unattached commands, one thousand one hundred and twenty-five; cavalry, eight thousand seven hundred and twenty-seven; artillery, four thousand eight hundred and fifty-four; while Longstreet had about ten thousand; putting the entire strength of Lee's Army, of all arms, at sixty-three thousand nine hundred and ninety-eight.

General Grant had, as heretofore mentioned, been made commander in chief of all the Union armies, while General Lee held the same position in the Confederate service. Grant had taken up his headquarters with the Army of the Potomac, giving the direction of this army his personal attention, retaining, however, General George S. Meade as its immediate commander.

Grant had divided his army into three corps—Second, under Major General W.S. Hancock; Fifth, Major General G.K. Warren; Sixth, Major General John Sedgwick—all in camp near Culpepper Court House, while a separate corps, under Major General A.E. Burnside, was stationed near the railroad crossing on the Rappahannock River.

Lee's Army was divided as follows: Rodes', Johnston's, and Early's Divisions, under Lieutenant General Ewell, Second Corps; R.H. Anderson's, Heath's, and Wilcox's Divisions, under Lieutenant General A.P. Hill, Third Corps.

Longstreet had no Major Generals under him as yet. He had two divisions, McLaws' old Division, under Brigadier General Kershaw, and Hood's, commanded by Brigadier General Fields. The division had been led through the East Tennessee campaign by General Jenkins, of South Carolina. Also a part of a division under General Bushrod Johnston, of the Army of the West.

Grant had in actual numbers of all arms, equipped and ready for battle, one hundred and sixteen thousand eight hundred and eighty-six men. He had forty-nine thousand one hundred and ninety-one more infantry and artillery than Lee and three thousand six hundred and ninety-seven more cavalry. He had but a fraction less than double the forces of the latter. With this disparity of numbers, and growing greater every day, Lee successfully combatted Grant for almost a year without a rest of a week from battle somewhere along his lines. Lee had no reinforcements to call up, and no recruits to strengthen his ranks, while Grant had at his call an army of two million to draw from at will, and always had at his immediate disposal as many troops as he could handle in one field. He not only outnumbered Lee, but he was far better equipped in arms, subsistence, transportation, and cavalry and artillery horses. He had in his medical, subsistence, and quartermaster departments alone nineteen thousand one hundred and eighty-three, independent of his one hundred and sixteen thousand eight hundred and eighty-six, ready for the field, which he called noncombatants. While these figures and facts are foreign to the "History of Kershaw's Brigade," still I give them as matters of general history, that the reader may better understand the herculean undertaking that confronted Longstreet when he joined his forces with those of Lee's. And as this was to be the deciding campaign of the war, it will be better understood by giving the strength and environment of each army. The Second South Carolina Regiment was commanded by Lieutenant Colonel Gaillard; the Third, by Colonel Jas. D, Nance; the Seventh, by Captain Jerry Goggans; the Eighth, by Colonel Henagan; the Fifteenth, by Colonel J.B. Davis; the Third Battalion, by Captain Whiter. The brigade was commanded by Colonel J.D. Kennedy, as senior Colonel.

Thus stood the command on the morning of the 4th of May, but by the shock of battle two days later all was changed. Scarcely a commander of a regiment or brigade remained. The two military giants of the nineteenth century were about to face each other, and put to the test the talents, tactics, and courage of their respective antagonists. Both had been successful beyond all precedent, and both considered themselves invincible in the field. Grant had tact and tenacity, with an overwhelming army behind him. Lee had talent, impetuosity, and boldness, with an army of patriots at his command, who had never known defeat; and considered themselves superior in courage and endurance to any body of men on earth. Well might the clash of arms in the Wilderness of these mighty giants cause the civilized world to watch and wonder. Lee stood like a lion in the path—his capital behind him, his army at bay—while Grant, with equal pugnacity, sought to crush him by sheer force of overwhelming numbers.

CHAPTER 29
Battle of the Wilderness

At midnight, on the 3rd of May, Grant put this mighty force of his in motion—the greatest body of men moving to combat that had ever been assembled on the continent. On the 4th his army crossed the Rapidan, at Germania and Ely's Fords, and began moving out towards the turn-pike, leading from Orange Court House by way of the Wilderness to Fredericksburg.

On the 5th Ewell had a smart engagement on the turn-pike, while Heath's and Wilcox's Divisions, of Hill's Corps, had met successfully a heavy force under Hancock, on the plank road—two roads running parallel and about one mile distant. Both armies closed the battle at night fall, each holding his own field. However, the enemy strongly entrenched in front, while Hill's troops, from some cause unexplainable, failed to take this precaution, and; had it not been for the timely arrival of Longstreet at a critical moment, might have been fatal to Lee's Army.

On the morning of the 5th we had orders to march. Foragers coming in the night before reported heavy firing in the direction of the Rapidan, which proved to be the cavalry engagement checking Grant at the river fords. All felt after these reports, and our orders to march, that the campaign had opened. All day we marched along unused roads—through fields and thickets, taking every near cut possible. Scarcely stopping for a moment to even rest, we found ourselves, at 5 o'clock in the evening, twenty-eight miles from our starting point. Men were too tired and worn out to pitch tents, and hearing the orders "to be ready to move at midnight," the troops stretched themselves upon the ground to get such comfort and rest as was possible. Promptly at midnight we began to move again, and such a march, and under such conditions, was never before experienced by the troops. Along blind roads, overgrown by underbrush, through fields that had lain fallow for years, now studded with bushes and briars, and the night being exceedingly dark, the men floundered and fell as they marched. But the needs were too urgent to be slack in the march now, so the men struggled with nature in their endeavor to keep in ranks. Sometimes the head of the column would lose its way, and during the time it was hunting its way back to the lost bridle path, was about the only rest we got. The men were already worn out by their forced march of the day before, and now they had to exert all their strength to its utmost to keep up. About daylight we struck the plank road leading from Orange Court House to Fredericksburg, and into this we turned and marched down with a swinging step. Kershaw's Brigade was leading, followed by Humphreys' and Wofford's, with Bryan bringing up the rear. The Second South Carolina was in front, then the Third, Seventh, Fifteenth, Third Battalion, and Eighth on extreme right, the brigade marching left in front.

After marching some two miles or more down the plank road at a rapid gait, passing Hill's field infirmary, where the wounded of the day before were being cared for, we heard a sharp firing in our immediate front. Longstreet's artillery was far in the rear, floundering along through the blind roads as the infantry had done the night before. Our wagons and subsistence supplies had not been since dawn of the 5th, although this made little difference to the men, as Longstreet's Corps always marched with three days' rations in their haversacks, with enough cooking utensils on their backs to meet immediate Wants. So they were never thrown off their base for want of food. The cartridge boxes were filled with forty rounds, with twenty more in their pockets, and all ready for the fray.

As soon as the musketry firing was heard, we hastened our steps, and as we reached the brow of a small elevation in the ground, orders were given to deploy across the road. Colonel Gaillard, with the Second, formed on the left of the road, while the Third, under Colonel Nance; formed on the right, with the other regiments taking their places on the right of the Third in their order of march. Field's Division Was forming rapidly on the left of the plank road, but as yet did not reach it, thus the Second was for the time being detached to fill up. The Mississippians, under Humphreys, had already left the plank road in our rear, and so had Wofford, with his Georgians, and were making their way as best they could through this tangled morass of the Wilderness, to form line of battle on Kershaw's right. The task was difficult in the extreme, but the men were equal to the occasion, Bryan's Georgia Brigade filed off to the right, in rear, as reserves.

The line had not yet formed before a perfect hail of bullets came flying overhead and through our ranks, but not a man moved, only to allow the stampeded troops of Heath's and Wilcox's to pass to the rear. It seems that these troops had fought the day before, and lay upon the battlefield with the impression that they would be relieved before day. They had not reformed their lines, nor replenished their ammunition boxes, nor made any pretention towards protecting their front by any kind of works. The enemy, who had likewise occupied their ground of the day before, had reformed their lines, strengthened their position by breastworks—all this within two hundred yards of the unsuspecting Confederates. This fault lay in a misunderstanding of orders, or upon the strong presumption that Longstreet would be up before the hour of combat. Hancock had ordered his advance at sunrise, and after a feeble defense by Heath's and Wilcox's skirmish line, the enemy burst upon the unsuspecting Confederates, while some were cooking a hasty meal, others still asleep—all unprepared for this thunderbolt that fell in their midst. While forming his lines of battle, and while bullets were flying all around, General Kershaw came dashing down in front of his column, his eyes flashing fire, sitting his horse like a centaur—that superb style as Joe Kershaw only could—and said in passing us, "Now, my old brigade. I expect you to do your duty." In all my long experience, in war and peace, I never saw such a picture as Kershaw and his war-horse made in riding down in front of his troops at the Wilderness. It seemed an inspiration to every man in line, especially his old brigade, who knew too well that their conduct to-day would either win or lose him his Major General's spurs, and right royally did he gain them. The columns were not yet in proper order, but the needs so pressing to check the advance of the enemy, that a forward movement was ordered, and the lines formed up as the troops marched.

The second moved forward on the left of the plank road, in support of a battery stationed there, and which was drawing a tremendous fire upon the troops on both sides of the road. Down the gentle slope the brigade marched, over and under the tangled shrubbery and dwarf saplings, while a withering fire was being poured into them by as yet an unseen enemy. Men fell here and there, officers urging ion their commands and ordering them to "hold their fire." When near the lower end of the declivity, the shock came. Just in front of us, and not forty yards away, lay the enemy. The long line of blue could be seen under the ascending smoke of thousands of rifles; the red flashes of their guns seemed to blaze in our very faces. Now the battle was on in earnest. The roar of Kershaw's guns mingled with those of the enemy. Longstreet had met his old antagonist of Round Top, Hancock, the Northern hero, of Gettysburg. The roar of the small arms, mingled with the thunder of the cannon that Longstreet had brought forward, echoed and re-echoed up and down the little valley, but never to die away, for new troops were being put rapidly in action to the right and left of us. Men rolled and writhed in their last death struggle; wounded men groped their way to the rear, being blinded by the stifling smoke. All commands were drowned in this terrible din of battle—the earth and elements shook and trembled with the deadly shock of combat. Regiments were left without commanders; companies, without officers. The gallant Colonel Gaillard, of the Second, had fallen. The intrepid young Colonel of the Third, J.D. Nance, had already died in the lead of his regiment. The commander of the Seventh, Captain Goggans, was wounded. Colonel John D. Kennedy, commanding the brigade, had left the field, disabled from further service for the day.

Still the battle rolled on. It seemed for a time as if the whole Federal Army was upon us—so thick and fast came the death-dealing missiles. Our ranks were being decimated by the wounded and the dead, the little valley in the Wilderness becoming a veritable "Valley of Hennom." The enemy held their position with a tenacity, born of desperation, while the confederates pressed them with that old-time Southern vigor and valor that no amount of courage could withstand. Both armies stood at extreme tension, and the cord must soon snap one way or the other, or it seemed as all would be annihilated, Longstreet seeing the desperate struggle in which Kershaw and Humphreys, on the right, and Hood's old Texans, on the left, were now engaged, sought to relieve the pressure by a flank movement with such troops as he had at his disposal. R.H. Andersen's Division, of Hill's Corps had reported to him during the time Kershaw was in such deadly throes of battle. Four brigades, Wofford's, of Kershaw's, and G.T. Anderson's, Mahone's, and Davis', of Anderson's Division, were ordered around on our right, to strike the left of Hancock But during this manoeuver the enemy gradually withdrew from our front, and Kershaw's Brigade was relieved by Bratton's South Carolina Brigade. I quote here from Colonel Wallace, of the Second.

"Kershaw's Division formed line in the midst of this confusion, like cool and well-trained veterans as they were, checked the enemy, and soon drove them back. The Second Regiment was on the left of the plank road, near a battery of artillery, and although completely flanked at one time by the giving away of the troops on the right, gallantly stood their ground, though suffering terribly; they and the battery, keeping up a well-directed fire, to the right oblique, until the enemy gave way. General Lee now appeared on our left, leading Hood's Texas Brigade. We joined our brigade on the right of the plank road, and again advanced to the attack.

"We were relieved by Jenkins' Brigade, under command of that able and efficient officer, General Bratton, and ordered to the rear and rest. We had scarcely thrown ourselves upon the ground, when General Bratton requested that a regiment be sent him to fill a gap in the lines, which the enemy had discovered and were preparing to break through. I was ordered to take the Second Regiment and report to him. A staff officer showed me the gap, when I double quicked to it, just in time, as the enemy were within forty yards of it. As we reached the point we poured a well-directed volley into them, killing a large number, and putting the rest to flight. General Bratton witnessed the conduct of the regiment on this occasion and spoke of it in the highest terms."

But, meanwhile, Longstreet's flanking columns were steadily making their way around the enemy's left. At ten o'clock the final crash came. Like an avalanche from a mountain side, Wofford, Mahone, Anderson, and Davis rushed upon the enemy's exposed flank, doubling up Hancock's left upon his center, putting all to flight and confusion. In vain did the Federal commander try to bring order out of confusion, but at this critical moment Wadsworth, his leading Division General, fell mortally wounded. Thus being left without a commander, his whole division gave way, having, with Stephen's Division, been holding Fields in desperate battle. The whole of Hancock's troops to the right of the plank road was swept across it by the sudden onslaught of the flanking column, only to be impeded by the meeting and mixing with Wadsworth's and Stephen's retreating divisions.

At this moment a sad and most regrettable occurrence took place, that, in a measure, somewhat nullified the fruits of one of the greatest victories of the war. One of Mahone's regiments, gaining the plank road in advance of the other portion of the flanking column, and seeing Wadsworth giving such steady battle to Fields, rushed over and beyond the road and assailed his right, which soon gave way. Generals Longstreet, Kershaw, and Jenkins, with their staffs, came riding down the plank road, just as the Virginia Regiment beyond the road was returning to join its brigade. The other regiments coming up at this moment, and seeing through the dense smoke what they considered an advancing foe, fired upon the returning regiment just as General Longstreet and party rode between. General Jenkins fell dead, Longstreet badly wounded. Captain Doby, of Kershaw's staff, also was killed, together with several couriers killed and wounded.

This unfortunate occurrence put a check to a vigorous pursuit of the flying enemy, partly by the fall of the corps commander and the frightful loss in brigade and regimental commanders, to say nothing of the officers of the line. Captain Doby was one of the most dashing, fearless, and accomplished officers that South Carolina had furnished during the war. The entire brigade had witnessed his undaunted valor on so many battlefields, especially at Mayree's Hill and Zoar Church, that it was with the greatest sorrow they heard of his death. Captain Doby had seemed to live a charmed life while riding through safely the storms upon storms of the enemy's battles, that it made it doubly sad to think of his dying at the hands of his mistaken friends. On this same plank road, only a few miles distant, General Jackson lost his life one year before, under similar circumstances, and at the hands of the same troops. Had it not been for the coolness of General Kershaw in riding out to where he heard Jenkins' rifles clicking to return the fire, and called out, "Friends," it would be difficult to tell, what might have been the result.

To show the light in which the actions of Kershaw's Brigade were held in thus throwing itself between Lee and impending disaster at this critical moment, and stemming the tide of battle single-handed and alone, until his lines were formed, I will quote an extract from an unprejudiced and impartial eye witness, Captain J.F.J. Caldwell, who in his "History of McGowan's Brigade" pays this glowing but just tribute to Kershaw and his men. In speaking of the surprise and confusion in which a part of Hill's Corps was thrown, be says:

> "We were now informed that Longstreet was near at hand, with twenty-five thousand fresh men. This was good

matter to rally on. We were marched to the plank road by special order of General Hill; but just as we were crossing it, we received orders to return to the left. We saw General Longstreet riding down the road towards us, followed by his column of troops. The firing of the enemy, of late rather scattering, now became fierce and incessant, and we could hear a reply to it from outside. Kershaw's South Carolina Brigade, of McLaws' (afterwards Kershaw's) Division, had met them. The fire on both sides of the road increased to a continuous roar. Kershaw's Brigade was extended across the road, and received the grand charge of the Federals. Members of that Brigade have told me that the enemy rushed upon them at the double-quick, huzzahing loudly. The woods were filled with Confederate fugatives. Three brigades of Wilcox's Division and all of Heath's were driven more or less rapidly, crowding together in hopeless disorder, and only to be wondered at when any of them attempted to make a stand. Yet Kershaw's Brigade bore themselves with illustrious gallantry. Some of the regiments had not only to deploy under fire, but when they were formed, to force their way through crowds of flying men, and re-established their lines. They met Grant's legions, opened a cool and murderous fire upon them, and continued it so steadily and resolutely, that the latter were compelled to give back. Here I honestly believe the Army of Northern Virginia was saved! The brigade sustained a heavy loss, beginning with many patient, gallant spirits in the ranks and culminating in Nance, Gaillard, and Doby."

No further pursuit being made by Kershaw's Brigade during the day, it was allowed to rest after its day and night march and the bloody and trying ordeal of the morning. Friends were hunting out friends among the dead and wounded. The litter-bearers were looking after those too badly wounded to make their way to the rear.

Dr. Salmond had established his brigade hospital near where the battle had begun in the morning, and to this haven of the wounded those who were able to walk were making their way. In the rear of a battlefield are scenes to sickening for sensitive eyes and ears. Here you see men, with leg shattered, pulling themselves to the rear by the strength of their arms alone, or exerting themselves to the utmost to get to some place where they will be partially sheltered from the hail of bullets falling all around; men, with arms swinging helplessly by their sides, aiding some comrade worse crippled than themselves; others on the ground appealing for help, but are forced to remain on the field amid all the carnage going on around them, helpless and almost hopeless, until the battle is over, and, if still alive, await their turn from the litter-bearers. The bravest and best men dread to die, and the halo that surrounds death upon the battlefield is but scant consolation to the wounded soldier, and he clings to life with that same tenacity after he has fallen, as the man of the world in "piping times of peace."

Just in rear of where Colonel Nance fell, I saw one of the saddest sights I almost ever witnessed. A soldier from Company C, Third South Carolina, a young soldier just verging into manhood, had been shot in the first advance, the bullet severing the great artery of the thigh. The young man seeing his danger of bleeding to death before succor could possibly reach him, had struggled behind a small sapling. Bracing himself against it, he undertook deliberative measures for saving his life. Tying a handkerchief above the wound, placing a small stone underneath and just over the artery, and putting a stick between the handkerchief and his leg, he began to tighten by twisting the stick around. But too late; life had fled, leaving both hands clasping the stick, his eyes glassy and fixed.

The next day was devoted to the burying of the dead and gathering such rest as was possible. It was my misfortune to be wounded near the close of the engagement, in a few feet of where lay the lamented Colonel Nance. The regiment in some way became doubled up somewhat on the center, perhaps in giving way for the Second to come in, and here lay the dead in greater numbers than it was ever my fortune to see, not even before the stone wall at Fredericksburg.

In rear of this the surgeons had stretched their great hospital tents, over which the yellow flag floated. The surgeons and assistant surgeons never get their meed of praise in summing up the "news of the battle." The latter follow close upon the line of battle and give such temporary relief to the bleeding soldiers as will enable them to reach the field hospital. The yellow flag does not always protect the surgeons and their assistants, as shells scream and burst overhead as the tide of battle rolls backward and forward. Not a moment of rest or sleep do these faithful servants of the army get until every wound is dressed and the hundred of arms and legs amputated, with that skill and caution for which the army surgeons are so proverbially noted. With the same dispatch are those, who are able to be moved, bundled off to some city hospital in the rear.

In a large fly-tent, near the roadside, lay dying the Northern millionaire, General Wadsworth. The Confederates had been as careful of his wants and respectful to his station as if he had been one of their own Generals. I went in to look at the General who could command more ready gold than the Confederate States had in its treasury. His hat had been placed over his face, and as I raised it, his heavy breathing, his eyes closed, his cold, clammy face showed that the end was near. There lay dying the multi-millionaire in an enemy's country, not a friend near to hear his last farewell or soothe his last moments by a friendly touch on the pallid brow. Still he, like all soldiers on either side, died for what he thought was right.

He fails not, who stakes his all,
Upon the right, and dares to fall;
What, though the living bless or blame
For him, the long success of fame.

Hospital trains had been run up to the nearest railroad station in the rear, bringing those ministering angels of mercy the "Citizens' Relief Corps," composed of the best matrons and maidens of Richmond, led by the old men of the city. They brought crutches by the hundreds and bandages by the bolt. Every delicacy that the, South afforded these noble dames of Virginia had at the disposal of the wounded soldiers. How many thousands of Confederate soldiers have cause to bless these noble women of Virginia. They were the spartan mothers and sisters of the South.

Colonel James D. Nance

I do not think I would be accused of being partial in saying that Colonel Nance was the best all round soldier in Kershaw's Brigade, none excepted. I have no allusion to the man, but the soldier alone. Neither do I refer to qualities of courage, for all were brave, but to efficiency. First to recommend him was his military education and training. He was a thorough tactician and disciplinarian, and was only equaled in this respect by General Connor. In battle he was ever cool and collected—he was vigilant, aggressive, and brave. Never for a moment was he thrown off his base or lost his head under the most trying emergencies. His evolution in changing the front of his regiment from columns of fours to a line of battle on Mayree's

Hill, under a galling fire from artillery and musketry, won the admiration of all who witnessed it. Socially, he had the manners of a woman—quiet, unassuming, tender of heart, and of refined feelings. On duty—the march or in battle—he was strict and exacting, almost to sternness. He never sought comfort or the welfare of himself—the interest, the safety, the well being of his men seemed to be his ruling aim and ambition.

I append a short sketch of Colonel Nance taken from Dr. Barksdale's book, "Eminent and Representative Men of the Carolinas:"

"Colonel James Drayton Nance, the subject of this sketch, Was born in Newberry, S.C., October 10th, 1837, and was the son of Drayton and Lucy (Williams) Nance. He received his school education at Newberry, and was graduated from the Citadel Military Academy, at Charleston. In 1859 he was admitted to the bar and began the practice of law at Newberry.

"When the State seceded from the Union, December, 1860, and volunteers for her defense were called for, he was unanimously elected Captain of 'The Quitman Rifles,' an infantry company formed at Newberry, and afterwards incorporated into the Third Regiment, South Carolina Volunteers. With his company he was mustered into the Confederate service at Columbia in April, 1861, and was in command of the company at the first battle of Manassas and in the Peninsula campaign in Virginia.

"On May 16th, 1862, upon the reorganization of the Third Regiment, he was chosen its Colonel, a position which he filled until his death. As Colonel, he commanded the regiment in the various battles around Richmond, June and July, 1862, Second Manassas, Maryland Heights, Sharpsburg, Fredericksburg (where he was severely wounded), Gettysburg, Chickamauga, Knoxville, and the Wilderness, where on the 6th of May, 1864, he was instantly killed. His body was brought home and interred at Newberry with fitting honors. He was a brave, brilliant young officer, possessing the confidence and high regard of his command in an extraordinary degree, and had he lived, would have risen to higher rank and honor. His valuable services and splended qualities and achievements in battle and in council were noted and appreciated, as evidenced by the fact that at the time of his death a commission of Brigadier General had been, decided upon as his just due for meritorious conduct.

"At the age of seventeen he professed religion and united with the Baptist Church at Newberry, and from that time to his death was distinguished for his Christian consistency."

Lieutenant Colonel Franklin Gaillard

Lieutenant Colonel Franklin Gaillard is not known to fame by his military record alone, but was known and admired all over the State as the writer of the fiery editorials in the "Carolinian," a paper published in Columbia during the days just preceding Secession, and noted for its ardent State Rights sentiment. These eloquent, forcible, and fearless discussions of the questions of the day by young Gaillard was a potent factor in shaping the course of public sentiment and rousing the people to duty and action, from the Mountains to the Sea. Through the columns of this paper, then the leading one in the State, he paved the way and prepared the people for the great struggle soon to take place, stimulating them to an enthusiasm almost boundless.

He was in after years as fearless and bold with the sword as he had been with the pen. He was not the man to turn his back upon his countrymen, whose warlike passions he had aroused, when the time for action came. He led them to the fray—a paladin with the pen, a Bayard with the sword. He was an accomplished gentleman, a brave soldier, a trusted and impartial officer, a peer of any in Kershaw's Brigade.

Colonel Gaillard was born in 1829, in the village of Pineville, in the present County of Berkeley. In his early childhood his father, Thomas Gaillard, removed to Alabama. But not long thereafter Franklin returned to this State, to the home of his uncle, David Gaillard, of Fairfield County. Here he attended the Mount Zion Academy, in Winnsboro under the distinguished administration of J.W. Hudson. In the fall of 1846 he entered the South Carolina College, and graduated with honor in the class of 1849, being valedictorian of the class. Shortly after graduation, in company with friends and relatives from this State and Alabama, he went to California in search of the "yellow metal," the find of which, at that time, was electrifying the young men throughout the States.

After two or three years of indifferent success, he returned to this State once more, making his home with his uncle, in Winnsboro. In 1853 (or thereabout) he became the proprietor of the "Winnsboro Register," and continued to conduct this journal, as editor and proprietor, until 1857, when he was called to Columbia as editor of the "Carolinian," then owned by Dr. Robert W. Gibbes, of Richland, and was filling that position at the time of the call to arms, in 1861, when he entered the service in Captain Casson's Company, as a Lieutenant, and became a member of the renowned Second Regiment.

In March, 1853, he was married to Miss Catherine C. Porcher, of Charleston, but this union was terminated in a few years by the death of the wife. Colonel Gaillard left two children, one son and one daughter, who still survive, the son a distinguished physician, of Texas, and the daughter the wife of Preston S. Brooks, son of the famous statesman of that name, now of Tennessee.

Colonel Gaillard was a descendant of a French Huguenot emigrant, who, with many others, settled in this State after the Revocation of the Edict of Nantes, in 1685.

CHAPTER 30

To North Anna

Having been wounded in the last assault, I insert here Adjutant Y.J. Pope's description of the operations of Kershaw's Brigade from the Wilderness to North Anna River, covering a period of perhaps two weeks of incessant fighting. The corps had been put under the command of Major General R.H. Anderson, known throughout the army as "Fighting Dick Anderson." His division had been assigned to Longstreet's Corps in the place of Pickett's, now on detached service. Colonel Henagan, of the Eighth, commanded the brigade as senior Colonel.

NORTH ANNA FIVER, VIRGINIA.

How many times, as soldiers, have we crossed this stream, and little did we imagine in crossing that on its banks we would be called upon to meet the enemy. "Man proposes, but God disposes." In May, 1864, after the battles of the Wilderness, Brock's Road, and Spottsylvania—stop a minute and think of these battles—don't you recall how, on that midnight of the 5th day of May, 1864, the order came, "Form your regiments," and then the order came to march? Through the woods we went. The stars shown so brightly. The hooting of the owls was our only music. The young Colonel at the head of his regiment would sing, in his quiet way, snatches of the hymns he had heard the village choir sing so often and so sweetly, and then "Hear me Norma." His mind was clear; he had made up his determination to face the day of battle, with a calm confidence in the power of the God he trusted and in the wisdom of His decrees. The Adjutant rode silently by his side. At length daylight appears. We have at last struck in our march the plank road. The sun begins to rise, when all of a sudden we hear the roll of musketry. The armies are at work. General Lee has ridden up the plank road with his First Lieutenant, the tried, brave old soldier, Longstreet.

Nance has fallen, pierced by five balls, but we knew it not. Every hand is full. Presently, our four companies came up, so gallantly they looked as they came. Promptly filling up the broken line, we now move forward once more, never to fall back. We have Nance's body. The wild flowers around about him look so beautiful and sweet, and some of them are plucked by his friend to send to his sister, Mrs. Baxter.

But go back to the fight. It rages wildly all around. Presently, a crash comes from the right. It is Longstreet at the head of the flanking column, and then Hancock is swept from the field in front. Joy is upon us. Hastily Longstreet rides to the front. Then a volley and he falls, not dead, but so shattered that it will be months before we see him again. Then comes the peerless chieftain, Lee, and he orders the pursuing columns to halt. A line of hastily constructed fieldworks arise. A shout—such a shout rolls from right to left of Lee's lines. It has a meaning, and that meaning is that Grant's advance is baffled! But the Federal commander is not to be shut off. If he cannot advance one way, he will another. Hence, the parallel lines are started—the farther he stretches to our right, we must stretch also.

So now comes the affair at Brock's Road, on the 8th of May. 1864. As before remarked, Grant commenced his attempt at a flank movement, by means of an extension of his columns parallel to ours, hoping to meet some opening through which he might pour a torrent of armed men. Early in the morning of the 8th of May, 1864, we are aroused and begin our march. Soon we see an old Virginia gentleman, bareheaded and without his shoes, riding in haste towards us. He reports that our cavalry are holding the enemy back on Brock's Road, but that the Federal infantry are seen to be forming for the attack, and, of course, our cavalry cannot stand such a pressure. General Kershaw orders us forward in double-quick. Still we are not then. Then it was that a gallant cavalryman rushes to us and said:

"Run for our rail piles; the Federal infantry will reach them first, if you don't run."

Our men sprang forward as if by magic.

We occupy the rail piles in time to see a column, a gallant column, moving towards us, about sixty yards away. Fire, deadening fire, is poured into that column by our men. A gallant Federal officer rides just in rear, directing the movement. "Pick that officer off of his horse," is the command given to two or three of our cool marksmen.

He falls. The column staggers and then falls back. Once more they come to time. We are better prepared for them.

Right here let me state a funny occurrence. Sim Price observed old man John Duckett, in the excitement, shooting his rifle high over the heads of the Yankees. This was too much for Sim Price, and he said, "Good God, John Duckett, are you shooting at the moon?"

Here is the gallant J.E.B. Stuart, Lieutenant General, commanding the cavalry of the Army of Northern Virginia, with hat off, waiving it in an enthusiastic cheering of the gallant men of the old Third. Well he may, for the line they held on that day was that adopted by General Lee for the famous Spottsylvania battle.

Just prior to the battle of Spottsylvania Court House, which was fought on the 12th of May, 1864, sharpshooters were posted in trees in the woods, and kept up a pretty constant fusilade when any head showed itself. It is recalled that when Major R.P. Todd returned to our command an officer, eager to hear from his home in South Carolina, entered a little fly-tent with Todd, and presently one of these sharpshooters put a ball through this tent, between the heads of the two. Maybe they didn't move quickly. Here it was, that lest a night attack might be made, one-third of the men were kept in the trenches all the time, day and night. One of these nights, possibly the 11th of May, a staff officer stole quietly where the Colonel and Adjutant were lying and whispered, "It is thought that the enemy have gotten betwixt our out posts and the breastworks and intend to make a night attack. So awaken the soldiers and put every man in the trenches." The Colonel went to one end of the line and the Adjutant to the other, and soon had our trenches manned. The Colonel was observed full of laughter, and when questioned, stated that on going to the left wing of the regiment to awaken the men, he came across a soldier with some small branches kindled into a blaze, making himself a cup of coffee. He spoke to the soldier, saying:

"Who is that?"

The soldier replied, not recognizing the Colonel's voice: "Who in the h——l are you?"

The Colonel said: "Don't you know the Yankees are between the pickets and the breastworks, and will soon attack our whole line?"

He reported the man at these words, saying: "The Jesus Christ, Colonel!" rolling as he spoke, and he never stopped rolling until he fell into the pit at the works. Never was a revolution in sentiment and action more quickly wrought than on this occasion with this soldier.

It is needless to speak of the battle of Spottsylvania Court House, except to remark that here our comrades of McGowan's Brigade showed of what stuff they were made, and by their gallantry and stubborn fighting, saved the day for General Lee.

Soon after this battle General Grant, though baffled by its result, renewed his effort to reach Richmond. By a rapid march, General Lee was before Grant's columns at the North Anna River. Here we hoped the enemy would attack us. On the South side of this river, on the road leading to Hanover Junction, good heavy works had been completed, while a fort of inferior proportions on the North side was intended to protect the bridge across the river from raiding parties of the enemy. To our surprise, when the part of our army that was designed to cross the river at this point, had crossed over, the Third Regiment, James' Battalion, and the Seventh Regiment were left behind about this fort. We had no idea that anything serious was intended; but after awhile it leaked out that General Lee needed some time to complete a line of works from one point of the river to another on the same stream, on the South side, and that it was intended that the bare handful of men with us were intended to hold the approach to the bridge in face of the tens of thousands of Grant's Army in our front. Trying to realize the task assigned us, positions were assigned the different forces with us. It was seen that the Seventh Regiment, when stretched to the left of the fort, could not occupy, even by a thin line, the territory near them. We were promised the co-operation of artillery just on the other side of the river. Presently the attack opened on the right and center, but this attack we repulsed. Again the same points were assailed, with a like result. Then the attack was made on our left, and although the Seventh Regiment did its whole duty, gradually our left was seen to give way. This emboldened the enemy to press our right and center again, but they were firm. It was manifest now that the enemy would soon be in our rear, and as the sun was sinking to rest in the West, we made a bold dash to cross the river in our rear, bringing down upon us the enemy's artillery fire of shot and shell, as well as musketry. It looked hard to tell which way across the river was best—whether by way of the bridge, or to wade across. It was said our Lieutenant Colonel, who was on foot when reaching the opposite bank, and finding his boots full of water, said to a soldier: "Tom, give me your hand." "No, no, Major," was the reply; "this is no time for giving hands." The ascent of the long hill on the South side was made under the heavy fire of the enemy. When at its height, a stuttering soldier proposed to a comrade to lay down and let him get behind him. Of course the proposition was declined without thanks. When we reformed at the top of the hill, there was quite a fund of jokes told. Amongst others, the one last stated, Tom Paysinger said: "Nels., if I had been there, I would have killed myself laughing." Whereupon, the stutterer said: "T-T-Tom Paysinger, I saw a heap of men down there, but not one that laughed."

War has its humorous as well as its serious side, and many a joke was cracked in battle, or if not mentioned then, the joke was told soon afterwards. It is recalled just here that in this battle an officer, who had escaped being wounded up to that time, was painfully wounded. When being borne on the way to the rear on a stretcher, he was heard to exclaim: "Oh! that I had been a good man. Oh! that I had listened to my mother." When he returned to the army, many a laugh was had at his expense when these expressions would be reported. But the officer got even with one of his tormentors, who was one of the bearers of the litter upon which the officer was borne away, for while this young man was at his best in imitating the words and tone of the wounded man, he was suddenly arrested by the words: "Yes, I remember when a shell burst pretty close you forgot me, and dropped your end of the litter." The laugh was turned. All this, however, was in perfect good humor.

It has been shown how Kershaw's South Carolina Brigade closed the breach in Lee's Army on the 6th of May, and turned disaster into a glorious victory, and as the 12th of May, at "Bloody Angle," near Spottsylvania Court house, will go down in history as one among the most memorable battles of all time, I wish to show how another gallant South Carolina Brigade (McGowan's) withstood the shock of the greater portion of Grant's Army, and saved Lee's Army from disaster during the greater part of one day. This account is also taken from Captain Caldwell's "History of McGowan's Brigade." Being an active participant, he is well qualified to give a truthful version, and I give in his own language his graphic description of the battle of the "Bloody Angle."

History Of McGowan's Brigade

Reaching the summit of an open hill, where stood a little old house, and its surrounding naked orchard, we were fronted and ordered forward on the left of the road....Now we entered the battle. There were two lines of works before us; the first or inner line, from a hundred and fifty to two hundred yards in front of us; the second or outer line, perhaps a hundred yards beyond it, and parallel to it. There were troops in the outer line, but in the inner one only what appeared to be masses without organization. The enemy were firing in front of the extreme right of the brigade, and their balls came obliquely down our line; but we could not discover, on account of the woods about the point of firing, under what circumstances the battle was held. There was a good deal of doubt as to how far we were to go, or in what direction.... The truth is, the road by which we had come was not at all straight, which made the right of the line front much farther north than the rest, and the fire was too hot for us to wait for the long loose column to close up, so as to make an entirely orderly advance. More than this, there was a death struggle ahead, which must be met instantly. We advanced at a double-quick, cheering loudly, and entered the inner works. Whether by order or tacit understanding, we halted here, except the Twelfth Regiment, which was the right of the brigade. That moved at once to the outer line, and threw itself with its wanted impetuosity into the heart of the battle.... The brigade advanced upon the works. About the time we reached the inner lines, General McGowan was wounded by a minnie ball in the arm, and forced to quit the field. Colonel Brockman, senior Colonel present, was also wounded, and Colonel Brown, of the Fourteenth Regiment, assumed command then or a little later. The four regiments, the First, Thirteenth, Fourteenth, and Rifles (the Twelfth had passed on to the outer line), closed up and arranged their lines. Soon the order was given to advance to the outer line. We did so with a cheer and a double-quick, plunging through mud knee deep and getting in as best we could. Here, however, lay Harris' Mississippi Brigade. We were ordered to close to the right. We moved by the flank, up the works, under the fatally accurate firing of the enemy, and ranged ourselves along the entrenchments. The sight we encountered was not calculated to encourage us The trenches dug on the inner side were almost filled with water. Dead men lay on the surface of the ground and in the pools of water. The wounded bled, stretched, and groaned, or huddled in every attitude of pain. The water was crimson with blood. Abandoned knapsacks, guns, and accoutrements, with ammunition boxes, were scattered all around. In the rear disabled caissons stood and limbers of guns. The rain poured heavily, and an incessant fire was kept upon us from front and flank. The enemy still held the works on the right of the angle, and fired across the traverses. Nor were these foes easily seen. They barely raised their heads above the logs at the moment of firing. It was plainly a question of bravery and endurance now.

We entered upon the task with all our might. Some fired at the line lying in our front on the edge of the ridge before described; others kept down the enemy lodged in the traverses on the right. At one or two places Confederates and Federals were only separated by the works, and the latter not a few times reached their guns over and fired right down upon the heads of the former. So continued the painfully unvarying battle for more than two hours. At the end of that time a rumor arose that the enemy was desirous to come in and surrender. Colonel Brown gives the following in his official report: "About two o'clock P.M. the firing ceased along the line, and I observed the enemy, standing up in our front, their colors flying and arms pointing upwards. I called to them to lay down their arms and come in. An officer answered that he was waiting our surrender—that we had raised a white flag, whereupon he had ceased firing. I replied, 'I command here,' and if any flag had been raised it was without authority, and unless he came in, firing would be resumed. He begged a conference, which was granted, and a subordinate officer advanced near the breastwork and informed me that a white flag was flying on my right. He was informed that unless his commander surrendered, the firing would be continued. He started back to his lines, and failing to exhibit his flag of truce, was shot down midway between the lines, which was not more than twenty yards at this point. The firing again commenced with unabating fury and was astonishingly accurate all along the line. No man could raise his shoulders above the works without danger of immediate death. Some of the enemy lay against our works in front. I saw several of them jump over and surrender during the relaxation of the firing. An ensign of a Federal regiment came right up to us during the "peace negotiations" and demanded our surrender. Lieutenant Carlisle, of the Thirteenth Regiment, replied that we would not surrender. Then the ensign insisted, as he had come under a false impression, he should be allowed to return to his command. Lieutenant Carlisle, pleased with his composure, consented. But as he went away a man from another part of the line shot him through the face, and he came and jumped over to us. This was the place to test individual courage. Some ordinarily good soldiers did next to nothing, while others excelled themselves. The question became pretty plainly, whether one was willing to meet death, not merely to run the chances of it. There was no further cessation of fire, after the pause before described. Every now and then a regular volley would be hurled at us from what we supposed a fresh line of Federals, but it would gradually tone down to the slow, particular, fatal firing of the siege. The prisoners who ran into us now and then informed us that Grant's whole energies were directed against this point. They represented the wood on the other side as filled with dead, wounded fighters, and skulkers. We were told that if we would hold the place till dark, we would be relieved. Dark came, but no relief. The water became a deeper crimson, the corpses grew more numerous. Every tree about us, for thirty feet from the ground, was marked by balls. Just before night a tree six or eight inches in diameter, just behind the works, was cut down by the bullets of the enemy. We noticed at the same time a large oak hacked and torn in such a manner never before seen. Some predicted its fall before morning, but the most of us considered that out of the question. But about 10 o'clock it did fall forward on our works, wounding some men and startling a great many more. An officer, who afterwards measured this tree, informed me that it was twenty-two inches in diameter. This was entirely the work of rifle balls. Midnight came, still no relief; no cessation of the firing. Numbers of the troops sank, overpowered, into the muddy trenches and slept soundly. The rain continued. Just before daylight we were ordered, in a whisper, which was passed along the line, to slowly and noiselessly retire from the works....Day dawned, and the evacuation was complete.

Thus ended one of the most stubbornly contested battles of the war, if not of the century. The whole army, from one end to the other, sung the praises of the gallant South Carolinians, who, by their deeds of valor, made immortal the "Bloody Angle."

CHAPTER 31

From North Anna to Cold Harbor

It was while entrenched south of North Anna that our troops heard of the death of our great cavalry leader, General J.E.B. Stuart, who fell mortally wounded at Yellow Tavern, on May the 18th. If the death of Jackson was a blow to the army and the South, the death of Stuart was equally so. He was the Murat of the Southern Army, equally admired and beloved by the infantry as the cavalry. The body of the army always felt safe when the bugle of Stuart could be heard on the flank or front, and universal sadness was thrown around the Army of Northern Virginia, as well as the whole South, by his death. It was conceded by the North, as well as the South, that Stuart was the finest type of cavalry leader in either army, Longstreet badly wounded, Stuart and Jenkins dead, certainly gave the prospects of the campaign just opening anything but an assuring outlook.

Twentieth South Carolina Regiment

About this time our brigade was reinforced by the Twentieth South Carolina Regiment, one of the finest bodies of men that South Carolina had furnished during the war. It was between one thousand and one thousand two hundred strong, led by the "silver-tongued orator," Lawrence M. Keitt. It was quite an acceptable acquisition to our brigade, since our ranks had been depleted by near one thousand since the 6th of May. They were as healthy, well clad, and well fed body of troops as anybody would wish to see, and much good-humored badgering was indulged in at their expense by Kershaw's "web feet." From their enormous strength in numbers, in comparison to our "corporal guards" of companies, the old soldiers called them "The Twentieth Army Corps." I here give a short sketch of the regiment prior to its connection with the brigade.

The Twentieth Regiment was organized under the call for twelve thousand additional troops from South Carolina, in 1862, along with the Seventeenth, Eighteenth, and Nineteenth, Holcomb Legion, and other regiments. The companies composing the Twentieth assembled at the race course, in Charleston, S.C., in the fall of 1862. The companies had already organized in the respective counties, and elected officers, and after assembling in Charleston and organizing the regiment, elected the following field officers:

Colonel	L.M. Keitt.
Lieutenant Colonel	O.M. Dansler.
Major	S.M. Boykin.
Adjutant	John Wilson.
Quartermaster	John P. Kinard.
Commissary	Brock.
Surgeon	Dr. Salley.
Assistant Surgeon	Dr. Barton.
Chaplain	Rev. W.W. Duncan.

Company A, Anderson and Pickens	Captain Partlow.
Company B, Orangeburg	Captain McMichael.
Company C, Lexington	Captain Leaphart.
Company D, Orangeburg	Captain Danley.
Company E, Laurens	Captain Cowen.
Company F, Newberry	Captain Kinard.
Company G, Sumter	Captain Moseley.
Company H, Orangeburg and Lexington	Captain Ruff.
Company I, Orangeburg and Lexington	Captain Gunter.
Company K, Lexington	Captain Harmon.

    Captain Jno. P. Kinard, of Company F, was made Quartermaster, and First Lieutenant Jno. M. Kinard was promoted to Captain.

    A singularity of one of the companies, I, was that it had twenty-eight members by the name of Gunter. The Captain and all three Lieutenants and seven non-commissioned officers were of the name of Gunter, and it is needless to add that it was called the Gunter Company.

Colonel Keitt, acting as Brigadier General while in Charleston, the entire management of the regiment was left to Lieutenant Colonel Dansler. He was a fine officer, a good tactician, and thorough disciplinarian. A courteous gentleman, kind and sociable to all, he was greatly beloved by officers and men, and it was with feelings of universal regret the regiment was forced to give him up, he having resigned in the spring of 1864, to accept the position of Colonel of the Twenty-Second Regiment.

The regiment remained at the race course for several months, for drill and instruction. In February, 1863, they were moved to the west end of James' Island, near Secessionville, for guard and picket duty. After this, they were transferred to Sullivan's Island, and quartered in the old Moultrie House and cottages adjacent. Four companies were ordered to Battery Marshall, on the east side of the Island, to assist in the management of the siege guns at that point.

On the 7th of May the Federal gunboats crossed the bar and made an attack upon Forts Sumter, Moultrie, and the batteries on Morris' Island. Here the regiment was subjected to a heavy cannonading from the three hundred pounders from the Federal ironclads. Colonel Dansler, however, moved the regiment to the east, in the sandhills, thus avoiding the direct fire of the enemy. One of the ironclads was sunk and others badly crippled, drawing off after dark. In December eight companies were moved over to Mt. Pleasant and two to Kinloch's Landing.

During the memorable siege of Morris' Island, the Twentieth did its turn at picketing on that island, going over after dark in a steamer and returning before day.

On the night of the 30th July, 1863, while the regiment was returning from Morris' Island, the tide being low, the steamer Sumter, on which the regiment was being transported, was forced to take the main ocean channel. It was the duty of those on garrison duty at Fort Sumter to signal Moultrie and the shore batteries of the movements of the transport steamer. For some cause or other Sumter failed to give the signals, and Moultrie being aware that there was a steamer in the harbor and no signals up, opened upon the ill-fated steamer with all her guns, thinking it one of the enemy's ironclads. This was a signal for the shore batteries to open their guns, and in a few moments shells came crashing through the decks and cabins of the crowded steamer from all sides. This created a panic among the troops, and had it not been for the self-possession and coolness of the captain of the steamer, the loss of life would have been appalling. The captain turned his boat and beached it as soon as possible, not, however, before the men began leaping over the sides of the vessel in one grand pell-mell. The dark waves of unknown death were below them, while the shells shrieked and burst through the steamer. There was but little choice for the panic stricken men. Fortunately the waters here were shallow enough for the men to touch bottom and wade out, some to Fort Johnson, some to Fort Sumter, while others remained in the shallows until relieved by small boats from shore. The regiment lost sixteen men, either killed or drowned.

On the 16th or 18th of May, 1864, the regiment was ordered to Virginia, and reached Richmond about the twenty-second, and was ordered to join Kershaw's Brigade, reaching it about the 28th of May, near South Anna River.

After the resignation of Lieutenant Colonel Dansler, Major Boykin was promoted to that position, and Captain Partlow made Major. By the death of Colonel Keitt, Boykin and Partlow were raised in regular grade, and Captain McMichael made Major. Lieutenant Colonel Partlow was wounded at Deep Bottom soon after this, and did Hot return to duty until near the close of the war. Colonel Boykin and Major McMichael were both captured at Cedar Creek, and neither returned until after peace was declared. The regiment was commanded during the remainder of the service, with short exceptions, by Captain Leaphart.

Colonel Keitt being senior Colonel now in the brigade, was placed in command. It was unfortunate for Colonel Keitt and his command, being transferred to our army just at the moment it was in one of the most active and vigorous campaigns of the war. The men were ill-prepared to meet the requirements expected of soldiers, to undergo forced marches in the burning heat of summer, to accustom themselves so suddenly to the scant and badly-prepared food, night pickets in the open, in face of the enemy, and all the hardships incident to a soldier's life in the field. These troops had seen but little of real service, having only done garrison duty around Charleston, quartered in barracks or good tents, while now they had to take the field, with no advantage of the veterans, in the way of supplies and in accommodations, and with none of their experience and strength of endurance. They had all the courage of the veteran troops, but lacked acclimation. Their company discipline was well enough, and had excellent company and field officers, but were sadly deficient in regimental and brigade drill. It is doubtful if either their commander or any of their field officers had ever been in brigade drill or executed a maneuver in a larger body than a regiment. Like all new troops in the field, they had overloaded themselves with baggage, and being thus overloaded, straggling was universal in the regiment, until they became endured to the fatigues and hardships of the march. Had they come out two or three months earlier, and taken on the ways and customs of the soldier in the field, it would have been much better. Still they deserve the highest degree of praise for their self-denials, their endurance, and fortitude in the march and in battle. The necessity of the occasion caused them to learn rapidly the intricacies in the life of the veteran, and their action in battle in a few days after their arrival, stamped them as a gallant body of men.

On the night of the 31st of May orders came to prepare to march. Grant had withdrawn from our front, and was still rolling along on Lee's right. Both armies were now moving in the direction of Cold Harbor, where McClellan, two years before, had tried to stay the flight of his troops and to check the victorious march of Jackson, Hill, and Longstreet. Now Grant was tempting fate by moving his beaten troops to this ill-fated field, there to try conclusions with McClellan's old antagonist.

The Federals were moving with rapid gait to this strategic point, but Lee having the inner line, was first on the field. It must be borne in mind that since the 4th of May the army had been idle scarcely a day. From that day to the 1st of June it had been one continual battle. If the infantry was not engaged, it was the artillery that kept hammering away, while Stuart's Cavalry hovered around the flanks and rear of the enemy, ready at a moment to swoop like an eagle upon his prey. We were continually under arms, either on a forced march night and day, checking the enemy here, baffling him there, driving back his advance lines, or assaulting his skirmishers. At night the sound of the enemy's drums mingled with that of our own, while the crack of the rifles in the sharpshooters' pits was almost continuous. Early on the morning of June 1st Kershaw's Brigade was aroused and put on the march at a rapid pace in a southeasterly direction.

When nearing the old battlefield of Cold Harbor the men began to snuff the scent of battle. Cartridge boxes were examined, guns unslung, and bayonets fixed, while the ranks were being rapidly closed up. After some delay and confusion, a line of battle was formed along an old roadway. Colonel Keitt had never before handled such a body of troops in the open field, and his pressing orders to find the enemy only added perplexity to his other difficulties. Every man in ranks knew that he was being led by one of the most gifted and gallant men in the South, but every old soldier felt and saw at a glance his inexperience and want of self-control. Colonel Keitt showed no want of aggressiveness and boldness, but he was preparing for battle like in the days of Alva or Turenne, and to cut his way through like a storm center.

As soon as the line was formed the order of advance was given, with never so much as a skirmish line in front. Keitt led his men like a knight of old—mounted upon his superb iron-gray, and looked the embodiment of the true chevalier that he was. Never before in our experience had the brigade been led in deliberate battle by its commander on horseback, and it was perhaps Colonel Keitt's want of experience that induced him to take this fatal step. Across a large old field the brigade swept towards a densely timbered piece of oakland, studded with undergrowth, crowding and swaying in irregular lines, the enemy's skirmishers pounding away at us as we advanced. Colonel Keitt was a fine target for the sharpshooters, and fell before the troops reached the timber, a martyr to the inexorable laws of the army rank. Into the dark recesses of the woods the troops plunged, creeping and crowding their way through the tangled mass of undergrowth, groups seeking shelter behind the larger trees, while the firing was going on from both sides. The enemy meeting our advance in a solid regular column, our broken and disorganized ranks could not cope with them. Some of the regimental officers seeing the disadvantage at which our troops were fighting, ordered a withdrawal to the old roadway in our rear. The dense smoke settling in the woods, shielded our retreat and we returned to our starting point without further molestation than the whizzing of the enemy's bullets overhead. The lines were reformed, and Colonel Davis, of the Fifteenth, assumed command (or perhaps Colonel Henagan).

Colonel William Wallace, of the Second, in speaking of this affair, says:

> "Our brigade, under the command of the lamented Colonel Keitt, was sent out to reconnoitre, and came upon the en-

emy in large force, strongly entrenched. Keitt was killed, and the brigade suffered severely. A few skirmishers thrown out would have accomplished the object of a reconnoissance, and would have saved the loss of many brave men. Our troops finding the enemy entrenched, fell back and began to fortify. Soon our line was established, and the usual skirmishing and sharpshooting commenced. That same evening, being on the extreme left of Kershaw's Division, I received orders to hasten with the Second Regiment to General Kershaw's headquarters. I found the General in a good deal of excitement. He informed me that our lines had been broken on the right of his division, and directed me to hasten there, and if I found a regiment of the enemy flanking his position, to charge them. I hurried to the point indicated, found that our troops to the extent of a brigade and a half had been, driven from their works, and the enemy in possession of them. I determined to charge, however, and succeeded in driving them from their position, with but little loss. Our regiment numbered one hundred and twenty-seven men. The enemy driven out consisted of the Forty-eighth and One Hundred and Twelfth New York. We captured the colors of the Forty-eighth, took some prisoners, and killed many while making their escape from the trenches. We lost in this charge one of our most efficient officers, Captain Ralph Elliott, a brother of General Stephen Elliott. He was a brave soldier and a most estimable gentleman."

Our lines were formed at right angles to that on which we had fought that day, and the soldiers were ordered to fortify. The Second and Third on the left were on an incline leading to a ravine in front of a thicket; the Fifteenth and Twentieth, on the right of the Third, were on the brow of a plateau; in front was the broad old field, through which we had marched to the first advance; the Third Battalion, Eighth, and Seventh, on extreme right, were on the plateau and fronted by a thicket of tall pines.

As nearly all regimental commanders had been killed since the 6th of May, I will give them as they existed on the 1st of June, three weeks later:

Second	Major Wm. Wallace.
Third	Lieutenant Colonel W.D Rutherford.
Seventh	Captain James Mitchel.
Eighth	Major E.S. Stackhouse.
Twentieth	Lieutenant Colonel S.M. Boykin.
Third Battalion	Captain Whitener.
Brigade Commander	Colonel James Henagan.

 Grant stretched his lines across our front and began approaching our works with his formidable parallels. He would erect one line of breastworks, then under cover of night, another a hundred or two yards nearer us; thus by the third of June our lines were not one hundred yards apart in places. Our pickets and those of the enemy were between the lines down in their pits, with some brush in front to shield them while on the look out. The least shadow or moving of the branches would be sure to bring a rifle ball singing dangerously near one's head—if he escaped it at all. The service in the pits here for two weeks was the most enormous and fatiguing of any in the service—four men being in a pit for twenty-four hours in the broiling sun during the day, without any protection whatever, and the pit was so small that one could neither sit erect nor lie down.

 Early on the morning of the 3rd of June, just three days after our fiasco at Cold Harbor, Grant moved his forces for the assault. This was to be the culmination of his plan to break through Lee's lines or to change his plans of campaign and settle down to a regular siege. Away to our right the battle commenced. Heavy shelling on both sides. Then the musketry began to roll along in a regular wave, coming nearer and nearer as new columns moved to the assault. Now it reaches our front, and the enemy moves steadily upon our works. The cheering on our right told of the repulse by our forces, and had a discouraging effect upon the Federal troops moving against us. As soon as their skirmish line made its appearance, followed by three lines of battle, our pickets in front of us were relieved, but many fell before gaining our breastworks, and those who were not killed had to lie during the day between the most murderous fire in the history of the war, and sad to say, few survived. When near us the first line came with a rush at charge bayonets, and our officers had great difficulty in restraining the men from opening fire too soon. But when close enough, the word "fire" was given, and the men behind the works raised deliberately, resting their guns upon the works, and fired volley after volley into the rushing but disorganized ranks of the enemy. The first line reeled and attempted to fly the field, but were met by the next column, which halted the retreating troops with the bayonet, butts of guns, and officers' sword, until the greater number were turned to the second assault. All this while our sharpshooters and men behind our works were pouring a galling fire into the tangled mass of advancing and retreating troops. The double column, like the first, came with a shout, a huzzah, and a charge. But our men had by this time reloaded their pieces, and were only too eager awaiting the command "fire." But when it did come the result was telling—men falling on top of men, rear rank pushing forward the first rank, only to be swept away like chaff. Our batteries on the hills in rear and those mounted on our infantry line were raking the field, the former with shell and solid shot, the latter with grape and canister. Smoke settling on the ground, soon rendered objects in front scarcely visible, but the steady flashing of the enemy's guns and the hail of bullets over our heads and against our works told plainly enough that the enemy were standing to their work with desperate courage, or were held in hand with a powerful grasp of discipline. The third line of assault had now mingled with the first two, and all lying stretched upon the ground and hidden by the dense smoke, caused the greater number of our bullets to fly over their heads. Our elevated position and the necessity of rising above the works to fire, rendered our breastworks of little real advantage; considering, too, the disparity of numbers, then three lines against our one, and a very weak line at that. The loud Rebel yell heard far to our right told us to be of good cheer, they were holding their own, and repulsing every assault. The conflict in front of Breckenridge's Division was the bloodiest, with the possible exception of that of Mayree's Hill, in front of Fredericksburg, and the "Bloody Angle," of any during the war. Negro troops were huddled together and forced to the charge by white troops—the poor, deluded, unfortunate beings plied with liquor until all their sensibilities were so deadened that death had no horrors. Grant must have learned early in the day the impossibility of breaking Lee's line by direct charge, for by twelve o'clock the firing ceased.

This last assault of Grant's thoroughly convinced the hero of Vicksburg and Missionary Ridge of the impossibility of breaking Lee's lines by direct advances. He could not surprise him at any point, or catch him off his guard, for Lee knew every foot of the ground too well, having fought all over if for two years. It was estimated and confirmed afterwards by official reports, that Grant had lost sixty thousand men from his crossing of the Rapidan to the end of the 3rd of June, just thirty days—more men than Lee had in the commencement of the campaign. Grant had become wiser the more familiar he became with Lee and his veterans, and now began to put in new tactics—that of stretching out his lines so as to weaken Lee's, and let attrition do the work that shells, balls, and the bayonet had failed to accomplish. The end showed the wisdom of the plan.

The two regiments on the left of the brigade did not suffer so greatly as the others, being protected somewhat by the timber and underbrush in their front. The enemy's dead lay in our front unburied until Grant's further move to the right, then it became our duty to perform those rites.

Colonel Lawrence Massillon Keitt

Colonel Lawrence Massillon Keitt was the second son of George and Mary Magdalene Wannamaker Keitt. He was born on the 4th day of October, 1824, in St. Matthews Parish, Orangeburg District, S.C. He received his early education at Asbury Academy, a flourishing institution near the place of his birth.

In his thirteenth year he entered Mt. Zion College at Winnsboro, Fairfield County, where he spent one year in preparation for the South Carolina College, which he entered in his fourteenth year, graduating third in his class. He read law in Attorney General Bailey's office in Charleston, S.C., and was admitted to the bar as soon as he was of legal age. He opened a law office at Orangeburg, the county seat.

At the first vacancy he was elected a member to the Lower House of the General Assembly of the State, in which body he served until his election to the Lower House of Congress in 1853. He served in that body until December, 1860, when he resigned his seat and returned to South Carolina on the eve of the secession of his State from the Union. He was a leading Secessionist and was elected a member of the Secession Convention. That body after passing the Ordinance of Secession elected him a delegate to the Provisional Congress of the Confederate States, which met at Montgomery, Ala. He was a very active member. On the adjournment of the Provisional Government of the Confederate States he returned to South Carolina and raised the Twentieth Regiment of South Carolina Volunteers and went into the Confederate Army. His command was ordered to Charleston. He served with his command on James' Island, Sullivan's Island, Morris' Island, and in Charleston in all the important engagements. He was in command of Morris' Island twenty-seven days and nights during its awful bombardment. When ordered to evacuate the island he did so, bringing off everything without the loss of a man. He was the last person to leave the island. General Beauregard in his report to the War Department said it was one of the greatest retreats in the annals of warfare.

The latter part of May, 1864, he left Charleston with his command and joined General Lee's Army thirteen miles from Richmond. He carried about sixteen hundred men in his regiment to Virginia. It was called the "Twentieth Army Corps." He was assigned to Kershaw's Brigade and put in command of the brigade. On the first day of June, 1864, while leading the brigade, mounted on a grey horse, against a powerful force of the enemy he was shot through the liver and fell mortally wounded. He died on the 2nd of June, 1864. By his request his remains were brought to South Carolina and laid by the side of his father in the graveyard at Tabernacle Church. Thus passed away one of South Carolina's brightest jewels.

Chapter 32
From Cold Harbor to Petersburg

The field in the front at Cold Harbor where those deadly assaults had been made beggars description. Men lay in places like hogs in a pen—some side by side, across each other, some two deep, while others with their legs lying across the head and body of their dead comrades. Calls all night long could be heard coming from the wounded and dying, and one could not sleep for the sickening sound "W—a—t—e—r" ever sounding and echoing in his ears. Ever and anon a heart-rending wail as coming from some lost spirit disturbed the hushed stillness of the night. There were always incentives for some of the bolder spirits, whose love of adventure or love of gain impelled them, to visit the battlefield before the burial detail had reached it, as many crisp five-dollar greenbacks or even hundred-dollar interest-bearing United States bonds could be found in the pockets of the fallen Federal either as a part of his wages or the proceeds of his bounty. The Federal Government was very lavish in giving recruits this bounty as an inducement to fill the depleted ranks of "Grant the Butcher." Tom Paysinger, of the Third, who had been detailed as a scout to General Longstreet, was a master hand at foraging upon the battlefield. Whether to gain information or to replenish his purse is not known, but be that as it may, the night after the battle he crept quietly through our lines and in the stillness and darkness he made his way among the dead and wounded, searching the pockets of those he found. He came upon one who was lying face downward and whom he took to be beyond the pale of resistance, and proceeded to rifle his pockets. After gathering a few trifles he began crawling on his hands and knees towards another victim. When about ten steps distant the wounded Federal, for such it proved to be, raised himself on his elbow, grasped the gun that was lying beside him, but unknown to Paysinger, and called out, "You d———n grave robber, take that," and bang! went a shot at his retreating form. He then quietly resumed his recumbent position. The bullet struck Paysinger in the thigh and ranging upwards lodged in his hip, causing him to be a cripple for several long months. It is needless to say Paysinger left the field. He said afterwards he "would have turned and cut the rascal's throat, but he was afraid he was only 'possuming' and might brain him with the butt of his gun."

We remained in our position for several days and were greatly annoyed by the shells thrown by mortars or cannon mounted as such, which were continually bursting overhead or dropping in our works. The sharpshooters with globe-sighted rifles would watch through the brush in front of their rifle pits and as soon as a head was thoughtlessly raised either from our pits, which were now not more than fifty yards apart, or our breastwork, "crack!" went a rifle, a dull thud, and one of our men lay dead. It is astonishing how apt soldiers are in avoiding danger or warding it off, and what obstacles they can overcome, what work they can accomplish and with so few and ill assortment of tools when the necessity arises. To guard against the shells that were continually dropping in our midst or outside of our works, the soldiers began burrowing like rabbits in rear of our earthworks and building covered ways from their breastwork to the ground below. In a few days men could go the length of a regiment without being exposed in the least, crawling along the tunnels all dug with bayonets, knives, and a few wornout shovels. At some of these angles the passer-by would be exposed, and in going from one opening to another, only taking the fraction of a second to accomplish, a bullet would come whizzing from some unseen source, either to the right or left. As soon as one of these openings under a covered way would be darkened by some one passing, away a bullet would come singing in the aperture, generally striking the soldier passing through. So annoying and dangerous had the practice become of shooting in our works from an unseen source that a detail of ten or twenty men was sent out under Lieutenant D.J. Griffith, of the Fifteenth, to see if the concealed enemy might not be located and an end put to the annoyance. Griffith and his men crept along cautiously in the underbrush, while some of our men would wave a blanket across the exposed places in the breastwork to draw the Federal fire, while Griffith and his detail kept a sharp lookout. It was not long before they discovered the hidden "Yank" perched in the top of a tall gum tree, his rifle resting in the fork of a limb. Griffith got as close as he well could without danger of being detected by some one under the tree. When all was ready they sighted their rifles at the fellow up the tree and waited his next fire. When it did come I expect that Yankee and his comrades below were the worst surprised of any throughout the war; for no sooner had his gun flashed than ten rifles rang out in answer and the fellow fell headlong to the ground, a distance of fifty feet or more. Beating the air with his hands and feet, grasping at everything within sight or reach, his body rolling and tumbling among the limbs of the tree, his head at times up, at others down, till at last he strikes the earth, and with a terrible rebound in the soft spongy needles Mr. "Yank" lies still, while Griffith and his men take to their heels. It was not known positively whether he was killed or not, but one thing Lieutenant Griffith and his men were sure of—one Yankee, at least, had been given a long ride in midair.

After Grant's repulse at Cold Harbor he gave up all hopes of reaching Richmond by direct assault and began his memorable change of base. Crossing the James River at night he undertook the capture of Petersburg by surprise. It appears from contemporaneous history that owing to some inexcusable blunders on our part Grant came very near accomplishing his designs.

To better understand the campaign around Petersburg it is necessary to take the reader back a little way. Simultaneous with Grant's advance on the Rapidan an army of thirty thousand under the Union General B.F. Butler was making its way up the James River and threatening Petersburg. It was well known that Richmond would be no longer tenable should the latter place fall. Beauregard was commanding all of North Carolina and Virginia on the south side of the James River, but his forces were so small and so widely scattered that they promised little protection. When Lee and his veterans were holding back Grant and the Union Army at the Wilderness, Brocks Cross Roads, and Spottsylvania C.H., Beauregard with a handful of veterans and a few State troops was "bottling up Butler" on the James. What Kershaw had been to Lee at the Wilderness, McGowan at Spottsylvania, General Hagood was to General Beauregard on the south side around Petersburg. General Beauregard does not hesitate to acknowledge what obligations he was under to the brave General Hagood and his gallant band of South Carolinians at the most critical moments during the campaign, and it is unquestioned that had not General Hagood come up at this opportune moment, Petersburg would have fallen a year before it did.

General Beauregard fought some splendid battles on the south side, and if they had not been overshadowed by the magnitude of

Lee's from the Wilderness to the James, they would have ranked in all probability as among the greatest of the war. But from one cause and then another during the whole campaign Beauregard was robbed of his legitimate fruits of battle.

The low, swampy nature of the country below Richmond, especially between the James and the Chickahominy, prevented Lee's scouts from detecting the movements of Grant's Army for some days after the movement began. Grant had established his headquarters at Wilcox's Landing, on the James, and had all his forces in motion on the south of the river by the 13th of June, while Lee was yet north of the Chickahominy.

General Beauregard and the gallant troops under him deserve the highest praise for their conduct in successfully giving Butler battle, while Petersburg was in such imminent peril, and Lee still miles and miles away. It is scarcely credible to believe with what small force the plucky little Creole held back such an overwhelming army.

When Grant made his first crossing of the James and began the movement against Petersburg, General Beauregard had only Wise's Brigade of infantry, twenty-two pieces of artillery, two regiments of cavalry under General Bearing, and a few regiments of local militia.

Grant had ordered the Eighteenth Corps (Smith's) by way of the White House to Bermuda Hundreds, and this corps had crossed the narrow neck of land between the James and the Appomattox, crossing the latter river on a pontoon bridge, and was at the moment firing on Petersburg with a force under his command of twenty-two thousand, with nothing between General Smith and Petersburg but Beauregard's two thousand men of all arms. Kant's Cavalry and one division of negro troops, under Hinks, had joined their forces with Smith after coming to the south side. Hancock's and Warren's Corps crossed the Chickahominy at Long Bridge and the James at Wilcox's Landing, and with Grant at the head, all were pushing on to Petersburg. Wright (Sixth) and Burnside (Ninth) crossed by way of Jones' Bridge and the James and Appomattox on pontoon bridges, pushing their way rapidly, as the nature of the ground permitted, in the direction of Petersburg. Beauregard in the meantime had been reinforced by his own troops, they having been transferred temporarily to Lee, at Spottsylvania Court House.

Hoke's Division reached Petersburg at twelve o'clock, on the 15th of June. Hagood's Brigade, of that division, being transported by rail from the little town of Chester, reached the city about night. Bushrod

Johnson's Brigade was ordered up from Bermuda on the 16th. Beauregard being thus reinforced, had ten thousand troops of all arms on the morning of the 16th, with which to face Meade's Army, consisting of Hancock's, Smith's, and Burnside's Corps, aggregating sixty-six thousand men. Meade made desperate and continuous efforts to break through this weak line of gray, but without effect Only one division of Federals gained any permanent advantage. Warren, with four divisions, now reinforced Meade, bringing the Federal Army up to ninety thousand, with no help for Beauregard yet in sight. From noon until late at night of the 17th the force of this entire column was hurled against the Confederate lines, without any appreciable advantage, with the exception of one division before alluded to. Lee was still north of the James with his entire army, and undecided as to Grant's future movements. He was yet in doubt whether Grant had designs directly against the Capital, or was endeavoring to cut his communications by the capture of Petersburg. Beauregard had kept General Lee and the war department thoroughly advised of his peril and of the overwhelming numbers in his front, but it was not until midnight of the 17th that the Confederate commander determined to change his base and cross to the south side of the James. It was at that hour that Kershaw's Brigade received its orders to move at once. For the last few days the army had been gradually working its way towards the James River, and was now encamped near Rice's Station. From the manner in which we were urged forward, it was evident that our troops somewhere were in imminent peril. The march started as a forced one, but before daylight it had gotten almost to a run. All the regiments stood the great strain without flinching, with the exception of the Twentieth. The "Old Twentieth Army Corps," as that regiment was now called, could not stand what the old veterans did, and fell by the way side. It was not for want of patriotism or courage, but simply a want of seasoning. Fully half of the "Corps" fell out. When we reached Petersburg, about sunrise, we found only Wise's Brigade and several regiments of old men and boys, hastily gotten together to defend their city, until the regulars came up. They had been fighting in the ranks, these gray-beards and half-grown boys, for three days, and to their credit be it said, "they weathered the storm" like their kinsmen in Wise's Brigade, and showed as much courage and endurance as the best of veterans. On the streets were ladies of every walk in life, some waving banners and handkerchiefs, some clapping their hands and giving words of cheer as the soldiers came by with their swinging step, their clothes looking as if they had just swum the river. Were the ladies refugeeing—getting out of harm's way? Not a bit of it. They looked equally as determined and defiant as their brothers and fathers in ranks—each and all seemed to envy the soldier his rifle. If Richmond had become famous through the courage and loyalty of her daughters, Petersburg was equally entitled to share the glories of her older sister, Richmond.

Kershaw's Brigade relieved that of General Wise, taking position on extreme right, resting its right on the Jerusalem plank road, and extending towards the left over the hill and across open fields. Wise had some hastily constructed works, with rifle pits in front. These later had to be relieved under a heavy fire from the enemy's battle line. As the other brigades of the division came up, they took position on the left. Fields' Division and R.H. Anderson's, now of this corps, did not come up for some hours yet. General Anderson, in the absence of General Longstreet, commanded the corps as senior Major General. Before our division lines were properly adjusted, Warren's whole corps made a mad rush upon the works, now manned by a thin skirmish line, and seemed determined to drive us from our entrenchments by sheer weight of numbers. But Kershaw displayed no inclination to yield, until the other portions of our corps came upon the field. After some hours of stubborn fighting, and failing to dislodge us, the enemy withdrew to strengthen and straighten their lines and bring them more in harmony with ours. About four o'clock in the afternoon Meade organized a strong column of assault, composed of the Second, Fifth, and the Ninth Army Corps, and commanded in person, holding one corps in reserve. The artillery of the four corps was put in position, and a destructive fire was opened upon us by fifty pieces of the best field artillery. The infantry then commenced the storming of our works, but Field's Division had come up and was on the line. General Lee had given strength to our position by his presence, coming upon the field about eleven o'clock, and gave personal direction to the movements of the troops. The battle raged furiously until nightfall, but with no better results on the enemy's side than had attended him for the last three days—a total repulse at every point. By noon the next day Lee's whole force south of the James was within the entrenched lines of the city, and all felt perfectly safe and secure. Our casualties were light in comparison to the fighting done during the day, but the enemy was not only defeated, but badly demoralized.

Kershaw and Fields, of Lee's Army, with ten thousand under General Beauregard, making a total of twenty thousand, successfully combatted Grant's whole army, estimated by the Federals themselves as being ninety thousand. These are some figures that might well be taken in consideration when deeds of prowess and Southern valor are being summed up.

Grant seemed determined to completely invest Petersburg on the south side by continually pushing his lines farther to the left, lengthening our lines and thereby weakening them. On the 21st of June the Second and Sixth Corps of the Federal Army moved on to the west of the Jerusalem plank road, while the Fifth was to take up position on the east side. In the manoeuver, or by some misunderstanding, the Fifth Corps became separated from those of the other divisions, thereby leaving a gap of about a division intervening. General Lee seeing this opportunity to strike the enemy a blow, and as A.P. Hill was then coming up, he ordered him to push his force forward and attack the enemy in flank. Moving his troops forward with that despatch that ever attended the Third Corps of our army, it struck the enemy a stunning blow in the flank and rear, driving them back in great disorder, capturing several thousand prisoners and a battery or two of artillery. The enemy continued to give way until they came upon their strong entrenched position; then Hill retired and took his place on the line. Again Grant started his cavalry out on raids to capture and destroy the railroads leading into Petersburg and Richmond, the route by which the entire army of Lee had to look for supplies. But at Reams' Station Hampton met the larger body of the enemy's cavalry and after a hard fought battle, in which he utterly routed the enemy, he captured his entire wagon train and all his artillery. A short time after this Grant sent Hancock, one of the ablest Generals in the Federal Army, (a true, thorough gentleman, and as brave as the bravest, and one whom the South in after years had the pleasure of showing its gratitude and admiration for those qualities so rare in many of the Federal commanders, by voting for him for President of the United States) with a large body of cavalry to destroy the Weldon Road at all hazard and to so possess it that its use to our army would be at an end. After another hard battle, in which the enemy lost five thousand men, Hancock succeeded in his mission and captured and retained the road. The only link now between the capital and the other sections of the South on which the subsistence of the army depended was that by

Danville, Va. This was a military road completed by the government in anticipation of those very events that had now transpired. Another road on which the government was bending all its energies to complete, but failed for want of time, was a road running from Columbia to Augusta, Ga. This was to be one of the main arteries of the South in case Charleston should fail to hold out and the junction of the roads at Branchville fall in the hands of the enemy. Our lines of transportation, already somewhat circumscribed, were beginning to grow less and less. Only one road leading South by way of Danville, and should the road to Augusta, Ga., via Columbia and Branchville, be cut the South or the Armies of the West and that of the East would be isolated. As gloomy as our situation looked, there was no want of confidence in the officers and the troops. The rank and file of the South had never considered a condition of failure. They felt their cause to be sacred, that they were fighting for rights and principles for which all brave people will make every sacrifice to maintain, that the bravery of a people like that which the South had shown to the world, the spirits that animated them, the undaunted courage by which the greatest battles had been fought and victories gained against unprecedented numbers, all this under such circumstances and under such leadership—the South could not fail. Momentary losses, temporary reverses might prolong the struggle, but to change the ultimate results, never. And at the North there were loud and widespread murmurings, no longer confined to the anti-abolitionist and pro slavery party, but it came from statesmen the highest in the land, it came from the fathers and mothers whose sons had fallen like autumn leaves from the Rapidan to the Appomattox. The cries and wails of the thousands of orphans went up to high Heaven pleading for those fathers who had left them to fill the unsatiate maw of cruel, relentless war. The tears of thousands and thousands of widows throughout the length and breadth of the Union fell like scalding waters upon the souls of the men who were responsible for this holocaust. Their voices and murmuring, though like Rachael's "weeping for her children and would not be comforted," all this to appease the Moloch of war and to gratify the ambition of fanatics. The people, too, of the North, who had to bear all this burden, were sorely pressed and afflicted at seeing their hard earned treasures or hoarded wealth, the fruits of their labor, the result of their toil of a lifetime, going to feed this army of over two millions of men, to pay the bounties of thousands of mercenaries of the old countries and the unwilling freedmen soldiers of the South. All this only to humble a proud people and rob them of their inherent rights, bequeathed to them by the ancestry of the North and South. How was it with the South? Not a tear, not a murmur. The mothers, with that Spartan spirit, buckled on the armor of their sons with pride and courage, and with the Spartan injunction, bade them "come home with your shield, or on it." The fathers, like the Scottish Chieftain, if he lost his first born, would put forward his next, and say, "Another one for Hector." Their storehouses, their barns, and graneries were thrown open, and with lavish hands bade the soldiers come and take—come and buy without money and without price. Even the poor docile slave, for whom some would pretend these billions of treasure were given and oceans of blood spilled, toiled on in peace and contentment, willing to make any and every sacrifice, and toil day and night, for the interest and advancement of his master's welfare. He was as proud of his master's achievements, of our victories, and was even as willing to throw his body in this bloody vortex as if the cause had been his own. The women of the South, from the old and bending grandmothers, who sat in the corner, with their needles flying steady and fast, to the aristocratic and pampered daughter of wealth, toiled early and toiled late with hands and bodies that never before knew or felt the effects of work—all this that the soldier in the trenches might be clothed and fed—not alone for members of their families, but for the soldiers all, especially those who were strangers among us—those who had left their homes beyond the Potomac and the Tennessee. The good housewife stripped her household to send blankets and bedding to the needy soldiers. The wheel and loom could be heard in almost every household from the early morn until late at night going to give not comforts, but necessities of life, to the boys in the trenches. All ranks were leveled, and the South was as one band of brothers and sisters. All formality and restraint were laid aside, and no such thing as stranger known. The doors were thrown open to the soldiers wherever and whenever they chose to enter; the board was always spread, and a ready welcome extended. On the march, when homes were to be passed, or along the sidewalks in cities, the ladies set the bread to baking and would stand for hours in the doorway or at some convenient window to cut and hand out slice after slice to the hungry soldiers as long as a loaf was left or a soldier found.

With such a people to contend, with such heroes to face in the field, was it any wonder that the North began to despair of ever conquering the South? There was but one way by which the Northern leaders saw possible to defeat such a nation of "hereditary madmen in war." It was by continually wearing them away by attrition. Every man killed in the South was one man nearer the end. It mattered not what the cost might be—if two or a dozen soldiers fell, if a dozen households were put in mourning, and widows and orphans were made by the score—the sacrifice must be made and endured. The North had found in Grant a fit weapon by which to give the blow—a man who could calmly see the slaughter of thousands to gain an end, if by so doing the end in view could be expedited. The absence of all feelings of humanity, the coolness and indifference with which he looked upon his dead, his calmness in viewing the slaughter as it was going on, gained for him the appellation of "Grant, the Butcher." Grant saw, too, the odds and obstacles with which he had to contend and overcome when he wrote these memorable words, "Lee has robbed the cradle and the grave." Not odds in numbers and materials, but in courage, in endurance, in the sublime sacrifice the South was making in men and treasure. Scarcely an able-bodied man in the South—nay, not one who could be of service—who was not either in the trenches, in the ranks of the soldiers, or working in some manner for the service. All from sixteen to fifty were now in actual service, while all between fourteen and sixteen and from fifty to sixty were guarding forts, railroads, or Federal prisoners. These prisoners had been scattered all over the South, and began to be unwieldy. The Federals under the policy of beating the South by depleting their ranks without battle in the field had long since refused the exchange of prisoners. They had, by offers of enticing bounties, called from the shores of the Old Country thousands of poor emigrants, who would enlist merely for the money there was in it. Thousands and thousands of prisoners captured could not speak a word of English. They had whole brigades of Irish and Dutch, while the Swedes, Poles, Austrians, as well as Italians, were scattered in the ranks throughout the army. In the capturing of a batch of prisoners, to a stranger who would question them, it would seem more like we were fighting the armies of Europe than our kinsmen of the North. In fact, I believe if the real truth of it was known, the greater part of the Federal Army in the closing days of the Confederacy was either foreigners or sons of foreigners.

Were there ever before such people as those of the Southland?

Were there ever such patriotic fathers, such Christian mothers, such brave and heroic sons and daughters? Does it look possible at this late day that a cause so just and righteous could fail, with such men and women to defend it? It is enough to cause the skeptic to smile at the faith of those who believe in God's interference in human affairs and in the efficacy of prayers. The cause of the South was just and right, and no brave men would have submitted without first staking their all upon the issue of cruel, bloody war. Impartial history will thus record the verdict.

Chapter 33

In the Trenches Around Petersburg

As soon as General Lee's Army was all up and his lines established, we began to fortify in earnest. The breastworks that were built now were of a different order to the temporary ones in the Wilderness and at Cold Harbor. As it was known now that a regular siege had begun, our breastworks were built proportionately strong. Our lines were moved to the left to allow a battery to occupy the brow of a hill on our right, Kershaw's Brigade occupying both slopes of the hills, a ravine cutting it in two. Field pieces were mounted at intervals along the line with the infantry, every angle covered by one or more cannon. The enemy commenced shelling us from mortars from the very beginning of our work, and kept it up night and day as long as we remained in the trenches. The day after Kershaw took position Grant began pressing our picket line and running his parallels nearer and nearer our works. It was said that Grant won his laurels in the West with picks and shovels instead of rifles and cannon, but here it looked as if he intended to use both to an advantage. As soon as he had his lines located, he opened a fusilade upon Petersburg, throwing shells into the city from his long-ranged guns, without intermission. It was in the immediate front of the right of the brigade and the battery on the hill that the enemy's mine was laid that occasioned the "Battle of the Crater" a month afterwards. Before we had finished our works, several night assaults were made upon us, notably the one up the ravine that separated the Second and Third on the night of the 21st of June. It was easily repulsed, however, with little loss on our side, the enemy firing too high. What annoyed the soldiers more than anything else was the continual dropping of shells in our works or behind them. We could hear the report of the mortars, and by watching overhead we could see the shell descending, and no one could tell exactly where it was going to strike and no chance for dodging. As every old soldier knows, card playing was the national vice, if vice it could be called, and almost all participated in it, but mostly for amusement, as the soldiers scarcely ever had money to hazard at cards. While a quartet was indulging in this pastime in the trenches, some one yelled, "Lookout, there comes a shell!" Looking up the disciples of the "Ten Spots" saw a shell coming down right over their heads. Nothing could be done but to stretch themselves at full length and await developments. They were not long in suspense, for the shell dropped right upon the oilcloth on which they had been playing. There it lay sizzling and spluttering as the fuse burned lower and lower, the men holding their breath all the while, the other troops scattering right and left. The thing could not last; the tension broke, when one of the card-players seized the shell in his hands and threw it out of the works; just before exploding. It was the belief in the brigade that those men did not play cards again for more than thirty days.

Another annoyance was the enemy's sharpshooters, armed with globe-sighted rifles. These guns had a telescope on top of the barrel, and objects at a distance could be distinctly seen. Brush screened their rifle pits, and while they could see plainly any object above our works, we could not see them. A head uncautiously raised above the line, would be sure to get a bullet in or near it.

About one hundred yards in our rear, up the ravine, was a good spring of water. The men could reach this in safety by going down the breastworks in a stooping posture, then up the ravine to the spring. A recruit in the Second Regiment had gone to this spring and was returning. When about twenty paces from the works he undertook, through a spirit of adventure; or to save a few steps, to run diagonally across the field to his regiment. It was his last. When about midway he was caught by a bullet from the enemy's picket, and only lived long enough to call out, "Oh, mother!" Many lost their lives here by recklessness or want of caution.

After remaining in the trenches about two weeks, Kershaw's Brigade was relieved by a part of Hoke's Division and retired to some vacant lots in the city in good supporting distance of the front line. We were not out of reach of the shells by any means; they kept up a continual screaming overhead, bursting in the city. The soldiers got passes to visit the town on little shopping excursions, notwithstanding the continual bursting of the shells in the city. The citizens of Petersburg, white and black, women and children, like the citizens of Charleston, soon became accustomed to the shelling, and as long as one did not drop in their immediate vicinity, little attention was paid to it. One night after a furious bombardment the cry was heard, "The city is on fire; the city is on fire." A lurid glare shot up out of the very heart of the city, casting a dim light over the buildings and the camps near about. Fire bells began ringing, and the old men rushing like mad to fight the fire. As soon as the enemy discovered that the city was on fire, they concentrated all their efforts to the burning buildings. Shells came shrieking from every elevated position on the enemy's lines, and fell like "showers of meteors on a frolic." Higher and higher the flames rose until great molten-like tongues seemed to lick the very clouds. The old men mounted the ladder like boys, and soon the tops of the surrounding buildings were lined with determined spirits, and the battle against the flames began in earnest. We could see their forms against the dark back-ground, running hither and thither, fighting with all the power and energy of the brave and fearless men they were. They paid no heed to the screaming, shrieking, bursting shells all around, but battled bravely to save the city. After the burning of several contiguous buildings, the flames were gotten under control, and eventually the fire was extinguished. I have seen many battles, but never more heroism displayed than by the old citizens and boys that night in Petersburg. The soldiers were not allowed to leave their camp, and all the citizens of military age were away in the army, so the old men and boys had to fight this fire single-handed and alone, and amid a perfect storm of shot and shell.

Grant had been daily reinforced by recruits and forces from the West. Butler had received a large reinforcement from Banks, on the lower Mississippi, and was gradually working his way up to Richmond. A great number of these troops, to judge from the prisoners we captured, were foreigners; many could not speak a word of English. Kershaw was ordered to reinforce the troops on the north side, and on the 13th of July we crossed the James on a pontoon bridge, near Chaffin's Bluff, after an all night's march over brush, briars, through field and bog, and took position on a high ridge running out from the river. In front of us was a vast swamp of heavy timber and underbrush, called Deep Bottom. Beyond Deep Bottom the enemy had approached and entrenched, being supported by gun boats in the James. This position it was determined to surprise and take by assault. Early at night the brigade was moved out in this swamp, along a dull road that ran along its edge, and advanced in the direction of the enemy. No attempt of assault, was ever more dreaded or looked on with such apprehension, save, perhaps, our charge on the works at Knoxville, than this night charge at Deep Bottom. When near the enemy's position, we formed line of battle, while it was so dark in the dense woods that an object ten feet away could not be distinguished. We had to take and give commands in whispers, for fear the enemy would discover our presence. We moved forward gradually, a few steps at a time, each step a little nearer the enemy, who lay asleep behind their works. We had advanced, perhaps, two hundred yards, and as yet had encountered none of the enemy's pickets or videttes, showing how securely they felt in regard to a night attack. While halting to adjust our lines, which had to be done every few paces, Colonel Rutherford and myself were reconnoitering in front, and discovered a white object a few feet away. The men saw it, too, and thought it a sheep. The Colonel advanced and gave it a slight jab with his sword. In a moment a white blanket was thrown off, and there lay, as nicely coiled up as little pigs, two of the Yankee sentinels. They threw up their hands in a dazed kind of way, and to our whispered threats and uplifted swords, uttered some unintelligible jargon. We soon saw they did not understand a word of English. So it was we captured almost their entire picket line, composed of foreigners of Banks' Army, of Louisiana. Just then, on our right, whether from friend or foe, I never learned, several discharges of rifles alarmed both armies. It was too late then to practice secrecy, so the command "charge" was given. With a tremendous yell, we dashed through the tangled, matted mass of undergrowth, on towards the enemy's line. Aroused thus suddenly from their sleep, they made no other resistance than to fire a few shots over our head, leaving the breastworks in haste. Some lay still, others ran a few rods in the rear, and remained until captured, while the greater part scampered away towards their gun boats.

Colonel Henagan, of the Eighth, being in command of the brigade, ordered breastworks to be thrown up on the opposite side of an old road, in which the enemy lay and which they had partly fortified. The next day, about 3 o'clock, the enemy opened upon us a heavy fusilade with their siege mortars and guns from their gun boats and ironclads in the James. These were three hundred-pounders, guns we had never before been accustomed to. Great trees a foot and a half in diameter were snapped off like pipe-stems. The peculiar frying noise made in going through the air and their enormous size caused the troops to give them the name of "camp kettles." They passed through our earthworks like going through mole hills. The enemy advanced in line of battle, and a considerable battle ensued, but we were holding our own, when some watchers that Colonel Henagan had ordered in the tops of tall trees to watch the progress of the enemy, gave the warning that a large body of cavalry was advancing around our left and was gaining our rear. Colonel Henagan gave the command "retreat," but the great "camp kettles" coming with such rapidity and regularity, our retreat through this wilderness of shrubbery and tangled undergrowth would have ended in a rout had not our retreat been impeded by this swamp morass. We reached the fortification, however, on the bluff, the enemy being well satisfied with our evacuation of the position so near their camp.

The brigade, with the exception of marching and counter-marching, relieving other troops and being relieved, did no further service than occupying the lines until the 6th of August. The brigade boarded the train on that day at Chester for destination at that time unknown.

About the first of July the enemy, commanded by General Burnside, undertook to blow up a portion of our lines by tunneling under the works at a convenient point suitable for assault, and attempted to take our troops by surprise. The point selected was that portion of the line first held by Kershaw's Brigade, near Cemetery Hill, and in front of Taylor's Creek, near Petersburg. The continual night assaults on us at that point and the steady advance of their lines were to gain as much distance as possible. From the base of the hill at Taylor's Creek they began digging a tunnel one hundred and seventy yards long, and at its terminus were two laterals, dug in a concave towards our works, of thirty-seven feet each. In these laterals were placed eight hundred pounds of powder, with fuse by which all could be exploded at once.

General Beauregard, who commanded at this point, had been apprised of this undertaking, and at first had sunk counter-mines. But this was abandoned, and preparations were made to meet the emergency with arms. At this point and near the "Crater," as it was afterwards called, were stationed Colquit's (Ga.), Gracie's (Ala.), and Elliott's (S.C.) Brigades. Elliott's was posted immediately over it with Pegram's Battery. Rear lines had been established by which the troops could take cover, and reinforcements kept under arms night and day, so that when the explosion did take place, it would find the Confederates prepared. Batteries were placed at convenient places to bear upon the line and the place of explosion.

On the morning of the 30th of July, everything being in readiness, the fuse was placed, and at 3.30 o'clock the light was applied. Before this terrible "Crater" were massed Ledlie's, Potter's, Wilcox's, and Ferrero's Divisions, supported by Ames'. In the front was Ferrero's Division of negro troops, drunk and reeling from the effects of liquor furnished them by the wagon loads. This body of twenty-three thousand men were all under the immediate command of Major General Ord. On the left of Burnside, Warren concentrated ten thousand men, while the Eighteenth Corps, with that many more, were in the rear to aid and support the movement—the whole being forty-three thousand men, with eight thousand pounds of gun-powder to first spring the mine. General Sheridan, with his cavalry, was to make a demonstration in our front and against the roads leading to Petersburg. Hancock, too, was to take a part, if all things proved successful—fifty thousand men were to make a bold dash for the capture of the city. Immediately over the mine was Elliott's Brigade, consisting of the Seventeenth, Twenty-sixth, Twenty-third, Twenty-second, and Eighteenth South Carolina Regiments. At 3.30 o'clock the fuse was lighted, and while the Confederates, all unconscious of the impending danger, lay asleep, this grand aggregation of men of Grant's Army waited with bated breath and anxious eye the fearful explosion that eight thousand pounds of powder, under a great hill, were to make. Time went on, seconds into minutes. The nerves of the assaulters were, no doubt, at extreme tension. Four o'clock came, still all was still and silent. The Federal commanders held their watches in hand and watched the tiny steel hands tick the seconds away. The streaks of day came peeping up over the hills and cast shadows high overhead. The fuse had failed! A call was made for a volunteer to go down into the mine and relight the fuse. A Lieutenant and Sergeant bravely step forward and offered to undertake the perilous mission. They reach the mouth of the tunnel and peer in. All was dark, silent, sombre, and still. Along they grope their way with a small lantern in their hands. They reach the barrel of powder placed at the junction of the main and the laterals. The fuse had ceased to burn. Hurriedly they pass along to the other barrels. Expecting every moment to be blown into space, they find all as the first, out. The thousands massed near the entrance and along Taylor's Creek, watched with fevered excitement the return of the brave men who had thus placed their lives in such jeopardy for a cause they, perhaps, felt no interest. Quickly they placed new fuses, lit them, and quickly left the gruesome pit.

Scarcely had they reached a place of safety than an explosion like a volcano shook the earth, while the country round about was lit up with a great flash. The earth trembled and swayed—great heaps of earth went flying in the air, carrying with it men, guns, and ammunition. Cannon and carriages were scattered in every direction, while the sleeping men were thrown high in the air.

But here I will allow Colonel F.W. McMaster, an eye witness, who commanded Elliott's Brigade after the fall of that General, to tell the story of the "Battle of the Crater" in his own words. I copy his account, by permission, from an article published in one of the newspapers of the State.

The Battle of the Crater
By Colonel F.W. McMaster

In order to understand an account of the battle of the "Crater," a short sketch of our fortifications should be given.

Elliott's Brigade extended from a little branch that separated it from Ransom's Brigade on the north, ran three hundred and fifty yards, joining Wise's Brigade on the south. Captain Pegram's Virginia Battery had four guns arranged in a half circle on the top of the hill, and was separated from the Eighteenth and Twenty-second South Carolina Regiments by a bank called trench cavalier.

The Federal lines ran parallel to the Confederate. The nearest point of Pegram's Battery to the Federal lines was eighty yards; the rest of the lines was about two hundred yards apart. The line called gorge line was immediately behind the battery, and was the general passage for the troops. The embankment called trench cavalier was immediately in rear of the artillery and was constructed for the infantry in case the battery should be taken by a successful assault.

The general line for the infantry, which has been spoken of as a wonderful feat of engineering, was constructed under peculiar circumstances. Beauregard had been driven from the original lines made for the defense of Petersburg, and apprehensive that the enemy, which numbered ten to one, would get into the city, directed his engineer, Colonel Harris, to stake a new line. This place was reached by General Hancock's troops at dark on the third day's fighting, and our men were ordered to make a breastwork. Fortifications without spades or shovels was rather a difficult feat to perform, but our noble soldiers went to work with bayonets and tin cups, and in one night threw up a bank three feet high—high enough to cause Hancock to delay his attack. In the next ten days' time the ditches were enlarged until they were eight feet high and eight feet wide, with a banquette of eighteen inches high from which the soldiers could shoot over the breastwork.

Five or six traverses were built perpendicularly from the main trench to the rear, so as to protect Pegram's guns from the enfilading fire of the big guns on the Federal lines a mile to the north. Besides these traverses there were narrow ditches five or six feet deep which led to the sinks.

The only safe way to Petersburg, a mile off, was to go down to the spring branch which passed under our lines at the foot of the hill, then go to the left through the covered way to Petersburg, or to take the covered way which was half way down the hill to Elliott's headquarters.

At this point a ravine or more properly a swale ran up the hill parallel to our breastworks. It was near Elliott's headquarters where Mahone's troops went in from the covered way and formed in battle array.

The soldiers slept in the main trench. At times of heavy rains the lower part of the trench ran a foot deep in water. The officers slept in burrows dug in the sides of the rear ditches. There were traverses, narrow ditches, cross ditches and a few mounds over officers' dens, so that there is no wonder that one of the Federal officers said the quarters reminded him of the catacombs of Rome.

An ordinary mortal would not select such a place for a three mouths' summer residence.

About ten days after the battle, and while I was acting Brigadier General and occupying General Elliott's headquarters, a distinguished Major General visited me and requested me to go over the lines with him. I gladly complied with the request. He asked me where the men rested at night. I pointed out the floor of the ditch. He said, "But where do the officers sleep?" We happened then to be in the narrow ditch in front of my quarters, and I pointed it out to him.

He replied, in language not altogether suitable for a Sunday School teacher, that he would desert before he would submit to such hardships.

THE "CRATER"

The explosion took place at 4.45 A.M. The "Crater" made by eight thousand pounds of gun powder was one hundred and thirty-five feet long, ninety-seven feet broad and thirty feet deep. Two hundred and seventy-eight men were buried in the debris—Eighteenth Regiment, eighty-two; Twenty-second, one hundred and seventy, and Pegram's Battery, twenty-two men.

To add to the terror of the scene the enemy with one hundred and sixty-four cannon and mortars began a bombardment much greater than Fort Sumter or battery were ever subjected to. Elliott's Brigade near the "Crater" was panic stricken, and more than one hundred men of the Eighteenth Regiment covered with dirt rushed down. Two or three noble soldiers asked me for muskets. Some climbed the counterscarpe and made their way for Petersburg. Numbers of the Seventeenth joined the procession. I saw one soldier scratching at the counterscape of the ditch like a scared cat. A staunch Lieutenant of Company E. without hat or coat or shoes ran for dear life way down into Ransom's trenches. When he came to consciousness he cried out, "What! old Morse running!" and immediately returned to his place in line.

The same consternation existed in the Federal line. As they saw the masses descending they broke ranks, and it took a few minutes to restore order.

FEDERAL CHARGE

About fifteen minutes after the explosion General Ledlie's Corps advanced in line. The *cheval-de-frise* was destroyed for fifty yards. Soon after General Wilcox's Corps came in line and bore to Ledlie's left. Then Potter's Corps followed by flanks and was ordered to the right of Ledlie's troops.

The pall of smoke was so great that we could not see the enemy until they were in a few feet of our works, and a lively fusillade was opened by the Seventeenth Regiment on the north side of the "Crater." I saw Starling Hutto, of Company H, a boy of sixteen, on the top of the breastworks, firing his musket at the enemy a few yards off with the coolness of a veteran. As soon as I reached him I dragged him down by his coat tail and ordered him to shoot from the banquette. On the south of the "Crater" a few men under Major Shield, of the Twenty-second, and Captain R.E. White, with the Twenty-third Regiment, had a hot time in repelling the enemy.

Adjutant Sims and Captain Floyd, of the Eighteenth Regiment, with about thirty men, were cut off in the gorge line. They held the line for a few minutes. Adjutant Sims was killed and Captain Floyd and his men fell back into some of the cross ditches and took their chances with the Seventeenth.

It was half an hour before the Federals filled the "Crater," the gorge line and a small space of the northern part of the works not injured by the explosion. All this time the Federals rarely shot a gun on the north of the "Crater."

Major J.C. Coit, who commanded Wright's Battery and Pegram's battery, had come up to look after the condition of the latter. He concluded that two officers and twenty men were destroyed. Subsequently he discovered that one man had gone to the spring before the explosion, that four men were saved by a casemate and captured.

Colonel Coit says he took twenty-five minutes to come from his quarters and go to Wright's Battery, and thinks it was the first gun shot on the Federal side. Testimony taken in the court of inquiry indicate the time at 5.30 A.M.

General Stephen Elliott

General Stephen Elliott, the hero of Fort Sumter, a fine gentleman and a superb officer, came up soon after the explosion. He was dressed in a new uniform, and looked like a game cock. He surveyed the scene for a few minutes; he disappeared and in a short time he came up to me accompanied by Colonel A.R. Smith, of the Twenty-sixth, with a few men, who were working their way through the crowd. He said to me: "Colonel, I'm going to charge those Yankees out of the 'Crater'; you follow Smith with your regiment."

He immediately climbed the counter scrape. The gallant Smith followed, and about half a dozen men followed. And in less than five minutes he was shot from the "Crater" through his shoulder. I believe it was the first ball shot that day from the northern side of the "Crater." He was immediately pulled down into the ditch, and with the utmost coolness, and no exhibition of pain turned the command over to me, the next ranking officer. Colonels Benbow and Wallace were both absent on furlough.

I immediately ordered John Phillips, a brave soldier of Company I, to go around the "Crater" to inform the commanding officer of the serious wounding of General Elliott, and to inquire as to the condition of the brigade on the south side. Major Shield replied that Colonel Fleming and Adjutant Quattlebaum, with more than half the Twenty-second, were buried up, but with the remainder of his men and with the Twenty-third, under Captain White, and a part of Wise's Brigade we had driven the Yankees back, and intended to keep them back.

Being satisfied that the object of the mine was to make a gap in our line by which General Meade could rush his troops to the rear, I ordered Colonel Smith to take his Regiment, and Captain Crawford with three of my largest Companies, Companies K, E and B, containing nearly as many men as Smith's, to proceed by Elliott's headquarters up the ravine to a place immediately in rear of the "Crater"—to make the men lie down—and if the enemy attempted to rush down to resist them to the last extremity. This was near 6 o'clock A.M., and the enemy had not made any advance on the North side of the "Crater."

By this time the "Crater" was packed with men. I counted fourteen beautiful banners. I saw four or five officers waiving swords and pointing towards Petersburg, and I supposed they were preparing for a charge to the crest of the hill.

Elliott's Brigade

The line and strength of the Brigade from left to right was as follows: Twenty-sixth Regiment, two hundred and fifty men; Seventeenth, four hundred; Eighteenth, three hundred and fifty; Twenty-second, three hundred; Twenty-third, two hundred. In all one thousand and five hundred men, a full estimate.

Benbow's Regiment

The first severe attack of the enemy was on the South of the "Crater," which was defended by a part of the Twenty-second under Major Shedd, and Benbow's Twenty-third under Captain White. The enemy attacked with fury. Our men fought nobly, but were driven down their ditch. Wise's Brigade then joined in, and our men rushed back and recovered the lost space. About this time they shot Colonel Wright, leading the Thirteenth Minnesota regiment, and then the Federals slacked their efforts and bore to their right, and multitudes of them climbed the "Crater" and went to the rear of it and filled the gorge line and every vacant space on the North side. No serious aggressive attack was made on the Twenty-third Regiment during the rest of the day. The principal reason I suppose was the direct line to Cemetery Hill was through the Seventeenth Regiment. Every Federal officer was directed over and over again to rush to the crest of the hill.

Seventeenth Regiment

The Federals being checked on the South of the "Crater" charged Company A, the extreme right Company, next to the "Crater." Captain W.H. Edwards was absent sick, and a few of the men were covered with dirt by the explosion and were consequently demoralized. Private Hoke was ordered to surrender—declared he never would surrender to a Yankee. He clubbed his musket and knocked down four of his assailants, and was bayoneted. There were five men killed in Company A. Company F was the next attacked, and private John Caldwell shot one man and brained two with the butt of his musket. Lieutenant Samuel Lowry, a fine young man of twenty years, and four privates were killed. Company D surrendered in a traverse, and twenty-seven men were killed. Had the splendid Lieutenant W.G. Stevenson been present the result would have been different. Fourteen out of twenty-seven of these men died in prison of scurvy at Elmira, N.Y. Private J.S. Hogan, of Company D, leaped the traverse. He joined in Mahone's charge, and after the fight was sickened by the carnage; went to the spring to revive himself, then went into the charge under General Sanders. After the battle he procured enough coffee and sugar to last him a month. This young rebel seemed to have a furor for fighting and robbing Yankees. At the battle of Fort Steadman he manned a cannon which was turned on the enemy, and in the retreat from Petersburg he was in every battle. He was always on the picket line, by choice, where he could kill, wound or capture the enemy. He feasted well while the other soldiers fed on parched corn, and surrendered at Appomattox with his haversack filled with provisions.

Company C, the next Company, had fourteen men killed. Its Captain, William Dunovant, was only eighteen years of age, and as fine a Captain as was in Lee's Army. lieutenant C. Pratt, a fine officer not more than twenty-five years old, was killed. The command devolved on Sergeant T.J. LaMotte. G and H had two each; I, three; K, five; and B, one; F, five.

The Federals had the advantage over the Seventeenth because there were some elevated points near the "Crater" they could shoot from. After being driven down about fifty yards there was an angle in the ditch, and Sergeant LaMotte built a barricade, which stopped the advance. A good part of the fighting was done by two men on each side at a time—the rest being cut off from view.

Looking After Smith's Men

About 6:30 I went down a narrow ditch to see if Smith and his men were properly located to keep the enemy from going down to the ravine before I got back. I saw there was a vacant space in our trench. I hustled in and saw two muskets poked around an angle, as I got in the muskets were fired and harmlessly imbedded the balls in the breastworks. I immediately concluded that it was not very safe for the commander being on the extreme right of his men and went lower down. In a short time I again went in a ditch a little lower down the hill, anxious about the weak point on our line. I was smoking a pipe with a long tie-tie stem. As I returned I observed a rush down the line. As I got in the ditch the bowl of the pipe was knocked off. A big brawny fellow cried out, "Hold on men! the Colonel can't fight without his pipe!" He wheeled around, stopped the men until he picked up the bowl and restored it to me. I wish I knew the name of this kind-hearted old soldier.

The principal fighting was done by the head of the column.

A few game fellows attempted to cross the breastworks. A Captain Sims and a negro officer were bayoneted close together on our breastworks, but hundreds of the enemy for hours stuck like glue to our outer bank.

A Long and Lazy Fight

The sun was oppressively hot. There was very little musketry, the cannonading had closed; it was after 7 o'clock, and the soldiers on both sides, as there was not much shooting going on, seemed to resort to devices to pass the time. I saw Captain Steele throwing bayonets over a traverse. I saw Lamotte on one knee on the ground, and asked what he was doing. He whispered, "I'm trying to get the drop on a fellow on the other side." They would throw clods of clay at each other over the bank. As an Irishman threw over a lump of clay I heard him say, "Tak thart, Johnny." We all wished that Beauregard had supplied us with hand grenades, for the battle had simmered down to a little row in the trenches.

The Battle that Conquered Meade

At 8.10 A.M. Ferrero's four thousand three hundred negroes rushed over and reached the right flank of the Seventeenth. This horde of barbarians added greatly to the thousands of white men that packed themselves to the safe side of the breastworks. Thousands rushed down the hill side. Ransom's Twenty-sixth and Twenty-fifth Regiments were crazy to get hold of the negroes. "Niggers" had been scarce around there during the morning, now they were packed in an acre of ground and in close range. The firing was great all down the hill side, but when it got down to the branch the musketry was terrific, and Wright's Battery two hundred yards off poured in its shells. About half past 8 o'clock, at the height of the battle, there was a landslide amongst the negroes. Colonel Carr says two thousand negroes rushed back and lifted him from his feet and swept him to the rear. General Delavan Bates, who was shot through the face, said at that time that Ransom's Brigade was reported to occupy those lines.

When the battle was at its highest the Seventeenth was forced down its line about thirty yards. Lieutenant Colonel

Fleming, of Ransom's Forty-ninth Regiment, came up to me and pointed out a good place to build another barricade. I requested him to build it with his own men, as mine were almost exhausted by the labors of the day. He cheerfully assented, stepped on a banquette to get around me, and was shot in the neck and dropped at my feet.

At this moment of time an aide of General Bushrod Johnson told me that the General requested me to come out to Elliott's headquarters. I immediately proceeded to the place, and General Mahone came up. I was introduced to him, and suggested to him when his men came in to form them on Smith's men who were lying down in the ravine. A few minutes afterwards, by order of General Johnson, Captain Steele brought out the remnant of the Seventeenth Regiment, and they marched in the ravine back of Mahone's men.

Mahone's Charge

By this time General Mahone's Brigade of Virginians, eight hundred men strong, was coming in one by one, and were formed a few steps to the left and a little in advance of Smith's and Crawford's men. I was standing with General Johnson, close to Elliott's headquarters, and could see everything that transpired in the ravine. It took Mahone so long to arrange his men I was apprehensive that the enemy would make a charge before he was ready. A few Federal officers began to climb out of the main ditch until they numbered perhaps twenty-five men. General Mahone was on the extreme right it seemed to me busy with some men—I have heard since they were some Georgians. Captain Girardey had gone to Colonel Weisinger, who was worried with the delay, and told him General Mahone was anxious to take some of the Georgians with him. But the threatening attitude of the enemy precipitated the charge.

The noble old Roman, Colonel Weisinger, cried out "Forward!" and eight hundred brave Virginians sprung to their feet and rushed two hundred yards up the hill. It had not the precision of a West Point drill, but it exhibited the pluck of Grecians at Thermopylae. The men disappeared irregularly as they reached the numerous ditches that led to the main ditch until all were hid from view. The firing was not very great for the bayonet and butt of the muskets did more damage than the barrel. If any one desires a graphic description of a hand to hand fight I beg him to read the graphic detailed account given by Mr. Bernard in his "War Talks of Confederate Veterans."

In a few minutes the enemy in the ditches up to fifty yards of the "Crater" were killed or captured. The whole battlefield of three acres of ground became suddenly quiet comparatively.

Mahone in an hour's time sent in the Georgia Brigade, under General Wright. There was such a heavy fire from the "Crater" the brigade was forced to oblique to the left and banked on Mahone's men. In a few minutes after they landed at the foot of the "Crater" in their second charge.

Sanders' Alabama Brigade came up at this time. Besides his Alabamians were Elliott's Brigade and Clingman's Sixty-first North Carolina. The charge was made about one o'clock P.M., and the Federal artillery poured all its fire on the "Crater" for some minutes, slaughtering many of their own men. At this charge Lieutenant Colonel Gulp, who was absent at the explosion, being a member of a courtmartial, came up and took charge of the Seventeenth in the ravine, where Captain Steele had them. In the charge of the "Crater" under Sanders were Colonel Gulp, Colonel Smith and Lieutenant Colonel J.H. Hudson with the Twenty-sixth, and a large number of privates, especially from the Seventeenth Regiment, which also had a good many in Mahone's charge.

A good many of the Twenty-third joined in the charge, and Private W.H. Dunlap, Company C, Twenty-third Regiment, now of Columbia, was the first man who got in the "Crater" on the south side.

While the men were piled up around the "Crater" Adjutant Fant heard some Alabama soldiers picking out the fine banners within, and he was lucky to get two of them. He laid them down, and in a minute they were spirited away.

A little incident recited by Honorable George Clark Sanders, Adjutant General, illustrates how true politeness smoothes the wrinkled brow of war. He says that he saw a fine looking Federal officer making his way out of the "Crater" with much pain, using two reversed muskets for crutches, seeing one leg was shot off. He said I'm very sorry to see you in so much pain. The soldier replied the pain occurred at Spottsylvania a year ago. This is a wooden leg shot off to-day—then gave his name as General Bartlett, but Colonel Sanders kindly helped him out.

The horrors of war are sometimes relieved with incidents which amuse us. Adjutant Fant tells an amusing incident of Joe Free, a member of Company B. The Adjutant had gone In the afternoon to the wagon yard to be refreshed after the labors of the day. There was a group of men reciting incidents. The Adjutant overheard Free say He had gone into an officer's den for a few minutes to shade his head from the heat of the sun, as he was suffering from an intense headache, and as he began to creep out he saw the trench full of negroes. He dodged back again. Joe says he was scared almost to death, and that he "prayed until great drops of sweat poured down my face." The Adjutant knew that his education was defective and said, "What did you say, Joe?" "I said Lord have mercy on me! and keep them damned niggers from killing me!"

It was an earnest and effective prayer, for Mahone's men in an hour afterwards released him.

In a recent letter received from Captain E.A. Crawford, he says the enemy formed three times to charge, but we gave them a well directed volley each time and sent them into the rear line in our trench. When Mahone came in and formed my three companies charged with him. Colonel Smith told me they charged four times. Cusack Moore, a very intelligent private of Company K, said they charged five times. After the charge Captain Crawford requested General Mahone to give him permission to report to his regiment, and he ordered him to report to General Sanders, and he joined in that charge with his men. Company K had fifty-three men, Captain Cherry; Company E, forty, and Captain Burley, Company B, twenty-five; in all, one hundred and eighteen men.

Lieutenant Colonel Culp was a member of a military court doing duty in Petersburg at the time of the explosion, and could not get back until he reported to me at Elliott's headquarters. I made some extracts from his letter recently received:

"I recollect well that in the charge (the final one) which we made that model soldier and Christian gentleman, Sergeant Williams, of Company K, was killed, and that one of the Crowders, of Company B, was killed in elbow touch of me after we got into the works. These casualties, I think, well established the fact that Companies K and B were with me in the charge, and, as far as I know now, at least a portion of all the companies were with me. I recollect that poor Fant was with as very distinctly, and that he rendered very efficient service after we got to the 'Crater' in ferreting out hidden Federals, who had taken shelter there, and who, for the most part, seemed very loath to leave their biding places. I feel quite confident that Capt. Crawford was also there, but there is nothing that I can recall at this late day to fasten the fact of his presence on my mind, except that he was always ready for duty, however perilous it might be, and I am sure his company was there, in part at least. So, too, this will apply to all of the officers of our regiment whose duty it was to be there on that occasion, and who were not unavoidably kept away. In the charge that we made we were to be supported by the Sixty-first North Carolina. They were on our left, and I suppose entered the works entirely to the left of the 'Crater,' for I am sure that our regiment, small as it was, covered the 'Crater,' and when I reached the old line with my command we found ourselves in the very midst of the old fort, which, I may say, had been blown to atoms in the early morning. When we arrived the Federals began, in some instances, to surrender to us voluntarily, others, as before intimated, had to be pulled out of their hiding places. And with these prisoners we captured quite a number of colors, probably as many as a dozen, certainly not less than eight or ten. I was so occupied in trying to clear the trenches of the enemy that I gave no attention to these colors after they fell into the hands of our men, and afterwards learned, to my sorrow, that they had fallen into hands which were not entitled to them. Suffice it to say that few, if any of them, could be found. After perfect quiet had been restored, and we were thus robbed of these significant trophies of our triumph at which we felt quite a keen disappointment, it is pleasing to me to say that I think that every man of our regiment who was present acted his part nobly in the performance of the hazardous duty assigned us on that memorable occasion. You gave me the order to make the final charge already referred to."

The Artillery

The Confederates only had twenty-six cannon, and only three of them were conspicuous. The Federals had one hundred and sixty-four cannon and mortars. They fired five thousand and seventy-five rounds. They had only one man killed and two wounded.

General Hunt and others spoke slightingly of our guns, with two exceptions, Wright's Battery and Davenport's, which is mentioned as the two-gun battery. General Hunt the day before had accurately prepared to silence all these guns, except the Davenport Battery. General Hunt said he expected a company of infantry would take us in fifteen minutes after Pegram's Battery was gone. But the Wright Battery was a complete surprise. It was constructed just behind Ransom's Brigade, about one hundred yards. General Hunt never could locate the place, and shot at short range above five hundred shells doing no damage, but honeycombing the surrounding ground.

Wright's Battery was in five hundred yards of the "Crater," and Colonel Coit informed me he shot about six hundred rounds of shell and shrapnel at short range.

In my opinion it did more damage than all our guns put together. Its concealed location gave it a great advantage overall other guns.

Davidson's Battery had only one gun, which only could shoot in one line. But it created more anxiety amongst the enemy than any other. The infantry officers constantly alluded to its destructive power, and they dug a trench to guard against its fire. Major Hampton Gibbes commanded it until he was wounded, and then Captain D.N. Walker for the rest of the day did his duty nobly, and no doubt killed many Federals. General Warren was ordered to capture this gun about 8.30, but at 8.45 he was ordered to do nothing "but reconnoitre." This was before Mahone came up.

The most interesting of our guns were the two coehorns of Major John C. Haskell, because all of his shells were emptied into the "Crater," which was packed with men. General Mahone says: "In the meantime Colonel Haskell, a brilliant officer of our artillery, hunting a place where he could strike a blow at our adversary, presented himself for any service which I could advise. There were two coehorn mortars in the depression already referred to, and I suggested to him that he could serve them. I would have them taken up to the outside of the 'Crater,' at which place he could employ himself until one o'clock, as perhaps no such opportunity had ever occurred or would be likely to occur for effective employment of these little implements of war. Colonel Haskell adopted the suggestion, and the mortars being removed to a ditch within a few feet of the 'Crater,' they were quickly at work emptying their contents upon the crowded mass of men in this horrible pit."

Lieutenant Bowley, a Federal officer, says:

"A mortar battery also opened on us. After a few shots they got our range so well that the shells fell directly among us. Many of them did not explode at all, but a few burst directly over us and cut the men down cruelly." He also speaks of a few Indians from Michigan. "Some of them were mortally wounded, and, drawing their blouses over their faces, they chanted a death song and died—four of them in a group."

A Feast After a Famine

About 3 o'clock p.m. absolute quietness prevailed over the battlefield where the carnage of war rioted a few hours before. My Orderly, M.C. Heath, a boy of sixteen, who now is a distinguished physician of Lexington, Ky., came to me at Elliott's headquarters and told me that the Lieutenant Colonel and Adjutant sent their compliments and requested me to come to dinner at my den in the trench. I went, and had to step over the dead bodies—all negroes. A narrow ditch led to a plaza six feet square, where a half dozen men, in fine weather, could sit on campstools. On the breastworks hung a dead negro. In the ditch I had to step over another dead negro. As I got to my plaza I saw two more negroes badly wounded in a cell two feet deeper than the plaza where I slept. One of the negroes was resting his bloody head on a fine copy of Paley's philosophy, which I came across in my wanderings. Heath's big basket was well stored with good viands, and we ate with the ferocity of starving men, regaling ourselves with the incidents of battle, without any expressions of sorrow for our friends, Colonel David Fleming and Adjutant Quattlebaum, who a few yards above were entombed in our old sleeping place in the "Crater" which we occupied as our quarters until they succeeded us ten days before, or any lamentations for the hundreds of dead and dying on the hillside around.

The joy of the glorious victory drowned out all sentiments of grief for a season, and it seemed a weird holiday.

A Blunder in Beauregard's Book

Mr. Barnard, in his interesting article on the "Crater," criticises a remarkable paragraph in Colonel Roman's work, "basing his statements made by General Bushrod Johnson and Colonel McMaster." The only objection to my statement was I said Mahone's charge was at 10 o'clock a.m.

The paragraph is as follows:

"Such was the situation. The Federals unable to advance and fearing to retreat, when, at 10 o'clock, General Mahone arrived with a part of his men, who had laid down in the shallow ravine to the rear of Elliott's salient held by the forces under Colonel Smith, there to await the remainder of the Division, but a movement having occurred among the Federals, which seemed to menace an advance, General Mahone then forwarded his Brigade with the Sixty-first North Carolina, of Hoke's Division, which had now also come up. The Twenty-fifth and Forty-ninth North Carolina, and the Seventeenth South Carolina, all under Smith, which were formed on Mahone's left, likewise formed in the 'Crater' movement, and three-fourths of the gorge line was carried with that part of the trench on the left of the 'Crater' occupied by the Federals. Many of the latter, white and black, abandoned the breach and fled under a scourging flank fire of Wise's Brigade."

This is confusion worse confounded. It is difficult to find a paragraph containing so many blunders as the report of General Johnson to Colonel Roman.

The Sixty-first North Carolina of Hoke's Brigade was not present during the day, except at Sander's charge two hours afterwards. The Twenty-fifth and Forty-ninth North Carolina were not present at all, but remained in their trench on the front line.

Smith's men on the extreme right did not as a body go into

Mahone's charge. Captain Crawford with one hundred and eighteen men did charge with Mahone. In fact he commanded his own men separate from Smith, although he was close by.

Colonel Roman's account taken from General Johnson's statement is unintelligible.

Time of Mahone's Charge

I dislike to differ with Mr. Bernard, who has been so courteous to me, and with my friend, Colonel Venable, for we literally carried muskets side by side as privates in dear old Captain Casson's company, the Governor's Guards, in Colonel Kershaw's Regiment, at the first battle of Manassas, and I shot thirteen times at Ellsworth's Zouaves. Venable was knocked down with a spent ball and I only had a bloody mouth. And the rainy night which followed the battle we sheltered ourselves under the same oilcloth. But I can't help thinking of these gentlemen as being like all Virginians, which is illustrated by a remark of a great Massachusetts man, old John Adams, in answering some opponent, said:

"Virginians are all fine fellows. The only objection I have to you is, in Virginia every goose is a swan."

Colonel Venable says:

"I am confident the charge of the Virginians was made before 9 o'clock a.m."

Mr. Bernard says, in speaking of the time:

"Mahone's Brigade left the plank road and took to the covered way."

"It is now half-past 8 o'clock." In a note he says: "probably between 8.15 and 8.30."

"At the angle where the enemy could see a moving column with ease the men were ordered to run quickly by, one man at a time, which was done for the double purpose of concealing the approach of a body of troops and of lessening the danger of passing rifle balls at these points."

It took Mahone's Brigade, above eight hundred men, to walk at least five hundred yards down this covered way and gulch, one by one, occasionally interrupted by wounded men going to the rear, at least twenty minutes. At a very low estimate it took them half an hour to form in the ravine, to listen to two short speeches, and the parley between Weisinger and

Girardey. With the most liberal allowance this will bring the charge at 9.15 A.M., but it took more time than that.

Captain Whitner investigated the time of the charge in less than a month after the battle. I extract the following, page 795, 40th "War of Rebellion:"

> "There is a great diversity of opinion as to the time the first charge was made by General Mahone. But one officer of the division spoke with certainty, Colonel McMaster, Seventeenth South Carolina Volunteers. His written statement is enclosed."

Unluckily the paper was "not found." But there is no doubt I repeatedly said it was about ten o'clock A.M.

General Mahone took no note of the time, but says:

> "According to the records the charge must have been before nine o'clock. General Burnside in his report fixes the time of the charge and recapture of our works at 8.45 A.M." *40th "War of Rebellion," page 528.*

He is badly mistaken. General Burnside says:

> "The enemy regained a portion of his line on the right. This was about 8.45 A.M., but not all the colored troops retired. Some held pits from behind which they had advanced severely checking the enemy until they were nearly all killed.
>
> "At 9.15 I received, with regret, a peremptory order from the General commanding to withdraw my troops from the enemy's lines."

Now this battle indicated as at 8:45 was a continuation, of the one that many officers said was about half-past eight o'clock. And both Mahone and Mr. Bernard were mistaken in stating that the great firing and retreat of soldiers was the result of the Virginian's charge, whereas at this time Mahone's Brigade was at the Jerusalem plank road. Moreover, when Mahone did come up his eight hundred men could not create one-fourth of the reverberation of the Seventeenth Regiment, Ransom's Brigade, and the thousands of the enemy. Besides Mahone's men's fighting was confined to the ditches, and they used mostly the butts and bayonets instead of the barrels of their muskets. No it was the fire of Elliott's men, Ransom's men, the torrent of shells of Wright's Battery and the enemy, Ord's men, and the four thousand negroes, all of them in an area of one hundred yards. The part of the line spoken of by Generals Delavan Bates and Turner and others as the Confederate line were mere rifle pits which the Confederates held until they had perfected the main line, and then gave up the pits. They were in the hollow, where the branch passes through to the breastworks.

Now the tumultuous outburst of musketry, Federal and Confederate, and the landslide of the Federals, was beyond doubt before I went out to Elliott's headquarters on the order of General Johnson.

For two hours before this Meade had been urging Burnside to rush to the crest of the hill until General B. was irritated beyond measure, and replied to a dispatch: "Were it not insubordination I would say that the latter remark was unofficerlike and ungentlemanly." Before this time Grant, Meade and Ord had given up hope. They had agreed to withdraw, hence the positive order to withdraw my troops from the enemy's line at 9.15.

Now this must have been before Mahone came up, for there is no allusion to a charge by any Federal General at the court of inquiry. With the 8.30 charge made at the hollow, there was a synchronous movement made by General Warren on the south of the "Crater," but at 8.45 he was informed that it was intended alone for a reconnoissance of the two-gun battery.

At 9.15 General Warren sends dispatch: "Just before receiving your dispatch to assault the battery on the left of the 'Crater' occupied by General Burnside the enemy drove his troops out of the place and I think now hold it. I can find no one who for certainty knows, or seems willing to admit, but I think I saw a Rebel flag in it just now, and shots coming from it this way. I am, therefore, if this (be) true no more able to take this battery now than I was this time yesterday. All our advantages are lost."

The advantages certainly were not lost on account of Mahone's men, but on account of the losses two hundred yards down the hill, of which he had doubtless been advised. He saw what he thought was a "Rebel flag," but for a half an hour he had heard of the terrific castigation inflicted on the Federals down the hill.

But here is something from the court of inquiry that approximates the time of Mahone's charge.

General Griffen, of Potter's Ninth Corps, in reply to the question by the court:

"When the troops retired from the 'Crater' was it compulsory from the enemy's operations, or by orders from your commanders?" Answer. "Partly both. We retired because we had orders. At the same time a column of troops came up to attack the 'Crater,' and we retired instead of stopping to fight. This force of the enemy came out of a ravine, and we did not see them till they appeared on the rising ground."

"What was the force that came out to attack you? The force that was exposed in the open?" Answer, "five or six hundred soldiers were all that we could see. I did not see either the right or left of the line. I saw the center of the line as it appeared to me. It was a good line of battle. Probably if we had not been under orders to evacuate we should have fought them, and tried to hold our position, but according to the orders we withdrew."

General Hartranft, of Ninth Corps, says in answer to the question "Driven out?"

"They were driven out the same time, the same time I had passed the word to retire. It was a simultaneous thing. When they saw the assaulting column within probably one hundred feet of the works I passed the word as well as it could be passed for everybody to retire. And I left myself at that time. General Griffen and myself were together at that time. The order to retire we had endorsed to the effect that we thought we could not withdraw the troops that were there on account of the enfilading fire over the ground between our rifle pits and the 'Crater' without losing a great portion of them, that ground being enfiladed with artillery and infantry fire. They had at that time brought their infantry down along their pits on both sides of the 'Crater,' so that their sharpshooters had good range, and were in good position. Accordingly we requested that our lines should open with artillery and infantry, bearing on the right and left of the 'Crater,' under which fire we would be able to withdraw a greater portion of our troops, and, in fact, everyone that could get away. While we were in waiting for the approach of that endorsement and the opening of the fire, this assaulting column of the enemy came up and we concluded—General Griffin and myself—that there was no use in holding it any longer, and so we retired."

This proves beyond doubt that Mahone's charge was after 9.15. It probably took Burnside some minutes to receive this order and some minutes for him and Griffin to send it down the line, and to send orders to the artillery to open on their flanks to protect them. This would bring Mahone's charge to 9.30 or 9.45.

Smith and Crawford Save Petersburg

I ordered Smith to take his regiment, the Twenty-sixth, and Crawford with Companies K, E, and B, to lie down in the ravine. Every General was ordered to charge to the crest. Had the enemy gotten beyond Smith's line fifty yards they could have marched in the covered way to Petersburg; not a cannon or a gun intervened. General Potter says his men charged two hundred yards beyond the "Crater," when they were driven back. Colonel Thomas said he led a charge which was not successful; he went three or four hundred yards and was driven back. General Griffin says he went about two hundred yards and was driven back. Colonel Russell says he went about fifty yards towards Cemetery Hill and "was driven back by two to four hundred infantry, which rose up from a little ravine and charged us." Some officer said he went five hundred yards beyond the "Crater." There was the greatest confusion about distances. General Russell is about right when he said he went about fifty yards behind the "Crater." When they talk of two or three hundred yards they must mean outside the breastworks towards Ransom's Brigade.

From the character of our breastworks, or rather our cross ditches, it was impracticable to charge down the rear of our breastworks. The only chance of reaching Petersburg was through the "Crater" to the rear. Smith and Crawford, whose combined commands did not exceed two hundred and fifty men, forced them back. Had either Potter, Russell, Thomas, or Griffin charged down one hundred yards farther than they did, the great victory would have been won, and Beauregard and Lee would have been deprived of the great honor of being victors of the great battle of the "Crater."

Elliott's Brigade

After the explosion, with less than one thousand two hundred men, and with the co-operation of Wright's Battery and Davenport's Battery, and a few men of Wise's Brigade, resisted nine thousand of the enemy from five to eight o'clock. Then four thousand five hundred blacks rushed over, and the Forty-ninth and Twenty-fifth North Carolina, Elliott's Brigade, welcomed them to hospitable graves at 9 o'clock A.M.

At about 9.30 A.M. old Virginia—that never tires in good works—with eight hundred heroes rushed into the trench of the Seventeenth and slaughtered hundreds of whites and blacks, with decided preference for the Ethiopians.

Captain Geo. B. Lake, of Company B, Twenty-second South Carolina, who was himself buried beneath the debris, and afterwards captured, gives a graphic description of his experience and the scenes around the famous "Crater." He says in a newspaper article:

Fighting at the 'Crater'
By Captain George B. Lake.

The evening before the mine was sprung, or possibly two evenings before, Colonel David Fleming, in command of the Twenty-second South Carolina Regiment—I don't know whether by command of General Stephen Elliott or not—ordered me to move my company, Company B, Twenty-second South Carolina, into the rear line, immediately in rear of Pegram's four guns. I had in my company one officer, Lieutenant W.J. Lake, of Newberry, S.C., and thirty-four enlisted men. This rear line was so constructed that I could fire over Pegram's men on the attacking enemy.

The enemy in our front had two lines of works. He

had more men in his line nearest our works than we had in his front. From this nearest line he tunnelled to and under Pegram's salient, and deposited in a magazine prepared for it not less than four tons of powder, some of their officers say it was six tons. We knew the enemy were mining, and we sunk a shaft on each side of the four-gun battery, ten feet or more deep, and then extended the tunnel some distance to our front. We were on a high hill, however, and the enemy five hundred and ten feet in our front, where they began their work, consequently their mine was far under the shaft we sunk. At night when everything was still, we could hear the enemy's miners at work. While war means kill, the idea of being blown into eternity without any warning was anything but pleasant.

That Terrible Saturday Morning

On that terrible Saturday morning, July 30, 1864, before day had yet dawned, after the enemy had massed a large number of troops in front of our guns, the fuse which was to ignite the mine was fired. The enemy waited fully an hour, but there was one explanation, the fuse had gone out. A brave Federal officer, whose name I do not know, volunteered to enter the tunnel and fire it again, which he did.

A minute later there was a report which was heard for miles, and the earth trembled for miles around. A "Crater" one hundred and thirty feet long, ninety-seven feet in breadth, and thirty feet deep, was blown out. Of the brave artillery company, twenty-two officers and men were killed and wounded, most of them killed. Hundreds of tons of earth were thrown back on the rear line, in which my command was.

A Whole Company Buried

Here was the greatest loss suffered by any command on either side in the war, myself, my only Lieutenant, W.J. Lake, and thirty-four enlisted men were all buried, and of that little band thirty-one were killed. Lieutenant Lake and myself and three enlisted men were taken out of the ground two hours after the explosion by some brave New Yorkers. These men worked like beavers, a portion of the time under perpetual fire.

Buried Thirty Feet Deep

Colonel Dave Fleming and his Adjutant, Dick Quattlebaum, were also in the rear line, only a few feet to my left, and were buried thirty feet deep; their bodies are still there. I do not know how many of the Federal troops stormed the works, but I do know the Confederates captured from them nineteen flags. The attacking columns were composed of white men and negroes; sober men and men who were drunk; brave men and cowards.

One of the latter was an officer high in command. I have lost his name, if I ever knew it. He asked me how many lines of works we had between the "Crater" and Petersburg, when I replied, "Three." He asked me if they were all manned. I said, "Yes." He then said, "Don't you know that I know you are telling a d———d lie?" I said to him. "Don't you know that I am not going to give you information that will be of any service to you?" He then threatened to have me shot, and I believe but that for the interference of a Federal officer he would have done so.

Death To Advance And Death To Retreat

I had just seen several of our officers and men killed with bayonets after they had surrendered, when the enemy, who had gone through the "Crater" towards Petersburg, had been repulsed, and fell back in the "Crater" for protection. There was not room in the "Crater" for another man. It was death to go forward or death to retreat to their own lines. It is said there were three thousand Yankees in and around the "Crater," besides those in portions of our works adjacent thereto.

Then the Coshorn mortars of the brave Major Haskell and other commanders of batteries turned loose their shells on the "Crater." The firing was rapid and accurate. Some of these mortars were brought up as near as fifty yards to the "Crater." Such a scene has never before nor never will be witnessed again. The Yankees at the same time were using one hundred and forty pieces of cannon against our works occupied by Confederate troops.

Elliott's Brigade in the day's fight lost two hundred and seventy-eight officers and men. Major General B.R. Johnson's

Division, Elliott's Brigade included, lost in the day, nine hundred and thirty-two officers and men. This was the most of the Confederate loss.

FEDERAL TOTAL LOSS OVER FIVE THOUSAND

While the enemy acknowledged a loss of from five to six thousand men—and that I am sure is far below their real loss—I make another quotation from Major General B.R. Johnson's official report:

> "It is believed that for each buried companion they have taken a tenfold vengeance on the enemy, and have taught them a lesson that will be remembered as long as the history of our wrongs and this great revolution endures."

Virginians, Georgians, North Carolinians, South Carolinians and others who may have fought at the "Crater," none of you have the right to claim deeds of more conspicuous daring over your Confederate brethren engaged that day. Every man acted well his part.

What about the four cannons blown up? you ask. One piece fell about half way between the opposing armies, another fell in front of our lines, not so near, however, to the enemy, a third was thrown from the carriage and was standing on end, half buried in the ground inside the "Crater," the fourth was still attached to the carriage, but turned bottom side up, the wheels in the air, and turned against our own men when the enemy captured it. That day, however, they all fell into the hands of the Confederates, except the one thrown so near the enemy's works, and in time we regained that also.

CAPTAIN LAKE A PRISONER

Before the fighting was over the Yankee officer who could curse a prisoner so gallantly ordered two soldiers to take charge and carry me to their lines, no doubt believing that the Confederates would succeed in recapturing the "Crater." We had to cross a plain five hundred and ten feet wide that was being raked by rifle balls, cannon shot and shell, grape and canister. It was not a very inviting place to go, but still not a great deal worse than Haskell's mortar shells that were raining in the center. I had the pleasure of seeing one of my guards die. The other conducted me safely to General Patrick's headquarters. Patrick was the Yankee provost marshall.

When I was placed under guard near his quarters he sent a staff officer to the front to learn the result of the battle.

After a short absence he galloped up to General Patrick and yelled out "We have whipped them!"

Patrick said: "I want no foolishness, sir!"

The staff officer then said: "General, if you want the truth, they have whipped us like hell."

CHAPTER 34
Leaving the Shenandoah Valley

To relieve the tension that oppressed both Richmond and Petersburg, General Lee determined to dispatch a force to the Valley to drive the enemy therefrom, to guard against a flank movement around the north and west of Richmond, and to threaten Washington with an invasion of the North. The Second Corps of the army was ordered Northwest. General Ewell being too enfeebled by age and wounds, had been relieved of his command in the field and placed in the command of Henrico County. This embraced Richmond and its defensive, the inner lines, which were guarded and manned by reserves and State troops. General Early, now a lieutenant General, was placed in command of the expedition. Why or what the particular reason a corps commander was thus placed in command of a department and a separate army, when there were full Generals occupying inferior positions, was never known. Unless we take it that Early was a Virginian, better informed on the typography of the country, and being better acquainted with her leading citizens, that he would find in them greater aid and assistance than would a stranger. The department had hopes of an uprising in the "Pan Handle" of Maryland in recruits from all over the States. The prestige of Early's name might bring them out. Early was a brave and skillful General. Being a graduate of West Point, he was well versed in the tactical arts of war; was watchful and vigilant, and under a superior he was second to none as a commander. But his Valley campaign—whether from failures of the troops or subaltern officers, I cannot say—but results show that it was a failure. There could be no fault found with his plans, nor the rapidity of his movements, for his partial successes show what might have been accomplished if faithfully carried out. Still, on the whole, his campaign in the Valley was detrimental, rather than beneficial, to our cause. Early had already made a dash through the Valley and pushed his lines beyond the Potomac, while his cavalry had even penetrated the confines of Washington itself. It was said at the time, by both Northern and Southern military critics, that had he not wavered or faltered at the critical moment, he could have easily captured the city. No doubt his orders were different—that only a demonstration was intended—and had he attempted to exceed his orders and failed, he would have received and deserved the censure of the authorities. The bane of the South's civic government was that the Executive and his military advisors kept the commanders of armies too much under their own leading strings, and not allowing them enough latitude to be governed by circumstances—to ride in on the flow tide of success when an opportunity offered. But the greatest achievements, the greatest of victories, that history records are where Generals broke away from all precedent and took advantage of the success of the hour, that could not have been foreseen nor anticipated by those who were at a distance. Be that as it may, Early had gone his length, and now, the last of July, was retreating up the Valley.

Kershaw, with his division, was ordered to join him, and on the 6th of August the troops embarked at Chester Station and were transported to Mitchel Station, on the Richmond and Mannassas Railroad, not far from Culpepper. On the 12th the troops marched by Flint Hill, crossed the Blue Ridge, and camped near the ancient little hamlet of Front Royal. The next day we were moved about one mile distant to a large spring, near the banks of the beautiful and now classic Shenandoah. How strange to the troops of the far South to see this large river running in the opposite direction from all our accustomed ideas of the flow of rivers—that water seeks its level and will therefore run South, or towards the coast. But here the stream rises in the south and runs due north towards the Potomac. After long and fatiguing marches, the soldiers here enjoyed a luxury long since denied them on account of their never ceasing activity. The delight of a bath, and in the pure, clear waters of the Shenandoah, was a luxury indeed. On the 17th of August the march was again resumed, and we reached Winchester, Va., on the next day. Remaining two days near the old city which had become so dear to the hearts of all the old soldiers through the hospitality and kindness of her truly loyal people, and being the place, too, of much of our enjoyment and pleasure while camping near it two years before, we left on the 21st, going in the direction of Charleston.

On nearing the latter place we found the enemy in force, and had to push our way forward by heavy skirmishing. When within two miles of Charlestown, we halted and went into camp, and threw our pickets beyond the town on the north. On the 25th we moved through the city and took the Harper Ferry Road, two miles beyond. Here we took up camp, and were in close proximity to the enemy, who lay in camp near us. A heavy skirmish line was thrown out about half a mile in our front. Lieutenant Colonel Maffett of the Third, but commanding the Seventh, was deployed in a large old field as support. We were encamped in line of battle in a beautiful grove overlooking and in full view of our skirmishers.

The enemy seemed to display little activity. Now and then a solitary horseman could be seen galloping away in the direction of his camp.

The want of alertness on the part of the enemy threw our pickets off their guard. Colonel Maffett was lounging under the shade of a tree in the rear of the skirmish line, with a few of the reserves, while those on the picket line lay at convenient distances, some with their coats off, others lying under the shade of trees or in the corners of a fence, all unconscious of an approaching enemy. The Federals had surveyed the field, and seeing our pickets so lax, and in such bad order for defense, undertook to surprise them. With a body of cavalry, concealed by the forest in their front, they made their way, under cover of a ravine, until within a short distance of the unsuspecting pickets. Then, with a shout and a volley, they dashed upon the line and over it, capturing nearly all, made their way to the rear, and there captured lieutenant Colonel Maffett and many of his reserves.

Commotion struck our camp. Drums beat, men called to arms, line of battle formed, and an advance at double-quick was made through the old field, in the direction of our unfortunate friends. But all too late. The surprise had been complete and the captured prisoners had been hurried to the rear. Colonel Maffett's horse, which was grazing near the scene of the skirmish, galloped through the enemy's disorganized lines, some trying to head him off, others to capture him, but he galloped defiantly on to camp. The enemy amused themselves by throwing a few shells into our lines.

The horse of Colonel Maffett was carried home by his faithful body servant, Harry, where both lived to a ripe old age. Not so with the unfortunate master. Reared in the lap of luxury, being an only son of a wealthy father and accustomed to all the ease and comforts that wealth and affluence could give, he could not endure the rigor and hardships of a Northern prison, his genial spirits gave way, his constitution and health fouled him, and after many months of incarceration he died of brain fever. But through it all he bore himself like a true son of the South. He never complained, nor was his proud spirit broken by imprisonment, but it chafed under confinement and forced obedience to prison rule and discipline. The Confederacy lost no more patriotic, more self-sacrificing soldier than Lieutenant Colonel Robert Clayton Maffett.

On the 27th we marched to Princeton, and remained until the 31st, picketing on the Opequan River, then returned to Charlestown. On the day before, the Third Regiment went out on the Opequan, being in hearing of the church bells and in sight of the spires of Washington. What an anomaly! The Federals besieging the Confederate capital, and the Confederates in sight of Washington.

From Charlestown we were moved back to Winchester and went into camp for a few days. So far Early's demonstration had been a failure. Either to capture Washington or weaken Grant, for day in and day out, he kept pegging away at Petersburg and the approaches to it and Richmond. These seemed to be the objective points, and which eventually caused the downfall of the two places. The enemy in our front had moved up to Berryville, a small hamlet about eight miles from Winchester, and on the 30th of September we were ordered out to attack the plan. The Federals had fortified across the turn-pike and had batteries placed at every commanding point. In front of this fortification was a large old field, through which we had to advance. The Brigade was formed in line of battle in some timber at the edge of the opening and ordered forward. The frowning redoubts lined with cannon and their formidable breastwork, behind which bristled the bright bayonets, were anything but objects to tempt the men as they advanced to the charge. As soon as we entered the opening the shells came plunging through our ranks, or digging up the earth in front. But the Brigade marched in good order, not a shot being fired, the enemy all the while giving us volley after volley. The men began to clamor for a charge, so much so that when we were about half way through the old field the command came "charge." Then a yell and a rush, each man carrying his gun in the most convenient position, and doing all in his power to reach the work first. The angle in front of the Third was nearer than the line in front of the other Regiments. Just before we reached the works the enemy fled to a grove in rear under an incline and began firing on our troops, who had now reached the work and began to fire from the opposite side. The firing in this way became general all along the line. The Artillery had withdrawn to the heights in rear and opened upon us a tremendous fire at short range. The enemy could be seen from our elevated position moving around our right through a thicket of pines, and some one called out to the troops immediately on the right of the Third Regiment, "The enemy are flanking us." This caused a momentary panic, and some of the Brigade left the captured work and began running to the rear. Colonel Rutherford ordered some of his officers to go down the line and get the demoralized troops to return to the ranks, which was accomplished without much delay.

The enemy in front began slackening their fire, which caused some of the men to leap over the works and advance to the brow of a hill just in front of us to get a better view. The enemy rallied and began pouring a heavy fire into the bold spirits who had advanced beyond the lines, wounding quite a number. General Kershaw, with a brigade of the division, crossed over the turn-pike and began a counter-move on the enemy's right, which caused such panic, that in a few minutes their whole line withdrew beyond the little town. Acting Assistant Adjutant General Pope, on the brigade staff, received a painful wound in the cheek, but outside of a sprinkling throughout the brigade of wounded, our loss was slight.

That night the enemy was reinforced, and about 9 o'clock next day there was a general advance. The enemy had changed his direction, and now was approaching parallel to the turn-pike. I was in command of the brigade skirmishers during the night, posted in a large old field on left of the turn-pike. Just as a detail, commanded by an officer of the Twentieth, came to relieve me, the enemy was seen advancing through a forest beyond the old field. The officer, not being familiar with the skirmish tactics, and never being on a skirmish line during action before, asked me to retain the command and also my line of skirmishers and conduct the retreat, which I did. The brigade at that time was on the retreat, and this double skirmish line covered and protected the rear. If there is any sport or amusement at all in battle, it is while on skirmish line, when the enemy is pressing you. On a skirmish line, usually, the men are posted about ten paces apart and several hundred yards in front of the main line of battle, to receive or give the first shock of battle. In our case the line was doubled, making it very strong, as strong, in fact, as some of the lines of General Lee's at that time holding Petersburg. When the enemy's skirmishers struck the opening our line opened upon them, driving them helter-skelter back into the woods. I ordered an advance, as the orders were to hold the enemy in check as long as possible to give our main line and wagon train time to get out of the way. We kept up the fire as we advanced, until we came upon the enemy posted behind trees; then, in our turn, gave way into the opening. Then the enemy advanced, so forward and backward the two lines advanced and receded, until by the support of the enemy's line of battle we were driven across the turn-pike, where we assembled and followed in rear of the brigade. There is nothing in this world that is more exciting, more nerve stirring to a soldier, than to participate in a battle line of skirmishers, when you have a fair field and open fight. There it takes nerve and pluck, however, it is allowed each skirmisher to take whatever protection he can in the way of tree or stump. Then on the advance you do not know when to expect an enemy to spring from behind a tree, stump, or bush, take aim and fire. It resembles somewhat the order of Indian warfare, for on a skirmish line "all is fair in war."

We returned without further molestation to the vicinity of Winchester, the enemy not feeling disposed to press us. It was never understood whose fault it was that a general engagement did not take place, for Early had marched and began the attack, and pressed the enemy from his first line of works, then the next day the enemy showed a bold front and was making every demonstration as if to attack us.

General Kershaw having been promoted to Major General, General James Connor was sent to command the brigade. He was formerly Colonel of the Twenty-second North Carolina Regiment, promoted to Brigadier, and commanded McGowan's Brigade after the battle of Spottsylvania Court House. After the return of General McGowan, he was assigned to the command of Laws' Brigade, and about the 6th or 7th of September reached us and relieved Colonel Henagan, of the Eighth, who had so faithfully led the old First Brigade since the battle of the Wilderness.

While in camp near Winchester, the Eighth Regiment, under Colonel Henagan, was sent out on picket on the Berryville road. In the morning before day General Sheridan, with a large force of cavalry, made a cautious advance and captured the videttes of the Eighth, which Colonel Henagan had posted in front, and passing between the regiment and the brigade, made a sudden dash upon their rear, capturing all of the regiment, with Colonel Henagan, except two companies commanded by the gallant Captain T.F. Malloy. These two companies had been thrown out on the right, and by tact and a bold front Captain

Malloy saved these two companies and brought them safely into camp. The whole brigade mourned the loss of this gallant portion of their comrades. Colonel Henagan, like Colonel Maffett, sank under the ill treatment and neglect in a Northern prison and died there.

Col. J. W. Henagan

Col. J.W. Henagan was born November 22nd, 1822, in Marlboro County, S.C., Was the son of E.L. Henagan and wife, Ann McInnis. His father was a Scotch-Irishman. His mother Scotch. Was educated at Academy in Bennettsville and Parnassus. Was elected Sheriff of Marlboro County in October, 1852, and went into office February, 1853. In 1860 was elected to the Legislature. Was re-elected to the Legislature in 1863.

Prior to the war was prominent in militia service, serving consecutively as Captain, Colonel and Brigadier General. In March, 1861, volunteered, and in April became Lieutenant Colonel of Eighth Regiment South Carolina Volunteers and went with the Regiment to Virginia. Was in battle of Bull Run or First Manassas. In 1862 he became by election Colonel of the Eighth South Carolina Volunteers and served in that capacity until his capture near Winchester in the fall of 1864 when he was sent a prisoner to Johnson's Island, Ohio. Here he died a prisoner of war, April 22, 1865.

No Regiment of the Confederacy saw harder service or was engaged in more battles than the Eighth South Carolina of Kershaw's Brigade and no officer of that Brigade bore himself with more conspicuous gallantry than Colonel Henagan. He was always at his post and ready to go forward when so ordered. There was little or no fear in him to move into battle, and he was always sure, during the thickest of the fight, cheering on his men to victory.

Colonel Henagan, as a citizen of the County, was as generous as brave. His purse was open to the needs of the poor. Did not know how or could not refuse the appeals to charity. He was the eldest son of a large family. When about twenty years old his father died and left on his shoulders the responsibility of maintaining and educating several younger brothers and sisters. He never swerved from this duty, but like the man that he was, did his work nobly. He was a dutiful son, a kind brother, a friend to all. He knew no deception, had no respect for the sycophant. Loved his country. A friend to be relied on. Was a farmer by profession. A good politician. Was a very quiet man, but always expressed his views firmly and candidly when called upon.

Colonel Robert Clayton Maffett

Colonel Robert Clayton Maffett was born in Newberry County, about the year 1836. Was the only son of Captain James Maffett, long time a member of the General Assembly of South Carolina. At the breaking out of the war Colonel Maffett was Colonel of the Thirty-ninth Regiment of State Militia. From this regiment two companies were formed in answer to the first call for volunteers. One of these companies elected him Captain, which afterwards became Company C, Third South Carolina Regiment. His company was one of the few that reorganized before the expiration of the term of the first twelve months' enlistment, and again elected Colonel Maffett as its Captain. After a thirty days' furlough, just before the seven days' battle, he returned with his company and became senior Captain in command. He soon became Major by the death of Lieutenant Colonel Garlington, Major Rutherford being promoted to Lieutenant Colonel. After the death of Colonel Nance, 6th of May, he became Lieutenant Colonel. He participated in nearly all the great battles in which the regiment was engaged, and was often in command. He was several times wounded, but not severely. At the time of his capture he was in command of the Seventh Regiment. Colonel Maffett was conspicuous for his fine soldierly appearance, being a perfect type of an ideal soldier.

He was loved and admired by the men as few officers of his station were. In camp he was the perfect gentleman, kind and indulgent to his men, and in battle he was cool, collected, and gallant. He died in prison only a short while before the close of the war, leaving a wife and one daughter of tender age.

CHAPTER 35

Reminiscences of the Valley

Y.J. Pope, Adjutant of the Third South Carolina, but then acting as Assistant Adjutant General on General Connor's Staff, gives me here a very ludicrous and amusing account of a "Fox hunt in the valley." A hunt without the hounds or without the fox. No man in Kershaw's Brigade was a greater lover of sport or amusement of any kind than Adjutant Pope. In all our big snow "festivals," where hundreds would engage in the contest of snow-balling, Adjutant Pope always took a leading part. It was this spirit of sport and his mingling with the common soldier, while off duty, that endeared Pope so much to the troop. With his sword and sash he could act the martinet, but when those were laid aside Adjutant Pope was one of the "boys," and engaged a "boat" with them as much as any one in the "Cross Anchors," a company noted for its love of fun.

Says, Adjutant Pope, now a staid Judge on the Supreme Court Bench:

> The Third South Carolina Infantry had been placed on pickets in front of Early in September, 1864. The point at which picket were posted were at two fords on the Opequan River, Captain Dickert, with his company, was posted at some distance from the place where the other portion of the Regiment was posted to cover one of the fords. I can see now the work laid cut for Captain Dickert, ought to have been assigned to the Cavalry for a company of Infantry, say a half mile from the Regiment, might have been surrounded too quickly for the company to be retired or to receive assistance from the Regiment. Well, as it was, no harm came of it for the company held the ford unassailable. A company of the Regiment was placed at a ford on the highway as it crossed the river. While a few officers were enjoying a nice supper here comes an order to call in the companies on picket and to follow the Regiment

with all possible speed towards Winchester, to which latter place the army of Early had already gone. Guides were sent to us, and our Regiment had marched by country road until we struck the turn-pike. The march was necessarily rapid lest the Regiment might be assailed by overwhelming numbers of the enemy. The soldiers did not fancy this rapid marching.

"To our surprise and horror, after we had reached the turn-pike road, and several miles from our destination, the soldiers set up an imitation of barking, just as if a lot of hounds in close pursuit of a fresh jumped fox. Now any one at all familiar with the characteristic of the soldier know imitation is his weak point, one yell, all yell, one sing, all sing, if one is merry, all are merry. We were near the enemy, and the Colonel knew the necessity of silence, and caution Colonel Rutherford was, of course indignant at this outburst of good humor in the dark watches of the night, and the enemy at our heels or flank. He sent back orders by me (Pope) to pass down the lines and order silence. But 'bow-wow,' 'bow,' 'bow-wow,' 'yelp, yelp,' and every conceivable imitation of the fox hound rent the air. One company on receiving the orders to stop this barking would cease, but others would take it up. 'Bow-wow,' 'toot,' 'toot,' 'yah-oon,' 'yah-oon,' dogs barking, men hollowing, some blowing through their hands to imitate the winding of the huntman's horn. 'Stop this noise,' 'cease your barking,' 'silence,' still the chase continued. 'Go it, Lead,' 'catch him, Frail,' 'Old Drive close to him,' 'hurah Brink,' 'talk to him old boys.' The valley fairly rung, with this chase. Officers even could not refrain from joining in the encouragement to the excited dogs as the noise would rise and swell and echo through the distant mountain gorges to reverberate up and down the valley—at last wore out by their ceaseless barking and yelling, the noise finally died out, much to the satisfaction of the Colonel commanding, myself and the officers who were trying to stop it. As mortified as I was at my inability to execute the orders of Colonel Rutherford, still I never laughed so much in my life at this ebullition of good feelings of the men, after all their toils and trials, especially as I would hear some one in the line call out as if in the last throes of exhaustion, 'Go on old dog,' 'now you are on him,' 'talk to him, old Ranger.' What the Yankees thought of this fox chase at night in the valley, or what their intentions might have been is not known, but they would have been mighty fools to have tackled a lot of old 'Confeds' out on a lark at night.

The negro cooks of the army were a class unique in many ways. While he was a slave, he had far more freedom than his master, in fact had liberties that his master's master did not possess. It was the first time in the South's history that a negro could roam at will, far and wide, without a pass. He could ride his dead master's horse from Virginia to Louisiana without molestation. On the march the country was his, and so long as he was not in the way of moving bodies of troops, the highways were open to him. He was never jostled or pushed aside by stragglers, and received uniform kindness and consideration from all. The negro was conscious of this consideration, and never took advantage of his peculiar station to intrude upon any of the rights or prerogatives exclusively the soldier's. He could go to the rear when danger threatened, or to the front when it was over. No negro ever deserted, and the fewest number ever captured. His master might fall upon the field, or in the hands of the enemy, but the servant was always safe. While the negro had no predilection for war in its realities, and was conspicuous by his absence during the raging of the battles, still he was among the first upon the field when it was over, looking after the dead and wounded. At the field hospitals and infirmaries, he was indispensable, obeying all, serving all, without question or complaint. His first solicitude after battle was of his master's fate—if dead, he sought him upon the field; if wounded, he was soon at his side. No mother could nurse a child with greater tenderness and devotion than the dark-skinned son of the South did his master.

At the breaking out of the war almost every mess had a negro cook, one of the mess furnishing the cook, the others paying a proportional share for hire; but as the stringency of the Subsistence Department began to grow oppressive, as the war wore on, many of these negroes were sent home. There was no provision made by the department for his keep, except among the officers of the higher grade; so the mess had to share their rations with the cook, or depend upon his ability as a "forager." In the later years of the war the country occupied by the armies became so devastated that little was left for the "forager." Among the officers, it was different. They were allowed two rations (only in times of scarcity they had to take the privates' fare). This they were required to pay for at pay day, and hence could afford to keep a servant. Be it said to the credit of the soldiers of the South, and to their servants as well, that during my four years and more of service I never heard of, even during times of the greatest scarcity, a mess denying the cook an equal share of the scanty supply, or a servant ever found stealing a soldier's rations. There was a mutual feeling of kindness and honesty between the two. If all the noble, generous and loyal acts of the negroes of the army could be recorded, it would fill no insignificant volume.

There was as much cast among the negroes, in fact more, as among the soldiers. In times of peace and at home, the negro based his claims of cast upon the wealth of his master. But in the army, rank of his master overshadowed wealth. The servant of a Brigadier felt royal as compared to that of a Colonel, and the servant of a Colonel, or even a Major, was far ahead, in superiority and importance, to those belonging to the privates and line officers. The negro is naturally a hero worshiper. He gloried in his master's fame, and while it might often be different, in point of facts, still to the negro his master was "the bravest of the brave."

As great "foragers" as they were, they never ventured far in front while on the advance, nor lingered too dangerously in the rear on the retreat. They hated the "Yankee" and had a fear of capture. One day while we were camped near Charlestown an officer's cook wandered too far away in the wrong direction and ran up on the Federal pickets. Jack had captured some old cast-off clothes, some garden greens and an old dominicker rooster. Not having the remotest idea of the topography of the country, he very naturally walked into the enemy's pickets. He was halted, brought in and questioned. The Federals felt proud of their capture, and sought to conciliate Jack with honeyed words and great promises. But Jack would have none of it.

"Well, look er here," said Jack, looking suspiciously around at the soldiers; "who you people be, nohow?"

"We are Federal soldiers," answered the picket.

"Well, well, is you dem?"

"Dem who?" asked the now thoroughly aroused Federal.

"Why dem Yankees, ob course—dem dat cotched Mars Clayt."

The Federal admitted they were "Yankees," but that now Jack had no master, that he was free.

"Is dat so?" Then scratching his head musingly, Jack said at last, "I don know 'bout dat—what you gwine do wid me, anyhow; what yer want?"

He was told that he must go as a prisoner to headquarters first, and then dealt with as contrabands of war.

"Great God Almighty! white folks, don't talk dat er way." The negro had now become thoroughly frightened, and with a sudden impulse he threw the chicken at the soldier's feet, saying, "Boss, ders a rooster, but here is me," then with the speed of a startled deer Jack "hit the wind," to use a vulgarism of the army.

"Halt! halt!"—*bang, whiz*, came from the sentinel, the whole picket force at Jack's heels. But the faithful negro for the time excelled himself in running, and left the Federals far behind. He came in camp puffing, snorting, and blowing like a porpoise. "Great God Almighty! good people, talk er 'bout patter-rollers, day ain't in it. If dis nigger didn't run ter night, den don't talk." Then Jack recounted his night's experience, much to the amusement of the listening soldiers.

Occasionally a negro who had served a year or two with his young master in the army, would be sent home for another field of usefulness, and his place taken by one from the plantation. While a negro is a great coward, he glories in the pomp and glitter of war, when others do the fighting. He loves to tell of the dangers (not sufferings) undergone, the blood and carnage, but above all, how the cannon roared round and about him.

A young negro belonging to an officer in one of the regiments was sent home, and his place as cook was filled by Uncle Cage, a venerable looking old negro, who held the distinguished post of "exhorter" in the neighborhood. His "sister's chile" had filled Uncle Cage's head with stories of war—of the bloodshed on the battlefield, the roar of cannon, and the screaming of shells over that haven of the negro cooks, the wagon yards—but to all the blood and thunder stories of his "sister's chile" Uncle Cage only shook his head and chuckled, "Dey may kill me, but dey can't skeer dis nigger." Among the other stories he had listened to was that of a negro having his head shot off by a cannon ball. Sometime after Uncle Cage's installation as cook the enemy made a demonstration as if to advance. A few shells came over our camp, one bursting in the neighborhood of Uncle Cage, while he was preparing the morning meal for his mess.

Some of the negroes and more prudent non-combattants began to hunt for the wagon yard, but Uncle Cage remained at his post. He was just saying:

"Dese yer young niggers ain't no account; dey's skeered of dere own shad—"

Boom, boom, a report, and a shell explodes right over his head, throwing fragments all around.

Uncle Cage made for the rear, calling out as he ran, "Oh, dem cussed Yankees! You want er kill er nudder nigger, don't you?" Seeing the men laughing as he passed by in such haste, he yelled back defiantly, "You can laff, if you want to, but ole mars ain't got no niggers to fling away."

"Red tape" prevailed to an alarming extent in the War Department, and occasionally a paroxysm of this disease would break out among some of the officers of the army, especially among the staff, "West Pointers," or officers of temporary high command—Adjutant Pope gives his experience, with one of those afflicted functionaries, "Where as Adjutant of the Third South Carolina," says he, I had remained as such from May, 1862, till about the 1st of September, 1864, an order came from brigade headquarters, for me to enter upon the responsibilities of acting Assistant Adjutant General of Kershaw's Brigade. When General Connor was disabled soon after, and the Senior Colonel of the brigade, present for duty, the gallant William D. Rutherford, received his death-wound, General Kershaw, commanding division, sent the Assistant Adjutant General of the division, (a staff officer), Major James M. Goggans, to command the brigade. About the 17th of October there came a delegation to brigade headquarters, to learn, if possible, whether there could be obtained a leave of absence for a soldier, whose wife was dead, leaving a family of children to be provided for.

I was a sympathetic man, and appreciated the sad condition of the poor soldier, who had left his all to serve his country, and now had at home, a house full of motherless children. I said "wait till I see the brigade commander," and went to Major Goggans, relating the circumstances, and was assured of his approval of the application for leave of absence in question. This news, the spokesman of the delegation, gladly carried back to the anxiously awaiting group. Soon papers were brought to headquarters, signed by all the officers below. When the papers were carried by me to the brigade commander for his approval, it raised a storm, so to speak, in the breast of the newly appointed, but temporary Chieftain.

"Why do you bring me this paper to sign this time of day?" it being in the afternoon. "Do you not know that all papers are considered at nine o'clock A.M.? In future, and as long as I am in command of the Brigade, I want it understood that under no considerations and circumstances, I wish papers to be signed, brought to me before or after nine o'clock A.M."

The faces of the officers composing the delegation, when the news was brought to them, plainly expressed their disgust; they felt, at the idea, that no grief, however great, would be considered by the self-exalted Chief; except as the clock struck nine in the morning.

Circumstances and occurrences of this kind were so rare and exceptional, that I record the facts given by Judge Pope, to expose an exception to the general rule of gentlemanly deportment of one officer to another, so universal throughout the army. The kindness, sympathy and respect that superiors showed to subalterns and privates became almost a proverb. While in a reminiscent mood, I will give a story of two young officers as given by the writer of the above. He claims to have been an eye witness and fully competent to give a true recital. It is needless to say that the writer of these memoirs was one of the participants, and as to the story itself, he has only a faint recollection, but the sequel which he will give is vivid enough, even after the lapse of a third of a century. Judge Pope writes, "It is needless to say that the Third South Carolina Regiment had a half-score or more young officers, whose conduct in battle had something to do with giving prestige to the regiment, whose jolly good nature, their almost unparallel reciprocal love of officers and men, helped to give tone and recognition to it, their buoyancy of spirits, their respect for superiors and kindness and indulgence to their inferiors, endeared them to all—the whole command seemed to embibe of their spirit of fun, mischief and frolic." Captains L.W. Gary, John W. Watts, John K. Nance, Lieutenants Farley and Wofford, Adjutant Pope and others, whom it may be improper to mention here, (and I hope I will not be considered egotistical or self praise, to include myself), were a gay set. Their temperatures and habits, in some instances, were as wide as the poles, but there was a kind of affinity, a congeniality of spirits between them, that they were more like brothers in reality than brothers in arms, and all might be considered a "chip of the old block." Nor would our dearly beloved, kind, generous hearted Colonel Rutherford, when off duty, feel himself too much exalted to take a "spin with the boys" when occasions and circumstances admitted. Many, many have been the jolly carousals these jolly knights enjoyed while passing through some town or city. The confinement and restrictions of camp life induced them, when off duty and in some city, to long for a "loosening of the bit" and an ebullition of their youthful spirits.

Judge Pope, continuing, says:

In the spring of 1864 Longstreet's soldiers were ordered from East Tennessee, to join Lee in Virginia, and it follows that there was joy in the camp among the soldiers, for who does not love Virginia? In route the command was halted in Lynchburg, and what was more natural for the fun-loving, jovial members of the old brigade, after being isolated so long, cut off from civilization as it seemed to them, shut up in the gorges of the mountains, than to long for a breath of fresh air—to wish for the society and enjoy the hospitality of the fair ladies of old Virginia, especially the quaint old city of Lynchburg. With such feelings, two handsome and gallant Captains of the Third Regiment applied for and obtained leave of absence for the day. I will call this jolly couple John and Gus. To say that these two young Captains—one of the right and the other of the left color company—were birds rare, would scarce express it. They were both in their 'teens,' and small of statue withal. They were two of the youngest, as well as the smallest, officers in the brigade. Notwithstanding their age and build, they would not hesitate to take a 'bout' with the strongest and the largest. As one would say to the other, 'When your wind fails you, I will leg him.' Now, these two knights, out on a lark and lookout for adventure, did not hesitate to shie their castors in the ring and cross lances the first opportunity presented. No doubt, after being a while with the famous Sancho Panza at the wine skins, they could see as many objects, changed through enchantment, as the Master Dan Quixote did, and demanded a challenge from them. In walking up a side street in the city, they, as by enchantment, saw walking just in front of them, a burly, stout built man, dressed out in the finest broad cloth coat. What a sight for a soldier to see! a broad cloth coat!" and he a young man of the army age. Ye gods was it possible. Did their eyes deceive them, or had they forgotten this was a Sabbath day, and the city guard was accustomed to wear his Sunday clothes. There were a set of semi-soldiers in some cities known as "city guards," whose duties consisted of examining soldier's furloughs and passes in cities and on trains. Their soft places and fine clothes were poison to the regular soldiers, and between whom, a friendly and good natured feud existed. There was another set that was an abomination to both, the gambler, who, by money or false papers, exempted themselves. Richmond was their city of refuge, but now and then one would venture out into a neighboring town.

"Come out of that coat; can't wear that in the city to-day," was the first salutation the jolly knights gave the fine dressed devotee of the blue cloth.

"What, do you wish to insult me?" indignantly replied the man, turning and glaring at the two officers with the ferocity of a tiger.

"Oh, no," says John, "we want that coat;" and instinctively the young Captains lay hands upon the garment that gave so much offense.

"Hands off me, you cowardly young ruffians!"

'Oh, come out of that coat,' replied the jolly couple.

Rip, rip, went the coat; *biff, biff,* went the non-combatant's fist. Right and left he struck from the shoulders, to be replied to with equal energy by the fists of the young men.

Rip, rip, goes the coat, *bang, biff,* goes the fists. Down in the street, over in the gutter, kicks and blows, still *rip, rip,* goes the coat.

"Help!" cries the non-combatant.

"Yes," cries Gus, "help with the coat John."

The noise gathered the crowd. With the crowd came Lieutenant H.L. Farley. The burly frame of Farley soon separated the fighters. The gambler seeing his hopelessness in the face of so much odds, rose to his feet, and made a dash for liberty, leaving in the hands of each of the boys a tail of the much prized coat, all 'tattered and torn.' The gambler made quite a ludicrous picture, streaking it through town with his coat-tails off."

This is Pope's story, but I will here tell the sequel which was not near so amusing to me.

Sometime afterwards, the writer and participant in the fray of the "coat-tail" was slightly wounded, and was sent to Lynchburg to the hospital, formerly a Catholic college, if I am not mistaken. After being there for a time with my wounded brother officers (this was a hospital for officers alone) I became sufficiently convalescent to feel like a stroll through the city. I felt a little tender, lest I might meet unexpectedly my unknown antagonist and erstwhile hostile enemy; but one night I accepted the invitation of a tall, robust-built Captain from Tennessee (a room-mate, and also convalescent from a slight wound) to take a stroll. Being quite small, friendless, and alone, I did not object to this herculean chaperone. After tiring of the stroll, we sauntered into a soldier's cheap restaurant and called for plates. While we were waiting the pleasure of "mine host," the tread of footsteps and merry laughter of a crowd of jolly roisters met our ears, and in walked some soldiers in the garb of "city police," and with the crowd was my man of the "long coat-tail." My heart sank into the bottom of my boots, my speech failed me, and I sat stupified, staring into space. Should he recognize me, then what? My thought ran quick and fast. I never once expected help from my old Tennessean. As we were only "transient" acquaintances, I did not think of the brotherhood of the soldier in this emergency. The man of the "long coat" approached our table and raised my hat, which, either by habit or force of circumstances, I will not say, I had the moment before pulled down over my eyes.

"Hey, my fine young man, I think I know you. Aren't you the chap that torn my coat sometime ago? Answer me, sir," giving me a vigorous shake on the shoulder. "You are the very d———n young ruffian that did it, and I am going to give you such a thrashing as you will not forget."

I have never yet fully decided what answer I was going to make—whether I was going to say yes, and ask his pardon, with the risk of a thrashing, or deny it—for just at that moment the "tall sycamore of the Holston" reached out with his fist and dealt my assailant a blow sufficient to have felled an ox of the Sweetwater. Sending the man reeling across the room, the blood squirting and splattering, he said:

"Gentlemen, I came here with this boy, and whoever whips him has first got to walk my log, and that is what few people can do."

The old "sycamore" from Tennessee looked to me at that precious moment as tall as a church steeple, and fully as large around. In all my whole life never was a man's presence so agreeable and his services so acceptable. It gave me a confidence in myself I never felt before nor since. His manly features and giant-like powers acted like inspiration upon me, and I felt for the time like a Goliath myself, and rose to my feet to join in the fray. But my good deliverer pushed me back and said:

"Stand aside, young man, I have tickets for both in here," and with that he began to wield his mighty blows first here and then there—first one and then another went staggering across the room, until the crowd gathered outside and put an end to the frolic. No explanations were given and none asked. Taking me by the arm, the big Captain led me away, saying, after we had gone some little distance:

"Young man, that was a narrow escape you made, and it was lucky I was on hand."

He spoke with so much candor and logic, that I did not have the heart nor disposition to doubt or contradict it.

I would be willing to qualify before a grand jury to my dying day that I had had a close call.

CHAPTER 36

The Second Valley Campaign

On the 15th of September we began our return to Lee, marching about six miles south of Middleton. The next day we took up the march again to within fifteen miles of Luray Court House, then to within eleven miles of Sperryville, on the turn-pike, between the two points. Virginia or that part of it is blessed for her good roads on the main thoroughfares. The road from Staunton to the Potomac is one of the finest in America, being laid with cobble stones the entire length, upwards of one hundred and twenty-five miles. Then the road engineers did one thing that should immortalize them, that is in going around hills instead of over them, as in our State. Those engineers of old worked on the theory that the distance around a hill was no greater than over it, and much better for travel.

Over the Blue Ridge at Thornton Gap and to within five miles of Woodville, reaching Culpepper at three o'clock P.M., the 9th. Our ears were greeted with the distant roar of artillery, which proved to be our artillery firing at a scouting party of United States cavalry. On through Culpepper we marched, to within one mile of Rapidan Station, our starting point of near two months before. And what a fruitless march—over the mountains, dusty roads, through briars and thickets, and heat almost unbearable—fighting and skirmishing, with nightly picketing, over rivers and mountain sides, losing officers, and many, too, being field officers captured. While in camp here we heard of Early's disaster in the Valley, which cast a damper over all the troops. It seems that as soon as Sheridan heard of our detachment from Early's command he planned and perfected a surprise, defeating him in the action that followed, and was then driving him out of the Valley. Could we have been stopped at this point and returned to Early, which we had to do later, it would have saved the division many miles of marching, and perhaps further discomfiture of Early and his men. But reports had to be made to the war department.

Orders came for our return while we were continuing our march to Gordonsville, which place we reached on the 23rd of September, at 4 o'clock, having been on the continuous march for exactly fifty days. On the morning of the 24th we received the orders to return to the relief of Early, and at daylight, in a blinding rain, we commenced to retrace our steps, consoling ourselves with the motto, "Do your duty, therein all honor lies," passing through Barboursville and Standardville, a neat little village nestled among the hills, and crossed the mountain at Swift Run Gap. We camped about one mile of the delightful Shenandoah, which, by crossing and recrossing its clear, blue-tinged waters and camping on its banks so often, had become near and dear to all of us, and nothing was more delightful than to take a plunge beneath its waters. But most often we had to take the water with clothes and shoes on in the dead of winter, still the name of the Shenandoah had become classic to our ears.

The situation of Early had become so critical, the orders so imperative to join him as soon as possible, that we took up the march next morning at a forced speed, going twelve miles before a halt, a feat never before excelled by any body of troops during the war. When within two miles of Port Republic, a little beyond its two roads leading off from that place, one to Brown's Gap, we encountered the enemy's cavalry. Here they made an attack upon our brigade, but were repulsed at first fire from the infantry rifles. There was one thing demonstrated during this war, that whatever might have been accomplished in days of old, the cavalry on either side could not stand the fire of the infantry. And it seemed that they had a kind of intuition of the fact whenever the infantry was in their front. Nothing better as an excuse did a cavalry commander wish, when met with a repulse, than to report, "We were driving them along nicely until we came upon the enemy's infantry, then we had to give way."

This report had been made over and over again, until it became threadbare; but a cavalry officer thought it a feather in his cap to report his defeat or repulse by, "We met their infantry." We made a junction with Early near Brown's Gap, on the 26th, and camped at night with orders to be prepared to march at daylight. The troops of Early's were in a despondent mood, but soon their spirits revived at the sight of Kershaw's Division. We moved forward in the direction of Harrisonburg, our duty being to guard the two roads leading thereto. Early sent the other part of the army to the left and forward of us, and in this order we marched on to Waynesboro. Reaching there next day, the enemy's cavalry scattered when our troops came in sight. We began, on October 1st, moving in the direction of the turn-pike, leading from Winchester to Staunton, striking near Harrisonburg on the 6th.

We began the forward movement down the Valley on the 7th, the enemy slowly giving way as we advanced. We passed through those picturesque little cities of the Valley, Harrisonburg, New Market, and Woodstock, marching a day or two and then remaining in camp that length of time to give rest to the troops, after their long march. It must be remembered we had been two months cut off from the outside world—no railroad nearer than Staunton, the men being often short of rations and barefooted and badly clad; scarcely any mail was received during these two months, and seldom a paper ever made its appearance in camp. We only knew that Lee was holding his own. We reached and passed through Strausburg on the 13th. In the afternoon of this day, while we were on the march, but at the time laying by the side of the turn-pike, the enemy tried to capture some of our artillery. We had heard firing all day in our front, but thought this the effects of the enemy's sullen withdrawal. While resting by the road side, the enemy made a spirited attack upon the troops in front. We were hurriedly rushed forward, put in line of battle, advanced through an uneven piece of ground, and met the enemy posted behind a hill in front. They opened upon us at close range, killing and wounding quite a number, but as soon as our brigade made the first fire, they fled to a brick wall, running at an angle from the turn-pike. General Connor fell at the first fire, badly wounded in the knee, from the effects of which he lost his leg, and never returned, only to bid his brigade farewell in the pine regions of North Carolina. Colonel Rutherford being next in command, advanced the troops to the top of the hill and halted. In going out in front to reconnoitre in the direction of the stone wall, a party of the enemy, who had concealed themselves behind it, rose and fired, mortally wounding the gallant and much beloved Colonel. A charge was made, and the enemy fled to a thicket of pine timber and made their escape. This was a bloody little battle for the brigade, and some of its loss was irreparable. We halted after driving the enemy away, and at night withdrew to Fisher's Hill and camped for the night. Fisher's Hill is a kind of bluff reaching out from the Massanutten Mountain on our right; at its base ran Cedar Creek. It is a place of great natural strength. In the presence of some of his friends Colonel Rutherford passed away that night, at one o'clock, and his remains were carried to his home by Captain Jno. K. Nance. General Connor had his leg amputated. The brigade was without a field officer of higher grade than Major, and such officer being too inexperienced in the handling of so large a number of men, Major James Goggans, of the division staff, was ordered to its command. While some staff officers may be as competent to handle troops in the field as the commanders themselves, still in our case it was a lamentable failure. Major Goggans was a good staff officer, a graduate of West Point, but he was too old and inexperienced to command troops of such vigor and enthusiasm as the South Carolinians who composed Kershaw's Brigade.

We remained a short time on Fisher's Hill, throwing up some slight fortifications. Kershaw's Brigade was encamped in a piece of woods on the left of the turn-pike as you go north.

Colonel William Drayton Rutherford

Colonel William Drayton Rutherford was the son of Dr. Thomas B. Rutherford and Mrs. Laura Adams Rutherford, his wife. He was born on the 21st of September, 1837, in Newberry District, South Carolina. By his father he was a descendant of Virginians, as well as of that sturdy and patriotic stock of Germans who settled what was known as the "Fork." By his mother he was a descendant of the New England Adams family—what a splendid boy and man he was! He was educated in the best schools in our State, and spent sometime abroad. At the sound of arms he volunteered and was made Adjutant of the Third South Carolina Infantry. At the reorganization of the regiment, in May, 1862, he was elected Major of his regiment. When Lieutenant Colonel B. Conway Garlington was killed at Savage Station, June 29th, 1862, Rutherford became Lieutenant Colonel of his regiment. When Colonel James D. Nance fell in the battle of the Wilderness, on the 6th day of May, 1864, he became Colonel of the Third South Carolina Regiment. He was a gallant officer and fell in the front of his regiment at Strausburg, Va., on the 13th of October, 1864.

He married the beautiful and accomplished Miss Sallie H. Fair, only daughter of Colonel Simeon Fair, in March, 1862, and the only child of this union was "the daughter of the regiment," Kate Stewart Rutherford, who is now Mrs. George Johnstone.

Colonel Rutherford was in the battles of First Manassas, Williamsburg, Savage Station, Malvern Hill, First Fredericksburg (12th December, 1862, where he was badly wounded), Knoxville, Wilderness, Brock's Road (and other battles about Spottsylvania), North Anna Bridge, Second Cold Harbor, Deep Bottom, Berryville, and Strausburg.

He was a delight to his friends, by reason of his fare intelligence, warm heart, and generous impulses; to his family, because he was always so considerate of them, so affectionate, and so brimful of courtesy; but to his enemies (and he never made any except among the vicious), he was uncompromisingly fierce.

I will state here that General James Connor had been in command of the brigade for about two or three months, Colonel Kennedy, the senior officer of the brigade, being absent on account of wounds received at the Wilderness. There is no question but what General Connor was one of the best officers that South Carolina furnished during the war. But he was not liked by the officers of the line or the men. He was too rigid in his discipline for volunteers. The soldiers had become accustomed to the ways and customs of Kershaw and the officers under him, so the stringent measures General Connor took to prevent straggling and foraging or any minor misdemeanor was not calculated to gain the love of the men. All, however, had the utmost confidence in his courage and ability, and were willing to follow where he led. Still he was not our own Joseph Kershaw. Below I give a short sketch of his life.

GENERAL JAMES CONNOR

General James Connor, son of the late Henry Connor, was born in Charleston, S.C., 1st of September, 1829. Graduated at the South Carolina College, 1849, same class with D. Wyatt Aiken, Theo G. Barker, C.H. Simonton, and W.H. Wallace (Judge). Read law with J.L. Pettigrew. Admitted to the bar in 1852. Practiced in Charleston. Appointed United States District Attorney for South Carolina in 1856, Hon. A.G. Magrath then District Judge. As District Attorney, prosecuted Captain Carrie, of the "Wanderer," who had brought a cargo of Africans to the State; also prosecuted T.J. Mackey for participation in Walker's filibustering expedition. Always justified the expectations of his friends in their high opinion of his talents and marked ability in all contingencies. Resigned as District Attorney in December, 1860. Was on the committee with Judge Magrath and W.F. Colcock, charged to urge the Legislature to call a convention of the people to consider the necessity of immediate Secession, and upon the passage of the Secession Ordinance, prepared for active service in the army. But upon the formation of the Confederate States Government he was appointed Confederate States of America District Attorney for South Carolina, but declined. Went into the service as Captain of the Montgomery Guards, and in May, 1861, was chosen Captain of the Washington Light Infantry, Hampton Legion. In July, 1861, he became Major, and in June, 1863, was appointed Colonel of the Twenty-second North Carolina Volunteers. Being disabled for field duty, temporarily, was detailed as one of the judges of the military court of the Second Army Corps. With rank of Colonel, June, 1864, was commissioned Brigadier General, and by assignment commanded McGowan's and Laws' Brigades. Subsequently, as Acting Major General, commanded McGowan's, Laws', and Bushrod Johnson's Brigades. On return of McGowan to duty, was assigned permanently to command of Kershaw's Brigade.

He engaged in the following battles: Fort Sumter, First Manassas, Yorktown, New Stone Point, West Point, Seven Pines, Mechanicsville, Chancellorsville, Riddle's Shop, Darby's Farm, Fossil's Mill, Petersburg, Jerusalem, Plank Road, Reams' Station, Winchester, Port Republic, and Cedar Run. Severely wounded in leg at Mechanicsville and again at Cedar Run, October 12th, 1864. Leg amputated.

Returning to Charleston after the war, he resumed law practice with W.D. Portier. Was counsel for the South Carolina Railway. In 1878 was Receiver of the Georgia and Carolina Railway. Was candidate for Lieutenant Governor in 1870. Elected Attorney General in 1876, resigned in 1877. Was at one time since the war M.W.G.M. of the Grand Lodge of Masons in this State.

One of the most distinguished looking and fearless officers of the Twentieth South Carolina Regiment was killed here, Captain John M. Kinard. Captain Kinard was one of the finest line officers in the command—a good disciplinarian and tactician, and a noble hearted, kind-hearted gentleman of the "Old School." He was rather of a taciturn bend, and a man of great modesty, but it took only a glimpse at the man to tell of what mould and mettle he was made. I give a short sketch of his life.

Captain John Martin Kinard

Captain John Martin Kinard was born July 5, 1833, in the section of Newberry County known as the Dutch Fork, a settlement of German emigrants, lying a few miles west of Pomaria. In 1838 his father, General Henry H. Kinard, was elected Sheriff of Newberry County, and moved with his family to the court house town of Newberry. Here Captain Kinard attended school until he was about seventeen years old, when he went to Winnsboro, S.C., to attend the famous Mount Zion Academy. He entered South Carolina College in 1852, but left before finishing his college course to engage in farming, a calling for which he had had a passionate longing from his boyhood days. Having married Mary Alabama, the daughter of Dr. P.B. Ruff, he settled on his grandfather's plantation now known as Kinards. While living here his wife died, and a few years afterwards he married Lavinia Elizabeth, the daughter of Dr. William Rook.

When the State called her sons to her defense, he answered promptly, and enlisted as First Lieutenant in a company commanded by his uncle, John P. Kinard. His company was a part of the Twentieth Regiment, Colonel Lawrence Keitt, and was known as Company F. During the first years of the war he was engaged with his company in the defense of Charleston Harbor, rising to the rank of Captain on the resignation of his uncle.

While serving with his regiment in Virginia, to which place it had been moved in 1864, Captain Kinard came home on furlough. Very soon, however, he set out for the front again, and was detailed for duty in the trenches around Richmond. While engaged here he made repeated efforts to be restored to his old company, and joined them with a glad heart in October, 1864. On the 13th of October, a few days after his return, he warned his faithful negro body-guard, Ham Nance, to keep near, as he expected some hot fighting soon. And it came. The next day the enemy was met near Strausburg, and Captain Kinard fell, with a bullet in his heart. He died the death of the happy warrior, fighting as our Anglo-Saxon forefathers fought, in the midst of his kinsmen and friends. Ham Nance bore his body from the field, and never left it until he returned it to his home in Newberry.

Captain Kinard left three children. By his first wife, a daughter, Alice, now the wife of Elbert H. Aull, Esq.; by his second wife, two sons, John M. Kinard, Commandant of the John M. Kinard Camp, Sons of Veterans, and James P. Kinard.

CHAPTER 37
Battle of Cedar Creek or Fisher's Hill

After the retreat of the enemy across Cedar Creek, on the 13th, the brigade returned to Fisher's Hill, and encamped in a beautiful grove. It was now expected that we would have a long, sweet rest—a rest so much needed and devoutly wished for, after two months of incessant marching and fighting. The foragers now struck out right and left over the mountains on either side to hunt up all the little delicacies these mountain homes so abounded in—good fresh butter-milk, golden butter—the like can be found nowhere else in the South save in the valleys of Virginia—apple butter, fruits of all kinds, and occasionally these foragers would run upon a keg of good old mountain corn, apple jack, or peach brandy—a "nectar fitting for the gods," when steeped in bright, yellow honey. These men were called "foragers" from their habit of going through the country, while the army was on the march or in camp, buying up little necessaries and "wet goods," and bringing them into camp to sell or share with their messmates. It mattered not how long the march, how tired they were, when we halted for the night's camp, while others would drop, exhausted, too tired to even put up their tents or cook a supper, these foragers would overcome every obstacle, climb mountains, and wade rivers in search of something to eat or drink, and be back in camp before day. In every regiment and in almost every company you could find these foragers, who were great stragglers, dropping in the rear or flanking to the right or left among the farm houses in search of honey, butter, bread, or liquors of some kind. Some of these foragers in the brigade were never known to be without whiskey during the whole war. Where, how, or when they got it was as a sealed book to the others. These foragers, too, when out on one of their raids, were never very particular whether the owner of the meat or spring house, or even the cellar, was present or not, should they suspicion or learn from outside parties that these places contained that for which they were looking. If at night, they would not disturb the old man, but while some would watch, others would be depredating upon his pig pen, chicken roost, or milk house. It was astonishing what a change in the morals of men army life occasioned. Someone has said, "A rogue in the army, a rogue at home;" but this I deny. Sometimes that same devilish, schoolboy spirit that actuates the truant to filch fruit or melons from orchards of others, while he had abundance at home, caused the soldier oftentimes to make "raids," as they called these nocturnal visits to the farm houses outlying the army's track. I have known men who at home was as honorable, honest, upright, and who would scorn a dishonest act, turn out to be veteran foragers, and rob and steal anything they could get their hands on from the citizens, friend or foe alike. They become to look upon all as "fish for a soldier's net." I remember the first night on Fisher's Hill, after fighting and marching all day, two of my men crossed over the Massanutton Mountain and down in the Luray Valley, a distance of ten miles or more, and came back before day with as unique a load of plunder as I ever saw. While in some of the mountain gorges they came upon a "spring house" a few hundred feet from the little cabin, nestled and hid in one of those impenetrable caves, where the owner, no doubt, thought himself safe from all the outside world. They had little difficulty in gaining an entrance, but all was dark, so kneeling down and examining the trough they found jars of pure sweet milk, with the rich, yellow cream swimming on top. This, of course, they could not carry, so they drank their fill. While searching around for anything else that was portable, they found a lot of butter in a churn, and to their astonishment, a ten-gallon keg of peach brandy. Now they were in the plight of the man who "when it rained mush had no spoon." They had only their canteens, but there was no funnel to pour through. But the mother of invention, as usual, came to their assistance. They poured out the milk in the jars, filled two for each, and returned over the mountain with a jar of brandy under each arm. The next morning I found, to my surprise, hanging to the pole of my tent, my canteen filled with the choicest brandy. Whiskey sold for $1.00 per drink, so their four jars of brandy added something to their month's pay. As a Captain of a company, I could not give leave of absence, nor could I excuse any who left camp against orders or without permission. So I had it understood that should any of my men wish to undertake a foraging expedition, not to ask my permission, but go; and if they did not get caught by outside guards, I would not report nor punish them, but if they got caught, not to expect any favors or mercy at my hands. While I never countenanced nor upheld foraging, unless it was done legitimately and the articles paid for, still when a choice piece of mutton or pork, a mess tin of honey, or canteen of brandy was hanging on my rifle pole in the morning, I only did what I enjoined on the men, "say nothing and ask no question." And so it was with nearly all the Captains in the army. And be it said to the credit of the Southern troops, pilfering or thieving was almost an unknown act while camping in our own country. It was only done in the mountains of Virginia or East Tennessee, where the citizens were generally our enemies, and who were willing to give aid and comfort to the Federals, while to the Southern troops they often denied the smallest favors, and refused to take our money.

On the night of the 18th of October we received orders to prepare for marching at midnight. No drums were to be beaten, nor noise of any kind made. From this we knew an advance was to be made, as Gordon's Division had orders to march soon after nightfall. The most profound secrecy, the absence of all noise, from rattling of canteens or tin cups, were enjoined upon the men. They were to noiselessly make their way over the spur of the Massanutton Mountain, which here butted out in a bold promontory, dividing the Shennandoah and the Luray Valleys, and strike the enemy in the flank away to our right. The other divisions were to be in readiness to attack as the roll of battle reached their front or right. The enemy was posted on an almost impregnable position on the bluff overlooking Cedar Creek, while in their rear was a vast plateau of several miles in extent. The enemy's breastworks were built of strong timbers, with earth thrown against them, with a deep trench on the inside, being deeper from the bottom of the trench to the top of the works than the heights of the soldiers when standing. Thus a step of three or four feet was built for the troops to stand on and fire. The breastworks wound in and out with the creek, some places jutting out almost to the very brink; at others, several hundred yards in the rear; a level piece of bottom land intervening. This ridge and plateau were some fifty feet or more above the level of the creek, and gave elegant position for batteries. In front of this breastwork, and from forty to fifty feet in breadth, was an abattis constructed of pine trees, the needles stripped, the limbs cut and pointed five to ten feet from the trunks. These were packed and stacked side by side and on top of each other, being almost impossible for a single man even to pick his way through, and next to impossible for a line of battle to cross over. All along the entire length of the fortifications were built great redoubts of earthwork in the form of squares, the earth being of sufficient thickness to turn any of our cannon balls, while all around was a ditch from twelve to fifteen feet deep—only one opening in the rear large enough to admit the teams drawing the batteries. Field pieces were posted at each angle, the infantry, when needed, filled the space between. These forts were built about two hundred yards apart, others being built in front of the main line. This I believe was the most completely fortified position by nature, as well as by hand, of any line occupied during the war, and had the troops not been taken by surprise and stood their ground, a regiment strung out could have kept an army at bay.

General Gordon's troops left camp earlier than did Kershaw's, beginning their winding march at single file around the mountain side, over the great promontory, down in the plain below, through brush and undergrowth, along dull trails, catching and pulling themselves along by the bushes and vines that covered the rough borders and ledges of the mountain. Sometime after midnight Kershaw moved out across the turn-pike in the direction of the river, the Second South Carolina in front, under Captain McCulcheon; then the Third, under Major Todd; then the Eighth, Twentieth, Fifteenth, and the Seventh. The James' or Third Battalion having some months before been organized into brigade sharpshooters, adding two companies to it, preceded the brigade, and was to charge the fords and capture the pickets. When near the river the brigade was halted, and scouting parties sent ahead to see how the land lay. A picked body moved cautiously along in front, and when all was in readiness, a charge was made—a flash, a report or two, and the enemy's out post at this point was ours. As we were feeling our way along the dull road that led to this ford, one poor fellow, who had been foremost in the assault on the pickets, was carried by us on a litter. Nothing but a low, deep groan was heard, which told too plainly that his last battle had been fought. The river crossed, the brigade continued in columns of fours, moving rapidly forward that all would be in readiness by the time Gordon's guns opened to announce that he was in position and ready.

Now our line of battle was formed, and never before or since was the brigade called in action with so few officers. Not a Colonel, nothing higher than a Major, in the entire brigade, the brigade itself being commanded by a staff officer, who had never so much as commanded a company before. At the close of the day there were but few officers in the command of the rank of Captain even.

Just at the beginning of dawn we heard the guns of Gordon belching forth far to our right. The cannon corps of the enemy roused up from their slumbers and met the attack with grape and cannister, but Gordon was too close upon them, the assault so sudden, that the troops gave way. Nearer and nearer came the roll of battle as each succeeding brigade was put in action. We were moving forward in double-quick to reach the line of the enemy's breastworks by the time the brigade on our right became engaged. Now the thunder of their guns is upon us; the brigade on our right plunges through the thicket and throw themselves upon the abattis in front of the works and pick their way over them. All of our brigade was not in line, as a part was cut off by an angle in Cedar Creek, but the Second and Third charged through an open field in front of the enemy's line. As we emerged from a thicket into the open we could see the enemy in great commotion, but soon the works were filled with half-dressed troops and they opened a galling fire upon us. The distance was too great in this open space to take the works by a regular advance in line of battle, so the men began to call for orders to "charge." Whether the order was given or not, the troops with one impulse sprang forward. When in a small swale or depression in the ground, near the center of the field, the abattis was discovered in front of the works. Seeing the impossibility to make their way through it under such a fire, the troops halted and returned the fire. Those behind the works would raise their bare heads above the trenches, fire away, regardless of aim or direction, then fall to the bottom to reload. This did not continue long, for all down the line from our extreme right the line gave way, and was pushed back to the rear and towards our left, our troops mounting their works and following them as they fled in wild disorder. "Over the works, cross over," was the command now given, and we closed in with a dash to the abattis—over it and down in the trenches—before the enemy realized their position. Such a sight as met our eyes as we mounted their works was not often seen. For a mile or more in every direction towards the rear was a vast plain or broken plateau, with not a tree or shrub in sight. Tents whitened the field from one end to the other for a hundred paces in rear of the line, while the country behind was one living sea of men and horses—all fleeing for life and safety. Men, shoeless and hatless, went flying like mad to the rear, some with and some without their guns. Here was a deserted battery, the horses unhitched from the guns; the caissons were going like the wind, the drivers laying the lash all the while. Cannoneers mounted the unhitched horses barebacked, and were straining every nerve to keep apace with caissons in front. Here and there loose horses galloped at will, some bridleless, others with traces whipping their flanks to a foam. Such confusion, such a panic, was never witnessed before by the troops. Our cannoneers got their guns in position, and enlivened the scene by throwing shell, grape, and cannister into the flying fugitives. Some of the captured guns were turned and opened upon the former owners. Down to our left we could see men leaving the trenches, while others huddled close up to the side of the wall, displaying a white flag. Our ranks soon became almost as much disorganized as those of the enemy. The smoking breakfast, just ready for the table, stood temptingly inviting, while the opened tents displayed a scene almost enchanting to the eyes of the Southern soldier, in the way of costly blankets, overcoats, dress uniforms, hats, caps, boots, and shoes all thrown in wild confusion over the face of the earth. Now and then a suttler's tent displayed all the luxuries and dainties a soldier's heart could wish for. All this fabulous wealth of provisions and clothing looked to the half-fed, half-clothed Confederates like the wealth of the Indies. The soldiers broke over all order and discipline for a moment or two and helped themselves. But their wants were few, or at least that of which they could carry, so they grab a slice of bacon, a piece of bread, a blanket, or an overcoat, and were soon in line again following up the enemy. There was no attempt of alignment until we had left the breastworks, then a partial line of battle was formed and the pursuit taken up. Major Todd, of the Third, having received a wound just as we crossed the works, the command of the regiment devolved on the writer. The angle of the creek cutting off that portion of the brigade that was in rear, left the Second and Third detached, nor could we see or hear of a brigade commander. The troops on our right had advanced several hundred yards, moving at right angle to us, and were engaging the enemy, a portion that had made a stand on the crest of a hill, around an old farm house. Not knowing what to do or where to go, and no orders, I accepted Napoleon's advice to the lost soldier, "When a soldier is lost and does not know where to go, always go to where you hear the heaviest firing." So I advanced the regiment and joined it on the left of a Georgia brigade. Before long the enemy was on the run again, our troops pouring volley after volley into them as they fled over stone fences, hedges, around farm houses, trying in every conceivable way to shun the bullets of the "dreaded gray-backs." I looked in the rear. What a sight! Here came stragglers, who looked like half the army, laden with every imaginable kind of plunder—some with an eye to comfort, had loaded themselves with new tent cloths, nice blankets, overcoats, or pants, while others, who looked more to actual gain in dollars and cents, had invaded the suttler's tents and were fairly laden down with such articles as they could find readiest sale for. I saw one man with a stack of wool hats on his head, one pressed in the other, until it reached more than an arm's length above his head. Frying-pans were enviable utensils in the army, and tin cups—these articles would be picked up by the first who came along, to be thrown aside when other goods more tempting would meet their sight.

After getting the various brigades in as much order as possible, a general forward movement was made, the enemy making only feeble attempts at a stand, until we came upon a stone fence, or rather a road hedged on either side by a stone fence, running parallel to our line of battle. Here we were halted to better form our columns. But the halt was fatal—fatal to our great victory, fatal to our army, and who can say not fatal to our cause. Such a planned battle, such complete success, such a total rout of the enemy was never before experienced—all to be lost either by a fatal blunder or the greed of the soldier for spoils. Only a small per cent comparatively was engaged in the plundering, but enough to weaken our ranks. It was late in the day. The sharpshooters (Third Battalion) had been thrown out in a cornfield several hundred yards in our front. The men lay in the road behind the stone fence without a dream of the enemy ever being able to rally and make an advance. Some were inspecting their captured plunder; others sound asleep, after our five miles' chase. The sun was slowly sinking in the west. Oh, what a glorious victory! Men in their imagination were writing letters home, telling of our brilliant achievements—thirty pieces of artillery captured, whole wagon trains of ordnance, from ten to twenty thousand stands of small arms, horses and wagons, with all of Sheridan's tents and camp equippage—all was ours, and the enemy in full retreat!

But the scenes are soon to be shifted. Sheridan had been to Winchester, twenty miles away. He hears the firing of guns in the direction of Fisher's Hill, mounts his black charger, and with none to accompany him but an orderly, he begins his famous ride from Winchester. Louder and louder the cannon roar, faster and faster his faithful steed leaps over the stoney pike, his rider plunging the steel rowels into the foaming sides. Now he is near enough to hear the deep, rolling sound of the infantry, accompanied by the dreaded Rebel yell. He knew his troops were retreating from the sound he hears. A few more leaps, and he comes face to face with his panic stricken troops. The road was crowded, the woods and fields on either side one vast swarm of fleeing fugatives. A few of the faithful were still holding the Confederates at bay, while the mass were seeking safety in flight. His sword springs from its scabbard, and waving it over his head, he calls in a loud voice, "Turn, boys, turn; we are going back." The sound of his voice was electrical. Men halt, some fall, others turn to go back, while a few continue their mad flight. A partial line is formed, Sheridan knowing the effect of a show of forward movement, pushes his handful of men back to meet the others still on the run. They fall in. Others who have passed the line in their rush, return, and in a few moments this wild, seething, surging, panic stricken mass had turned, and in well formed lines, were now approaching the cornfield and woods in which our pickets and skirmishers lay, all unconscious of the mighty change—a change the presence of one man effected in the morale of the routed troops. They rush upon our sharpshooters, capturing nearly the whole line, killing Captain Whitner, the commander, and either capturing or wounding nearly all the commissioned officers. Before we knew it, or even expected it, the enemy was in our front, advancing in line of battle. The men hadn't time to raise a gun before the bullets came whizzing over our heads, or battering against the stone wall. We noticed away to our right the lines give way. Still Kershaw's Brigade held their position, and beat back the enemy in our front. But in the woods on our left some troops who were stationed there, on seeing the break in the line beyond us, gave way also. Someone raised the cry and it was caught up and hurried along like all omens of ill luck, that "the cavalry is surrounding us." In a moment our whole line was in one wild confusion, like "pandemonium broke loose." If it was a rout in the morning, it was a stampede now. None halted to listen to orders or commands. Like a monster wave struck by the head land, it rolls back, carrying everything before it by its own force and power, or drawing all within its wake. Our battle line is forced from the stone fence. We passed over one small elevation, down through a vale, and when half way up the next incline, Adjutant Pope, who was upon the staff of our brigade commander, met the fleeing troops and made a masterly effort to stem the tide by getting some of the troops in line. Around him was formed a nucleus, and the line began to lengthen on either side, until we had a very fair battle line when the enemy reached the brow of the hill we had just passed. We met them with a stunning volley, that caused the line to reel and stagger back over the crest. Our lines were growing stronger each moment. Pope was bending all his energies to make Kershaw's Brigade solid, and was in a fair way to succeed. The troops that had passed, seeing a stand being made, returned, and kept up the fire. It was now hoped that the other portion of the line would act likewise and come to our assistance, and we further knew that each moment we delayed the enemy would allow that much time for our wagon train and artillery to escape. But just as all felt that we were holding our own, Adjutant Pope fell, badly wounded by a minnie ball through the eye, which caused him to leave the field. Then seeing no prospects of succor on our right or left, the enemy gradually passing and getting in our rear, the last great wave rolls away, the men break and fly, every man for himself, without officers or orders—they scatter to the rear. The enemy kept close to our heels, just as we were rising one hill their batteries would be placed on the one behind, then grape and cannister would sweep the field. There were no thickets, no ravines, no fences to shield or protect us. Everything seemed to have been swept from off the face of the earth, with the exception of a lone farm house here and there. Every man appeared to be making for the stone bridge that spanned the creek at Strausburg. But for the bold, manly stand made by Y.J. Pope, with a portion of Kershaw's Brigade (the brigade commander was seldom seen during the day), the entire wagon train and hundreds more of our troops would have been lost, for at that distance we could hear wagons, cannons, and caissons crossing the stone bridge at a mad gallop. But in the rush some wagons interlocked and were overturned midway the bridge, and completely blocked the only crossing for miles above and below. Teamsters and wagoners leave their charge and rush to the rear. In the small space of one or two hundred yards stood deserted ambulances, wagons, and packs of artillery mules and horses, tangled and still hitched, rearing and kicking like mad, using all their strength to unloosen themselves from the matted mass of vehicles, animals, and men, for the stock had caught up the spirit of the panic, and were eager to keep up the race. As by intuition, the flying soldiers felt that the roadway would be blocked at the bridge over Cedar Creek, so they crossed the turn-pike and bore to the left in order to reach the fords above. As I reached the pike, and just before entering a thicket beyond, I glanced over my shoulder toward the rear. One glance was enough! On the hill beyond the enemy was placing batteries, the infantry in squads and singly blazing away as rapidly as they could load and fire, the grape and cannister falling and rattling upon the ground like walnuts thrown from a basket. The whole vast plain in front and rear was dotted with men running for life's sake, while over and among this struggling mass the bullets fell like hail. How any escaped was a wonder to the men themselves. The solid shot and shell came bouncing along, as the boys would laughingly say afterwards, "like a bob-tailed dog in high oats"—striking the earth, perhaps, just behind you, rebound, go over your head, strike again, then onward, much like the bounding of rubber balls. One ball, I remember, came whizzing in the rear, and I heard it strike, then rebound, to strike again just under or so near my uplifted foot that I felt the peculiar sensation of the concussion, rise again, and strike a man twenty paces in my front, tearing away his thigh, and on to another, hitting him square in the back and tearing him into pieces. I could only shrug my shoulders, close my eyes, and pull to the rear stronger and faster.

 The sun had now set. A squadron of the enemy's cavalry came at headlong speed down the pike; the clatter of the horses hoofs upon the hard-bedded stones added to the panic, and caused many who had not reached the roadway to fall and surrender. About one hundred and fifty of the Third Regiment had kept close at my heels (or I had kept near their front, I can't say which is the correct explanation), with a goodly number of Georgians and Mississippians, who had taken refuge in a thicket for a moment's breathing spell, joining our ranks, and away we continued our race. We commenced to bend our way gradually back towards the stone bridge. But before we neared it sufficiently to distinguish friend from foe, we heard the cavalry sabering our men, cursing, commanding, and yelling, that we halted for a moment to listen and consult. In the dim twilight we could distinguish some men about one hundred yards in front moving to and fro. Whether they were friends, and like ourselves, trying to escape the cavalry in turn and creep by and over the bridge, or whether they were a skirmish line of the enemy, we could not determine. The Captain of a Georgia regiment (I think his name was Brooks), with four or five men, volunteered to go forward and investigate. I heard the command "halt," and then a parley, so I ordered the men to turn towards the river. The command came after us to "halt, halt," but we only redoubled our speed, while "bang, bang," roared their guns, the bullets raining thick and fast over our head. I never saw or heard of my new found friends again, and expect they, like many captured that day, next enjoyed freedom after Lee and Johnston had surrendered. When we reached the river it was undecided whether we could cross or not. So one of my men, a good swimmer, laid off his accoutrement and undertook to test the depth. In he plunged, and was soon out of sight in the blue waters. As he arose he called out, "Great God! don't come in here if you don't want to be drowned. This river has got no bottom." Our only alternative was to go still higher and cross above the intersection of the north and south prongs of the Shenandoah, where it was fordable. This we did, and our ranks augmented considerable as we proceeded up the banks of the stream, especially when we had placed the last barrier between us and the enemy. We had representatives of every regiment in Early's Army, I think, in our crowd, for we had no regiment, as it naturally follows that a man lost at night, with a relentless foe at his heels, will seek company.

We returned each man to his old quarters, and as the night wore on more continued to come in singly, by twos, and by the half dozens, until by midnight the greater portion of the army, who had not been captured or lost in battle, had found rest at their old quarters. But such a confusion! The officers were lost from their companies—the Colonels from their regiments, while the Generals wandered about without staff and without commands. The officers were as much dazed and lost in confusion as the privates in the ranks. For days the men recounted their experiences, their dangers, their hair-breadth escapes, the exciting chase during that memorable rout in the morning and the stampede in the evening, and all had to laugh. Some few took to the mountains and roamed for days before finding an opportunity to return; others lay in thickets or along the river banks, waiting until all was still and quiet, then seek some crossing. Hundreds crowded near the stone bridge (the Federal pickets were posted some yards distance), and took advantage of the darkness to cross over under the very nose of the enemy.

One man of the Fifteenth came face to face with one of the videttes, when a hand to hand encounter took place—a fight in the dark to the very death—but others coming to the relief of their comrade beat the Confederate to insensibility and left him for dead. Yet he crawled to cover and lay concealed for a day and night, then rejoined his regiment in a sickening plight.

A man in my company, Frank Boozer, was struck by a glancing bullet on the scalp and fell, as was thought, dead. There he lay, while hundreds and hundreds trampled over him, and it was near day when he gained consciousness and made his way for the mountain to the right. There he wandered along its sides, through its glens and gorges, now dodging a farm house or concealing himself in some little cave, until the enemy passed, for it was known that the mountains and hills on either side were scoured for the fugitives.

Captain Vance, of the Second, with a friend, Myer Moses, had captured a horse, and they were making their way through the thickets, Moses in front, with Vance in rear, the darkness almost of midnight on them. They came upon a squad of Federal pickets. They saw their plight in a moment, but Moses was keen-witted and sharp-tongued, and pretended that he was a Yankee, and demanded their surrender. When told that they were Federals, he seemed overjoyed, and urged them to "come on and let's catch all those d——n Rebels." But when they asked him a few questions he gave himself away. He was asked:

"What command do you belong to?"

"Eighty-seventh New York," Moses answered, without hesitation.

"What brigade?" "What division?" etc. "We have no such commands in this army. Dismount, you are our prisoners."

But Captain Vance was gone, for at the very outset of the parley he slid off behind and quietly made his escape. In such emergencies it was no part of valor to "stand by your friend," for in that case both were lost, while otherwise one was saved.

What was the cause of our panic, or who was to blame, none ever knew. The blame was always laid at "somebody else's" door. However disastrous to our army and our cause was this stampede—the many good men lost (killed and captured) in this senseless rout—yet I must say in all candor, that no occasion throughout the war gave the men so much food for fun, ridicule, and badgering as this panic. Not one man but what could not tell something amusing or ridiculous on his neighbor, and even on himself. The scenes of that day were the "stock in trade" during the remainder of the war for laughter. It looked so ridiculous, so foolish, so uncalled for to see twenty thousand men running wildly over each other, as it were, from their shadows, for there was nothing in our rear but a straggling line of Federals, which one good brigade could have put to rout.

Both Colonel Boykin and Lieutenant Colonel McMichael, of the Twentieth, were captured and never returned to the service, not being parolled until after the surrender. The Twentieth was commanded by Major Leaphart until the close.

As Adjutant Pope never returned in consequence of his wounds. I will give a few facts as to his life. No officer in the army was parted with greater reluctance than Adjutant Pope.

Adjutant Young John Pope

Y.J. Pope was born in the town of Newberry, S.C., on the 10th of April, 1841. Was the son of Thomas Herbert Pope and Harriett Neville Pope, his wife. He was educated in the Male Academy, at Newberry, and spent six years at Furman University, Greenville, S.C., from which institution he graduated in August, 1860. After studying law under his uncle, Chief Justice O'Neall, he entered the Confederate Army on April 13th, 1861, as First Sergeant in Company E, of Third South Carolina Regiment of Infantry. He participated in the battles of First Manassas and Williamsburg while in his company. In May, 1862, he was made Adjutant of the Third South Carolina Regiment, and as such participated in the battles of Savage Station, Malvern Hill, Maryland Heights, Sharpsburg, First Fredericksburg (where he was slightly wounded), Chancellorsville, Gettysburg (where he received three wounds), Chickamauga (where he was severely wounded), Wilderness, Brock's Road and other battles around Spottsylvania Court House, North Anna River Bridge, Second Cold Harbor, Berryville (where he was shot through the mouth), Strausburg, and Cedar Creek, on the 19th of October, 1864, where he lost his left eye, which was totally destroyed by a minnie bullet.

Since the war he has been elected Mayor of his native town at five elections. He was elected by the Legislature District Judge of Newberry, in December, 1865, and served as such until June, 1868, when Radicals abolished that office. He was elected to the House of Representatives of his State in the year 1877, and was by the Joint Assembly of the Legislature elected Associate Counsel for the State to test the legality of State bonds, when more than two million dollars were saved the State. He was elected State Senator in 1888, and served until he was elected Attorney General of the State, in 1890. He served in this office until the 3rd of December, 1891, when he was elected Associate Justice of Supreme Court of the State, and on the 30th of January, 1896, he was unanimously re-elected Associate Justice of the Supreme Court of South Carolina.

On the 3rd of December, 1874, he married Mrs. Sallie H.F. Rutherford. By this union there were two daughters, Mary Butler Pope and Neville Pope. The former died in October, 1893, and left a wound which has never healed.

During a part of the year 1864 Adjutant Pope served on the brigade staff as Assistant Adjutant General, and was acting in this capacity when he received the wound that incapacitated him from further service in the field.

Lieutenant U.B. Whites, formerly of my company, but later in command of Company G, Third Battalion, writes a very entertaining sketch of prison life, which I very willingly give space to, so that the uninitiated may have some idea of prison life, and the pleasure of being called "fresh fish" by the old prison "rats." Lieutenant Whites was a gallant soldier and a splendid officer. He was what is called in common parlance "dead game" in battle and out. He is a commercial man, and at present a member of the South Carolina colony of Atlanta, Ga.

How it Feels to be Taken a Prisoner of War.

After being flushed with the most signal victory of more than half a day's fighting, and while gloating over the brilliant success and planning and scheming future glories, and after having captured a great number of Federal soldiers, together with a large number of field pieces, and then in turn to be captured yourself, especially after having boasted and affirmed oftentimes that you never would be taken a prisoner unless sick or wounded, is exceedingly humiliating, to say the least of it, and the feelings of such an one can better be imagined than described. Yet such was the exact condition of the writer on the evening of October 19th, 1864, at the battle of Strausburg, or as it is known at the present day among the veterans, "Early's Stampede."

It is proper to note here that the writer was a line officer belonging to Company H, Third Regiment South Carolina

Volunteers, but several months previous had been assigned to command a company of "picked" men made from the various companies and regiments of the old brigade (Kershaw's), and this company was assigned to duty in the Third Battalion. This battalion was to do the skirmishing and sharpshooting for the brigade. This explanation is necessary in order that the reader may better understand my position and place when captured.

Late in the afternoon of this exciting day General Phil Sheridan succeeded in rallying his routed columns and led the attack on our line. Our skirmish line was in excellent condition. We had no trouble in effectually resisting and driving back the enemy's skirmish line. When within short range of our rifles we opened fire, and for nearly half an hour held them in check, while they fairly rained lead into our ranks. The command "retreat" was given, and we retired, firing. During the retreat brave Captain Whitener was killed. I rallied the remnant of my company in rear of the Third South Carolina. General Kershaw rode rapidly up to where I had rallied what few men I had left and enquired for Captain Whitener. I replied, "He is killed, General." He then ordered me to take what few I had and could gather and double-quick to a point on the extreme left of his division. When I arrived at the point designated, which was in thick woods, to my horror I found the place literally alive with Yankees. I had double-quicked right into the midst of the "blue bellies." "Surrender," came in tones of thunder. I stood amazed, astonished beyond conception. "Surrender," again came the command. There was absolutely no alternative. There was no chance to fight and less chance to run. My brave boys and I were prisoners of war. This was one of the consequences of war that I had never figured upon, and was wholly unprepared for it. I said to the officer who demanded my sword that I would rather give him my right arm. He preferred the sword and got one—I had two, having captured one that morning. Just then an unusual incident occurred.

"Hello, Lieutenant Whites, my old friend, I am glad to see you."

I looked and recognized a Federal Sergeant, whom I had befriended while en route with him and many other Federal prisoners from East Tennessee to Richmond. I replied:

"My dear fellow, I know, under the circumstances, you will excuse me when I tell you that I am truly sorry that I cannot return the compliment."

I was ordered to the rear under guard of one soldier. I was turned over to the provost guard. My other sword was demanded. Of course I gave it up without a word. My emotions were too intense for utterance. I was a disarmed, helpless prisoner of war. My feelings can better be described by relating an incident which occurred later on. After Lee's surrender, a few uncompromising, unconquered Confederates attempted to make their way to Johnston's Army in North Carolina. The way was full of obstacles, and one of the party, nearly overcome, sat with his elbows on his knees and his face in his hands, when a comrade accosted him with—

"Hello, John, what is the matter with you?"

"O, I was just thinking," replied John.

"Well, what in the world were you thinking so deeply about that you were lost to every other environment?"

"Well, Jim, to tell you the truth, I was thinking I wished I was a woman."

"Wish you were a woman! Great Scotts, John, are you gone crazy? A brave soldier like you wishing to be a woman!"

"Now, Jim, I'll tell you the truth; if I were a woman I could just cry as much as I pleased, and no one would think that I was a fool."

I felt very much like John. I wished I was a woman, so that I could cry as much as I pleased.

That night all the prisoners were marched to General Sheridan's headquarters, where we went into camp without supper. Some said their prayers, while others cursed the Yankees inaudibly, of course. Next morning we were lined up and counted. Eleven hundred Confederates answered at Sheridan's roll call. It looked like Kershaw's whole Brigade was there, though there were many Georgians among us. Sheridan then inspected the prisoners, and at his personal instance—shame be it said to his memory—we were all robbed of our good blankets and dirty, worn out ones given in their stead.

After the inspection by Sheridan, we began the march (we knew not where to) under a heavy guard—a whole regiment of infantry to guard eleven hundred prisoners. This guard was old soldiers, who knew how to treat a prisoner. They were kind to us. Nothing of special interest occurred on this day. We arrived at Winchester about sundown. We got some rations, ate supper, lay down to sleep, when we were hurriedly aroused and ordered to "fall in line quickly," "fall in," "fall in."

"What is the trouble?" I ventured to ask.

"Mosby! Mosby is coming."

The name of Mosby was a holy terror to the Federals in that part of Virginia. Silently we prayed that Mosby might make a dash and rescue us. All night long we vainly listened for the clatter of the hoops of Mosby's troopers. But, alas! Mosby did not come. The rumor was false. We took up the night march under double guard. A line of cavalry was placed outside the already heavy infantry guard. The night was dark and drizzly—a good night to escape, had not the guard been so heavy. There were two infantry guards to every four prisoners, besides the outer cavalry guard. The hope of an escape was a forlorn one, but I made the attempt and succeeded in passing both guards, but in my ecstacy I foolishly ran in the dark, and ran right squarely against a plank fence with so much force as to attract the attention of a cavalryman, who was soon at my side and escorted me back with a "d——n you, stay in your place." Several prisoners more fortunate than myself did succeed in making their escape in the darkness.

The guards had kindly informed us that at Harper's Ferry we would be searched and relieved of all valuables, and if we had a knife or anything that we desired to retain, they would keep it for us until after the search. This promise they sacredly kept. The search, or robbery as I call it, was very rigid. Like vandals, they searched every pocket and relieved us of all money, pocket-books, knives, keys, and every other thing, except our tobacco. I beat them a little, notwithstanding their rigid search. I had a five-dollar greenback note inside of my sock at the bottom of my boot. This they failed to find.

From Harper's Ferry to Baltimore, the trip was by rail at night. The guard had now been greatly reduced, only eight to each coach. They had got plenty of whiskey for themselves and for all who wanted it. We were having a jolly good time. At this point, knowing that we were in a friendly part of Maryland, I conceived the idea of making a dash for the guns of the guard, uncoupling the rear coaches, put on the brakes, and make our escape across the Potomac. This plan was quietly communicated to all the prisoners in this the rear coach. All agreed to the plan, except Lieutenant Colonel McMichael, of the Twentieth South Carolina Regiment. He protested so strongly that the plan was abandoned. The trip from this on to Fort Delaware was without incident or special interest.

On our arrival at Fort Delaware we were again subjected to a rigid examination and search, and what few trinkets the kind guards saved for us at Harper's Ferry, were now taken away from us. I, however, saved my five-dollar greenback note, which was safely ensconced inside my sock at the bottom of my foot. Here officers and privates were separated and registered, each as to command, rank, and state. The heavy gates swung open with a doleful noise. We marched in amid the shouts of the old prisoners, "fresh fish," "fresh fish." I wanted to fight right then and there. I did not want to be guyed. I wanted sympathy, not guying. "Fresh fish" was the greeting all new arrivals received, and I being an apt scholar, soon learned to shout "fresh fish" as loud as a Texas cowboy.

The heavy prison gates closed around with a dull sepulchral sound, and prison life began in earnest, with Brigadier General Schoeff master of ceremonies. The prison was in the shape of an oblong square, with the "shacks" or "divisions" on the long side and at the short sides or ends. At the other long side was built a plank fence twelve or fifteen feet high. This fence separated the officers and privates. Near the top of this fence was erected a three-foot walk, from which the strictest guard was kept over both "pens" day and night. Fifteen feet from this plank fence on either side was the "dead line." Any prisoner crossing the "dead line" was shot without being halted. There was not an officer shot during my eight months' sojourn there, but it was a frequent occurrence to hear the sharp report of a guard's rifle, and we knew that some poor, unfortunate Confederate soldier had been murdered. The cowardly guards were always on the lookout for any semblance of an excuse to shoot a "d———n Rebel."

There was a rigid censorship placed over all mail matter being sent from or received at the "pen." All letters were read before being mailed, and all being received were subjected to the same vigilant censorship. They were all opened and read by an official to see that they contained nothing "contraband of war." Money was "contraband." Only such newspapers as suited the fastidious taste of General Schoeff were permitted to come inside the "pen." The officers and privates were supposed to be strictly "incommunicado," but even these found means of communication. The open, spacious courts on both sides of the separating fence, on fair days, were always thronged with men taking exercise. A short note—a small piece of coal was the "mail coach"—the route was the "air line"—the note securely tied to the piece of coal, and at an opportune moment, when the guard's face was in a favorable direction, the "mail" passed over the "air line" into the other pen, and vice versa. This line kept up a regular business, but was never detected.

A large majority of prisoners (officers) had some acquaintance, friend, or relative in Baltimore, New York, or other Northern cities, who would gladly furnish money or clothing to them. Provisions were not permissible under the rules and regulations of the prison authorities. Baltimore, especially, and New York did much toward relieving the burdens of prison life. Such inestimable ladies as Mrs. Mary Howard, of Baltimore, and Mrs. Anna Hoffman, of New York, deserve an everlasting monument of eternal gratitude for the great and good service rendered the unfortunate Confederate prisoners. These philanthropic ladies, with hundreds of other sympathizing men and women of the North, kept many of us furnished with money and clothing. The money itself we were not permitted to have. In its stead the prison officials issued the amounts of money on bits of parchment in denominations of five cents, ten cents, twenty-five cents, fifty cents, and one dollar pieces. This was the prison currency. The prison name for it was "sheepskin." The prison officials would not allow us to have the "cold cash," lest we should enter into a combination and bribe an important guard, thereby effecting an escape. The "sheepskin" answered every other purpose for trade. We had a suttler who was a suttler right. He was a real, genuine, down-east Yankee. He loved money ("sheepskins" were money to him), and he would furnish us with anything we wanted for plenty "sheepskins." He would even furnish whiskey "on the sly," which was positively prohibited by the prison regulations.

He had only to go to headquarters at the close of the day and have his "sheepskins" cashed in genuine greenbacks, and he went away happy and serene, to dream of more "sheepskins."

The amusements and diversions of prison life are wonderful to contemplate. They were numerous and varied. A man could find anything to suit his inclinations. Of all the many diversions, gaming was probably the most prominent, and stands at the head of the list. By common consent, it seemed that a certain part of the open court was set aside for gaming purposes. It made no difference how severe the weather was, these gaming tables were always in full blast. A man could amuse himself with any game at cards that he desired. There were "farrow bank," "chuck-a-luck," "brag," "eucher," "draw poker," "straight poker," "seven-up," "five-up," and most prominent of all, a French game, pronounced in Fort Delaware "vang-tu-aug," meaning twenty-one. All these were games for "sheepskins"—bets, five cents; limit, ten cents. All were conducted on a high plane of honor. If a dealer or player was detected in attempting anything that was unclean, he was tried in court, convicted, and punished.

There were courts and debating societies; classes in French, Spanish, and Greek. There were Bible students and students in the arts and sciences prosecuting their varied studies. The gutta-percha ring-makers were quite numerous, and it was really astonishing to see the quality of the work turned out, being handsomely engraved and inlaid with silver. There were diversion and amusement for everybody and every class of men, except croakers and grumblers. They had no lot, parcel, or place, and such characters were not permitted to indulge in their evil forebodings. They had to be men, and real live men, too. The reader may desire to know whence all the books, cards, materials, etc., came. I answer, from the Yankee suttler, for "sheepskins."

It must be said to the credit of the Federal prison officials, that the sanitary and hygienic arrangements were as near perfect as man could well make them. These officials were exceedingly jealous of the health of the place. In fact, it was often thought they were unnecessarily strict in enforcing their hygienic rules. Everything had to be thoroughly clean. Cleanliness was compulsory. A laundry machine was furnished, and a kind of laundrying was accomplished. Blankets were required to be dusted and sunned regularly. Every few weeks the whole army of prisoners were turned out into the cold, and there remained until the "shacks" were thoroughly white-washed, both inside and outside. This work was performed by "galvanized Yankees." A "galvanized Yankee" was a Confederate prisoner who had "swallowed the yellow pup," i.e., had taken the oath of allegiance to the United States Government. These men were looked upon even by the Federal officers as a contemptible set, and were required to do all kinds of menial service.

The water was good and plentiful. There could be no just criticism along this line. I am constrained to believe that it was owing to these stringent health laws that the percentage of sickness was so very small. Of course, I can only speak of the officers in Fort Delaware.

The prison fare is the most difficult, as well as unpleasant, part of prison life of which to treat. However, I will give the simple facts, and allow the reader to draw his own conclusions as to the justice and necessity for such treatment. To say that the fare was entirely insufficient, is putting it mildly, and would not be more than might be expected under similar circumstances and conditions; but the reader will more fully understand the situation when this insufficiency is exemplified by the facts which follow. Think of being compelled to live on two ounces of meat and six ounces of bread per day. Yet this was a prison ration for us towards the close of the war. This was totally inadequate to appease hunger. Men who had no other means of procuring something to eat were nearly starved to death. They stalked about listlessly, gaunt looking, with sunken cheeks and glaring eyes, which reminded one of a hungry ravenous beast. Hungry, hungry all the time. On lying down at night, many, instead of breathing prayers of thankfulness for bountiful supplies, would lie down invoking the most severe curses of God upon the heads of the whole Federal contingent, from President Lincoln down to the lowest private. Hunger makes men desperate and reckless. The last six or eight months of the war the fare was much worse than at any time previous. It was at this period that the Federal administration was retaliating, as they claimed, for the treatment their prisoners were receiving at Andersonville, Ga.

This inhuman condition of affairs was absolutely brought about by the United States Government itself by positively refusing time and again an exchange of prisoners, and it can not escape the just odium and stigma of the inhuman treatment, the untold suffering, and agonies of both the Confederate and Union prisoners of war.

As already observed, there were not a great number of officers who suffered so intensely, but there were some, who, like nearly all the privates, had no friends or acquaintances in the North to render any assistance, and they suffered greatly. Of course, we endeavored to relieve one another as far as we could. Often have I and others given our entire day's ration from the mess hall to some brother officer less fortunate than ourselves. I have seen an officer peal an apple, throw the pealing upon the ground, and immediately an unfortunate one would pick it up and ravenously devour it. There were a great many wharf rats burrowing under the plank walks which traversed the open court of the prison. These rodents are much larger than our common barn rats, and they were eagerly sought by the starving officers. There was a general warfare declared on the wharf rat in prison. When these rats were taken and being prepared, the odor arising therefrom was certainly tempting to a hungry man, and when ready they were eaten with a keen relish. The rats did not require any of Lee's and Perin's Worcester sauce to make them palatable, or to give them zest. This will give the reader some idea of the straits to which some of the Confederate officers, and nearly all the privates, in prison at Fort Delaware were reduced to by gaunt hunger.

I must here chronicle an event which I desire to go down in history. After being in prison and being hungry for about two months, I received a letter, addressed in a lady's handwriting, to "Lieut. U.B. White, Division 28, Fort Delaware," and postmarked "Baltimore, Md." My surprise was great, but on opening it and finding the writer's name to be "Mrs. Mary Howard, of Lexington Avenue, Baltimore," my surprise was unbounded. I knew no such person as Mrs. Mary Howard, and, in fact, at that time I did not know a soul in Baltimore. I felt sure that there must be some mistake about it. I read and re-read that letter. I scrutinized and examined the address again and again. It was plain, except that the final "s" in my name was wanting, which was and is, to my mind, a very natural and correct omission. Mrs. Howard said in her letter that she had been informed that I was a prisoner of war and that I was in Division Twenty-eight, Fort Delaware, and that I was in need of both money and clothing, and that if this was true she would be glad to relieve my wants. I immediately answered that letter. I said to Mrs. Howard that her information was only too true, which I very much regretted. From that time my hunger was appeased and my nakedness clad. Thirty-five years have elapsed since Mrs. Mary Howard wrote that letter, and to-day it is as much of a mystery to me as it was on the day I received it—by whom or by what means or device Mrs. Howard ever found out who I was, or what my condition and circumstances were, I will never know. She and I corresponded regularly during the balance of my prison life, and for sometime after the war when I returned to South Carolina, and yet that mystery was never explained. Mrs. Mary Howard! Grand, noble, heroic, Christian woman! "She hath done what she could." Through her agency and her means and her efforts she not only assisted and relieved me, but hundreds of other poor, helpless Confederate prisoners. To-day she is reaping her sublime reward, where there are no suffering hungry, starving prisoners to relieve. God bless her descendants!

When General Lee surrendered we refused to believe it, notwithstanding the prison was flooded with various newspapers announcing the fact, and the nearby cities were illuminated, the big guns were belching forth their terrific thunder in joy of the event. However, the truth gradually dawned upon us, and we were forced to realize what we at first thought impossible—that Lee would be forced to surrender. A few days later we were all ordered into line, and officially notified of General Lee's surrender. The futility of further resistance was emphasized, and we were urgently requested to take the oath of Allegiance to the United States Government. This was "a bitter pill," "the yellow pup," to swallow, and a very few solemnly complied. The great majority still had a forlorn hope. Generals Johnston, Kirby Smith, Mosby, and others were still in the field, and it seemed to be a tacit understanding, that we would never take the oath of allegiance as long as one Confederate officer contended in the field.

Finally, when there was no disguising the fact that General Johnston and all others had honorably surrendered—that all was lost—on the 19th day of June, 1865, the last batch of officers in prison took the oath of allegiance to the United States Government, bade farewell to Fort Delaware, and inscribed on its walls, on its fences, in books, and divisions the French quotation, "*Font est perdeu l'honeur*"—All is lost but honor.

A prison! Heavens, I loath the hated name,
Famine's metropolis, the sink of shame,
A nauseous sepulchre, whose craving womb
Hourly inters poor mortals in its tomb;
By ev'ry plague and ev'ry ill possessed,
Ev'n purgatory itself to thee's a jest;
Emblem of hell, nursery of vice,
Thou crawling university of lice;
When wretches numberless to ease their pains,
With smoke and all delude their pensive chains.
How shall I avoid thee? or with what spell
Dissolve the enchantment of thy magic cell?
Ev'n Fox himself can't boast so many martyrs,
As yearly fall within thy wretched quarters.
Money I've none, and debts I cannot pay,
Unless my vermin, will those debts defray.
Not scolding wife, nor inquisition's worse;
Thou'rt ev'ry mischief crammed into one curse.

CHAPTER 38

Leaving the Valley for the Last Time

The retreat from Fisher's Hill to New Market will never be forgotten by those who participated therein as long as they live. To recapitulate the movements of the last thirty-six hours and reflect upon what had been accomplished, it seems beyond human endurance. No retreat in history, even the famous retreat of Xenophon, while of greater duration and under different circumstances, still it did not equal that of Early during the same length of time. From midnight of the 18th the troops were in line, crossing the river some miles in the distance before daylight, storms and takes the enemy's lines by nine o'clock, incessant fighting for five or six miles (either fighting or on the run), then a stampede of the same distance, then back across the river and to camp, a two hours' halt, a forced march of thirty-five miles—making over fifty miles in all—without eating or drinking, only as could be "caught up" on the march or run. Up the valley this routed, disorganized rabble (it could not be called an army) marched, every man as he saw fit, here a General at the head of a few squads called regiments, or a Colonel or Captain with a few men at his heels, some with colors and some without; here a Colonel without a man, there a score or two of men without a commissioned officer. A great number had abandoned their arms and accoutrements, others their scanty baggage. Some regiments had lost their whole supply trains that hauled their cooking utensils and provisions. Then we could see artillerymen with nothing but a few jaded horses, their cannons and caissons left in the general upheaval and wreck at the Stone Bridge, or on the field of battle; Quartermasters, with their teamsters riding or leading their horses, their wagons abandoned or over run by others in the mad rush to escape across the bridge before it was blocked. Along the road loose horses roamed at will, while the sides of the pike were strewn with discarded blankets, tent flies, oilcloths and clothing, the men being forced to free themselves of all surplus incumbrances in order to keep up with the moving mass. At one place we passed General Early, sitting on his horse by the roadside, viewing the motley crowd as it passed by. He looked sour and haggard. You could see by the expression of his face the great weight upon his mind, his deep disappointment, his unspoken disappointment. What was yesterday a proud, well-disciplined army that had accomplished during the first part of the day all, or more, that even the most sanguine General could have expected—crossed rivers, pulled themselves over the mountains, assaulted and surprised an enemy who lay in feeling security behind almost impregnable fortifications, routed and driven them from the field, capturing almost the whole camp equipage with twenty field pieces—now before him poured, the same victorious army, beaten, stampeded, without order or discipline, all the fruits of victory and his own camp equipage gone, his wagon trains abandoned, the men without arms, his cannoneers without cannonry and every color trailing in the dust. And what caused it? The sudden change from victory to defeat. It was not the want of Generalship, for General Early had wisely planned. It was not for lack of courage of the troops, for that morning they had displayed valor and over come obstacles which would have baffled and dismayed less bold spirits. Was it for the superior gallantry of the enemy's troops or the superior Generalship of their adversary? The latter was awry, and the former had been routed from their entrenchments by the bayonet of the Confederates. Sheridan did not even hope to stop our victorious march, only to check it sufficiently to enable him to save the remnant of his army. A feeble advance, a panic strikes our army, and all is lost, while no individual, officer, brigade, or regiment could be held responsible. It shows that once a panic strikes an army all discipline is lost and nothing but time will restore it. For nearly one hundred years historians have been framing reasons and causes of Napoleon's Waterloo, but they are as far from the real cause to-day as they were the night of the rout. It will ever remain the same sad mystery of Early at Cedar Creek. Men are, in some respects, like the animal, and especially in large bodies. A man, when left alone to reason and think for himself, and be forced to depend upon his own resources, will often act differently than when one of a great number. The "loss of a head" is contagious. One will commit a foolish act, and others will follow, but cannot tell why. Otherwise quiet and unobtrusive men, when influenced by the frenzy of an excited mob, will commit violence which in their better moments their hearts would revolt and their consciences rebel against. A soldier in battle will leave his ranks and fly to the rear with no other reason than that he saw others doing the same, and followed.

The stampede of Early was uncalled for, unnecessary, and disgraceful, and I willingly assume my share of the blame and shame. My only title to fame rests upon my leading the Third South Carolina Regiment in the grandest stampede of the Southern Army, the greatest since Waterloo, and I hope to be forgiven for saying with pardonable pride that I led them remarkably well to the rear for a boy of eighteen. A General could not have done better.

We passed the little towns and villages of the Valley, the ladies coming to their doors and looking on the retreat in silence. Were we ashamed? Don't ask the pointed question, gentle reader, for the soldiers felt as if they could turn and brain every Federal soldier in the army with the butt of his rifle. But not a reproach, not a murmur from those self-sacrificing, patriotic women of the Valley. They were silent, but sad—their experience during the time the enemy occupied the Valley before told them they had nothing to expect but insult and injury, for their bold, proud Virginia blood would not suffer them to bend the knee in silent submission. Their sons and husbands had all given themselves to the service of their country, while rapine and the torch had already done its work too thoroughly to fear it much now or dread its consequences. But the presence alone of a foreign foe on their threshold was the bitterness of gall.

On reaching New Market, men were gathered together in regiments and assigned to camping grounds, as well as the disorganized state of the army would allow. All night long the stragglers kept coming in, and did so for several days. We were suffering for something to eat more than anything else. Rations of corn were issued, and this was parched and eaten, or beaten up, when parched, and a decoction which the soldiers called "coffee" was made and drunk.

The troops remained in camp until the last of October, then began their march to rejoin Lee. The campaign of Early in the Valley had been a failure, if measured by the fruits of victory. If, however, to keep the enemy from occupying the Valley, or from coming down on the north or rear of Richmond was the object, then it had accomplished its purpose, but at a heavy loss and a fearful sacrifice of life. We arrived at Richmond early in November, and began building winter quarters about seven miles from the city, on the extreme left of the army. Everything north of the James continued quiet along our lines for a month or more, but we could hear the deep baying of cannon continually, away to our right, in the direction of Petersburg.

When we had about finished our huts we were moved out of them and further to the right, in quarters that Hoke's Division had built. These were the most comfortable quarters we occupied during the war. They consisted of log huts twelve by fourteen, thoroughly chinked with mud and straw, some covered with dirt, others with split boards. We had splendid breastworks in front of us, built up with logs on the inside and a bank of earth from six to eight feet in depth on the outside, a ditch of three or four feet beyond and an escarpment inside. At salients along the line forts for the artillery were built, but not now manned, and in front of our lines and around our forts mines or torpedoes were sunk, which would explode by tramping on the earth above them.

At these mines were little sticks about three feet long stuck in the ground with a piece of blue flannel tied to the end to attract the attention of our pickets going out. But hundreds of white sticks, exactly like those above the mines, were stuck into the earth every three feet for a distance of forty feet all around, but these were marked red instead of blue. This was so that the enemy, in case of a charge, or spies coming in at night, could not distinguish harmless stakes from those of the torpedo. We picketed in front and had to pass through where these stakes were posted single file, along little paths winding in and out among them. The men were led out and in by guides and cautioned against touching any, for fear of mistake and being blown up. It is needless to say these instructions were carried out to the letter and no mistake ever made. On several occasions, even before we had our first quarters completed, a report would come occasionally that the enemy was approaching or quartered near our front, and out we would go to meet them, but invariably it proved to be a false alarm or the enemy had retired. Once in December the enemy made a demonstration to our right, and we were called out at night to support the line where the attack was made. After a few rounds of shelling and a few bullets flying over our heads (no harm being done), at daylight we returned to our camp. Our lines had been so extended that to man our works along our front we had not more than one man to every six feet. Still with our breastworks so complete and the protection beyond the line, it is doubtful whether the enemy could have made much headway against us. All the timber and debris in our front for more than one thousand yards had been felled or cleared away.

The ladies of Richmond had promised the soldiers a great Christmas dinner on Christmas day, but from some cause or other our dinner did not materialize. But the soldiers fared very well. Boxes from home were now in order, and almost every day a box or two from kind and loving friends would come in to cheer and comfort them. Then, too, the blockaders at Wilmington and Charleston would escape the Argus eyes of the fleet and bring in a cargo of shoes, cloth, sugar, coffee, etc. Even with all our watchfulness and the vigilance of the enemy on the James, that indefatigable and tireless Jew, with an eye to business, would get into Richmond with loads of delicacies, and this the soldier managed to buy with his "Confederate graybacks." They were drawing now at the rate of seventeen dollars per month, worth at that time about one dollar in gold or one dollar and seventy cents in greenbacks. The Jews in all countries and in all times seemed to fill a peculiar sphere of usefulness. They were not much of fighters, but they were great "getters." They would undergo any hardships or risks for gain, and while our government may not have openly countenanced their traffic, still it was thought they "winked" at it. I do know there were a lot of Jews in Richmond who could go in and out of our lines at will. Sometimes they were caught, first by one army and then by another, and their goods or money confiscated, still they kept up their blockade running. I was informed by one of General Gary's staff officers since the war, that while they were doing outpost duty on the lower James, Jews came in daily with passports from the authorities at Richmond, authorizing them to pass the lines. On many occasions they claimed they were robbed by our pickets. Once this officer allowed two Jews to pass out of the lines, with orders to pass the pickets, but soon they returned, saying they were robbed. General Gary, who could not tolerate such treachery, had the men called up and the Jews pointed out the men who had plundered them. But the men stoutly denied the charge, and each supported the other in his denials, until a search was ordered, but nothing was found. They cursed the "lying Jew" and threatened that the next time they attempted to pass they would leave them in the woods with "key holes through them." "While at the same time," continued the officer, "I and so was General Gary satisfied these same men had robbed them."

We were now again under our old commander, Lieutenant General Longstreet. He had recently returned to the army, convalescent from his severe wound at the Wilderness, and was placed in command of the north side. Scarcely had he assumed command, and prior to our arrival, before he was attacked by General Butler, with twenty thousand men. He defeated him, sustaining little loss, with Fields' and Hokes' Divisions, and Gary's Cavalry. Butler lost between one thousand two hundred and one thousand five hundred men. The year was slowly drawing to a close, with little perceptible advantage to the South. It is true that Grant, the idol and ideal of the North, had thrown his legions against the veterans of Lee with a recklessness never before experienced, and with a loss almost irreparable, still the prospects of the Confederacy were anything but encouraging. Yet the childlike faith and confidence of the Confederate privates in their cause and in their superiors, that disaster and defeat never troubled them nor caused them worry or uneasiness. General Hood had gone on his wild goose chase through Middle Tennessee, had met with defeat and ruin at Franklin and Nashville; Sherman was on his unresisted march through Georgia, laying waste fields, devastating homes with a vandalism unknown in civilized warfare, and was now nearing the sea; while the remnant of Hood's Army was seeking shelter and safety through the mountains of North Georgia. Still Lee, with his torn and tattered veterans, stood like a wall of granite before Richmond and Petersburg. What a halo of glory should surround the heads of all who constituted the Army of Lee or followed the fortunes of Longstreet, Hill, Ewell, and Early. At Chickamauga, Chattanooga, East Tennessee, Wilderness, or wherever the plumes of their chieftains waved or their swords flashed amid the din of battle, victory had ever perched upon their banners. It was only when away from the inspiration and prestige of Longstreet did the troops of Kershaw fail or falter, and only then to follow in the wake of others who had yielded.

Owing to the casualties in battle during the last few months and the disasters of the two Valley campaigns, many changes in the personnel of the companies and regiments necessarily took place, once we got fairly settled in camp.

Brigadier General Kershaw had been made Major General in place of General McLaws soon after the battle of the Wilderness. His Aid-de-Camp, Lieutenant Doby, having been killed on that day, I.M. Davis, Adjutant of the Fifteenth, was placed upon the personnel staff of the Major General.

Colonel John D. Kennedy, of the Second, having recovered from the wounds received on the 6th of May, was promoted in place of General Connor to the position of Brigadier General.

The Colonel and Lieutenant Colonel of the Twentieth both being captured on the 19th of October, Lieutenant Colonel F.S. Lewie, of the Fifteenth, was assigned temporarily to the command of the Twentieth. Captain G. Leaphart, senior Captain, was afterwards promoted to Major, and commanded the "Twentieth Army Corps" until the close of the war.

Lieutenant Colonel Stackhouse was made Colonel of the Eighth after the death of Henagan, and either Captain McLucas or Captain T.F. Malloy was promoted to Major (I am not positive on this point). Captain Rogers was also one of the senior Captains, and I think he, too, acted for a part of the time as one of the field officers.

The Third Battalion was commanded by one of the Captains for the remainder of the war, Colonel Rice and Major Miller both being permanently disabled for field service, but still retained their rank and office.

There being no Colonel or Lieutenant Colonel of the Seventh, and Major Goggans having resigned soon after the Wilderness battle, Captain Thomas Huggins was raised to the rank of Colonel. I do not remember whether any other field officers of this regiment were ever appointed, but I think not. Lieutenant John R. Carwile, who had been acting Adjutant of the Seventh for a long time, was now assigned to duty on the brigade staff.

Captain William Wallace was promoted to Colonel of the Second, with Captain T.D. Graham and B F. Clyburn, Lieutenant Colonel and Major respectively.

Colonel Rutherford, of the Third, having been killed on the 13th of October, and Lieutenant Colonel Maffett, captured a short while before, Captain R.P. Todd was made Major, then raised to the rank of Lieutenant Colonel, and Captain J.K.G. Nance, Major.

Many new Captains and Lieutenants were made, to fill the vacancies occasioned by the above changes and deaths in battle, but I have not the space to mention them.

Our last Brigadier General, J.D. Kennedy, was a very good officer, however, his kindness of heart, his sympathetic nature, his indulgent disposition caused him to be rather lax in discipline. There was quite a contrast in the rigidity of General Connor's discipline and the good, easy "go as you please" of General Kennedy. But the latter had the entire confidence of the troops, and was dearly loved by both officers and men. He was quite sociable, courteous, and kind to all. The men had been in service so long, understood their duties so well, that it was not considered a necessity to have a martinet for a commander. General Kennedy's greatest claim to distinction was his good looks. He certainly was one of the finest looking officers in the army. I fear little contradiction when I say General Kennedy and Major W.D. Peck, of the Quartermaster Department, were two of the finest looking men that South Carolina gave to the war. I give a short sketch of General Kennedy.

General John D. Kennedy

General John D. Kennedy was born in Camden, South Carolina, January 5th, 1840, the son of Anthony M. and Sarah Doby Kennedy. His mother was the grand-daughter of Abraham Belton, a pioneer settler of Camden and a patriot soldier in the Revolution. His father was born in Scotland, having emigrated to the United States about the year 1830, at which time he settled in Kershaw County, S.C., where he married. (He has been engaged in planting and merchandising for many years. Two sons and two daughters were the issue of this marriage.) General Kennedy obtained his early scholastic training in the Camden schools, and in 1855, at the age of fifteen, entered the South Carolina College at Columbia. He entered the law office of Major W.Z. Leitner soon after, and was admitted to practice in January, 1861, and in April of that year joined the Confederate Army as Captain of Company E, Second South Carolina Regiment, under the command of Colonel J.B. Kershaw. In 1862 he was made Colonel of the Second South Carolina Regiment, and in 1864 was promoted to the rank of Brigadier General, and held that position to the close of the war, having surrendered with General Johnston at Greensboro, North Carolina, in 1865. General Kennedy was six times wounded, and fifteen times was hit by spent balls. At the close of the war he resumed his practice of law at Camden, but abandoned it soon after and turned his attention to farming. In 1877 he once more returned to the bar, and has since been actively and prominently engaged in his practice. In 1876 he was a member of the State Democratic Executive Committee, and was its chairman in 1878. In December, 1865, he was elected to Congress, defeating Colonel C.W. Dudley, but did not take his seat, as he refused to take the ironclad oath. In 1878-9 he represented his county in the Legislature, and was Chairman of the Committee on Privileges and Elections. He was elected Lieutenant Governor of the State in 1880, and in 1882 was a prominent candidate for Governor, but Colonel Hugh Thompson received the nomination over General Bratton and himself. He was elected Grand Master of the Grand Lodge A.F.M. of South Carolina in 1881, and served two years. As a member of the National Democratic Convention in 1876, he cast his vote for Tilden and Hendricks, and in 1884 was Presidential Elector at large on the Democratic ticket. President Cleveland sent him as Consul General to Shanghai, China, in 1886. In 1890 he was Chairman of the State Advisory Committee, of the straightout Democratic party. In early life he was married to Miss Elizabeth Cunningham, who died in 1876. In 1882 Miss Harriet Boykin became his wife.

The above is taken from Cyclopaedia of Eminent and Representative Men of the Carolinas of the Nineteenth Century.

Notes on General Kennedy's life, furnished by one of his soldiers:

> He was born at Camden, S.C., January 5th, 1840. While in his 'teens he became a member of the Camden Light Infantry, of which J.B. Kershaw was Captain; elected First Lieutenant in 1860. Upon the secession of South Carolina, December 20th, 1860, Captain Kershaw was elected Colonel of the Second South Carolina Volunteers, and Lieutenant Kennedy was chosen Captain of the Camden Volunteers, a company composed of members of the Camden Light Infantry and those who united with them for service in the field. This company became Company E, Second South Carolina Volunteers, was ordered to Charleston April 8th, 1861, and witnessed from their position on Morris Island the siege of Fort Sumter, April 12th, 1861. The Second Regiment formed part of the First Brigade, commanded by General M.L. Bonham, of the Army of the Potomac, as the Confederate Army in Northern Virginia was then called. In the spring of 1862 the troops who had volunteered for twelve months reorganized for the war, the Second South Carolina Volunteers being, I believe, the first body of men in the army to do so. At reorganization Captain Kennedy was elected Colonel, in which capacity he served until 1864, when he was promoted to the command of the brigade, which he held until the close of the war. In 1862 the name of the army was changed to the Army of Northern Virginia, the Federals having called theirs the Army of the Potomac. The Second was engaged in every battle fought by the army in Virginia, from the first Manassas to Petersburg, except Second Manassas, and was also in battle of Chickamauga, battles around Knoxville, Averysboro, and Bentonville, and surrendered at Greensboro April 27th, 1865. General Kennedy was in every battle in which his command was engaged, and was wounded six times and struck fifteen times. He died in Camden, S.C., April 14th, 1896.

Colonel R. P. Todd

Colonel R.P. Todd was born in Laurens County, about the year 1838. Graduated at a literary college (I think the South Carolina), read law, and entered upon the practice of his profession a year or two before the beginning of hostilities. At the first call by the State for twelve months' volunteers, Colonel Todd enlisted in the "Laurens Briars," afterwards Company G, Third South Carolina Regiment, and was elected Captain. He took his company with him into the Confederate service, and at the reorganization in 1862, was again elected Captain. Was made Major in 1864 and Lieutenant Colonel in the early part of 1865. He was in most of the great battles in which the regiment was engaged, and was several times severely wounded. He surrendered at Greensboro, N.C.

After the war he again took up the practice of law and continued it until his death, which took place several years ago. He represented his county in the Senate of the State for one term.

Soon after the close of the war he married Miss Mary Farley, sister of General Hugh L. Farley, formerly Adjutant and Inspector General of South Carolina, and of Captain William Farley, one of the riders of General Stuart, and a famous character in John Estin Cook's historical romances.

Colonel Todd was a good officer, gallant soldier, and loyal and kind to his men. He was a man of brilliant attainments and one of the most gifted and fluent speakers in the brigade.

The writer regrets his inability to get a more enlarged sketch of this dashing officer, talented lawyer, and perfect gentleman.

Captain John K. Nance

Captain John K. Nance was one of the most jovial, fun-loving, light-hearted souls in the Third Regiment. He was all sunshine, and this genial, buoyant disposition seemed to be always caught up and reflected by all who came about him. He was truly a "lover of his fellow-men," and was never so happy as when surrounded by jolly companions and spirits like his own. He was a great lover of out-door sports, and no game or camp amusement was ever complete without this rollicksome, good-natured knight of the playground.

He was born in Laurens County, in 1839. Graduated from Due West College and soon afterwards joined the "Quitman Rifles," Company E, of the Third Regiment, then being organized by his kinsman, Colonel James D. Nance. He was first Orderly Sergeant of the company, but was soon elected Lieutenant. At the reorganization of his company, in 1862, he was elected First Lieutenant, and on

James D. Nance being made Colonel of the Third, he was promoted to Captain. Many times during the service he was called upon to command the regiment, and in the latter part of 1864 or the first of 1865 he was promoted to Major.

Captain John K. Nance was one of the best officers upon the drillground in the regiment, and had few equals as such in the brigade. He was a splendid disciplinarian and tactician, and could boast of one of the finest companies in the service. His company, as well as himself, was all that could be desired upon the battlefield.

In 1864 he married Miss Dolly, daughter of Dr. Thomas B. Rutherford, and sister of the lamented Colonel W.D. Rutherford. After the war he was engaged in planting in Newberry County. He was three times elected Auditor of the county. He was a leading spirit among the Democrats during the days of reconstruction, and lent all energies and talents to the great upheaval in politics in 1876 that brought about the overflow of the negro party and gave the government to the whites of the State. He died about 1884, leaving a widow and several children.

COLONEL WILLIAM WALLACE

Colonel William Wallace, of the Second South Carolina Regiment, was undoubtedly the Murat of the Old First Brigade. His soldierly qualities, his dashing courage, and the prestige that surrounds his name as a commander, especially upon the skirmish line, forcibly recalls that impetuous prince, the Roland of Napoleon's Army. Upon the battle line he was brave almost to rashness, and never seemed to be more in his element or at ease than amidst the booming cannon, the roar of musketry, or the whirl of combat. Colonel Wallace was a soldier born and a leader of men. He depended not so much upon tactics or discipline, but more upon the cool, stern courage that was in himself and his men.

His life as a soldier and civilian has been fortunate and brilliant, in which glory and promotion followed hand in hand. A comrade gives a few facts in his life.

Colonel William Wallace was born in Columbia, S.C., November 16th, 1824, and was graduated at the South Carolina College in 1844. He then studied law under Chancellor James J. Caldwell. Was admitted to the bar in 1846, and began the practice of law at Columbia, in which he continued, with the exception of his military service, giving attention also to his planting interests.

At the beginning of the Confederate War he held the rank of General in the State Militia. At the call for troops, ordered out the Twenty-third Regiment, State Troops, and was the first man of the Regiment to volunteer. He was elected Captain of the "Columbia Grays," afterwards Company C of the Second South Carolina Volunteer Infantry, Colonel Kershaw commanding. After the reduction of Fort Sumter, with his company and three others of the Second, he volunteered for service in Virginia, and about a month after their arrival in Virginia the regiment was filled up with South Carolinians. He was promoted to Major in 1863, to Lieutenant Colonel after the battle of the Wilderness, and to Colonel after the battle of Bentonville.

He had the honor of participating in the capture of Fort Sumter and the battles of Blackburn's Ford, First Manassas, Williamsburg, Savage Station, Malvern Hill, Sharpsburg, Fredericksburg, Chancellorsville, Gettysburg, Chattanooga, Knoxville, Wilderness, Spottsylvania Court House, Second Cold Harbor, the defense of Petersburg until the winter of 1864-1865, and the campaign in the Carolinas, including the battles of Averysboro and Bentonville.

During the desperate struggle at Second Cold Harbor, in June, 1864, with the Second Regiment alone, he recaptured our breastworks on Kershaw's right and Hoke's left, from which two of our brigades had been driven. The enemy driven out consisted of the Forty-eighth and One hundred and Twelfth New York, each numbering one thousand men, while the Second numbered only one hundred and twenty-six men all told. So rapid was the assault that the color bearer of the Forty-eighth New York, with his colors, was captured and sent to General Kershaw, who was at his proper position some distance in rear of his division.

During his service Colonel Wallace was twice wounded—in the foot, at Charlestown, W. Va., and in the arm, at Gettysburg. After the conclusion of hostilities he returned to his home and the care of his plantation. Previous to the war he had an honorable career in the Legislature, and immediately afterwards he was a member of the Convention of 1865 and of the Legislature next following, and was elected to the State Senate for four years, in 1881. From 1891 to 1894 he was engaged in the correction of the indexes of the records of the Secretary of State's office, and in 1894 was appointed postmaster of Columbia by President Cleveland.

By his marriage, in 1848, to Victoria C., daughter of Dr. John McLemore, of Florida, Colonel Wallace has five children living, Andrew, William, Bruce, Edward Barton, and Margaret. After the death of his first wife he married, in 1876, Mrs. Fannie C. Mobley, nee Means.

Captain John Hampden Brooks

John Hampden Brooks was Captain of Company G, Seventh South Carolina Regiment, from its entry into State service to the end of its twelve months' enlistment. At the reorganization of the regiment he declined re-election, and served for a short time as Aidde-Camp on General Kershaw's staff. At this time, upon recommendation of Generals Kershaw and Jos. E. Johnston, he raised another company of Partisan Rangers, and was independent for awhile. Upon invitation, he joined Nelson's Seventh South Carolina Battalion, Hagood's Brigade, and served with this command (save a brief interval) to the end of the war. He was in the first battle of Manassas and in Bentonville, the last great battle of the war. At Battery Wagner his company was on picket duty the night of the first assault, and it was by his order that the first gun was fired in that memorable siege, and one of his men was the first Confederate killed. At the battle of Drewry's Bluff, Va., Captain Brooks was three times wounded, and lost sixty-eight out of the seventy-five men carried into action, twenty-five being left dead upon the field. Upon recovery from his wounds he returned to his command, but was soon detached by request of General Beauregard and order of General Lee, to organize a foreign battalion from the Federal prisoners at Florence, S.C., with distinct promise of promotion. This battalion was organized and mustered into Confederate service at Summerville, S.C., as Brooks' Battalion, and in December, 1864, Captain Brooks took a part of the command to Savannah (then being invested by General Sherman) and they served a short time on the line of defense. In consequence of bad behavior and mutiny, however, they were soon returned to prison. Captain Brooks was now placed in command of all unattached troops in the city of Charleston, but he became tired of inactivity, at his own request was relieved, and upon invitation of his old company, ignoring his promotion, he returned to its command.

Captain Brooks was born at Edgefield Court House and was educated at Mt. Zion, Winnsboro, and the South Carolina College. His father, Colonel Whitfield Brooks, was an ardent nullifier, and named his son, John Hampden, in honor of that illustrious English patriot. That Captain Brooks should have displayed soldierly qualities was but natural, as these were his by inheritance. His grandfather, Colonel Z.S. Brooks, was a Lieutenant in the patriotic army of the Revolutionary War, and his grandmother a daughter of Captain Jas. Butler, killed in the "Cloud's Creek massacre." His brothers, Captain Preston S. and Whitfield B. Brooks, were members of the Palmetto Regiment in the Mexican War; the latter mortally wounded at Cherubusco and promoted to a Lieutenant in the Twelfth Regulars for gallantry in action.

Captain Brooks is the sole survivor of the first Captains of the Seventh Regiment, and resides at Roselands, the old family homestead, formerly in Edgefield, but now Greenwood County.

Captain Andrew Harllee

Captain Andrew Harllee, of Company I, Eighth South Carolina Regiment, when a boy went with a number of the best young men of the State to Kansas Territory, in 1856, and saw his first service with the Missourians in the border troubles in that Territory, and took part in several severe engagements at Lawrence, Topeka, and Ossawattonic Creek with the Abolition and Free State forces, under old John Brown and Colonel Jim Law; the Southern or pro-slavery forces being under General David R. Atchison and Colonels Stingfellow and Marshall. After remaining in Kansas a year, he returned to his home and commenced the study of law at Marion Court House, but after a short time was appointed to a position in the Interior Department at Washington by the Hon. Thos. A. Hendrix, under whom he served as a clerk in a land office while in Kansas. This position in the Interior Department he held at the time of the secession of the State, and was the recipient of the first dispatch in Washington announcing the withdrawal of South Carolina from the Union, which was sent him by his uncle, General W.W. Harllee, then Lieutenant Governor and a member of the Secession Convention. He at once began preparations for his departure from Washington for Charleston, but was notified from Charleston to remain until the Commissioners appointed by the Convention to proceed to Washington and endeavor to treat with the authorities should arrive, which he did, and was appointed their Secretary. The Commission consisted of Senator Robert W. Barnwell, General James H. Adams, and Honorable James L. Orr. After many fruitless efforts, they finally got an audience with President Buchanan, who refused to treat with them in any manner whatever, and Mr. Harllee was directed to proceed at once to Charleston, the bearer of dispatches from the Commissioners to the Convention still in session, and after delivering the same he reported to Governor Pickens for duty. The Governor appointed him Assistant Quartermaster, with the rank of Captain, and he discharged the duties of that office around Charleston until the fall of Fort Sumter.

Anxious for service at the front, he resigned from the Quartermaster Department and enlisted as a private in Company I, Eighth South Carolina Regiment, and fought through the battles of Bull Run and Manassas with a musket. General Bonham, in command of the brigade, detailed him for scouting duty in and near Alexandria and Washington, and he had many thrilling adventures and narrow escapes in the discharge of those duties. In October, 1861, Lieutenant R.H. Rogers, of his company, resigned, and Private Harllee was elected Second Lieutenant in his stead. At the reorganization of the regiment and companies, in April, 1862, he was elected Captain of his company, which he commanded to the surrender. He was several times severely wounded, and bears upon his person visible evidences of the battle-scarred veteran. He was regarded by all his comrades as a daring and intrepid officer.

He lives upon his plantation, near Little Rock, where he was born and reared, is a bachelor, a professional farmer, and one of the leading citizens of his section of the State.

Captain William D. Carmichael

Captain William D. Carmichael volunteered in 1861, and assisted in raising Company I, Eighth South Carolina Regiment, and was elected Second Lieutenant at reorganization. In April, 1862, he assisted Captain Stackhouse in raising Company L for the same regiment, and was elected First Lieutenant of that company, and upon the promotion of Captain Stackhouse to Major, he was promoted Captain of Company L and commanded it to the surrender.

He was three times wounded, twice severely, and was one of the most gallant and trusted officers of that gallant regiment. After the war he settled on his plantation, near Little Rock, married, and has lived there ever since, raising a large family of children, and is one of the most successful farmers of that progressive section. He is one of the foremost citizens of Marion County.

Captain Duncan McIntyre

Captain Duncan McIntyre, of Company H, Eighth South Carolina Regiment, Kershaw's Brigade, was born at Marion S.C., on August 30th, 1836. Was prepared for college at Mount Zion Institute, at Winnsboro, S.C. Entered Freshman Class of South Carolina College, December, 1853.

Married Julia R., daughter of General William Evans, December, 1858. Commenced life as a planter on the west side of Pee Dee River, in Marion County, January 1st, 1860.

On secession of the State, he volunteered for service in the Jeffries' Creek Company. Was elected First Lieutenant of the company, Captain R.G. Singletary having been elected as commander. On Governor Pickens' first call for troops the company offered its services and was assigned to the Eighth South Carolina Regiment, Colonel E.B.C. Cash commanding. The company was ordered to Charleston on fall of Fort Sumter, where it remained until the last of May, when it was ordered to Florence, S.C., where, about the 1st of June, it was mustered into Confederate service by General Geo. Evans, and immediately ordered to Virginia to form a part of Bonham's Brigade.

Captain McIntyre was with the regiment at the first battle of Manassas or Bull Run, and with the exception of two short leaves of absence from sickness and from wounds, was with the regiment in nearly all of its campaigns and important skirmishes and battles, Williamsburg, battles around Richmond, Va., Maryland Heights, Sharpsburg, Fredericksburg, Chancellorsville, Wilderness, Spottsylvania Court House, and all of the battles against Grant up to the investment of Petersburg, Va. He was with the regiment and Longstreet's Corps in the campaign in Tennessee.

In the Tennessee campaign he commanded the Eighth Regiment at the battle of Ream's Station, and when the Second, Eighth, and Third Battalion, under the command of the gallant Colonel Gaillard, of the Second, made a daring and successful attack (at night) on the picket line of the enemy, the Eighth was on the right and first to dislodge the enemy and occupy the pits.

Captain McIntyre was twice wounded—first, in the chest at the battle of Fredericksburg, Va., and second time, severely in the thigh at Deep Bottom, Va.

Colonel William Drayton Rutherford

When Colonel William Drayton Rutherford fell in battle at Strasburg, Virginia, on the 13th of October, 1864, he was but a little more than twenty-seven years of age, having been born in Newberry, S.C., on the 23rd day of September, 1837.

The life thus destroyed was brimful of hope, for he was gifted with a rare intelligence, and possessed of an affectionate nature, with a deep sympathy for his fellow men and a patriotism which could only terminate with his own life. His father, Dr. Thomas B. Rutherford, was a grandson of Colonel Robert Rutherford, of Revolutionary fame, and his mother, Mrs. Laura Adams Rutherford, was a direct descendant of the Adams family of patriots who fought for their country in the State of Massachusetts.

The boyhood of Colonel Rutherford was spent on the plantation of his father, in Newberry County. Here was laid the foundation of his splendid physical nature, and his mind as well. While not beyond the height of five feet and ten inches, and with not an ounce of spare flesh, physically he was all bone and muscle, and was the embodiment of manly beauty. His early training was secured in the Male Academies of Greenville and Newberry. At the age of sixteen years he entered the Citadel Academy in Charleston, S.C. It was at this school he first exhibited the remarkable power arising from his ability to concentrate every faculty of his mind to the accomplishment of a single purpose, for, by reason of his fondness for out door sports and reading, he had fallen in stand amongst the lowest members of a large class, but, conceiving that some persons thought he could do no better, by a determined effort to master all the branches of study in an incredible space of time he was placed among the first ten members of his class. Military discipline was too restrictive for him, hence he left the Citadel Academy and entered the Sophomore Class of the South Carolina College at Columbia, S.C. In a few months after entering this college he was advanced from the Sophomore Class to that of the Junior. However, he never took his degree, for owing to a so-called college rebellion, he left college. Afterwards he regretted his step. Not content with the advantages be had already enjoyed, he went to Germany to complete his education, but the war between the States caused him to return to America. He espoused with heart and soul the cause of his native State. Before going to Germany he had been admitted to the practice of the law. Chief Justice John Belton O'Neall expressed himself as delighted with young Rutherford's examination for the bar, and predicted for him a brilliant career as a lawyer.

He was made Adjutant of the Third South Carolina Regiment of Infantry, and so thoroughly did he perform his duties as a soldier, and so delighted were his comrades in arms with his courage and generous nature, that he was elected, without opposition, on 16th of May, 1862, Major of his regiment, and on the 29th of June, 1862, he became Lieutenant Colonel, and on the 6th of May, 1864, he was promoted to the Colonelcy of his regiment. General James Connor was so much delighted with him as an officer that he recommended him for promotion to Brigadier General. When this gallant officer fell in the front of his regiment, there was naught but sorrow for his untimely end.

In March, 1862, he married the beautiful and accomplished Miss Sallie Fair, only daughter of Colonel Simeon Fair, of Newberry. The only child of this union was Kate Stewart Rutherford, who was known as the "daughter of the regiment." Kate is now the wife of the Honorable George Johnstone.

CHAPTER 39
Peace Conference

The civilized world, especially the Monarchies of Europe, which at first viewed with satisfaction this eruption in the great Republic across the waters, now anxiously watched them in their mad fury, tearing to tatters the fabric of Democratic government. This government, since its withdrawal from the Old World influence, had grown great and strong, and was now a powerful nation—a standing menace to their interest and power. But they began to look with alarm on the spectacle of these two brothers—brothers in blood, in aims, ambition, and future expectations, only an imaginary line separating them—with glaring eyes, their hands at each others throat, neither willing to submit or yield as long as there was a vestige of vitality in either. Even the most considerate and thoughtful of the North began to contemplate the wreck and ruin of their common country, and stood aghast at the rivers of blood that had flown, the widows and orphans made, and the treasures expended. They now began to wish for a call to halt. This useless slaughter caused a shudder to run through every thinking man when he contemplated of the havoc yet to come. The two armies were getting nearer and nearer together, one adding strength as the other grew weaker—the South getting more desperate and more determined to sacrifice all, as they saw the ground slipping inch by inch beneath their feet; the North becoming more confident with each succeeding day. It began to look like a war of extermination of American manhood. The best and bravest of the North had fallen in the early years of the war, while the bulk of the army now was composed of the lowest type of foreigners, who had been tempted to our shores by the large bounties paid by the Union Government. Taking their cue from their native comrades in arms, they now tried to outdo them in vandalizing, having been taught that they were wreaking vengeance upon the aristocracy and ruining the slave-holders of the South. The flower of the South's chivalry had also fallen upon the field and in the trenches, and now youths and old men were taking the places of soldiers who had died in the "Bloody Angles" and the tangled Wilderness.

A talk of peace began once more, but the men of the South were determined to yield nothing as long as a rifle could be raised. Nothing but their unrestricted independence would satisfy them. The man who could call nothing his own but what was on his back was as much determined on his country's independence as those who were the possessors of broad acres and scores of negroes.

Congressman Boyce, of South Carolina, began to call for a peace conference in the Confederate Congress. Montgomery Blair, the father of General Frank P. Blair, then commanding a corps in Sherman's Army, begged the North to halt and listen to reason—to stop the fratricidal war. Generals, soldiers, statesmen, and civilians all felt that it had gone on long enough. Some held a faint hope that peace could be secured without further effusion of blood. A peace conference was called at Hampton Roads, near the mouth of the Potomac. President Lincoln and Secretary of State William H. Seward, on the part of the North, and Vice-President Stephens, Honorable R.T.M. Hunter, and Judge Campbell, on the part of the South, attended. Lincoln demanded an "unconditional surrender" of the army—emancipation of the slaves and a return to our former places in the Union. Mr. Stephens and his colleagues knew too well the sentiment of the Southern people to even discuss such a course. Not a soldier in ranks would have dared to return and face the women of the South with such a peace and on such terms as long as there was the shadow of an organized army in the field.

General Ord, of the Union Army, a humane and Christian gentleman, wrote and sought an interview with General Longstreet. He wished that General to use his influence with General Lee and the officers of the army to meet General Grant, and with their wives mingling with the wives of the respective Generals, talk over the matter in a friendly manner, and see if some plan could not be framed whereby peace could be secured honorable to all parties. All had had glory enough and blood sufficient had been shed to gratify the most savage and fanatical. These officers or the most of them had been old school-mates at West Point, had been brother officers in the old army, their wives had mingled in pleasant, social intercourse at the army posts, and they could aid as only women can aid, in a friendly way, to bring back an era of good feelings.

General Ord further intimated that President Lincoln would not turn a deaf ear to a reasonable proposition for compensation for the slaves. General Longstreet accepted the overtures with good grace, but with a dignity fitting his position. He could not, while in the field and in the face of the enemy, with his superior present, enter into negotiations for a surrender of his army, or to listen to terms of peace. He returned and counseled Lee. Urged him to meet Grant, and as commander-in-chief of all the armies in the South, that he had a wide latitude, that the people were looking to him to end the war, and would be satisfied with any concessions he would recommend. That the politicians had had their say, now let the soldiers terminate the strife which politicians had begun. That Napoleon while in Italy, against all precedent and without the knowledge of the civil department, had entered into negotiations with the enemy, made peace, and while distasteful to the authorities, they were too polite to refuse the terms. But General Lee was too much a soldier to consider any act outside of his special prerogatives. He, however, was pleased with the idea, and wrote General Grant, asking an interview looking towards negotiations of peace. But General Grant, from his high ideals of the duty and dignity of a soldier, refused, claiming that the prerogatives of peace or war were left with the civil, not the military arm of the service. So it all ended in smoke.

General Lee began making preparations to make still greater efforts and greater sacrifices. He had been hampered, as well as many others of our great commanders, by the quixotic and blundering interference of the authorities at Richmond, and had become accustomed to it. There can be no question at this late day that the end, as it did come, had long since dawned upon the great mind of Lee, and it must have been with bitterness that he was forced to sacrifice so many brave and patriotic men for a shadow, while the substance could never be reached. His only duty now was to prolong the struggle and sacrifice as few men as possible.

General Bragg, that star of ill omen to the Confederacy, was taken out of the War Department in Richmond and sent to Wilmington, N.C., and that brilliant, gallant Kentuckian, General John C. Breckenridge, was placed in his stead as Secretary of War. General Breckenridge had been the favorite of a great portion of the Southern people in their choice of Presidential candidates against Lincoln, and his place in the cabinet of Mr. Davis gave hope and confidence to the entire South.

General Lee, no doubt acting on his own good judgment, and to the greatest delight of the army, placed General Joseph E. Johnston at the head of the few scattered and disorganized bands that were following on the flanks of Sherman. Some few troops that could be spared from the trenches were to be sent to South Carolina to swell, as far as possible, the army to oppose Sherman.

Governor Brown had called out a great part of the Georgia State Troops, consisting of old men and boys, to the relief of General Hardee, who was moving in the front of Sherman, and a great many of this number crossed over with General Hardee to the eastern side of the Savannah, and remained faithful to the end. Governor McGrath, of South Carolina, too, had called out every man capable of bearing arms from fifteen to sixty, and placed them by regiments under Beauregard and Johnston. The forts along the coast in great numbers were abandoned, and the troops thus gathered together did excellent service. North Carolina brought forward her reserves as the enemy neared her border, all determined to unite in a mighty effort to drive back this ruthless invader.

In this imperfect history of the times of which I write, I cannot resist at this place to render a deserved tribute to the noble women of the South, more especially of South Carolina. It was with difficulty that the soldiers going to the army from their homes after the expiration of their furloughs, or going to their homes when wounded or sick, procured a night's lodging in Richmond, for it must be remembered that that city was already crowded with civilians, officers of the department, surgeons of the hospitals, and officials of every kind. The hotels and private residences were always full. Scarcely a private house of any pretentions whatever, that did not have some sick or wounded soldier partaking of the hospitalities of the citizens, who could better care for the patient than could be had in hospitals. Then, again, the entire army had to pass through the city either going to or from home, and the railroad facilities and the crowded conditions of both freight and passenger cars rendered it almost obligatory on the soldiers to remain in the city over night. And it must be remembered, too, that the homes of hundreds and thousands of soldiers from Tennessee, Maryland, Kentucky, Mississippi, and all from the Trans-Mississippi were in the hands of the enemy, and the soldiers were forbidden the pleasure of returning home, unless clandestinely. In that case they ran the risk of being shot by some bushwhacker or "stay outs," who avoided the conscript officer on one side and recruiting officer on the other. In these border States there was a perpetual feud between these bushwhackers and the soldiers. It was almost invariably the case that where these "lay outs" or "hide outs" congregated, they sympathized with the North, otherwise they would be in the ranks of the Confederacy. Then, again, Richmond had been changed in a day from the capital of a commonwealth to the capital of a nation. So it was always crowded and little or no accommodation for the private soldier, and even if he could get quarters at a hotel his depleted purse was in such condition that he could not afford the expense. Nor was he willing to give a month's wages for a night's lodging. A night's lodging cost five dollars for supper, five for breakfast, and five for a bed, and if the soldiers were any ways bibulously inclined and wished an "eye opener" in the morning or a "night cap" at supper time, that was five dollars additional for each drink. Under such circumstances the ladies of South Carolina, by private contributions alone, rented the old "Exchange Hotel" and furnished it from their own means or private resources. They kept also a store room where they kept socks for the soldiers, knit by the hands of the young ladies of the State; blankets, shirts, and under clothing, from the cloth spun, woven, and made up by the ladies at home and shipped to Richmond to Colonel McMaster and a staff of the purest and best women of the land. Only such work as washing and scrubbing was done by negro servants, all the other was done by the ladies themselves. Too much praise cannot be given to Colonel McMaster for his indefatigable exertions, his tireless rounds of duty, to make the soldiers comfortable. The ladies were never too tired, night nor day, to go to the aid of the hungry and broken down soldiers. Hundreds and thousands were fed and lodged without money and without price. Car loads of the little comforts and necessities of life were shared out to the passing soldiers whenever their wants required it. Never a day or night passed without soldiers being entertained or clothing distributed. One night only was as long as a soldier was allowed to enjoy their hospitality, unless in cases of emergency. The officers of the army, whenever able, were required to pay a nominal sum for lodging. Better beds and conveniences were furnished them, but if they were willing to take private's "fare," they paid private's "fee," which was gratuitous. As a general rule, however, the officers kept apart from the men, for the officer who pushed himself in the private's quarters was looked upon as penurious and mean. It was only in times of the greatest necessity that a Southern officer wished to appear thus. If the Southern soldier was poor, he was always proud. This hotel was called the "South Carolina Soldiers' Home," and most of the other States inside the lines had similar institutions. In every home throughout the whole South could be heard the old "hand spinning wheel" humming away until far in the night, as the dusky damsel danced backwards and forwards, keeping step to the music of her own voice and the hum of the wheel. The old women sat in the corners and carded away with the hand-card, making great heaps of rolls, to be laid carefully and evenly upon the floor or the wheel. Great chunks of pine, called "latewood," were regularly thrown into the great fire place until the whole scene was lit up as by an incandescent lamp. What happiness, what bliss, and how light the toil, when it was known that the goods woven were to warm and comfort young "massa" in the army. The ladies of the "big house" were not idle while these scenes of activity were going on at the "quarter." Broaches were reeled into "hanks" of "six cuts" each, to be "sized," "warped," and made ready for the loom. Then the little "treadle wheel" that turned with a pedal made baskets of spools for the "filling." By an ingenious method, known only to the regularly initiated Southern housewife, the thread was put upon the loom, and then the music of the weaver's beam went merrily along with its monotonous "bang," "bang," as yard after yard of beautiful jeans, linsey, or homespuns of every kind were turned out to clothe the soldier boys, whose government was without the means or opportunity to furnish them. Does it look possible at this late day that almost the entire Southern Army was clothed by cloth carded, spun, and woven by hand, and mostly by the white ladies of the South?

    Hats and caps were made at home from the colored jeans. Beautiful hats were made out of straw, and so adapt had the makers become in utilizing home commodities, that ladies' hats were made out of wheat, oat, and rice straw. Splendid and serviceable house shoes were made from the products of the loom, the cobbler only putting on the soles. Good, warm, and tidy gloves were knit for the soldier from their home-raised fleece and with a single bone from the turkey wing. While the soldiers may have, at times, suffered for shoes and provisions, still they were fairly well clothed by the industry and patriotism of the women, and for blankets, the finest of beds were stripped to be sent voluntarily to the camps and army. As for tents, we had no need to manufacture them, for they were invariably captured from the enemy. Think of going through an army of sixty or seventy thousand men, all comfortably housed, and all through capture upon the battlefield. As for cooking utensils, nothing more nor better were wanted by the soldiers than a tin cup and frying-pan.

Salt was an article of great scarcity in the South. Coming over from Liverpool in ante bellum times as ballast, made it so cheap that little attention was given to the salt industry, and most of our best salt mines were in the hands of the enemy. But the Southern people were equal to any emergency. Men were put along the sea coast and erected great vats into which was put the salt sea water, and by a system of evaporation nice, fine salt was made. Farmers, too, that had the old-time "smoke" or meat houses with dirt floors, dug up the earth in the house and filtered water through it, getting a dark, salty brine, which answered exceedingly well the purpose of curing their meats.

All taxes, as I said before, were paid in "kind," and the tenth of all the meat raised at home was sent to the army, and with the few cattle they could gather, was sufficient to feed the troops. There were no skulking spirits among the people. They gave as willingly and cheerfully now as they did at the opening of the war. The people were honest in their dealings with the government, and as cheerful in their gifts to the cause as the Israelites of old in their "free will offerings" to the Lord. There were no drones among them, no secretion or dishonest division. The widows, with houses filled with orphans, gave of their scanty crops and hard labor as freely as those who owned large plantations and scores of slaves. In fact, it was noticeable that the poorer class were more patriotic and more cheerful givers, if such could be possible, than the wealthy class.

Negroes were drafted to go upon the coast to work in salt mills or to work upon the fortifications. This duty they performed with remarkable willingness, until, perhaps, some Federal gunboat got their range and dropped a few shells among them. Then no persuasion nor threat could induce them to remain, and numbers of them would strike out for home and often get lost and wander for days, half starved, through the swamps of the lower country, being afraid to show themselves to the whites for fear of being "taken up" and sent back. Many were the adventures and hair-breath escapes these dusty fugitives had, and could tell them in wonderful yarns to the younger generation at home. It may be that the negro, under mental excitement, or stimulated with strong drink, could be induced to show remarkable traits of bravery, but to take him cool and away from any excitement, he is slow at exposing himself to bodily dangers, and will never make a soldier in the field.

CHAPTER 40

The Return Home

The opening of the year 1865 looked gloomy enough for the cause of the Confederacy. The hopes of foreign intervention had long since been looked upon as an ignis fatuus and a delusion, while our maritime power had been swept from the seas. All the ports, with the exception of Charleston, S.C., and Wilmington, N.C., were now in the hands of the Federals. Fort Fisher, the Gibraltar of the South, that guarded the inlet of Cape Fear River, was taken by land and naval forces, under General Terry and Admiral Porter. Forts Sumter and Moultrie, at the Charleston Harbor, continued to hold out for a while longer. The year before the "Alabama," an ironclad of the Confederates, was sunk off the coast of France. Then followed the "Albemarle" and the "Florida." The ram "Tennessee" had to strike her colors on the 5th of August, in Mobile Bay. Then all the forts that protected the bay were either blown up or evacuated, leaving the Entrance to Mobile Bay open to the fleet of the Federals.

Sherman was recuperating his army around Savannah, and was preparing a farther advance now northward after his successful march to the sea. At Savannah he was met by a formidable fleet of ironclads and men of war, which were to accompany him by sailing along the coast in every direction. These were to form a junction with another army at Newburn, N.C.

Another matter that caused the South to despond of any other solution of the war than the bloody end that soon followed, was the re-election of Abraham Lincoln as President of the United States. The South felt that as long as he was at the head of the nation nothing but an unconditional surrender of our armies and the emancipation of the slaves would suffice this great emancipator. To this the South could not nor would not accede as long as there were rifles in the field and men to wield them. A great problem now presented itself to the Confederate authorities for solution, but who could cut the

Gordion knot? The South had taken during the war two hundred and seventy thousand prisoners, as against two hundred and twenty-two thousand taken by the Federals, leaving in excess to the credit of the South near fifty thousand. For a time several feeble attempts had been made for an equitable exchange of prisoners, but this did not suit the policy of the North. Men at the North were no object, and to guard this great swarm of prisoners in the South it took an army out of the field, and the great number of Southern soldiers in Northern prisons took quite another army from the service. In addition to the difficulty of supplying our own army and people with the necessities of life, we were put to the strain of feeding one hundred thousand or more of Federal prisoners. Every inducement was offered the North to grant some cortel of exchange or some method agreed upon to alienate the sufferings of these unfortunates confined in the prison pens in the North and South. The North was offered the privilege of feeding and clothing their own prisoners, to furnish medical aid and assistance to their sick. But this was rejected in the face of the overwhelming sentiments of the fathers, mothers, sisters, and brothers of those who were suffering and dying like flies in the Southern pens. Thousands and thousands of petitions were circulated, with strings of signatures from all classes in the Union, urging Congress to come in some way to the relief of their people. But a deaf ear was turned to all entreaties, this being a war measure, and no suffering could be too great when the good of the service required it. Taking it from a military point of view, this was the better policy, shocking as it was to humanity.

At one time it was considered in the Confederate Congress the propriety of turning loose and sending home as early as practicable these thousands of prisoners, trusting alone to their honor the observance of the parole. It was thought by the majority that the indiscriminate mingling and mixing of these fanatical agitators with the peaceable slaves in the country might incite insurrection and a bloody social war break out should the prisoners be released at the prison pens. Under all the varying circumstances the South was still busily engaged in mobilizing these prisoners in certain quarters, to protect them as far as possible from liberation by raiding parties. At Andersonville, Ga., there were twenty-two thousand; at Florence, S.C., two thousand; Salisbury, N.C., ten thousand; several hundred in Columbia, and detached numbers scattered along at various points on the railroads, at such places where convenient quarters could be secured and properly guarded. Quite a large number were at Bell

Isle, on the James River, as well as at the Liby Prison, in Richmond. These prisoners were sometimes guarded by the State militia and disabled veterans. Those at Florence were guarded by boy companies, under command of Colonel Williams, the former commander of the Third South Carolina. The stockades, as the prison pens were called, consisted of tall pine trees set into the ground some six or eight feet, standing upright and adjoining. The space thus enclosed covered several acres or as much more as there were prisoners or troops to guard them. The stockade fence was about fifteen feet above the level of the ground, with a walk way three feet from the top, on which the guards watched. There was a "dead line" some fifteen or twenty paces from the inside of the wall, over which no prisoner was allowed to cross, on penalty of being shot. And to prevent any collusion between the prisoners and the guard, none were permitted to speak to the sentinels under any circumstances. To better carry out these orders, the soldier who detected a prisoner speaking to a guard and shot him, a thirty days' furlough was given as an acknowledgment of his faithful observance of orders. On more occasions than one the prisoners in their attempt to draw inexperienced guards into a conversation, and perhaps offer a bribe, met their death instantly. Inside the enclosure some of the prisoners huddled under little tents or blankets, but the greater number burrowed under the ground like moles or prairie dogs. Numbers made their escape by tunnelling under the wall.

When Sherman began his march through Georgia, the major portion at Andersonville were removed to Salisbury, N.C., where a great national cemetery was set apart after the war, and kept under the authority of the war department, containing thousands of graves—monuments to the sufferings and death of these unfortunate people—a sacrifice to what their government called a "military necessity." Our prisoners were scattered in like manner at Camp Chase, in Ohio; Fort Johnston, in Lake Michigan; Fort Delaware, in the Delaware River; and many other places, subject to greater sufferings and hardships than the Federal prisoners in our hands.

The Government of the South had nothing to do but accept the conditions imposed upon the sufferers by the authorities in Washington.

In January, 1865, rumors were rife in camp of the transfer of some of the South Carolina troops to their own State to help swell the little band that was at that time fighting on the flanks and front of Sherman. Of course it was not possible that all could be spared from

Lee, but it had become a certain fact, if judged from the rumors in camp, that some at least were to be transferred. So when orders came for Kershaw's Brigade to break camp and march to Richmond, all were overjoyed. Outside of the fact that we were to be again on our "native heath" and fight the invader on our own soil, the soldiers of Kershaw's Brigade felt not a little complimented at being selected as the brigade to be placed at such a post of honor. It is a settled feeling among all troops and a pardonable pride, too, that their organization, let it be company, regiment, brigade, or even division or corps, is superior to any other like organization in bravery, discipline, or any soldierly attainments. Troops of different States claim superiority over those of their sister States, while the same rivalry exists between organizations of the same State. So when it was learned for a certainty that the old First Brigade was to be transferred to South Carolina, all felt a keen pride in being thus selected, and now stamped it as a settled fact, that which they had always claimed, "the best troops from the State." The State furnished the best to the Confederacy, and a logical conclusion would be "Kershaw's Brigade was the best of the service." Thus our troops prided themselves. Under such feelings and enthusiasm, it is little wonder that they were anxious to meet Sherman, and had circumstances permitted and a battle fought in South Carolina, these troops would have come up to the expectations of their countrymen.

But here I will state a fact that all who read history of this war will be compelled to admit, and that is, the department at Richmond had no settled or determined policy in regard to the actions of the army at the South. It would appear from reading contemporary history that Mr. Davis and his cabinet acted like Micawber, and "waited for something to turn up." His continual intermeddling with the plans of the Generals in the field, the dogged tenacity with which he held to his policies, his refusals to allow commanders to formulate their own plans of campaigns, forced upon Congress the necessity of putting one at the head of all the armies whom the Generals, soldiers, as well as the country at large, had entire confidence. General Lee filled this position to the perfect satisfaction of all, still his modesty or a morbid dislike to appear dictatorial, his timidity in the presence of his superiors, often permitted matters to go counter to his own views. It appears, too, that when General Sherman allowed Hood to pass unmolested to his right, and he began tearing up the railroads in his rear, it was a move so different to all rules of war, that it took the authorities with surprise. Then when he began his memorable march through the very heart of Georgia—Hood with a great army in his rear, in his front the sea—the South stood stupified and bewildered at this stupendous undertaking. It was thought by the army and the people that some direful blow would be struck Sherman when he was well under way in Georgia, and when too far from his base in the rear, and not far enough advanced to reach the fleet that was to meet him in his front.

How, when, or by whom this blow was to be struck, none even ventured an opinion, but that the authorities had Sherman's overthrow in view, all felt satisfied and convinced. But as events have shown since, it seems that our authorities in Richmond and the commanders in the field were as much at sea as the soldiers and people themselves. It was the purpose of General Beauregard to collect out all the militia of Governor Clark of Mississippi, of Governor Watts of Alabama, Governor Brown of Georgia, and of Governor Bonham of South Carolina to the southern part of Georgia, there, as Sherman approached, to reinforce General Hardee with all these State troops and reserves, under General Cobb, which numbered in all about eight thousand, and hold him in check until Hood came upon Sherman's rear, or forced him to retire. Of course it was expected, as a matter of fact, that Hood would be successful against the hastily concentrated army of Thomas, and Sherman would be forced to return for the protection of Kentucky and Ohio. But in military matters, as in others, too much must not be taken for granted, and where great events hinge on so many minor details, it is not surprising that there should be miscarriages. Hood was totally defeated and routed in Tennessee. The Governors of the sister States, on false principles of safety and obsolete statutes, refused to permit the State troops to leave the borders of their respective States, leaving nothing before Sherman but the handful of wornout veterans of Hardee and the few State troops of Georgia, to be beaten in detail as Sherman passed through the State. The women and children of our State were in the same frenzied condition at this time as those of Georgia had been when the Federals commenced their march from Atlanta. In fact, more so, for they had watched with bated breath the march of the vandals across the Savannah—the smoke of the burning homesteads, the wreck and ruin of their sister State—left little hope of leniency or mercy at the hands of the enemy, while all their strength and dependence in the way of manhood were either in the trenches with Lee or with the reserves along the borders of the State. Companies were formed everywhere of boys and old men to help beat back the mighty annaconda that was now menacing with its coils our common country. These were quite unique organizations, the State troops of the South. The grandfathers and grandsons stood side by side in the ranks; the fathers and sons had either fallen at the front or far away in a distant State, fighting for the Southland.

The people of this day and generation and those who are to come afterwards, will never understand how was it possible for the women of the South to remain at their homes all alone, with the helpless little children clustering around their knees, while all that had the semblance of manhood had gone to the front. Yet with all this, a merciless, heartless, and vengeful foe stood at their threshold, with the sword in one hand and the torch in the other. Not only thus confronted, they were at the mercy of four or five millions of negro slaves, waiting for freedom, as only a people could after two centuries of slavery. The enemy was ready and willing to excite these otherwise harmless, peaceful, and contented negroes to insurrection and wholesale butchery. But be it said to the everlasting credit and honor of the brave women of the South, that they never uttered a reproach, a murmur, or a regret at the conditions in which circumstances had placed them. But the negro, faithful to his instincts, remained true, and outside of an occasional outburst of enthusiasm at their newly found freedom, continued loyal to the end to these old masters, and looked with as much sorrow and abhorence upon this wanton destruction of the old homestead, around which clustered so many bright and happy memories, as if they had been of the same bone and the same flesh of their masters. Notwithstanding the numberless attempts by Federal soldiers now spread over an area of fifty miles to excite the negro to such frenzy that they might insult and outrage the delicate sensibilities of the women of the South, still not a single instance of such acts has been recorded.

Such were the feelings and condition of the country when Kershaw's Brigade, now under General Kennedy, boarded the train in Richmond, in January, 1865. We came by way of Charlotte and landed in Columbia about nightfall. The strictest orders were given not to allow any of the troops to leave or stop over, however near their homes they passed, or how long they had been absent. In fact, most of the younger men did not relish the idea of being seen by our lovely women just at that time, for our disastrous valley campaign and the close investiture of Richmond by Grant—the still closer blockade of our ports—left them almost destitute in the way of shoes and clothing. The single railroad leading from our State to the capital had about all it could do to haul provisions and forage for the army, so it was difficult to get clothing from home. We were a rather ragged lot, while the uniforms of the officers looked shabby from the dust and mud of the valley and the trenches around Richmond. Our few brief months in winter quarters had not added much, if any, to our appearance. By some "underground" road, Captain Jno. K. Nance, of the Third, had procured a spick and span new uniform, and when this dashing young officer was clad in his Confederate gray, he stood second to none in the army in the way of "fine looking." New officers did not always "throw off the old and on with the new" as soon as a new uniform was bought, but kept the new one, for a while at least, for "State occasions." These "occasions" consisted in visiting the towns and cities near camp or in transit from one army to another. An officer clad in a new uniform on ordinary occasions, when other soldiers were only in their "fighting garments," looked as much out of place as the stranger did at the wedding feast "without the wedding garments." But the day of our departure from Richmond Captain Nance rigged himself out in the pomp and regulations of war, his bright new buttons flashing in the sunlight, his crimson sash tied naughtily around his waist, his sword dangling at his side, he looked the "beheld of all beholders" as the troops marched with a light and steady step along the stone-paved streets of Richmond. He had married a year or so before the beautiful and accomplished sister of our lamented Colonel, and had telegraphed her to meet him at Columbia on our arrival. He dared not trust these innoculate garments to the dirty and besmeared walls of a box car so he discarded the new on our entrance to the train and dressed in his old as a traveling suit. All the way during our trip he teased his brother officers and twitted them with being so "shabbily dressed," while he would be such a *beau idea*" in his new uniform when he met his wife. He had never met his wife since his honeymoon a year before, and then only with a twenty-one days' furlough, so it can be well imagined with what anticipations he looked forward to the meeting of his wife. He was so happy in his expectations that all seemed to take on some of his pleasant surroundings, and shared with him his delight in the expected meeting of his young wife. He would look out of the car door and hail a comrade in the next car with, "Watch me when we reach Columbia, will you," while the comrade would send back a lot of good-natured railery. It was an undisputed fact, that Captain Nance was a great favorite among officers and men, and while all were giving him a friendly badgering, everyone was glad to see him in such a happy mood. He had given his new suit in charge of his body servant, Jess, with special injunction to guard it with his life. Now Jess was devoted to his master, and was as proud of him as the "squires" of old were of the knights. Jess, to doubly secure this "cloth of gold" so dear to the heart of his master, folded the suit nicely and put it in his knapsack and the knapsack under his head, while he slept the sleep of the just in the far corner of the box car. When we reached Charlotte Captain Nance concluded to rig himself out, as this was to be our last place of stoppage until Columbia was reached, and should his wife meet him there, then he would be ready. So he orders water and towel, and behind the car he began preparations for dressing, all the while bantering the boys about his suit.

At last he was ready to receive the treasured gray. He called out to his man Jess, "Bring out the uniform."

Jess goes into the car. He fumbles, he hunts—knapsacks thrown aside, guns and accoutrements dashed in every direction—the knapsack is found, hastily opened, and searched, but no uniform! The more impatient and more determined to find the missing clothes, the idea began more forcibly to impress Jess that he might have slept on the way. So engrossed was he in the search for the missing suit, that he failed to hear the orders from his master to—

"Hurry up! If you don't soon bring on that coat I'll frail you out. You think I can wait out here naked and freeze?"

But still the hunt goes on, haversacks once again thrown aside, knapsacks overhauled for the third time, while beads of perspiration begin to drop from the brow of Jess. The real facts began to dawn more surely upon him. Then Jess spoke, or I might say gave a wail—

"Marse John, 'fore God in heaven, if some grand rascal ain't done stole your clothes." His great white eyes shone out from the dark recesses of the car like moons in a bright sky.

Nance was speechless. Raising himself in a more erect position, he only managed to say: "Jess, don't tell me that uniform is gone. Don't! Go dig your grave, nigger, for if you black imp of Satan has gone to sleep and let some scoundrel steal my clothes, then you die."

Such a laugh, such a shout as was set up from one end of the train to the other was never heard before or since of the "Lone Pine

Tree State." All of us thought at first, and very naturally, too, that it was only a practical joke being played upon the Captain, and that all would be right in the end. But not so. What became of that uniform forever remained a mystery. If the party who committed the theft had seen or knew the anguish of the victim for one-half hour, his conscience would have smote him to his grave.

But all is well that ends well. His wife failed to reach him in time, so he wore the faded and tattered garments, as momentous of the Valley, through all the tangled swamps and morasses of the Saltkahatchie, the Edisto, and the Santee with as much pride as if clothed in the finest robes of a king.

We remained at Branchville for several days, and from thence we were transported by rail to Charleston and took up quarters on the "Mall." The citizens hailed us with delight and treated us with the greatest hospitality. The greater number of the best-to-do citizens had left the city, and all that lived on the bay and in reach of the enemies guns had moved to safer quarters in the city or refugeed in the up country. But every house stood open to us. Flags and handkerchiefs waved from the windows and housetops, and all was bustle and commotion, notwithstanding the continual booming of cannon at Sumter and on Sullivan's Island. Every minute or two a shell would go whizzing overhead or crashing through the brick walls of the buildings. Soldiers were parading the streets, citizens going about their business, while all the little stores and shops were in full blast, the same as if the "Swamp Angel" was not sending continually shells into the city. The people had become accustomed to it and paid little attention to the flying shells.

On one occasion, while a bridal ceremony was being performed in one of the palatial residences in the city, the room filled with happy guests, a shell came crashing into the apartment, bursting among the happy bridal party, killing one of the principals and wounding several of the guests.

While I and several other officers were eating breakfast at one of the hotels, a great noise was heard in the upper portion of the building, giving quite a shock to all. Someone asked the colored waiter, "What was that noise?" "Only a shell bursting in one of the upper rooms," was the reply.

Women and children walked leisurely to market or about their daily vocations, the shells roaring overhead, with no more excitement or concern than had it only been a fourth of July celebration.

Even the negroes, usually so timid and excitable, paid but momentary attention to the dangers.

The Confederates had abandoned the greater part of Morris' Island, and great batteries had been erected on it by General Gillmore, with the avowed purpose of burning the city. Some weeks before this he had erected a battery in the marshes of the island and a special gun cast that could throw shells five miles, the greatest range of a cannon in that day. The gun was named the "Swamp Angel" and much was expected of it, but it did no other execution than the killing of a few civilians and destroying a few dwellings. The citizens were too brave and patriotic to desert their homes as long as a soldier remained on the islands or in the forts. The gallant defenders of Sumter, after a month of the most terrific connonading the world had ever seen, were still at their guns, while the fort itself was one mass of ruins, the whole now being a huge pile of stone, brick, and masonry. Fort Moultrie, made famous by its heroic defense of Charleston in the days of the Revolution, and by Jasper leaping the sides of the fort and replacing the flag over its ramparts, still floated the stars and bars from its battlements. All around the water front of Charleston bristled great guns, with ready and willing hands to man them. These "worthy sons of noble sires," who had, by their unflinching courage, sent back the British fleet, sinking and colors lowered, were now ready to emulate their daring example—either to send the fleet of Gillmore to the bottom, or die at their post. No wonder the people of South Carolina felt so secure and determined when such soldiers defended her borders.

The city guards patrolled the streets of Charleston to prevent the soldiers from leaving their camps without permits, and between these two branches of the service a bitter feud always existed. The first night we were in the city some of the soldiers, on the Verbal permission of their Captains, were taking in the city. Leaving their arms at camp, they were caught "hors de combat," as it were, and locked up in the city guardhouse over night. The next morning I went to look for my absentees, and away up in the top story of the lower station house I saw them, their heads reaching out of the "ten of diamonds" and begging to be released. After much red tape, I had them turned out, and this incident only added to the ill will of the two parties. After the soldiers began to congregate and recount their grievances as they thought, they used the city guards pretty roughly the remainder of our stay. But the most of all these differences were in the nature of "fun," as the soldiers termed it, and only to give spice to the soldier's life.

There were two young Captains in the Third, who, both together, would only make one good man, physically. So small in stature were they that on some previous occasion they had agreed to "whip the first man they ever met that they thought small enough to tackle." This personage they had never as yet met, but walking down King street they entered a little saloon kept by a Jew. The Jew could scarcely see over the counter, so low was he, but otherwise well developed. On seeing the little Jew, the two young officers eyed each other and said one gleefully:

"John, here's our man."

"Yes, yes," said D, "You tackle him in front and I'll leg him in rear. By all that's sacred, we can say we whipped one man, at least."

So telling the little Jew of their agreement, and that they thought he was the man they were looking for, ordered him out to take his medicine like a little man. The Jew took it good humoredly and told the officers he was their friend and did not care to fight them, etc. But the officers persisted so, to "humor them and to show friendship for the young men," said he would "accommodate them." At that the Jew struck out with his right on John's jaw, hitting the ceiling with the little officer. Then with his left he put one in the pit of D.'s stomach, lifting him clear of the floor and dropping him across a lot of barrels. Then John was ready by this time to receive a "header" under the chin, piling him on top of D. The boys crawled out as he was preparing to finish up the two in fine style, but—

"Hold on! hold on! young man," cried both in a breath, "we are not mad; we are only in fun; don't strike any more."

"All right," said the Jew, "if you are satisfied I am. Come let's have a drink."

So all three took a friendly sip, and as the two wiser, if not stronger, young men left the shop, one said to the other:

"We'll have to get a smaller man yet before we can say we whipped anybody."

"You are right," said the other; "I was never worse mistaken in all my life in the size of the man, or he grew faster after he began to fight than anything I ever saw. He stretched out all over, like a bladder being blown up."

They found out afterwards that the Jew was a professional boxer, and was giving lessons to the young men of the city.

The soldiers seemed to be getting rather demoralized by the influences of the city, and were moved over the Ashley River and encamped about four miles of the city, in a great pine forest, near the sea. This was a great sight for many, for as much travelling as the troops had done during the last four years, this was their first close quarters to the ocean, and many had never before witnessed the great rolling waters of the sea. Oysters were plentiful, and negroes on the plantation brought out boat loads for the soldiers, and gave them out for a little tobacco or a small amount of Confederate "shin-plasters." These were about the only articles they had seen in a long time that they could buy with a "shin-plaster" (fractional currency), as almost every other commodity was worth from one dollar up. Great fires were built at night, and eight or ten bushels of the sweet, juicy bi-valves were poured over the heap, to be eaten as the shells would pop by the heat.

From this place, after a week's sojourn, we were carried by rail to the Saltkahatchie River, at the crossing of the Charleston and Savannah Railroad.

CHAPTER 41

On the Saltkahatchie

When we reached our destination on the Saltkahatchie, we were met by our old commander of Virginia and Tennessee, Major General McLaws, from whom we had been separated for more than a year. The soldiers were glad to see him, and met him with a rousing cheer, while the old veteran was equally delighted to see us. It was like the meeting of father and absent children, for General McLaws was kind and indulgent to his men, even if not a very successful General. After being relieved of his command in East Tennessee and succeeded by General Kershaw, he had commanded the post at Augusta, Ga., to which place he returned after the close of hostilities and remained until his death. He was the greater part of the time postmaster of the city of Augusta. There being few occupations that the old West Pointers of the South could fill, they generally accepted any office in the gift of the government that would insure them an honest livelihood.

General McLaws was facing two corps of Sherman's Army at this place with some few veterans, State troops, and reserves. Sherman had been quiet for some time, recruiting his army with negroes from the great plantations along the coast, and resting up his army for his march through the State. Negroes flocked to his army by the thousands, and were formed into regiments and brigades, officered by white men. Even our own Generals and some of our statesmen at this time and before were urging Congress to enlist the negroes, but the majority were opposed to the movement. To show how confident were our leaders even at this late day of the Confederacy, I will quote from Wm. Porcher Miles, then in the Confederate Congress, in reply to General Beauregard urging the enlistment of the slaves. It must be understood that at this time Lee had all he could do to hold his own against Grant, growing weaker and weaker as the days rolled by, while Grant was being reinforced from all over the United States. Lee had the solitary railroad by which to subsist his army. Sherman had laid waste Georgia and was now on the eve of marching; through South Carolina. The Army of the Trans-Mississippi was hopelessly cut off from the rest of the Confederacy. The Mississippi River was impassable, to say nothing of the Federal pickets that lined its banks and the gunboats that patrolled its waters, so much so that one of our Generals is said to have made the report "that if a bird was dressed up in Confederate gray, it could not cross the Mississippi." Hood's Army was a mere skeleton of its former self—his men, some furloughed, others returned to their home without leave, so disheartened were they after the disastrous defeat in Tennessee. Still all these conditions being known and understood by the authorities, they were yet hopeful. Says Mr. Miles in Congress:

"I cannot bring my mind to the conviction that arming our slaves will add to our military strength, while the prospective and inevitable evils resulting from such measures make me shrink back from such a step. This can be when only on the very brink of the brink of the precipice of ruin."

From such language from a Confederate Congressman, dark as the day looked on February 4th, 1865, the date of the letter, the people did not seem to feel that they were on the "brink of the precipice." Continuing, Mr. Miles goes on in a hopeful strain:

"But I do not estimate him [speaking of Grant] as a soldier likely to decide the fate of battle. We have on our rolls this side of the Mississippi four hundred and one thousand men, one hundred and seventy-five thousand effective and present. We can easily keep in the field an effective force of two hundred thousand. These are as many as we can well feed and clothe, and these are sufficient to prevent subjugation or the overrunning of our territory."

How a man so well informed and familiar with the foregoing facts could hope for ultimate results, is hard to comprehend by people of this day and generation. It was the plan of General Beauregard to concentrate all the available troops in North and South Carolina on the Saltkahatchie, to keep Sherman at bay until Dick Taylor, with the remnant of Hood's Army, could come up, then fall back to the Edisto, where swamps are wide and difficult of passage, allow Sherman to cross over two of his corps, fall upon them with all the force possible, destroy or beat them back upon the center, then assail his flanks, and so double him up as to make extrication next to impossible. But in case of failure here, to retire upon Branchville or Columbia, put up the strongest fortifications possible, withdraw all the troops from Charleston, Wilmington, and in the other cities, put in all the State troops that were available from the three States, push forward as many veterans as Lee could temporarily spare from the trenches, barely leaving a skirmish line behind the works around Richmond and Petersburg, then as Sherman approached, fall upon him with all the concentrated force and crush him in the very heart of the State, or to so cripple him as to make a forward movement for a length of time impossible; while the railroads in his rear being all destroyed, his means of supplies would be cut off, and nothing left but retreat. Then, in that event, the whole of Beauregard's troops to be rushed on to Lee, and with the combined army assault, the left flank of Grant and drive him back on the James. That the soldiers in the ranks and the subaltern officers felt that some kind of movement like this was contemplated, there can be no doubt. It was this feeling that gave them the confidence in the face of overwhelming numbers, and nerved them to greater efforts in time of battle. It was this sense of confidence the soldiers had in the heads of departments and in the commanding Generals that gave the inspiration to the beaten army of Hood that induced these barefoot men to march half way across the continent to place themselves in battle lines across the pathway of Sherman. It was this confidence in the wisdom of our rulers, the genius of the commanders, the stoicism of the soldiers, and above all, the justness of our cause and the helping hand of the Omnipotent, that influenced the women of the South to bear and endure the insults of the Federal soldiers, and view with unconcern the ruin of their homes and the desecration of their country. From the standpoint of the present, this would have been the only possible plan whereby any hopes of ultimate success were possible. But to the people of this day and time, the accomplishment of such an undertaking with the forces and obstacles to be overcome looks rather far-fetched, especially when we reflect that Johnston, with fifty or sixty thousand of the best troops in the service, had failed to check Sherman among the mountain passes of North Georgia, or even to prevent his successful advance to the very walls of Atlanta. That General Beauregard, with his handful of regular troops and a contingent of boys and old men, could accomplish what General Johnston, with a well equipped army of veterans, failed in, was simply a blind faith in the occult influence of Providence.

But it seems as if the department at Richmond had lost its head, and had no settled policy. Telegrams were being continually sent to the Generals in the field to "Crush the enemy," "You must fight a great battle," "Either destroy him or so cripple his efforts to reach Grant, that reinforcements would be taken from Lee's front," "Why don't you fight?" etc. These were the encouraging messages Generals Beauregard and Hardee were receiving, but where were the troops to accomplish such work? Generals from every direction were calling for aid—to be reinforced, or that the enemy was making advances, without means to stop him. The answer to all these calls were the same, in substance at least, as that given by Napoleon to the request of Ney of Waterloo, when that marshal called upon the Emperor for reinforcements, "Where does he expect me to get them? Make them?" It seems that the people, with the exception of the privates in the field and the women and children at home, had become panic stricken.

On the 3rd of February General Sherman began crossing the Saltkahatchie at places between Broxton's and Rivers' Bridges (and above the latter), and was moving by easy stages in the direction of Branchville. It was not conclusively known whether Sherman, on reaching that place, would turn towards Augusta or in the direction of Charleston, or continue his march to Columbia. President Davis having declined the proposition of General Beauregard to evacuate all the cities on the coast and make a stand on the Edisto, declined also a like proposition to fight the great battle at either Branchville or Columbia, without offering any better policy himself. The only alternative the latter had was to keep out of Sherman's way as well as possible and to allow him to continue laying waste the entire center of the State. His only encouragements were dispatches from the President to "Turn and Crash Sherman," "Call on the Governors," "Bring out the militia," etc.

Sherman's columns of advance consisted of four great patrolled lines, with a corps on each. His extreme right was made up of the Seventeenth Corps, under General Frank P. Blair, the Fifteenth next, under General Jno. A. Logan, the two being the right wing of the army, commanded by General Howard. The left wing, under General Slocum, consisted of the Fourteenth Corps, on extreme left, General Jeff. C. Davis commanding; the next, the Twentieth, under General A.S. Williams, the whole numbering sixty thousand. The cavalry, numbering four thousand additional, was on either flank.

To meet this formidable array, Beauregard had under his immediate command Hardee, with thirteen thousand seven hundred (three thousand being State militia); around Augusta and on the march in Georgia and upper South Carolina was the remnant of Hood's Army—Steven D. Lee, with three thousand three hundred and fifty; Dick Cheatham, with two thousand five hundred.

Stewart's Corps was far back in Georgia, and too far away to give any hopes of meeting Beauregard in this State. It consisted of Loring's Division, one thousand eight hundred and eighty-seven; Wathals' Division, one thousand and thirty-six; French's Division, one thousand five hundred and nineteen.

It must not be forgotten that the number under Hardee included the troops in and around Charleston, and all the cities and towns in the State where soldiers were stationed.

General Wheeler, in command of several brigades of cavalry, now reduced to a mere skeleton organization, was hovering around the enemy's flanks and in front between Branchville and Augusta.

Just prior to the evacuation of Columbia, General Beauregard applied to the war department for the promotion of General Wade Hampton to Lieutenant General, to take precedence over Major General Wheeler, now in command of all the cavalry in this army. He further asked that he be assigned to the command of the cavalry of his department, all of which was granted. Generals Hampton and Butler were both at home at the time, the former on furlough, the latter recruiting and mounting his troops. These two Generals being natives of the State, and General Hampton so familiar with the topography of the country through which the army had to pass, General Beauregard thought him a desirable officer for the post. Furthermore, Wheeler's Cavalry had become thoroughly demoralized and undisciplined. From their long, continual retreats the cavalry had become to look upon "retreat" as the regular and national order. Acting on the principle that all which was left in their wake of private property would be appropriated by the enemy, they fell with ruthless hands upon whatsoever property their eyes took a fancy to, consoling themselves with the reasoning "that if we don't take it, the enemy will." So audacious had become the raids of Wheeler's command that citizens had little choice between the two evils, "Wheeler's Cavalry or the Federals." The name of "Wheeler's men" became a reproach and a by-word, and remains so to this day with the descendants of those who felt the scourge of these moving armies.

These are matters that are foreign to the subject or to the "History of Kershaw's Brigade," but as the greater part of the soldiers of South Carolina were away during the march through their State and ignorant of the movements of the armies, I write for their information, and the concluding part of this work will be rather a history of the whole army than of one brigade.

CHAPTER 42
March Through South Carolina

When Sherman put this mighty machine of war in motion, Kershaw's Brigade was hurried back to Charleston and up to George's Station, then to the bridge on the Edisto. Raiding parties were out in every direction, destroying bridges and railroads, and as the Southern Army had no pontoon corps nor any methods of crossing the deep, sluggish streams in their rear but by bridges, it can be seen that the cutting of one bridge alone might be fatal to the army. It was discovered early in the march that Sherman did not intend to turn to the right or the left, but continue on a direct line, with Columbia as the center of operations. We were removed from the Edisto back to Charleston, and up the Northeastern Railroad to St. Stephen's, on the Santee. It was feared a raiding party from Georgetown would come up the Santee and cut the bridge, thereby isolating the army Hardee had in Charleston and vicinity. Slowly Sherman "dragged his weary length along." On the 13th of February the corps of General Blair reached Kingsville and drove our pickets away from the bridge over the Congaree.

On the 15th of February the advance column of the Twentieth Corps came in sight of Columbia. All the bridges leading thereto were burned and the Southern troops withdrawn to the eastern side. Frank Blair's Corps left the road leading to Columbia at Hopkin's, and kept a direct line for Camden. Another corps, the Fifteenth, crossed the Broad at Columbia, while the Fourteenth and Twentieth were to cross at Freshley's and Alston. Orders had been given to evacuate Charleston, and all the troops under General McLaws, at Four Hole Swamp, and along the coast were to rendezvous at St. Stephen's, on the Santee, and either make a junction with the Western Army at Chester, S.C., or if not possible, to continue to Chesterfield or Cheraw. The plan of the campaign was now to concentrate all the forces of Hood's State Troops and Hardee's at some point in upper

South Carolina or in North Carolina, and make one more desperate stand, and by united action crash and overthrow Sherman's Army, thereby relieving Lee.

On the morning of the 16th of February the enemy, without any warning whatever, began shelling the city of Columbia, filled with women and children. Now it must be remembered that this was not for the purpose of crossing the river, for one of Sherman's corps had already crossed below the city and two others above. One shell passed through the hotel in which General Beauregard was at the time, others struck the State House, while many fell throughout the city. General Hampton withdrew his small force of cavalry early on the morning of the 17th, and the Mayor of the city met an officer of the Federal Army under a flag of truce and tendered him the surrender of the city, and claimed protection for its inhabitants. This was promised.

All during the day thousands of the enemy poured into the city, General Sherman entering about midday. Generals Davis' and Williams' Corps crossed the Saluda and continued up on the western bank of Broad River, one crossing ten, the other twenty-five miles above Columbia. The people of Columbia had hopes of a peaceful occupation of the city, but during the day and along towards nightfall, the threatening attitude of the soldiers, their ominous words, threats of vengeance, were too pretentious for the people to misunderstand or to expect mercy. These signs, threats, and mutterings were but the prelude to that which was to follow.

About 9 o'clock P.M. the alarm of fire was given and the dread sound of the fire bells, mingled with the hum and roar of ten thousand voices and the tread of as many troops hurrying to and fro on their cursed mission, could be heard by the now thoroughly frightened populace. The people, with blanched countenances, set features, looked in mute silence into the faces of each other. All knew and felt, but dared not even to themselves to whisper, the unmistakable truth. Now another alarm, another fire bell mingles its sound with the general chorus of discord, shouts of the soldiery, the frightened cries of the people—jells of the drunken troops all a scathing, maddening turbulance in the crowded streets. A lurid glare shoots up above the housetops, then the cracking and roaring of the dread elements told but too plainly that the beautiful city was soon to be wrapped in flames. The sack and pillage had begun!

Few men being in the city, the women, with rare heroism, sought to save some little necessities of life, only to see it struck to the floor or snatched from their hands and scattered in the streets. Here would be a lone woman hugging an infant to her breast, with a few strips of clothing hanging on her arms; helpless orphans lugging an old trunk or chest, now containing all they could call their own—these would be snatched away, broken open, contents rifled by the drunken soldiers, or if not valuable, trampled under foot.

Soldiers, with axes and hammers, rushed from house to house, breaking in doors, smashing trunks, boxes, bureaus, and robbing them of all that was valuable, then leaving the house in flames. Helpless women, screaming children, babes in the arms, invalids on beds, jolted and jostled against the surging mob—none to help, none to advise—these defenseless sufferers rushed aimlessly about, their sole purpose being to avoid the flames and seek a place of safety. The fires originated principally in the southern section of the city, and as the fire eat its way up, the howling throng followed, driving the innocent and helpless ahead.

As the night wore on, the drunken soldiers, first made intoxicated by the wine in private cellars or the liquors in the government buildings, now became beastly drunk in their glee at the sight of the destruction they had wrought. The women and children followed the dark back-ground of that part of the city not yet in flames. The Federal officers, instead of offering assistance or a helping hand to the ruined and distressed people, added insult to injury by joining in with the private soldiers in the plundering of the city, insulting the women and adding fuel to the flame.

All night long did the flames rage, leap, and lick the clouds as one block of buildings after another fell—food for the devouring elements. This drunken orgies was kept up until their craven hearts were fully satisfied. A few squares in the north-eastern part of the city were left, also several churches, and into these the women and children were huddled and packed, and had to remain for days and some for weeks, almost on the verge of starvation. The Federal commander, through the boundless dictates of his sympathetic heart, after destroying all that fire and rapine could reach, left the starving thousands a few rations each of the plunder he had robbed of the planters in the country.

No vehicles nor horses were left in the city's limits—the bridges burned that led across the river to the west. To the east, Blair's Corps was laying waste everything in their pathway, while above and below the city, for a distance of fifty miles, Sherman had swept the country as bare as if a blight had fallen upon it. How the people of Columbia subsisted during the time they were penned in the city churches and the few buildings left, will ever remain a mystery, and to none so much as the sufferers themselves.

Grains of corn were eagerly picked up in the streets as they dropped from the wagons, and the women and children of the lower class and the negroes flocked to the deserted camps to gather up the crumbs left by the soldiers or the grains trampled under foot of the horses.

Every house in a stretch of fifty miles was entered and insults and indignities offered the defenseless women which would have shamed the savage Turk. Ladies were forced to disclose, at the point of the pistol or the sabre, the hiding-place of their little valuables. Some were forced to cook meals and wait upon the hell hounds, while they regaled themselves upon the choice viands of medicinal wines of the planters' wives. But be it known to their immortal honor, that it was only on the most rare occasions that these proud dames of the South could, either by threat or brutal treatment, be forced to yield to their insolent demands. With the orders from the soldiers to "prepare a meal" or "disclose the whereabouts of their money or valuables," came the threat, "We will burn your house if you do not." But almost invariably came the quick response, "Burn it, burn it, you cowardly wretches, and kill me, if you wish, and all of us, but I will never soil my hands by waiting upon a cowardly Yankee, nor tell you the place of concealment—find it if you can." The soldiers would question the negroes to find out if there were any watches, silver plate, or money belonging to the household; if so, they would, by a system of inquisition, attempt to force the women to give it up, but in vain.

A woman, Mrs. Miller, the wife of a neighbor of mine, had her husband's gold watch in her bosom, and refused to give it up when demanded, even when a cocked pistol was at her head. The vandal struck her a stunning blow with the butt end of the pistol—all in vain. The brave heroine held to the heirloom, and stoutly resisted all entreaties and threats.

Two old people living near me, brother and maiden sister, named Loner, both pass three scores, were asked to give their money. They had none. But one of the ruffians threw a fire brand under the bed, saying:

"I will put it out if you will tell me where you keep your money; you have it, for I've been so informed."

"Let it burn," answered the old women. "Do you think to frighten or intimidate me by burning my house that I will tell what I choose to conceal? Do you think I care so much for my house and its belongings? No, no; you mistake the women of the South. You will never conquer her people by making war upon defenseless women. Let the house go up in flames, and my ashes mingle with its ashes, but I will remain true to myself, my country, and my God."

Soon all that was left of the once happy home was a heap of ashes. Will God, in His wisdom, ever have cause to again create such women as those of the Southland? Or were there ever conditions in the world's history that required the presence of such noble martyrdom as was displayed by the women of the South during the Civil War?

But a Nemesis in this case, as in many others, was lurking near. Bands of Confederates and scouts had scattered themselves on the flanks and rear of the enemy; old men and boys and disabled veterans were lying in wait in many thickets and out of the way places, ready to pounce upon the unsuspecting freebooters and give to them their just deserts. Was it any wonder that so many hundreds, nay thousands, of these Goths failed to answer to Sherman's last roll call? Before the sun was many hours older, after the burning of the Loner homestead, the dreaded "bushwhackers" were on the trail of the vandals.

For years afterwards people, from curiosity, came to look at a heap of human bones in a thicket near, bleached by winter's rain and summer's sun, while some of the older men, pointing to the ghostly relics, would say, "Those are the remains of Sherman's houseburners." And such were the scenes from the Saltkahatchie to the Cape Fear. Who were to blame?

Sherman now directs his march towards Winnsboro and Chester, still in the four great parols, burning and plundering as they go. It seems that in their march through Georgia they were only whetting their appetites for a full gorge of vandalism in South Carolina. After their carnival of ruin in Columbia the Federals, like the tiger, which, with the taste of blood, grows more ravenous, they became more destructive the more destruction they saw. Great clouds of black smoke rose up over the whole county and darkened the sky overhead, while at night the heavens were lit up by the glare of the burning buildings. The railroad tracks were torn up and bridges burned, the iron being laid across heaps of burning ties, then when at red heat, were wrapped around trees and telegraph posts—these last through pure wantonness, as no army was in their rear that could ever use them again.

While that part of Sherman's Army was crossing Broad River at Alston and Freshley's, and the other near Ridgeway, General Hampton wrote General Beauregard to concentrate all his forces at or near the latter place by shipping Hardee and all forces under him at once by railroad—Stephenson's Division of Western men, now with Hampton and all the cavalry to fall upon the Fifteenth Corps, under Blair, and crush it before the other portions of the army could reach it. He argued that the enemy was marching so wide apart, the country so hilly, and the roads in Fairfield County almost impassable, that one wing of the army could be crushed before the other could reach it. But General Beauregard telegraphed him, "The time is past for that move. While it could have been done at the Edisto or Branchville, it is too late now."

On the night of the 17th and morning of the 18th Charleston was evacuated. Before the commencement of the retirement, orders were given by General Beauregard to General Hardee to withdraw the troops in the following order, but General Hardee being sick at this time, the execution of the order devolved upon General McLaws: One brigade of Wright's Division, in St. Paul's Parish, to move by railroad to Monk's Corner, then march by Sandy Run to the Santee; the other portion of Wright's Division to move by Summerville to St. Stephen's. The troops in Christ Church Parish to go by steamer to St. Stephen's. The troops from James' Island to move out by Ashley's Ferry and follow the Northeastern railroad, to be followed in turn by all the troops in the city. McLaws was to withdraw from Sherman's front at Branchville and follow on to St. Stephen's. After all the troops were here congregated, the line of march was taken up in the direction of Cheraw. Away to our left we could see the clouds of smoke rise as houses went up in flames, while forest fires swept the country far and wide. It was not fully understood to what point Sherman was making, until he reached Winnsboro. Here he turned the course of direction by turning to the right, crossing the Catawba at Pea's Ferry and Rocky Mount, the right wing under General Howard, at Pea's; the left, under General Slocum, at Rocky Mount, all marching to form a junction again at Cheraw. Sherman did not dare to trust himself far in the interior for any length of time, but was marching to meet the fleet that had left him at Savannah and the troops under Schofield, at Newbern, N.C. This is the reason he turns his course towards the sea coast. Raiding parties, under Kilpatrick, were sent out in the direction of Darlington and Lancaster, burning and plundering at will.

About this time Fort Fisher and all the works at the mouth of the

Cape Fear River fell into the hands of the enemy. Wilmington surrendered and General Bragg, who was in command there, retreated to Goldsboro.

How, in the face of all these facts, could it be possible for Generals to deceive themselves or to deceive others, or how President Davis could have such delusive hopes, is now impossible to comprehend. On February 22nd, after the fall of Wilmington, the Army of Sherman was on the border of North Carolina, while Hood's was straggling through the upper part of this State, with no prospects of forming a junction with Beauregard. President Davis wrote on that day: "General Beauregard: I have directed General J.E. Johnston to assume command of the Southern Army and assign you to duty with him. Together, I feel assured you will beat back Sherman."

To add one man, even if a great commander, would add but little strength to any army, already exhausted beyond the hope of recuperation, still "You will beat Sherman back!" the President writes. I for one cannot see how a General could receive such an order at such time in any other spirit than ridicule. President Davis, even after the fall of Richmond and the battle of Bettonville fought, where Johnston tried once more to "beat back Sherman" and failed—after all the circumstances and conditions were given to him in detail—said, "The struggle could be still carried on to a successful issue by bringing out all our latent resources; that we could even cross the Mississippi River, join forces with Kirby Smith, and prolong the war indefinitely." Was there ever such blind faith or dogged tenacity of purpose? Did Mr. Davis and our Generals really believe there was still a chance for a successful issue at this late day, or was it the knowledge of the disposition of the troops whom they knew would rather suffer death than defeat.

It must, within all reason, have been the latter, for no great commander cognizant of all the facts could have been so blind. Even while the Confederate troops were overwhelmed by numbers, communications cut on all sides, all out posts and the borders hemmed in one small compass, some of our soldiers entered a publishing house in Raleigh, destroyed all the type, broke the presses, and demolished the building—all this because the editor of the paper advised the giving up of the contest! Did the soldiers of the South believe as yet that they were beaten? Circumstances and their surly moods say not. Well might a commander or executive have apprehensions of his personal safety should he counsel submission as long as there was a soldier left to raise a rifle or draw a lanyard. I ask again was there ever before such troops as those of the South? Will there ever be again?

Kershaw's Brigade, now attached to Hardee's Corps, reached Cheraw about the first of March, but the enemy's advance was at Chesterfield, causing Hardee to continue his march by Rockinham on to Fayetteville, N.C., near which place the two armies, that is the one under Hampton and the other under Hardee, came together. Hardee having recovered from his indisposition, relieved General McLaws, the latter returning to Augusta, Ga. Kershaw's Brigade was soon after put in Wathal's Division.

On the 22nd of February General Jos. E. Johnston, who was then living at Lincolnton, N.C., was called from his retirement and placed in command of all the troops in North and South Carolina and Georgia. Although the army was nothing more than detachments, and widely separated and greatly disorganized when he reached them, still they hailed with delight the appointment of their former faithful old commander. His one great aim was the convergence of the various armies to one point in front of the enemy and strike a blow at either one or more of his columns, either at Fayetteville or at the crossing of the Cape Fear River. Hardee had been racing with Sherman to reach Cheraw and cross the PeeDee before Sherman could come up. He only accomplished this after many forced marches by "the skin of his teeth," to use a homely expression. He crossed the PeeDee one day ahead of the enemy, burning the bridge behind him, after moving all the stores that were possible. The right wing, under General Howard, crossed the PeeDee at Cheraw, while the left, under Slocum, crossed higher up, at Sneedsboro. Hampton was forced to make a long detour up the PeeDee and cross at the fords along the many little islands in that stream.

On the 8th of March General Bragg, with Hoke's Division, reinforced by a division under D.H. Hill, of Johnston's command, numbering in all about two thousand, attacked three divisions under General Cox, at Kiniston, defeating him with much loss, capturing one thousand five hundred prisoners and three pieces of artillery.

During the campaign our cavalry was not idle on the flanks or front of Sherman, but on the contrary, was ever on the alert, striking the enemy wherever possible. General Butler intercepted and defeated a body of Federals on their way to destroy the railroad at Florence, at or near Mount Elan. General Wheeler, also, at Homesboro, came up with the enemy, and after a spirited brush, drove the enemy from the field, capturing a number of prisoners. Again, near Rockinham, the same officer put the enemy to rout. General Kilpatrick had taken up camp on the road leading to Fayetteville, and commanding that road which was necessary for the concentration of our troops. In the night General Hampton, after thoroughly reconnoitering the position, surrounded the camp of Kilpatrick, and at daybreak, on the 10th, fell like a hurricane upon the sleeping enemy. The wildest confusion prevailed; friend could not be distinguished from foe. Shooting and saber slashing were heard in every direction, while such of the enemy who could mounted their horses and rode at break-neck speed, leaving their camp and camp equippage, their artillery and wagon trains. The enemy was so laden with stolen booty, captured in the Carolinas and Georgia, that this great treasure was too great a temptation to the already demoralized cavalry. So, instead of following up their victory, they went to gathering the spoils. Hundreds of horses were captured, but these ran off by our troops forcing all the artillery captured to be abandoned, after cutting the wheels to pieces. But the long train of wagons, laden with supplies, was a good addition to our depleted resources. A great number of the enemy were killed and wounded, with five hundred prisoners, besides recapturing one hundred and fifty of our own troops taken in former battles.

General Johnston now ordered the troops of General Bragg who had come up from Kiniston and the Western troops, under Stuart, Cheatham, and Lee, as well as a part of Hardee's, to concentrate at Smithfield. The bulk of Hardee's Corps, of which Kershaw's Brigade was a part, withdrew from Cheraw in the direction of Goldsboro, and at Averysboro the enemy came up with Hardee, and by the overpowering weight of numbers forced the Confederates from their position. The density of the pine forest was such, that after a few fires, the smoke settled among the undergrowth and under the treetops in such quantity that a foe could not be seen even a short distance away. The level condition of the country prevented our artillery from getting in any of its work, and a flank movement by the Federals could be so easily made, unnoticed, that Hardee was forced to retire in the direction of Smithfield and to an elevation.

General Johnston having learned that the enemy was marching in the direction of Goldsboro, instead of Raleigh, and that the right wing was a day's advance of the left, ordered a concentration of his troops near the little hamlet of Bentonville, situated near the junction of the roads, one leading to Raleigh and the other to Goldsboro, and there fall upon the one wing of the army and defeat it before the other came up. This was not so difficult in contemplation as in the performance, under the present condition of the troops and the topography of the country. General Johnston was misled by the maps at hand, finding afterwards that the Federal General, Howard, was much nearer Bentonville than was General Hardee. But General Hampton put General Butler's Division of Cavalry in front of this whole force, behind some hastily constructed breastworks, and was to keep Slocum at bay until the troops had all gotten in position.

General Hardee began moving early on the morning of the eighth, and on reaching Bentonville we now, for the first time, came up with all the other troops of the army. Hoke's Division lead off to take position and stood on both sides of a dull road leading through the thickets. Batteries were placed on his right. Next to the artillery was posted the Army of Tennessee, its right thrown forward. Before Hardee could get in position the enemy attacked with the utmost vigor, so much so that General Bragg, who was commanding in person at this point, asked for reinforcements. General Hardee, moving by at this juncture, ordered McLaws' Old-Division to the aid of Hoke. But the almost impenetrable thicket prevented hasty movement, and the smoke in front, overhead and the rear, with bullets passing over the heads of Hoke's men, made it impossible for these unacquainted with the disposition of the troops to know whether it was friend or foe in our front. The troops became greatly entangled and some of the officers demoralized. Some troops on our right, by mistaking the head of direction, began to face one way, while Kershaw's Brigade was facing another. But after much maneuvering, McLaw's got the troops disentangled and moved upon the line, and after several rounds at close range, the enemy retreated. Hardee was then ordered to charge with his wing of the army, composed of troops under Stuart and a division under Taliaferro, while Bragg was to follow by brigades from right to left. The firing was now confusing, our troops advancing in different direction, and the sound of our guns and cannon echoing and reverberating through the dense forest, made it appear as if we were surrounded by a simultaneous fire. But finding our way the best we could by the whizzing of the bullets, we rushed up to the enemy's first line of entrenchments, which they had abandoned without an effort, and took position behind the second line of works. After firing a round or two, the Confederates raised the old Rebel yell and went for their second line with a rush. Here General Hardee led his men in person, charging at their head on horseback. The troops carried everything before them; the enemy in double columns and favorably entrenched, was glad to take cover in the thicket in the rear. On the extreme left our troops were less successful, being held in check by strong breastworks and a dense thicket between the enemy and the troops of General Bragg. After sweeping the enemy from the field, General Hardee found it necessary to halt and reform his line and during this interval the enemy made an unsuccessful assault upon the troops of General Stuart. After nightfall and after all the killed and wounded had been removed from the field, General Johnston moved the troops back to the line occupied in the morning and threw up fortifications. Here we remained until the 21st; McLaws was detached and placed on the left of Hoke; the cavalry deployed as skirmishers to our left. There was a considerable gap between our extreme left and the main body of cavalry, and this break the writer commanded with a heavy Hue of skirmishers. Late in the day the enemy made a spirited attack upon us, so much so that General McLaws sent two companies of boys, formerly of Fizer's Brigade of Georgia Militia. The boys were all between sixteen and eighteen, and a finer body of young men I never saw. He also sent a regiment of North Carolina Militia, consisting of old men from fifty to sixty, and as these old men were coming up on line the enemy were giving us a rattling fire from their sharpshooters. The old men could not be induced to come up, however. The Colonel, a Venerable old gray-beard, riding a white horse, as soon as the bullets began to pelt the pines in his front, leaped from his horse and took refuge behind a large tree. I went to him and tried every inducement to get him to move up his men on a line with us, but all he would do was to grasp me by the hand and try to jerk me down beside him. "Lie down, young man," said he, "or by God you'll be shot to pieces. Lie down!" The old militiaman I saw was too old for war, and was "not built that way." But when I returned to the skirmish line, on which were my own brigade skirmishers, reinforced by the two boy companies, the young men were fighting with a glee and abandon I never saw equalled. I am sorry to record that several of these promising young men, who had left their homes so far behind, were killed and many wounded.

 This ended the battle of Bentonville, and we might say the war. The sun of the Confederacy, notwithstanding the hopes of our Generals, the determination of the troops, and the prayers of the people, was fast sinking in the west. The glorious rising on the plains of Manassas had gone down among the pine barriers of North Carolina. The last stroke had been given, and destiny seemed to be against us. For hundreds of miles had the defeated troops of Hood marched barefooted and footsore to the relief of their comrades of the East, and had now gained a shallow victory. They had crossed three States to mingle their blood with those of their friends who had fought with dogged resistence every step that Sherman had made. But their spirits were not broken. They were still ready to try conclusions with the enemy whenever our leaders gave the signal for battle. The South could not be conquered by defeat—to conquer it, it must be crashed. The tattered battle flags waved as triumphantly over the heads of the shattered ranks of the battle-scared veterans here in the pine barriers as it ever did on the banks of the Rapidan.

It is sad to chronicle that on this last day, in a battle of the cavalry, in which the infantry had to take a part, the gallant son of the brave General Hardee fell at the head of his column as the Eighth Texas Cavalry was making a desperate charge.

In the battle of Bentonville the Confederates had fourteen thousand infantry and cavalry. The cavalry being mostly on the flanks, and General Wheeler on the north side of Mill Creek, could not participate in the battle in consequence of the swollen stream. The Federal Army had thirty-five thousand engaged on the 19th and seventy thousand in line on the 20th. The loss on the Confederate side was one hundred and eighty killed, one thousand two hundred and twenty wounded, and five hundred and fifteen missing. The enemy's losses in killed and wounded far exceeded the Confederates, besides the Confederates captured nine hundred prisoners.

On the night of the 21st the army began its retreat, crossing Mill Creek on the morning of the 22nd, just in time to see the enemy approach the bridge as our last troops had crossed.

On the 23rd General Sherman marched his army to Goldsboro, there uniting with General Schofield. It was the intention of General Lee that as soon as General Sherman had approached near enough, to abandon the trenches at Petersburg, and, with the combined armies, turn and fall upon his front, flank, and rear.

CHAPTER 43

The Surrender

The army took up quarters for a while around Smithfield. The troops were as jolly and full of life as they ever were in their lives. Horse racing now was the order of the day. Out in a large old field, every day thousands of soldiers and civilians, with a sprinkling of the fair ladies of the surrounding country, would congregate to witness the excitement of the race course. Here horses from Kentucky, Tennessee, Georgia, and North and South Carolina tried each others mettle. They were not the thoroughbreds of the course, but cavalry horses, artillery horses, horses of Generals, Colonels, and the staff—horses of all breeds and kinds, all sizes and description—stood at the head of the track and champed their bits with eagerness, impatient to get away. Confederate money by the handfuls changed owners every day. It was here that Governor Zeb Vance, of North Carolina, visited us, and was a greater favorite with the soldiers than any man in civil life. It was here, too, our old disabled commander, General James Connor, came to bid us an affectionate farewell. General Kennedy formed the brigade into a hollow square to receive our old General. He entered the square on horseback, accompanied by General Kennedy and staff. He had come to bid us farewell, and spoke to us in feeling terms. He recounted our many deeds of valor upon the field, our sufferings in camp and upon the march, and especially our supreme heroism and devotion in standing so loyally to our colors in this the dark hour of our country's cause. He spoke of his great reluctance to leave us; how he had watched with sympathy and affection our wanderings, our battles, and our victories, and then envoking Heaven's blessings upon us, he said in pathetic tones, "Comrades, I bid you an affectionate farewell," and rode away.

While in camp here there was a feeble attempt made to reorganize and consolidate the brigade by putting the smaller companies together and making one regiment out of two. As these changes took place so near the end, the soldiers never really realizing a change had been made, I will do no more than make a passing allusion to it, as part of this history. The only effect these changes had was the throwing out of some of our best and bravest officers (there not being places for all), but as a matter of fact this was to their advantage, as they escaped the humiliation of surrender, and returned home a few days earlier than the rest of the army.

After passing through South Carolina and venting its spleen on the Secession State, the Federal Army, like a great forest fire, sweeping over vast areas, stops of its own accord by finding nothing to feed upon. The vandalism of the Union Army in North Carolina was confined mostly to the burning of the great turpentine forests. They had burned and laid waste the ancestral homes of lower South Carolina, left in ashes the beautiful capital of the State, wrecked and ruined the magnificent residences and plantations of the central and upper part of the country, leaving in their wake one vast sheet of ruin and desolation, so that when they met the pine barrens of North Carolina, their appetites for pillage, plunder, and destruction seems to have been glutted.

It was the boast of the Federal commander and published with delight in all the Northern newspapers, that "where his army went along a crow could not pass over without taking its rations along." Then, too, this very country was to feed and support, while in transit to their homes almost the whole of Johnston's and the greater part of Lee's Army. All these, in squads or singly, were fed along the way from house to house wherever they could beg a little meal or corn, with a morsel of meat or molasses. A great number of negro troops also passed through this country on their way to the coast to be disbanded. But the noble women of South Carolina never turned a hungry soldier from their doors as long as there was a mouthful in the house to eat.

Another terror now alarmed the people—the news of a great raid, under Stoneman, being on its way through North Carolina and upper South Carolina, coming across the country from East Tennessee, laying waste everything in its track. General Sherman had concentrated his whole army at Goldsboro, and was lying idle in camp, preparatory to his next great move to connect with Grant. He had at his command the right wing, under General Howard, twenty-eight thousand eight hundred and thirty-four; its left wing, under General Slocum, twenty-eight thousand and sixty-three. General Schofield had come up from Newbern with twenty-six thousand three hundred and ninety-two and constituted the center, besides five thousand six hundred and fifty-nine cavalry, under Kilpatrick, and ninety-one pieces of artillery. General Johnston had encamped his army between two roads, one leading to Raleigh, the other to Weldon. The Confederate Government, after the evacuation of Richmond, had now established its quarters at Danville, Va., awaiting the next turn of the wheel. Lee had fallen back from Petersburg; while Johnston, before Sherman, was awaiting the move of that General to fall back still nearer to his illustrious chieftain. The government and all the armies were now hedged in the smallest compass. Still our leaders were apparently hopeful and defiant, the troops willing to stand by them to the last.

On the 10th of April President Davis and a part of his cabinet left Danville on his way to Greensboro. Even at this late day President Davis was urging the concentration of the troops under General Walker, the scattered troops at Salisbury and Greensboro, and those under Johnston at same place on the Yadkin, and crush Sherman, and then it is supposed to turn on Grant. All this with less than twenty thousand men!

The last conference of the great men of the Confederacy met at Greensboro, on the 13th of April, 1865. Those present were President Davis, Messrs. Benjamin, Secretary of State; Mallory, of the Navy; Reagin, Postmaster General; Breckinridge, Secretary of War, and General Johnston. The army had been falling back daily through Raleigh, and was now encamped near Greensboro. President Davis still clung to the delusion that by pressing the conscript act and bringing out all absentees, they could yet prolong the struggle, even if they had to cross the Mississippi and join with Kirby Smith. General Johnston urged in his and General Beauregard's name its utter impracticability, and informed the President plainly and positively that it was useless to continue the struggle—that they had as well abandon all hope of any other issue than that which they could gain through the Federal authorities, and besought Mr. Davis to open negotiations looking to peace—that he was yet the executive and head of the Confederate Government; that he was the proper one to commence such negotiations. This Mr. Davis refused, saying the Federal authorities would refuse to treat with him. Then General Johnston proposed doing so in his own name. This was agreed to, and a letter written by Mr. Mallory, he being the best penman in the group, and signed and sent by General Johnston to General Sherman. The letter recapitulated the results in the army in the last few days, changing the status of the two armies and the needless amount of bloodshed and devastation of property that the continuance of the struggle would produce, and asked for a conference looking to an armistice in the armies until the civil government could settle upon terms of peace. The letter was sent to General Hampton, and by him to the Federal commander the next day. General Sherman acknowledged the receipt of the letter on the 14th, and it reached General Johnston on the 16th, agreeing to a cessation of hostilities until further notice. General Sherman expressed in his letter a great desire to spare the people of North Carolina the devastation and destruction the passing of his army through the State would necessitate. When it began to be noised about in the camp that the army was about to be surrendered, the soldiers became greatly excited. The thought of grounding their arms to an enemy never before entered their minds, and when the news came of a surrender the greatest apprehension and dread seized all. So different the end to their expectation. None could even think of the future without a shudder. Some anticipated a term in Federal prisons; others, the higher officers, a military trial; others thought of their private property and their arms. Even in a prison camp, where our soldiers would be kept confined under a Federal guard, all was mystery and uncertainty. The wives and helpless children, left in the rear to the mercy of the negroes (now for the first time known to be free), agitated the minds of not a few. Men began to leave the army by twos and by squads. Guards were placed on all roads and around camps, and the strictest orders were given against leaving the army without leave. Cavalrymen in great numbers had mounted their horses and rode away. General Sherman sent guards to all fords and bridges to examine all the paroles of the troops of Lee now swarming through the country.

General Johnston met General Sherman at Durham, on the 17th of April, at the house of Mr. Bennett, but after a long and tedious controversy, nothing was agreed upon. A second meeting took place at the same house next day, at which General Breckinridge was unofficially present, when terms of an armistice were agreed to until the department at Washington could be beard from. President Davis had already gone South with such of his cabinet as chose to follow him, the whole settlement of difficulties now devolving upon General Johnston alone.

But just as all negotiations were progressing finely the news came of President Lincoln's assassination, throwing the whole of the Federal Army in a frenzy of excitement. While the troops of the South may not have given their assent to such measures, yet they rejoiced secretly; in their hearts that the great agitator, emancipator—the cause of all our woes—was laid low. To him and him alone all looked upon as being the originator, schemer, and consummater of all the ills the South had suffered. However the hearts of the Southern people may have changed in the thirty years that have passed, or how sadly they deplored his death, even in a decade afterwards, I but voice the sentiment of the South at the time when I say they hated Lincoln with all the venom of their souls, and his untimely taking off by the hands of the assassin partly consoled them for all they had suffered.

Orders came from General Sherman to General Johnston to the effect that part of their agreement was rejected by the Washington Authority, and notifying the latter that the truce would be called off in forty-eight hours. This occasioned a third meeting between the two commanders to make such changes that were required by the authorities. On the 26th General Johnston sent a communication to General Sherman requesting a meeting at same place for further conference. This was agreed to and the meeting took place, where such terms were agreed upon and signed as was thought to be in accordance with the wishes of the Washington Government. Rolls were made out in duplicate of all the officers and soldiers, and on the 2nd of May the troops marched out, stacked their arms, were given paroles, and slowly turned away and commenced their homeward journey.

A military chest, containing $39,000, had been received from the Government in Richmond and divided out among the soldiers, being $1.29 apiece. All the Wagon and artillery horses and wagons, also, were loaned to the soldiers and divided by lot. A few days' rations had been issued, and with this and the clothes on their back, this remnant at a once grand army bent their steps towards their desolate homes. It was found advisable to move by different routs and in such numbers as was most agreeable and convenient. Once away from the confines of the army, they took by-ways and cross country, roads, avoiding as much as possible the track of the late army. The troops of Kershaw's Brigade, on reaching the borders of their State, each sought for himself the easiest and nearest path home. The Western Army made their way, the most of them at least, to Washington, Ga., where there was yet railroad communication a part of the way through Georgia.

And now, gentle reader, my task is done—my pen laid aside, after days and days of earnest toil to give a faithful and correct account of your daring, your endurance, your patriotism, and your fidelity to the cause you had espoused. Your aims have been of the highest, your performances ideal, and while you were unsuccessful, still your deeds of daring will live in history as long as civilization lasts. While your cherished hopes ended in a dream, still your aspirations have been of the loftiest, and your acts will be copied by generations yet unborn, as a fitting pattern for all brave men. You have fought in all the great battles of the East, from the trenches of Petersburg to the rugged heights of Round Top. Your blood mingled with that of your comrades of the West, from Chickamauga to the storming of Fort London. You combatted the march of Sherman from the Saltkahatchie to the close, and stacked your arms more as conquering heroes than beaten foes. You have nothing to regret but the results—no hope but the continued prosperity of a reunited people. This heritage of valor left to posterity as a memorial of Southern manhood to the Southern cause will be cherished by your descendants for all time, and when new generations come on and read the histories of the great Civil War, and recall to their minds the fortitude, the chivalry, and the glories of the troops engaged, Kershaw's Brigade will have a bright page in the book of their remembrance.

CHAPTER 44

Retrospect

It would be supposed that the writer, who had fought by the side of nearly all, and who had visited battlefields where troops from every State had fallen, could form an idea of "Which were the best troops from the South?" The South has furnished a type of the true soldier that will last as a copy for all time. She had few regulars, and her volunteer troops were brought into service without preparation or without the knowledge of tactical drill, but in stoicism, heroism, and martyrdom they excelled the world.

I give in these pages a brief synopsis of the characteristics of the troops from different States, and while this is the view of the author alone, still I feel assured that the great mass of the old soldiers will admit its correctness. To the question, "Which were the best troops from the South?" there would be as many answers and as much differences of opinions as there were States in the Confederacy, or organizations in the field, as each soldier was conscientious in his belief that those from his own State were the best in the army, his brigade the best in the division, his regiment the best in the brigade, and his own company the best in the regiment. This is a pardonable pride of the soldier, and is as it should be to make an army great. Where all, individually and collectively, were as good or better than any who ever before faced an enemy upon a battlefield, there really are no "best."

But soldiers from different States, all of the same nationality and of the same lineage, from habits, temperaments, and environments, had different characteristics upon the field of battle. From an impartial standpoint, I give my opinion thus:

The Virginians were the cavaliers of the South, high-toned, high-bred, each individual soldier inspired by that lofty idea of loyalty of the cavalier. They were the ideal soldiers in an open field and a fair fight. They were the men to sweep a battle line that fronts them from the field by their chivalrous and steady courage. Virginia, the mother of Presidents, of great men, and noble women, the soldier of that State felt in honor bound to sustain the name and glory of their commonwealth. As a matter of fact, the Virginians, as a rule, with exceptions enough to establish the rule, being one of the oldest of the sister States, her wealth, her many old and great institutions of learning, were better educated than the mass of soldiers from the other States. They were soldiers from pride and patriotism, and courageous from "general principles." In an open, fair field, and a square and even fight, no enemy could stand before their determined advance and steady fire. They were not the impulsive, reckless, head-strong soldiers in a desperate charge as were those from some other Southern States, but cool, collected, steady, and determined under fire. They were of the same mettle and mould as their kinsmen who stood with Wellington at Waterloo.

The North Carolinians were the "Old Guard" of the Confederacy. They had little enthusiasm, but were the greatest "stickers" and "stayers" on a battle line of any troops from the South. They fought equally as well in thicket or tangled morass as behind entrenchments. To use an army expression, "The North Carolinians were there to stay." It was a jocular remark, common during the war, that the reason the North Carolina troops were so hard to drive from a position was "they had so much tar on their heels that they could not run." They were obstinate, tenacious, and brave.

South Carolinians took on in a great measure the inspirations of some of their French Huguenot ancestors and the indomitable courage of their Scotch and German forefathers of the Revolution. They were impulsive, impetuous, and recklessly brave in battle, and were the men to storm breastworks and rush to the cannon's mouth at the head of a "forlorn hope." They possibly might not stay as long in a stubbornly contested battle as some from other States, but would often accomplish as much in a few minutes by the mad fury of their assault as some others would accomplish in as many hours. They were the Ironsides of the South, and each individual felt that he had a holy mission to fulfill. There were no obstacles they could not surmount, no position they would not assail. Enthusiasm and self-confidence were the fort of South Carolinians, and it was for them to raise the Rebel yell and keep it up while the storm of battle raged fierce and furious. They were the first to raise the banner of revolt, and right royally did they sustain it as long as it floated over the Southland.

What is said of the South Carolinians can be truthfully said of Georgians. People of the same blood, and kindred in all that makes them one, they could be with propriety one and the same people. The Georgians would charge a breastwork or storm a battery with the same light-heartedness as they went to their husking bees or corn-shucking, all in a frolick. To illustrate their manner of fighting, I will quote from a Northern journal, published just after the seven days' battles around Richmond, a conversation between Major D., of the —— New York, and a civilian of the North. The Major was boasting in a noisy manner of the courage, daring, and superiority of the Northern soldiers over those of the South. "Well, why was it," asked the civilian, "if you were so superior in every essential to the Rebels, that you got such an everlasting licking around Richmond?" "Licking, h——l," said the wounded Major, "who could fight such people? Indians! Worse than an Apache. Just as we would get in line of battle and ready for an advance, a little Georgia Colonel, in his shirt sleeves and copperas breeches, would pop out into a corn field at the head of his regiment, and shout at the top of his voice, 'Charge!' Man alive! here would come the devils like a whirlwind—over ditches, gullies, fences, and fields, shouting, yelling, whooping, that makes the cold chills run up your back—flash their glittering bayonets in our very faces, and break our lines to pieces before you could say 'boo.' Do you call that fighting? It was murder." No more need be said of the Georgians.

Little Florida did not have many troops in the field, but little as she was, she was as brave as the best. Her troops, like those of Georgia and South Carolina, were impulsive, impetuous, and rapid in battle. They were few in numbers, but legions in the fray.

The Alabamians and Mississippians came of pioneer stock, and like their ancestry, were inured to hardships and dangers from childhood; they made strong, hardy, brave soldiers. Indifferent to danger, they were less careful of their lives than some from the older States. They were fine marksmen; with a steady nerve and bold hearts, they won, like Charles Martel, with their hammer-like blows. They were the fanatical Saraceus of the South; while nothing could stand before the broad scimeters of the former, so nothing could stand in the way of the rifle and bayonet of the latter.

The Louisianians were the Frenchmen of the South. Of small stature, they were the best marchers in the army. Like their ancestors in the days of the "Grand Monarch," and their cousins in the days of the

"Great Napoleon," they loved glory and their country. Light-hearted and gay in camp, they were equally light-hearted and gay in battle. Their slogan was, "Our cause and our country." The Louisianians were grand in battle, companionable in camp, and all round soldiers in every respect.

The Texan, unlike the name of Texan immediately after the war, when that country was the city of refuge for every murderer and cutthroat of the land, were gallant, chivalrous, and gentlemanly soldiers. Descendants of bold and adventurous spirits from every State in the South, they were equally bold and daring in battle, and scorned the very word of fear or danger. Hood's old Texas Brigade shared honors with the old Stonewall Brigade in endurance, courage, and obstinacy in action. The soldiers of Texas were tenacious, aggressive, and bold beyond any of their brethren of the South.

The Tennesseeans, true to the instincts of their "back woods" progenitors, were kind-hearted, independent, and brimful of courage. Driven from their homes and firesides by a hostile foe, they became a "storm center" in battle. They were combative and pugnacious, and defeat had no effect upon their order, and they were ever ready to turn and strike a foe or charge a battery. Their courage at Chickamauga is distinguished by showing the greatest per cent of killed and wounded in battle that has even been recorded, the charge of the Light Brigade not excepted, being over forty-nine per cent.

What is said of the Tennesseeans is equally true of the Arkansans. Of a common stock and ancestry, they inherited all the virtues and courage of their forefathers. The Confederacy had no better soldiers than the Arkansans—fearless, brave, and oftentimes courageous beyond prudence.

The border States' soldiers, Missourians, Kentuckians, and Marylanders, were the free lance of the South. They joined the fortunes of the South with the purest motives and fought with the highest ideals. Under Forrest and Morgan and the other great riders of the West, they will ever be the soldiers of story, song, and romance. Their troops added no little lustre to the constellation of the South's great heroes, and when the true history of the great Civil War shall be written, they will be remembered. Indomitable in spirits, unconquerable and unyielding in battle, they will ever stand as monuments to the courage of the Southern Army.

Appendices

The Magnitude of the War 211
The Confederate Dead 217
Regimental Rolls 222
   Second South Carolina Volunteer Regiment 223
   Third South Carolina Volunteer Regiment 235
   Seventh South Carolina Volunteer Regiment 246
   Eighth South Carolina Volunteer Regiment 256
   Fifteenth South Carolina Volunteer Regiment 266
   Third Battalion (James) 276
   Twentieth South Carolina Volunteer Regiment 282

The Magnitude of the War
its Losses in Killed and Died

What were the Confederate losses during the war? Where are the Confederate dead? Which State lost the most soldiers in proportion to the number furnished the war? These are questions which will perhaps be often asked, but never answered. It can never be known, only approximately. The cars containing the Confederate archives were left unguarded and unprotected at Greensboro on its way from Richmond, until General Beauregard noticed papers from the car floating up and down the railroad track, and had a guard placed over them and sent to Charlotte. There was a like occurrence at this place, no protection and no guard, until General Johnston had them turned over to the Federal authorities for safe keeping. Consequently, the Confederate rolls on file in Washington are quite incomplete, and the loss impossible to ever be made good.

The Federal authorities commenced immediately after the war to collect their dead in suitable cemeteries, and the work of permanently marking their graves continued systematically until the Federal loss in the war can be very accurately estimated. There are seventy-five public cemeteries for the burial of the Federal soldiers, in which are buried three hundred and sixty thousand two hundred and seven; of these, one hundred and thirty-nine thousand four hundred and ninety-six are marked unknown. There were thirty-three thousand five hundred and twenty negro soldiers buried in the cemeteries, and more than fifty thousand Union dead never accounted for A great number of these fell by the wayside during "Sherman's march to the sea;" lost by "Sherman's rear guard," called by the Federal soldiers "Confederate bushwhackers"

The rolls of the Confederate dead in the archives at Washington, given by States, are very unsatisfactory and necessarily incomplete Only two States can even approximate their loss. But as this is the record in Washington, I give it.

	Killed	Died of Wounds	Died of Disease
Virginia	5,328	2,519	6,947
North Carolina	14,522	5,151	20,602
South Carolina	9,187	3,725	4,700
Georgia	5,553	1,716	3,702
Florida	793	506	1,047
Alabama	552	190	724
Mississippi	5,807	2,651	6,807
Louisiana	2,612	858	3,059
Texas	1,348	1,241	1,260
Arkansas	2,165	915	3,872
Tennessee	2,115	874	3,425
Regulars	1,007	468	1,040
Border States	1,959	672	1,142
Totals	**52,954**	**21,570**	**59,297**

In the above it will be seen that North Carolina, which may be considered approximately correct, lost more than any other State. Virginia furnished as many, if not more, troops than North Carolina, still her losses are one-third less, according to the statistics in Washington. This is far from being correct. Alabama's dead are almost eliminated from the rolls, while it is reasonable to suppose that she lost as many as South Carolina, Mississippi, or Georgia. South Carolina furnished more troops in proportion to her male white population than any State in the South, being forty-five thousand to August, 1862, and eight thousand reserves. It is supposed by competent statisticians that the South lost in killed and died of wounds, ninety-four thousand; and lost by disease, one hundred and twenty-five thousand.

In some of the principal battles throughout the war, there were killed out right, not including those died of wounds:

First Manassas	387	Gettysburg	3,530
Wilson's Creek	279	Chickamauga	2,380
Fort Donelson	466	Missionary Ridge	381
Pea Ridge	360	Sabine Cross Roads	350
Shiloh	1,723	Wilderness	1,630
Seven Pines	980	Atlanta Campaign	3,147
Seven Days Battles	3,286	Spottsylvania	1,310
Second Manassas	1,553	Drury's Bluff	355
Sharpsburg	1,512	Cold Harbor	960
Corinth	1,200	Atlanta, July 22, 1864	1,500
Perryville	510	Winchester	286
Fredericksburg	596	Cedar Creek	339
Murfreesboro	1,794	Franklin	1,750
Chancellorsville	1,665	Nashville	360
Champion Hill	380	Bentonville	289
Vicksburg Siege	875	Five Forks	350

There were many other battles, some of greater magnitude than the above, which are not here given. There are generally five wounded to one killed, and nearly one-third of the wounded die of their wounds, thus a pretty fair estimate of the various battles can be had. There were more men killed and wounded at Gettysburg than on any field of battle during the war, but it must be born in mind that its duration was three days. General Longstreet, who should be considered a judge, says that there were more men killed and wounded on the battlefield at Sharpsburg (or Antietam), for the length of the engagement and men engaged, than any during this century.

The Union losses on the fields mentioned above exceeded those of the Confederates by thirteen thousand five hundred in killed and died of wounds.

There were twenty-five regular prison pens at the North, at which twenty-six thousand seven hundred and seventy-six Confederate prisoners died, tabulated as follows:

PRISONS.	No. Deaths.
Alton, Ill	1,613
Camp Butler, Ill	816
Camp Chase, Ohio	2,108
Camp Douglass, Ill	3,750
Camp Horton, Ind	1,765
Camp Randall, Wis	137
Chester, Penn	213
David's Is., N.Y. Harbor	178
Elmira, N.Y.	2,960
Fort Delaware, Del	2,502
Fort Warren, Bos'n H'b'r	13
Frederick, Md	226
Gettysburg, Penn	210
Hart's Is., N.Y. Harbor	230
Johnson's Island, Ohio	270
Knoxville, Tenn	138
Little Rock, Ark	220
Nashville, Tenn	561
New Orleans, La	329
Point Lookout, Md	3,446
Richmond, Va	175
Rock Island, Ill	1,922
St. Louis, Mo	589
Ship Island, Miss	162
Washington, DC	457

War is an expensive pastime for nations, not alone in the loss of lives and destruction of public and private property, but the expenditures in actual cash—gold and silver—is simply appalling. It is claimed by close students of historical data, those who have given the subject careful study, that forty million of human beings lose their lives during every century by war alone. Extravagant as this estimate may seem, anyone who will carefully examine the records of the great conflicts of our own century will readily be convinced that there are not as much extravagance in the claim as a cursory glance at the figures would indicate. Europe alone loses between eighteen, and twenty million, as estimated by the most skillful statisticians. Since the time of the legendary Trojan War (three thousand years), it is supposed by good authority that one billion two hundred thousand of human, beings have lost their lives by the hazard of war, not all in actual battle alone, but by wounds and diseases incident to a soldier's life, in addition to those fallen upon the field.

In the wars of Europe during the first half of this century two million and a half of soldiers lost their lives in battle, and the country was impoverished to the extent of six billions eight hundred and fifty millions of dollars, while three millions of soldiers have perished in war since 1850. England's national debt was increased by the war of 1792 to nearly one billion and a half, and during the Napoleonic wars to the amount of one billion six hundred thousand dollars.

During the last seventy years Russia has expended for war measures the sum of one billion six hundred and seventy million dollars, and lost seven hundred thousand soldiers. It cost England, France, and Russia, in the Crimean war of little more than a year's duration, one billion five hundred million dollars, and five hundred thousand lives lost by the four combined nations engaged.

But all this loss, in some cases lasting for years, is but a bagatelle in comparison to the loss in men and treasure during the four years of our Civil War.

According to the records in Washington, the North spent, for the equipment and support of its armies during the four years of actual hostilities, four billion eight hundred million in money, outside of the millions expended in the maintenance of its armies during the days of Reconstruction, and lost four hundred and ten thousand two hundred and fifty-seven men. The war cost the South, in actual money on a gold basis, two billion three hundred million, to say nothing of the tax in kind paid by the farmers of the South for the support of the army. The destruction and loss in public and private property, outside of the slaves, is simply appalling. The approximate loss in soldiers is computed at two hundred and nineteen thousand.

The actual cost of the war on both sides, in dollars and cents, and the many millions paid to soldiers as pensions since the war, would be a sum sufficient to have paid for all the negroes in the South several times over, and paid the national debt and perhaps the debts of most of the Southern States at the commencement of the war.

This enormous loss in blood and treasure on the part of the South was not spent in the attempts at conquest, the subversion of the Union, or the protection of the slave property, but simply the maintenance of a single principle—the principle of States Rights, guaranteed by the Federal Constitution.

The Confederate Dead
The Battlefields of The Civil War
The Two Civilizations

The North has gathered up the bones of the greater part of her vast armies of the dead, commencing the task immediately after the war, and interred them in her vast national cemeteries. At the head of each is an imperishable head-stone, on which is inscribed the name of the dead soldier, where a record has been kept, otherwise it is simply marked "unknown." The North was the victor; she was great, powerful, and rolling in wealth; she could do this, as was right and just.

But where are the South's dead? Echo answers from every hill and dale, from every home where orphan and widow weep and mourn, "Where?" The South was the vanquished, stricken in spirits, and ruined in possessions; her dead lie scattered along every battle ground from Cemetery Ridge and the Round Top at Gettysburg, to the Gulf and far beyond the Father of Waters. One inscription on the head-stones would answer for nearly all, and marked "unknown." One monument would suffice for all the army of the dead, and an appropriate inscription would be a slight paraphrase of old Simonides on the shaft erected to the memory of the heroes of Thermopylae—

> *Go, stranger, and to Southland tell*
> *That here, obeying her behest, we fell.*

The names of the great majority have already been forgotten, only within a circumscribed circle are they remembered, and even from this they will soon have passed into oblivion. But their deeds are recorded in the hearts of their countrymen in letters everlasting, and their fame as brave and untarnished soldiers will be remembered as long as civilization admires and glories in the great deeds of a great people. Even some of the great battle grounds upon which the South immortalized itself and made the American people great will soon be lost to memory, and will live only in song and story. Yet there are others which, through the magnificent tribute the North has paid to her dead, will be remembered for all time.

Looking backwards through the lapse of years since 1861, over some of the great battlefields of the Civil War, we see striking contrasts. On some, where once went carnage and death hand in hand, we now see blooming fields of growing grain, broad acres of briar and brush, while others, a magnificent "city of the dead." Under the shadow of the Round Top at Gettysburg, where the earth trembled beneath the shock of six hundred belching cannon, where trampling legions spread themselves along the base, over crest and through the gorges of the mountain, are now costly parks, with towering monuments—records of the wonderful deeds of the dead giants, friend and foe.

Around the Capital of the "Lost Cause," where once stood forts and battlements, with frowning cannon at each salient, great rows of bristling bayonets capping the walls of the long winding ramparts, with men on either side standing grim and silent, equally ready and willing to consecrate the ground with the blood of his enemy or his own, are now level fields of grain, with here and there patches of undergrowth and briars. Nothing now remains to conjure the passer-by that here was once encamped two of the mightiest armies of earth, and battles fought that astounded civilization.

On the plains of Manassas, where on two different occasions the opposing armies met, where the tide of battle surged and rolled back, where the banners of the now vanquished waved in triumph from every section of the field, the now victors fleeing in wild confusion, beaten, routed, their colors trailing in the dust of shame and defeat, now all to mark this historic battle ground is a broken slab or column, erected to individuals, defaced by time and relic seekers, and hidden among the briars and brush.

From the crest and along the sides of Missionary Ridge, and from the cloud-kissed top of Lookout Mountain, to Chickamauga, where the flash of cannon lit up the valley and plain below, where swept the armies of the blue and the gray in alternate victory and defeat, where the battle-cry of the victorious mingled with the defiant shouts of the vanquished, where the cold steel of bayonets met, and where brother's gun flashed in the face of brother, where the tread of contending armies shook the sides and gorges of the mountain passes, are now costly granite roadways leading to God's Acre, where are buried the dead of the then two nations, and around whose border runs the "River of Death" of legend, Chickamauga. Over this hallowed ground floats the flag of a reunited country, where the brother wearing the uniform of the victor sleeps by the side of the one wearing the uniform of the vanquished. Along the broad avenues stand lofty monuments or delicately chiseled marble, erected by the members of the sisterhood of States, each representing the loyalty and courage of her respective sons, and where annually meet the representatives of the Frozen North with those of the Sunny South, and in one grand chorus rehearse the death chants of her fallen braves, whose heroism made the name of the nation great. To-day there stands a monument crowned with laurels and immortelles, erected by the State to the fallen sons of the "Dark and Bloody Ground," who died facing each other, one wearing the blue, the other the gray, and on its sides are inscribed: "As we are united in life, and they in death, let one monument perpetuate their deeds, and one people, forgetful of all aspirations, forever hold in grateful remembrance all the glories of that terrible conflict, which made all men free and retaining every star in the Nation's flag."

The great conflict was unavoidable; under the conditions, it was irresistable. It was but the accomplishment, by human agencies, the will of the Divine. Its causes were like paths running on converging lines, that eventually must meet and cross at the angle, notwithstanding their distances apart or length. From the foundation of the government these two converging lines commenced. Two conflicting civilizations came into existence with the establishment of the American Union—the one founded on the sovereignty of the States and the continuance of slavery was espoused by the hot-blooded citizens of the South; the other, upon the literal construction of the Declaration of Independence, that "all men are created free and equal," and the supremacy of the general government over States Rights, and this was the slogan of the cool, calculating, but equally brave people of the North. The converging lines commenced in antagonism and increased in bitterness as they neared the vertex. The vertex was 1861. At this point it was too late to make concessions. There was no room for conciliation or compromise, then the only recourse left is what all brave people accepts—the arbitrament of the sword.

The South sought her just rights by a withdrawal from the "Unholy Alliance." The North sought to sustain the supremacy and integrity of the Union by coercing the "Erring Sisters" with force of arms. The South met force with force, and as a natural sequence, she staked her all. The North grew more embittered as the combat of battles rolled along the border and the tread of a million soldiers shook the two nations to their centers. First, it was determined that the Union should be preserved, even at the expense of the South's cherished institution; then, as the contest grew fiercer and more unequaled, that the institution itself should die with the re-establishment of the Union. Both played for big stakes—one for her billions of slave property, the other for the forty or more stars in her constellation. Both put forward her mightiest men of war. Legions were mustered, marshalled, and thrown in the field, with an earnestness and rapidity never before witnessed in the annals of warfare. Each chose her best Captains to lead her armies to battle, upon the issue of which depended the fate of two nations. The Southern legions were led by the Lees, Johnstons, Beauregards, Jacksons, Stuarts, Longstreets, and other great Lieutenants; the North were equally fortunate in her Grants, Shermans, Thomases, Sheridans, and Meads. In courage, ability, and military sagacity, neither had just grounds to claim superiority over the other. In the endurance of troops, heroism, and unselfish devotion to their country's cause, the North and South each found foemen worthy of their steel. Both claimed justice and the Almighty on their side. Battles were fought, that in the magnitude of the slaughter, in proportion to the troops engaged, has never been equalled since the days of recorded history; Generalship displayed that compared favorably with that of the "Madman of the North," the Great Frederick, or even to that of the military prodigy of all time—Napoleon himself. The result of the struggle is but another truth of the maxim of the latter, that "The Almighty is on the side of the greatest cannon."

I close my labors with an extract from a speech of one of the Southern Governors at Chickamauga at the dedication of a monument to the dead heroes from the State.

"A famous poem represents an imaginary midnight review of Napoleon's Army. The skeleton of a drummer boy arises from the grave, and with his bony fingers beats a long, loud reveille. At the sound the legions of the dead Emperor come from their graves from every quarter where they fell. From Paris, from Toulon, from Rivoli, from Lodi, from Hohenlinden, from Wagram, from Austerlitz, from the cloud clapped summit of the Alps, from the shadows of the Pyramids, from the snows of Moscow, from Waterloo, they gather in one vast array with Ney, McDonald, Masenna, Duroc, Kleber, Murat, Soult, and other marshals in command. Forming, they silently pass in melancholy procession before the Emperor, and are dispersed with 'France' as the pass word and 'St. Helena' as the challenge.

"Imagine the resurrection of the two great armies of the Civil War. We see them arising from Gettysburg, from the Wilderness, from Shiloh, from Missionary Ridge, from Stone River, from Chickamauga—yea, from a hundred fields—and passing with their great commanders in review before the martyred President. In their faces there is no disappointment, no sorrow, no anguish, but they beam with light and hope and joy. With them there is no 'St. Helena,' no 'Exile,' and they are dispersed with 'Union' as a challenge and 'Reconciliation' as a pass word."

Regimental Rolls

I have in this appendix endeavored to give a complete roll of all the members who belonged to Kershaw's Brigade. I have taken it just as it stands in the office of the State Historian in Columbia. The work of completing the rolls of the Confederate soldiers from this State was first commenced by the late General, H.L. Farley and finished by Colonel John P. Thomas, to whose courtesy I am indebted for the use of his office and archives while completing these rolls. There may be some inaccuracies in the spelling of names or in the names themselves, but this could not be avoided after the lapse of so many years. Then, again, the copy sent to the State Historian was often illegible, causing the same names to appear different and different names to look the same. But I have followed the records in the office in Columbia, and am not responsible for any mistakes, omissions, or inaccuracies.

In the list of officers there will appear some seeming irregularities and inaccuracies, but this is accounted for by the fact that the duplicate rolls were those taken from the companies' muster rolls when first enlisted in the Confederate service, and little or no record kept of promotions. Thus we will see Captains and Lieutenants in these rolls marked as non-commissioned officers. This was occasioned by those officers being promoted during the continuance of the war, and no record kept of such promotions.

Roll of Second South Carolina Volunteer Regiment

Colonels:
Kershaw, J.B
Jones, E.P
Kennedy, Jno. D
Wallace, Wm.

Lieutenant Colonels:
Goodwin, A.D
Gaillard, Frank
Graham, J.D.

Majors:
Casson, W.H
Clyburn, B
Leaphart, G.

Adjutants:
Sill, E.C
Goodwin, A.D
McNeil, A.

Assistant Quartermasters:
Wood, W.S
Peck, W.D.

Assistant Commissary Sergeant:
Villipigue, J.J.

Surgeon:
Salmond, F.

Assistant Surgeons:
Nott, J.H
Maxwell, A.

Chaplains:
McGruder, A.I

Smith, ——

COMPANY "A."

Captains:
Casson, W.H
Shelton, M.A
Gaillard, F
Leaphart, S.L
Maddy, M.M.

First Lieutenant:
Shuler, P.H.B.

Second Lieutenants:
Brown, R
Myers, W.M
Eggleston, D.B.

Sergeants:
West, W.H
Reid, J.C
Bryant, J.F
Livingston, J.B
Cooper, G.F
Gilbert, J.G
Wells, J.F
McTurious, E.C.
Joiner, B
DuBose, J.

Corporals:
Sulaff, W.C
Bruns, G
Newman, R
Rowan, S.W
Mack, J.M
Goodwin, C.T.

Privates:
Atta, T.M
Andre, Geo
Anderson, M.J
Anderson, Geo
Andrews, T.P
Blackwell, Jas
Bryant, B.F
Brown, C.K
Brown, Jessie,
Baker, J.L
Burns, L
Benjamin, T
Banks, C.C
Casson, J.H
Cavis, J.W
Canning, Thos
Clowdy, ——
Cannon, M
Calais, W.J
Cooper, J.W
DuBose, J.B
Durin, Thos
Deckerson, Geo
Dwight, W.M
Emlyn, H.N
Field, G.R
Forde, Edwin
Griffin, J.W
Gasoue, W
Gibson, J
Graham, J
Graham, Thos
Glass, W.G
Hall, J.R
Hoeffir, Chas

Hartnett, M
Hinton, S.P
Hinkle, E
Howard, W.P
Hays, A.G
Hall, J.W
Hennies W
Holmes, C.R
Hollis, M
Hollis, Carles,
Howell, O.F
Hutchinson, B.B
Halsey, M.P
Johnson, D.B
Joiner, P.H
Kelly, Tames
Kind, Wm
Kelly, J.G
Kindman, J.D
Loomis, H.H
Ladd, P.B
Lee, Isom,
Lindsey, S.J
Landrum, A.P
Leaphart, J.E
Landrum, L.M
Magillan, C
McGee, Alex
McFie, Joseph
Mathews, Jno
McDonald, D.J
McCarter, W.E
McCully, W.H
Miller, R.L
Mitchell, D
Marsh, J.A
Murphy, Geo
Myers, John,
Maw, R.E
Martin, E.R
Marsh. Thos
Martin, Saml
Newman, J.M
Neuffer, C.E
Nott, Carles.
Norton, R
Nott, W.J

Pritchard, D
Pelfry, J
Roberts, L.D
Roberts, J.F
Radcliff, L.J
Rentiers, J.G
Roach, W.J
Rose, J.C
Rulland, C.L
Randolph, W.J
Reilly, W.T
Stubbs, W.G
Stubbs, J.D
Starling, W.D
Starling, R
Starling. Jno
Smith, B
Smith, Richard
Stokes, E.R
Thurston, J
Taylor, H
Vaughn, B
Williams. Jno
Winchester, J.M
Winchester, J.

COMPANY "B."

Captains:
Hoke, A.D
Pulliam, R.C
Cagle, J.W.

First Lieutenants:
Isaacs, A
Holland, Wm.

Second Lieutenant:
Elford, Geo.E.

Sergeants:
Price, W.P
Watson, Wm. C
Dyer, G.B
Clyde, S.C
Pool, R.W. Pickle, O.A
Moore, T.H.L
Stall, Thos
Sudwith. Peter P

Jones, Jno. M
Towns, John M
Bacon, Randolph.

Corporals:
Harris, Frank E
Jennings, Jno. A
West, L.M
Ingram, H.G
Roberts, J.M
Shumate, W.T.

Privates:
Anderson, G.T
Allen, D
Beacham, E.F
Bowen, O.E
Brown, H.C
Bacon, A
Baldwin, Jas
Baldwin, W.W
Baldwin, E
Blakely, R.L
Bramlett, R.H
Bramlett, Joseph,
Barbary, Wm
Carson, Joseph M
Carson, John,
Carson, C.H
Carpenter, S.J
Carpenter, J.F
Cureton, A.H
Chandler, W.G
Coxe, F
Cooper, M
Cox, J.A
Cox, Wm. F
Dyer, G.W
Dyer, J.N
Diver, W.S
Diver, J.E
Diver, R.F
D'Oyle, C.W
Duncan, A.S
Duncan, W.H
Duncan, J.M
Duncan, Robert
Donaldson, Thos. R

Davis, Saml
Dauthit, S.J
Foster, A.A
Goodlett, F.M
Goodlett, L.M
Goodlett, J.H
Goodlett, J.Y
Garmany, W.H
Grogan, T.R
Gibson, S.K
Gibson, J
Gosett, I.P
Gibreath, W.W
Gibreath, L.P
Goldsmith, W.H
Gwin, R.A
Harris, R.A
Hawkins, L.P
Henning, N.P
Hirch, G.W
Hill, J.W
Hudson, W.A
Huff, P.D
Huff, P.W
Holland, D.W
Holland, A.J
Holland, Jno
Irvin, D.P
Ingram, W.P
Jones, E.P
Jones, E.T
Jones, B
Johnson, I.T
Kilburn, T.C
Kirkland, P
Long, W.D
Long, S.F
Mauldin, Jas
McKay, R.W
Miller, J.P
Miller, W.S
Markley, H.C
Markley, Jno
Markley, Charles
Morgan, W.N
Moore, F
Moore, Lewis M

Moore, John
Moore, J.T
Mills, J
Payne, J
Parkins, G.W
Parkins, J.D
Pickett, J.H
Price, J.M
Poole, J.W
Pool, Cartery Y
Poor, G.B
Rowley, E.F.S
Roe, H.D
Rice, J.H
Ramsey, W.H
Smith, L.R
Scrugg, W. L.M.A
Shumate, J.S
Shumate, R.Y.H
Shumate, L.J
Sullivan, J.N
Smyer, M.A
Sinder, J
Salmons, J.M
Turpin, W.P
Tracy, Fred. S
Thompson, W.D
Thornley, J.L
Turner, J.L
West, R.W
Wisnant, W.F
Wisnant, Alex
Whitmire, Wm
Walton, D.S
Williams, G.W
Watson, P.D
Watson, W.W
Watkins, Lynn
Yeargin, J.O.

COMPANY "C."

Captains:
Wallace, Wm
Lorick, S
Vinson, A.P.

First Lieutenants:
Wood, W.S
Bell, J.C
Peck, W.D
Wallace, E
Youmans, O.J
Scott, J.T
McGregor, W.C
Stenhouse, E.

Sergeants:
Myers, Jno. A
Howie, Wm
Radcliff, L.J
Beck, Chas, J
Shand, R. W
Clarkson, I.O.H
Bell, Jacob
Hill, Wm
Medlin, N
Corrall. Jno
Edwards, J.G
Bell, E.H.

Corporals:
McCullough, Jno
Owens, Peter
Garner, Thos
Robertson, R.D
Lee, J.W.G
Osment, J.R
Davis, H
Freeman, R.G
Loomis, T.D.

Privates:
Ballard, J.N
Boyer, Thomas
Busard, Sam
Boyle, J.C
Brown, S
Brice, Robert
Campbell, James
Campbell, J.M
Copeland, J
Cook, P
Chestnut, ——
Chambers, E.R
Cupps, C.M

Douglass, Jno
Dougherty, J
Dickens, H.C
Davis, R.A
Flaherty, M
Freeman, Wm
Glaze, Jno
Garner, Wm
Goodwin, E.M
Gruber, Jno
Gruber, S
Goins, Henry
Gunnell, J.S
Gunnell, W.H
Grier, J
Heminnis, M
Hurst, J.P
Harrison, B
Hauleely, Henry
Hendricks, Jno
Hunt, J
Hammett, H.B
Hamilton, D
Isbell, Walter
King, W.H
Kallestrane, M.H
Lee, U
Lee, L.W
Lee, A.J
Leach, C
Lochlier, ——
Martin, J.M
Martin, Joel
Martin, C.B
Martin, Daniel
Martin, Saml
Manville, A.T
Medlin, C
McPherson, S.
McPherson, W
McPherson, Jno
McGregor, P.C
Murrell, W.S
Medlin, P
Perry, J
Perry, C
Palmer, W.R

Pearson, Robt
Poag, R.P
Ramsay, J
Robertson, F.L
Ransom, Wm
Scarborough, Wm
Scott, J.R
Sheely, W.C
Sharp, G.W
Stubblefield, W.H
Tate, I.O
Vinson, Wm
Wailes, R
Wilson, K
Walker, C.A
Williamson, W.I
Woolen, James
Zesterfelt, F.

COMPANY "D."

Captains:
Richardson, Jno. S
Bartlett, L.W
Graham, I.D

First Lieutenants:
Wilder, J.D
Wilder, W.W
Jacob, I

Second Lieutenants:
Durant, T.M
Pelot, W.L
Rembert, L.M.

Third Lieutenants:
Nettles, J.H
Gardner, H.W.

Sergeants:
Gayle, I.P
Nettles, J.D
Hodge, J.W
Brennan, J.P
Bowman, S.J
McQueen, W.A
Pringle, S.M.

Corporals:
Wilson, S.T
Thompson, R.M
Gardner, A
Reams, H.M
Miller, J.I
Cole, S.R.

Privates:
Ard, J.P
Alsobrooks, J.E
Alsobrooks, Bog
Baker, W. T
Beard, D
Beck, I.S
Bradford, J.P
Brogdon, J.D
Brogdon, T. M
Brown, F.H
Brown, H.J
Browning, T.S
Brumby, G.S
Brunson, W.E
Brunson, W.J
Ballard, W.R
Blight, J
Burkett, I.L
Burkett, T.H
Brunson, I.R
Brown, S.J
Bird, J.P
Bass, S.C
Blanding, O
Britton, J.J
Caraway, P.T
Clyburn, B
Cook, W.H
Davis J.L
DeLorme, W.M
DeLorme, T.M
DeLorme, C
Dennis, John W
Dennis, J.M
Dennis, S.M
Dennis, R.E
Dennis, E.E
Dougherty, J
Dalrymple, S

Eubanks, A
Flowers, S.P
Flowers, T. E
Felder, W.E.A
Freman, I.H
Gallagher, P.B
Garden, H.R
Green, H.D
Graham, J.A
Gibson, H
Grooms, A
Haynsworth, J.H
Haynsworth, M.E
Hodge, I.B
Hodge, W.T
Holladay, D.J
Holladay, T.J
Huggins, W.H
Ives, J.E
Jenkins, W.W
Jackson, J.H
Jones, C.H
Jones, E.C
Jones, P.H
Kavanagh, T.D
Kelly, H.T
Kinney, Jno
Lesesne, J.I
London, Peter
Lynam, T.M
Lucas, A.P
Mellett, J.Y
McLaurin, J.C
McNeal, W.M
Moses, M.B
McKagan, G.P
Moses, H.C
Moses, Perry
Moses, Perry
Muldrow. I.R
Myers, R.C
Norton, J.J
Newman, S.I
O'Neil, W.J
Pry, J.C
Pool, W.M
Patterson, J.S

Ramsay, W.M
Redford, J.B
Richardson, G.
Rhame, J.F
Ross, D.J
Rodgers, I
Shaw, J.H
Scott, J
Sledge, W.A
Smith. F.H
Smith, T.J
Thompson, W.T
Troublefield, A.D
Troublefield, T.J
Troublefield. W.B
Vaughn, F.O
Watts, W.D
Wheeler. C.O
Wilson, C.A
Wilson, T.D
Witler, O
Wedekind, H
Wilder, Saml
Wilder, J
Frazer. J.B
Gilbert, J.C.T
Kirkland, J.G
McCoy, W.P
Myers, J.B
Richburg, J.B
Sims, E.R
Wells, J.A
Wilson, Robt
Hartley, T.J.

COMPANY "E."

Captains:
Kennedy, Jno. D
Leitner, Wm. S.

Lieutenants:
Dunlop, Josp. D
Sill, E.E
Drakeford, Jos. J
DePass, W.J
McKain, Jno. J

Riddle, James M.

Sergeants:
Dutton, W.C
Pegues, R.H
Hodgson, H.F
McKalgen, H.G
Ryan, D.R
Gerald, R.L
Nettles, Hiram.

Corporals:
Niles, A
Boswell, J.P
Perry, J.A
Honnet, B
Devine, F.G
Gardner. E
Polk, J.W.

Privates:
Allen, W.R
Ancrum, Thos. J
Arrants, J.H
Arrants, W.T
Arrants, R.H
Arrants, J.R
Barnes, J.B
Barnes, S.Y
Brown, John
Brown, Jas. R
Baum, Marcus
Buchanan. W.L
Baker, M
Beaver, Jno. R
Barrett, E
Barrington, J
Burchfield, E.C
Bowen, A
Bowen, W
Baer, B.M
Boykin, ——
Campell, Alex
Cook, M
Cook, J
Cook, John, Cook,
Joseph, Croft, J
Coker, R
Crump, T.M

Cusick, P
Cunningham, J.S
Cooper, J.C
Cooper, J.D
Crenshaw, W.J
Davis, J.T
DeBruhl, ——
Dunlap, E.R
Dunlap, C.J
Durant, J.A
Dawkins, W.B
Doby, A.E
Delton, B.Z
Evans, D
Evans, G
Elkins, E.E
Francis. Jno
Freeman, J
Freeman, M
Fullerton, G.P
Ford, A
Gardner, T.B
Gibson, H.B
Graham. D
Graham, T.T
Goens, E
Howell, M
Haile, J.S
Harrison, B
Heath, B.D
Hinson, J.E
Jeffers, L
Jinks, E.W
Johnson, W.E
Kendrick, James
Kelly, B.E
Kelly, D.H
Kirkland, R.R
Kirkley, R
King, G
Legrand, J.M
Leitner, B.F
Love, Wm
Love, L.W
Lawrence, E.H
Middleton, D.P
Munroe, G

Munroe, J
Munroe, Alex
Munroe, Jno
Mickie, Jno. P
Murchison, A.A
Moroh, L.C
Moore, Levi,
Maddox, Tom
McDaniel, I
Miller, J.A
McCown, J
McMillan, J
McKain, Wm
McIntosh, T.R
Means, S.B
McRea, D
Nelson, G
Nettles, W.N
Nettles, J.T
Nettles, J.E
Nettles, Joseph S
Pegue, C.J
Picket, J
Pope, T.W
Prichard, D
Proctor, R.W
Pennington, R.A
Pierson, P.J
Ryan, P.H
Rembert, T.M
Scarborough, H.G
Scarborough, L.W
Scott, Jno
Strawbridge, B.R
Small, R.E
Smith, Jno
Stokes, W
Smith, Geo
Smyth, J
Team, J
Tidwell, D
Turner, W
Vaughn, Lewis
Wethersbee, J.A
Wethersbee, T.C
Waner, J.O
Watts. Wm

Wilson, Roland
Wilson, T.R
Wilson, J.S
Winder, J.R
Witherspoon, T.M
Wood, J. Mc
Wood, Jno
Wood, Pinckney
Wells, D.E
Wright, W.H.

COMPANY "F."

Captains:
Perryman, W.W
McDowell, G.W
Vance, W. Cal.

Lieutenants:
Fouche, ——
Maxwell, J.C
McNeil, A
Parks, J.T
Adams, J.J
Koon, S.A
Lunbecker, W.A
Appleton W.L
Connor, G.W
Johnson, W.A.

Sergeants:
Moore, A.W
Fuller, H.F
Smith, J.W
Bond, S. Lewis
Brooks, Chas. E
Seaborn, ——

Privates:
Anderson, J.W
Anderson, James
Bailey, W.H
Benson, V.S
Blake, A.W
Burrell, W.J
Butler, Jno
Brooks, Stanmore,
Boozer, S.P

Boozer, William
Benson, Thos
Brownlee, J.A
Barratt, Jno. G
Bell, Wm. S
Bell, Wm. P
Carr, Jno. L
Chaney, Willis
Chaney, J.S
Chaney, R.E
Chaney, Ransom,
Cheatham, J.T
Cheatham, Jno
Crews, C.W
Crews, M.A
Carter, V.C
Creswell, I.D
Creswell, P
Caldwell, G.R
Chipley, W.W
Chipley, T.W
Cobb, C. A
Calvert, J.H
Crawford, H. Henry
Cason, Richard
Cason, J.F
Day, M
Davis, Dr. Frank
Davis, Jno. F.H
Deal, S.C
Douglass, W.W
Ellis, A.B
Fisher, C.D
Fouche, Jno
Fouche, Ben
Fuller, P.M
Fennel, J.L
Gilmer, Robt. P
Gilmer, Wm
Gillam, J.M
Griffin, V
Griffin, G.W
Grant, W.H
Grant, Jno
Goodwin, Jno
Hancock, W.H
Harris, G.M

Heffernan, J.L
Hearst, T.J
Hughey, J.E
Hughey, Fred. T
Hughey, N
Hodges, J.W
Harris, T
Hutchison, Soule,
Hutchison, Jno. W
Hutchison, R.F
Henderson, W.E
Hunter, W.C
Henderson, J.T
Ingraham, M.S
Jackson, C.
Johnson, F.P
Johnson, Saml
Johnson, J.W
Johnson, D.Q
Johnson, G. W
Jones, J.R
Johnson, J.W
Jones, C.C
Jones, Thomas
Jones, Willie
Jester, Benj
Lomax, W.G
Lenard, V.A
Lenard, J.J
Meriwether, W.N
Moreen, Jno. A
Milford, J.T
Marshall, G.W
McKellar, L.W
McKellar, G.W
McKellar, J.R
McCord, D.W
McNeill, H.B
McKensie, Jno
Major, R.W
Major, J.M
Moore, J.R
Moore, Robt
Moore, Henry
McCrary, B
Malone, A
Malone, Jno

Partlow, Jno. E
Powers, J.W
Pinson, A
Pinson, T.R
Pinson, Jno. V
Parks, Wm
Pelot, Dr. J.M
Rampey, G.W
Rampey, S.D
Reynolds, B
Reynolds, A.D
Reynolds, Jno. M
Roderick, W.F
Riley, E.C
Rykard, T.J
Riley, W.N
Rykard, L.H
Robertson, Jno
Ross, T.M
Ross, Jno
Ross. G.P
Ross, Wiley
Reed, J.S
Saddler, J.H
Saddler, Willis
Shadrick, W.S
Shepard, E.Y
Shepard, J.S
Selby, E.C
Selleck, C.W
Smith. R.G
Smith, T.N
Seal, J.R
Silk, Jas
Turner, J.S
Townsend, J.F
Turner, Ira
Teddards, D.F
Vance, J. C
Watson, G. McB
Waller, W.W
Waller, C.A.C
Walker, W.L
Wiss, E
Younge, J.C.

COMPANY "G."

Captains:
Haile, C.C
Clyburn, T.J.

Lieutenants:
Cantley, T. R
Jones, W.J.

Sergeants:
Cunningham, J.P
Tuesdale, J.E
Benton, F.J
Cauthen, A.J.

Corporals:
West, W.S
Coats, D.W
Jones, B.N
Williams, R.H
Jones, S.D
Kirkland, B.M.

Privates:
Alexander, J.H.R
Baskin, J.C.J
Blackburn, B.J
Blackwell, J.A
Boone. J
Boone. W
Boone, J.W
Bruce, J.H
Bowers, G.M
Baskin, C.E
Baskin, R.C
Bird, W.L
Blackmon, J.E
Blackmon, W.N
Belk. J.M
Cauthen, J.S
Coats, H.J
Coats, G.H
Copeland, W.W
Crawford, S
Chancy, B
Clark, J.W
Croxton, J. Q
Cook, J.E
Cook, T
Cato, A.D
Coon, S.S
Dixon, B.S
Dixon, F.L
Downs, A.J
Dixon, G.L
Davis, D
Davis, H.G
Davis, H
Dumm, J.W
Falkinberry, J.W
Falkinberry, W.J
Fletcher. D.G
Falkenberry, J
Fail, J
Gaftin, J.B
Gardner. R.C
Gray, W
Graham, J
Gaskin, D
Gaskin, J
Hall, J.D
Holly, J
Howie. F.P
Howie, S.D
Hough, N
Hough, J
Hough, W.P
Haile, G.W
Hunter, W.J
Johnson, W
Johnson, W.M
Johnson, A.A
Knight, J.A
Knox, W.L
Kelly, M.P
Kirby, J
Kirkland, R.R
Knight, W.A.
Love, McD. R
Mahaffy, W.W
Martin, J.S
Martin, W.H
Marshall, W.S
Marshall, J.S
Mosely, C
Mosely, F
Murchison, J.J
McLure, J
McDowell, J.E.C
McKay, H.C
Mahaffy, O.C
Mason, T.E
McMahan, A. W.
Marshall. W.D
Marshall, W.H
Mason, L.R
Nelson, T.J
Patterson, R.B
Patterson, W.W
Perry. T.J
Peach, W
Parker, B
Phaile, J
Powers, W.T
Philipps, W.P.
Redick. R
Reaver, D.R
Robertson, L.D
Robertson, E.H
Roe, J
Ray, D
Raysor, J.C
Rasey, B
Stover, D.G.
Sheorn, Morris D
Sheorn, James,
Sowell, J. A
Suggs, Wm
Button, E
Small, A.J
Trantham, W.D
Tuesdel, W.J
Tuesdel, B
Tuesdel, W.M
Tuesdel. H
Tuesdel, J.T
West, T.A
West, T.G
West, S
West, W.M
Williams, Jno
Williams, J. N

Williams, C.D
Wilkerson, J
Whitehead. S
Young, C.P
Young, G.W
Young, J.N
Young, W.C
Young, W.J.

COMPANY "H."

Captains:
McManus, A
Clyburn, B.R.

Lieutenants:
Perry, A. M
Welsh, S.J
Brasington, G.C
Reeves, T.J
Hinson, M.R.

Sergeants:
Perry, J.F
Gardener, S.C
Kennington, W.R
Williams, D. A
McKay, Dr. J.P
Ingram, I.N
Moody, J.J
Love, M.C
Sowells, W.S.

Corporals:
Baker, A.J
Small, J.M
Johnson, G.D
Johnson, D.G
Small, J.M
Douglass, S.A
Kelly, B.L
Cook, J.C
McHorton, W
Williams, T.E
Hilton, R.P
Boiling, R.A.

Privates:
Adkins, W.C
Baker, J.J.T
Baker, W
Bailey, J.D
Bailey, Jno
Bell, W.T
Bunnett, G.W
Bowers, N.H
Bowers, W. J
Brasington, W.M
Blackman, B
Bridges, P.H
Caston, W.J
Cato, R.E
Cauthen, G.L
Cauthen, L.D
Craige, W.M
Cauthen, J. M
Deas, A
Ellis, G.W
Ellis, W.W
Funderburk, W.B
Funderburk, J.C
Faulkenberry, J.T
Gardener, C.L
Gardener, S
Gardener, W.W
Gregory, W.T
Gregory, Willis
Harris, G.T
Harris, J. K
Harrell, D
Hilkon, T
Hinson, E
Hinson, W.L
Horton, A.J
Hough, M.J
Horton, W.C
Horton, J.B
Horton, J.T
Harvel, D. B
Jones, B.B
Johnson, J.D
Johnson, F.M
Johnson, D.T
Kennington, B.R
Kennington, R.W
Kennington, G.W
Kennington, J
Kennington, N
Kennington, R
Kennington, R
Kennington, W. J
Kennington, S.L
Knight, E.R
Lucas, M
Lowery, R.J
Lowery, W.W
Minor, L
Lyles, W.J
Lynn, W.T
Lathan, J.T
Lucas, J. R
Love, V.H
McManus, W.H
McManus. C.W
McManus, W.A
McManus, G.B
Neal, W.M
Perry, B.C
Phifer, W.T
Phillips, A
Phillips. J
Phillips. H.S
Phillips, A.L
Reaves, T.C
Robertson, W. U.R
Robertson, V.A
Reaves, J.J
Short, J.G
Small, J.M
Small, W.F
Sowell, S.F
Snipes, A
Sowell, A
Sodd, W
Swetty, A.M
Woeng. W.D
Welsh, T.J
Wilkinson, H.W
Williams, C.H
Williams, D.A
Williams, J.F
Williams, W.J
Wilson, G.B

Wright, W
Williams, A.M
Witherspoon, J.B.

COMPANY "I."

Captains:
Cuthbert, G.B
Elliott, R.E
Fishburn, Robt.

Lieutenants:
Holmes, C.R
Brownfield, T.S
Webb, L.S
Robinson, S
Darby, W.J
Brailsford, A.M
Bissell, W.S
Daniel, W.L.

Sergeants:
Wright, J.E
Lalane, G.M
Hanahan, H.D.

Corporals:
Boyd, J.B
Gaillard, T.E
DeSausure, E
Duttard, J.E
Bellinger, E. W
Mathews, O.D
Miller, R.S.

Privates:
Vincent, A.M
Artes, P.F
Bedon, H.D
Bellinger, J
Bellinger, C.C.P
Bird, J.B
Brownfield. R.I
Brailford, D.W
Brisbane, W
Bull, C.S
Baynord, E.M
Calder, S.C
Chaplain. D.J

Chaplain, E.A
Claney, T.D
Crawford, J.A
Cambell. J.E
Carr, J, T
Colcock, C.J
Davis, W.C
Dwight, C.S
Dyer, G.B
DeCavadene, F
Dupont, A
Elliott, W.S
Fludd, W.R
Farman, C.M
Gadsden, T.S
Galliard, T.G
Girardeau, G.M
Glover, J.B
Godfrey, W
Goodwin, J.J
Green, W.G
Hanckel, J.S
Hane, W.C
Harllee, J
Harllee, W.S
Harllee. P
Jackson, A
Jacobs, H.R
Kerrison, C
Kerrison, E
Larrisey, O
Lawton, W.M
Lawton, J.C
Miller, J.C
Mackey, J.J
Mackey, W.A
Mathews, P.F
Miller. A.B
Miller, P, G
Mills, E.J
Moses, J.L
Moses, P
Mortimer, Le. B
Munnerlyn, J.K
Mitchell, F.G
Myers. S.C
Montgomery, ——

McCoy, H.A
McLean, M.M
Pinckney, S.G
Palmer, J.J
Pinckney, H
Palmer, G
Palmer, K.L
People, H.M
Pendergrass, M.G
Prentiss, O.D
Prentiss, C.B
Ruffin, E
Ruffin, C
Raysor, J.C
Reeder, T.H
Rice, L.L
Rivers. R.H
Rivers. W
Roumillat, A.J.A
Royal, J.P
Sanders, A.C
Sanders, J.B
Shipman, B.M
Screven, R.H
Seabrook, J. C
Scott. M.O
Shoolbred, J
Shoolbred, R.G
Smith, G. McB
Stocker, T.M
Strobhart, James,
Thompson. T.S
Tillinghast, E.L
Trapier, E.S
Walker, W.A
Walker, W.J
Wescoat, W.P
Wescoat, T.M
Wickenberg, A.V
Zealy, J.E.

COMPANY "K."

Captains:
Rhett, A.B
Moorer, J.F
Webb, J

232

Dutart, J.E.

Lieutenants:
Elliott, W
Dwight, W.M
Lamotte, C.O
Edwards, D
Bradley, T.W.

Sergeants:
Fickling, W.W
Gilbert S.C
Webb J. J
Phillips, S.R
Fell, T.D
Hamilton, J
Phillips, L.R
Goldsmith, A.A
Moorer, R.G
Burrows, F.A
Williams, D.F
Wayne, R
Ferriera, F.C
O'Neill, E.F
Simmonds, J.R.

Corporals:
Purse, E.L
Lawson, P.A
Calvitt, W.L
Rushe, F.R
Sheller, D.A
Sparkman, A.J
Murphy, M
Plunkett, J
O'Neill, E.F
Heirs, G.S
Wooley A
Ackis, R.W
Autibus, G
Lord, R.

Privates:
Anderson, Wm
Allgood, J.F
Ackison, R.W
Allgood, J.L
Adams, D.A
Appleby, C.E

Baily, J
Barrett, R
Blatz, J.B
Brum, H
Brown, R.M
Brown. W
Brady, J
Buckner, J
Buckner, A
Buckner, J.A
Buckner, A.H
Burrows, F.A
Bruning, H
Ballentine, J.C
Byard, D.E
Bartlett, S.C
Bartlett, F.C
Boag, W
Braswell, T.T
Bell, C.W
Bell, W.P
Bull, C.J
Bull, E.E
Bazile, J.E
Bishop, J.S
Blume, C.C
Benson, J.N
Bailey, J
Bruce, J.H
Calvitt, W.T
Campsen, B
Casey, W.T
Conway, P
Cartigan, J.M
Cole, C
Cotchett, A.H
Creckins, A
Castills, M
Coward, R.M
Craige, W.S
Copeland, W.J
Deagen, P
Daly, F.R
Dillon, J.P
Dinkle, J
Dorum, W.D
Doran, J

Douglass, C.M
Day, M
Duncan, W.M
Estill, W
Elle, A
Tarrell, J.F
Ferria, R.C
Fisher, W.S
Fant, T.R
Furt, W
Fleming, A.H
Froysell, J.D
Gammon, J.E
Gammon, E.M
Goldsmith, A.A
Gibbs, W.H
Grubbs, W.L
Green, W.H
Grenaker, J.A
Griffeth, A
Gruber, J.T
Hammond, C.S
Hoys, T
Hibbard, F.C
Happoldd, D
Hoeffer, C.M
Haganes, H.C
Harris, J
Hendricks, J.A
Hendricks, M
Hunt, H.D
Hunt, J.H
Hunt, R
Hunter, T.T
Haigler, E.N
Haigler, W.L
Heirs, J.A
Howard, R.P
Hough, H.J
Heirs, G
Harley, J.M
Harley, P
Jones, G.T
Jones, D.H
Joseph, A.H
Jowers, J.P
Johnson, W.G

233

Kerney, G
Kelly, J.G
Kunney, A.A
Kennedy, J
Kennedy, H.R
Kennedy, J.A
Lavell, A.J
Lawson, T.A
Lonergan, J.D
Maher, E
Marshall, W
McCollum, E
Meylick, F.W
Meyleick, W
McKensie, A
McLure, A
Meyers, A.C
Murphy, M
Martin, W
McGellom, B
Martin, A
Moorer, R.A
Mitchel, D.H
Mitchel, F.G
Musgrove, W.W
Martin, J
Neill, R.T
Noll, C
Nicklus, J
Nevek, R.P
Nesmith, E.C

Nix, J.B
O'Neill, J
Oppenhimer, E.H
Oppenheimer, H. H
Platt, W.W
Philipps, L.R
Prace, A
Purse, E
Purse, W.G
Page, J.J
Phunkett, J
Pearson. J.H
Payne, J.P
Richardson, C.O
Ryan, T.A
Randolph, L.A
Robinson, S.L
Reentz, J.W
Righter, J.A
Reid, J.W
Reeves, J.P
Rushe, F.D
Schmitt, T
Scott, W
Shepard, D.H
Sammonds, J.R
Sporkman, A.J
Sellick, C.H
Street, E
Summers, E
Sutherland, J.P

Sherer, J.R
Sandifer, J
Shuler, S.N
Spillers, W.F
Schmitt, R
Smith, J.C
Simons, J.R
Smith, O.A.C
Thompson, M.N
Timmonds, G.C
Turner, J.W
Taylor C.M
Turner, C
Welmer, M.W
Wallace, J.L
Walsh, P
Wilkins, J.R
Wilkins, T.K
Willis. J.V
Watts, W.D
Williams, T. A
Weeks, T.S
Wolley, A
Wolly, H.A
Williman, W.H
Yates, M. J
Youngblood, J
Zimmerman, U.A
Zeigler, J.B.E.

Roll of Third South Carolina Volunteer Regiment

Colonels:
Williams, James H
Nance, James D
Rutherford, W.D
Moffett, R.C.

Lieutenant Colonels:
Foster, B.B
Garlington, B.C
Todd, R.P. Majors:
Baxter, James M
Nance, J.K.G.

Adjutants:
Rutherford, W.D
Pope, Y.J.

Majors:
Williams, J.W
Simpson, O.A
Garlington, J.D.

Quartermasters:
McGowan, Jno. G. (Captain)
Shell, G.W. (Captain)

Commissaries:
Hunt, J.H. (Captain),
Lowrance, R.N. (Captain)

Surgeons:
Ewart, D.E
Evans, James.

Assistant Surgeons:
Dorroah, Jno. F
Drummond, ——

Brown, Thomas

COMPANY "A."

Captains:
Garlington, B.C
Hance, W.W
Richardson, R.E.

Lieutenants:
Gunnels, G.M
Arnold, J.W
Garlington, H.L
Hollingsworth, J
Hudgens, W.J
Mosely, Jno. W
Shell, G.W.
Shell, Henry D
Simpson, C.A
Fleming, H.F.

Sergeants:
Simpson, T.N
Robertson, V.B
Wilson, T.J
Teague, A.W
Motte, Robert P
Garlington, Jno
McDowells, Newman
Griffin, W.D
Jones, P.C
Gunnels, W.M.

Corporals:
Mosely, R.H
Sullivan, W.P
Martin, R.J

Richardson, S.F
West, E
Atwood, I.L
Richardson, W.M.

Privates:
Anderson, D.A
Anderson, W.J
Allison, T.W
Anderson, W.Y
Allison, W.I
Adams, Jno. S
Atwood, W.M
Ballew, J.B
Ballew, B.F
Bass, John
Beard, W.F
Boyd, W.T
Black, W.E
Ball, J.S
Bolt, T.W
Bolt, W.T
Bolt, Pink
Bolt, John L
Bolt, H
Bradford, W.A
Bright, Jno. M
Beasley, B.H
Cason, W.B
Clark, J.Q.A
Campton, L.D
Crasy, J.B
Chappell, W.T
Day, N.T
Day, John,
Davenport, T.J

235

Donaldson, W.M
Davis, J.J
Donnon, J.M
Evans, Wm
Elmore, ——
Fleming, J.O.C
Finley, C.G
Finley, J.M
Finley, J.R
Franks, N.D
Franks, C.M
Franks, T.B
Franks, J.W.W
Gray, Duff
Gary, J.D
Going, Wm
Garrett, W.H
Garlington, S.D
Hall, J.F
Hance, Theodore
Ham, James E
Harrison, P.M
Harrison, J.A
Hill, L.C
Hellams, D.L
Henderson, W.H
Henderson, Lee A
Hix, E.M
Hawkins, J.B
Hix, W.P
Hix, Willis
Hix, C.E
Hudgens, J.M
Hudgens, J.H
Hudgens, W.H
Hudgens, J.B
Irby, G.M
Irby, A.G
Jennings, A
Jennings, R
Jenerette, Wm
Jones, B.P
Kirk, C.E
Lovelace, J.H
Monroe, W
Medlock, J.T
McKnight, H.W

McDowell. Baker
McCollough, J.L
Milan, Jno. A
Milan, W.W
Milan, M.F
McAbee, A
McAbee, ——
McAbee, ——
Metts, J.A
Miller, Harry
Neal, S.H
Nolan, Jno
Oliver, S.A
Odell, L.M
Parks, John M
Pinson, W.V
Pinson. W.S
Pinson, M.A
Pope, D.Y
Ramage, Frank
Robertson, Z
Robertson, A
Rodgers, W.S
Simpson, B.C
Simpson, R.W
Simpson, J.D
Simpson, O.F
Sullivan, M.A
Sullivan, J.M
Smith, P
Shell, Frank
Simmons, S.P
Sharp, A.L
Speke, S.A
Teague, Thomas J
Teague, M.M
Templeton, J.L
Templeton, P
Templeton, S.P
Templeton, W.A
Tribble, M.P
Tribble, J.C.C
Tobin, Thos. A
Todd, S.F
Vance, S.F
Vaughan, Jno
Winebrenner, George

Williams, Jno
Williams, W.A
Wilson, J.M
West, S.W.
West, Joseph
Wilbanks, John S
Woods, Harvey
Willis, E.R
Young, Martin J
Young, Robert H.

COMPANY "B."

Captains:
Davidson, Samuel N
Gary, Thomas W
Connor, Thompso

Lieutenants:
Hunter, W.P
Lipscomb, T.J
Buzhardt, M.P
Davenport, C.S
Pulley, S.W.

Sergeants:
Summer, M.B
Reeder, J.R.C
Moffett, R.D
Clark, J.P
Spears, L.M
Copeland, J.A
Peterson, W.G
Livingston, A.J
Smith, J.D
Bradley, E.P
Tribble, A.K.

Corporals:
Davis, T.M
Gary, Jno. C
Dean, Julius
Lark, Dennis
Chalmers, Joseph H
Anderson, W.A
Wallace, W.W
Spears, A.S
Perkins, H.S

Gibson, B.W
Workman, Robt
Stephens, P.J
Suber, Mid.

Privates:
Brooks, E.A
Burton, Kay
Butler, J.C
Bishop, W.F
Bishop, Jno
Bailey, A.W
Brown, D
Brown, J.A
Butler, E.A
Butler, J.N
Butler, B.R
Butler, D.M
Cannon, Isaac P
Crooks, L.T
Crooks, J.A.B
Chalmers, E.P
Craddock, D.F
Craddock, S
Chupp, J.G
Cole, John
Campell, Jno. B
Cleland, J.P
Clark, E.G
Connor, Robt
Clamp, D.L
Chappells, J.B
Davenport, H
Davenport, W.P
Davenport, E.W
Dalrymple, John
Davis, A.P
Davis, D.P
Davis, J.T
Dumas, J.H
Davenport, J.C
Floyd, Jno. S
Floyd, J.N
Gary, J.W
Gary, M.H
Gary, C.M
Gary, Jessie
Griffin, S.B

Griffin, W.B
Grimes, W.M
Grimes, T.A
Gibson, M
Gibson, W.W
Golding, James W
Golding, Jno. P
Galloway, Jno
Graham, T.J
Greer, R.P
Hopkins, G.T
Harp, David
Harmon, W.C
Harmon, H.T
Jones, J.S.B
Johnson, W
Johnson, W.R
James, W.A
King, W.H
Keller, W.J
Lank, J.W
Lyles, I.E
Livingston, H
Livingston, E
Longshore, E.C
Longshore, A.J
McKettrick, J.W
Middleton, J.H
Moates, J.L
Moates, F
Montgomery, G.B
McEllunny, R.N
Neel, J.M
Neel, T.M
Pitt. J.M
Pitt, W
Pitt, J
Pitt, D
Pitt, A.N
Reeder, A.M
Richey, E
Robertson, S.J
Reid, W.W
Reeder, W
Spruel, J.S
Spruel, W.F
Stewart, J.P

Senn, D.R
Satterwhite, R.S
Scurry, J.R
Sterling, G.P
Saddler, G.W
Suber, G.A
Suber, A
Thrift, C
Thrift, G.W
Templeton, R.W
Willinghan, W.W
Workman, J.A
Workman, J.M
Workman, H
Workman, P
Whitman, J.C
White, G.F
Wells, G.F
Waldrop. W.W
Williams, B.

COMPANY "C."

Captains:
Moffett, R.C
Herbert, C.W.

Lieutenants:
Moffett, D.S
Wilson, Jno. C
Culbreath, Joseph,
Speake, J.L
Piester, ——

Sergeants:
Kibler, A.A
Moffett, T.J
Cromer, E.P
Wilson, T.R
Long, G.F
Fellers, J.B.

Corporals:
Young, N.H
Boozer, D.W
Fulmer, J.B
Bowers, J.S
Sites, George,

Kelly, James M
Paysinger, S.S.

Privates:
Adams, W.H.
Albritton, Joseph
Banks, James C.
Baird, Henry
Baughn, Henry
Bouknight, F
Blair, T.S
Blair, J.P
Boland, S.D
Boland, James M
Boozer, C.P
Boozer, S.D
Boulware, I.H
Boyd, G.M
Cannon, H.D
Calmes, Jno. T
Calmes, Wash
Carmichael, J.D
Counts, W.F
Cromer, A.B
Crosson, H.S.N
Crosson, D.A
Crouch, Jacob
Crouch, Wade
Davenport, Wm
Davenport, J.M
Davis, Jno
Duncal, J.W
Dominick, D.W.S
Elmore, J.A
Enlow, Nathan
Ferguson, G
Fellers, J.P
Fellers, S.H
Folk, H.S
Frost, Eli
Gallman, D.F
Gallman, Henry G
Gallman, J.J
George, James M
George, N.B
George, L.O
Griffeth, G.W
Gruber, I.H

Grimes, Thos
Guise, Albert
Hair, J.B
Hartman, J.M
Hawkins, P.M
Hawkins, J.M
Hawkins, E.P
Hendricks, J.E
Herbert, J.W
Hussa, Carwile
Halfacre, D.N
Huff, Andrew
Kelly, J.H
Kelly, Y.S
Kelly, W.J
Kinard, Levi
Kibler, Levi
Kibler, I.M
Kibler, J.H
Kibler, H.C
Lane, G.G
Lane, W.R
Lester, Alen
Lester, Alfred
Lester, Charles
Long, A.J
Long, M.J
Long, L.W
Livingston, J.M
McGraw, P.T
McGraw, B.F
McCracken, L.C
McCracken, Jno
McNealus, Jno
Mansel, R.J
Moffett, R.D
Martin, Allen
Moon, Frank
Morris, S
Nates, J.C
Neill, J.B
Neill, J. Calvin
Neill, J. Spencer
Nelson, J.G
Paysinger, H.M
Paysinger, T.M
Pugh, Wm

Pugh, H
Quattlebaum, I.E
Quattlebaum, D.B
Rankin, A.J
Rankin, G.W
Rawls, S.
Sanders, Reagen James B
Reagen, H.W
Reagen, Jno. W
Reid, Newt
Reid, J.P
Richardson, D
Rikard, J.A
Rikard, J.W
Kinard, L.C
Sease, N.A
Sease, J. Luke,
Shepard, Jno. R
Seigman, Jesse E
Spence, Saml
Spence, Jno. D
Sligh, J.W
Sligh, D.P
Stillwell, J.T
Stockman, J.Q.A
Stribbling, J.M
Stockman, Jno. C
Stuart, W
Stuart, C.T
Sultan, R.J
Thompson, T.J
Whites, J.D
Werts, M
Whites, G.J
Werts, Andrew
Werts, Jno. A
Wilson, Wm
Willingham, Hav.

COMPANY "D."

Captains:
Fergerson, Thos. B
Walker, F.N.

Lieutenants:
Bobo, Y.J

Abernathy, C.P
Moore, J.P
Floyd, N.P
Ray, P. John
Walker, J
Henry, Allen
Wade, Gordon F.M
Bobo, Hiram.

Sergeants:
Campell, Levi
Allen, Garland Floyd
Chance, M
Ray, Hosea
Roy, Robt. Y
Ducker, H.W
Davis, M.M.

Corporals:
Abernathy, J.D.C
Hill, T.F.C
Dillard, Geo. M
Fergerson, Jno. W
Welburn, Robt. C.

Privates:
Allen, B.R
Bobo, J.P
Sardine, T.C
Barrett, J
Browning, Hosea
Carson, John
Cathcart, H.P
Cooper, J
Dodd, W.T
Cooper, T.M
Fergerson, H.T
Floyd, A.F
Floyd, J.M
Farmer, W
Fergerson, E
Franklin, Y.P
Farrow, A.T
Finger, Mark
Graham, Isaac
Graham, J.F
Gentry, J.W
Gentry. E
Huckaby, P

Hill, B.M
Hollis, P.W
Hembree, C.B
Andrew, ——
Jackson, Drewy
Graham, A
Kelly, Wm
Kelly, M
Lamb, Thomas
Lamb, Robert
Lynch, W.E
Lynch, A
Lynch, John
Lynch, B.S
Murphy, R.C
Myers, J.D
McCravy, A.F
McCravy, R.S
McCravy, Sam
Murray, Peter
Murray, F.H
Nix, Stephen
McMillen, Wm
Ramsay, Robt
Ramsay, P
Mullens, Wm
Pruitt, E.A
Pope, C
Poole, Robt
Smith, Caspar
Smith, Wm
Stephens, M
Stephens, J.F
Shands, Anthony,
Shands, Frank
Stone, T.B
Stearns, A.B
Shands, Saml
Pruitt, John
Sexton, J.W
Tinsley, J.L
Tinsley, A.R
Tinsley, J.P
Taylor, W.B
Varner, Andrew
Varner, M.S
Varner, J.W

Vaugh, Jas
Williams, C.M
Williams, J.D
Workman, H
Wesson, Frank
Woodbanks, Thomas,
Woodbanks, Jno
Lynch, Pink
Ray, Thos
Poole, Robt.

COMPANY "E."

Captains:
Nance, J.D
Nance, Jno. K.G
Wright, Robt. H.

Lieutenants:
Bailey, E.S
Moorman, Thos. S
Hair, Jno. S
Hentz, D.J
Haltiwanger, Richard,
Martin, J.N
James, B.S
Langford, P.B
Weir, Robt. L
Cofield, Jas. E.

Sergeants:
Pope, Y.J
Lake, T.H
Boyd, C.F
Chapman, S.B
Ruff, Jno. S
Kingore. A.J
Buzzard, B.S
Reid, H.B
Hood, Wm
Duncan, T.S
Rutherford, W.D
Paysinger, T.M
Thompson, W.H
Ramage, D.B
Leavell, R.A
Horris, T.J
Glymph, L.P

Sloan, T.G
Blatts, Jno
Harris, J.R.

Privates:
Abrams, J.N
Abrams, J.K
Abrams, C.R
Atchison, S.L
Atkins, R.W
Assman, H.M
Brandy, H
Bernhart, H.C
Blatts, W.H
Bell, Jno. F
Bruce, J.D
Boazman, W.W
Boazman, Grant
Eramlett, A.W
Boozer, D.C
Boozer, E.P
Boyd, M.P
Burgess, C.H
Brown, T.C
Brown, J.E
Blackburn, James
Bailey, A. Wm
Butler, J.C
Canedy, A.B
Clend, M.P
Caldwell, J.E
Collins, A.B
Clamp, G
Cameron, J.S
Cameron, J.P
Cromer, S.D
Davis, J.H
Davis, Jas
Davis, Jno
Derick, S.S
Duckett. Jno. G
Duckett, J.C
Duckett, J
Duckett. G.T
Faeir, W.Y
Fair, Robt
Faeir, G.A
Foot, M

Gary, J.N
Glasgow, L.K
Graham, C.P
Gall man, H
Harris, M.M
Hargrove, P.H
Hiller, S.J
Hiller, G.E
Haltin, Wm
Haltin, R
Johnson, J.A
Johnson, W
Kelly, I.J
Keom, G
Keney, G
Keitler, J.N
Lindsey, J
Lovelace, B.H
Lake, T.W
Lake, E.G
Lee, W
Lindsey, W.R
Marshall, J.R
Mayes, J.B
McCrey, S.T
McCaughrin, S.T
McMillen, W.J
Miller, J.W
Mathis, J.M
Marshal, J.L
Melts, W
Metts, McD
Metts, W.G
Murtishaw, S.W
Nance, A.D
O'Dell, I.N
Pratt, S
Price, S
Pope, B.H
Pope, W.H
Pope, T.H
Pope, H
Reid, J.M
Reid, W.W
Renwick, H
Ruff, J.H
Ruff, W.W

Ruff, J.M.H
Ruff, R.S
Rodlesperger, T
Rice, J
Riser, J.W
Riser, W.W
Riser, Joe, Ruff, M
Sligh, T.W
Sloan, E.P
Sligh, G
Sligh, W.C
Suber, W.H
Suber, G.B
Souter, F.A
Summer, F.M
Schumpert, B
Schumpert, P.L
Sawyer, F.A
Sultsbacer, W
Stribling, M
Scurry, D.V
Tarrant, W.T
Tribble, J.R
Turnipseed, J.O
Wheeler, D.B
Wright, J.M
Witt, M.H
Wilson, T.R
Wilson, C
Wood, S.J
Wingard, H.S
Wideman, S
Wilson, J.W
Willingham, W.P
Weir T.W
Willingham, ——
Zoblel, J
Hornsby, J.D
Harris, J.Y.

COMPANY "F."

Captain:
Walker, T.

Lieutenants:
McGowan, H.L

Williams, J.G
Loaman, S.

Sergeants:
East, I.H.L
Hill, J.C
Neil, W.W
Bailey, W.F
Gray, W.S
Madden, J
Wells, B.W.

Privates:
Alston, F.V
Andrews, H.A
Andrews, T
Ballew, R
Bryson, H.H
Byson, R
Boyd, W.M.J
Boyd, W
Bryson, H.J
Bryson, J.E
Byson, J.A
Burrill, B
Burrill, W
Byson, J.G
Boseman, L.J
Bale, A
Cannon, J.L
Cole, J
Conner, J.B
Coleman, O.A
Cook, M.C
Crisp, J.T
Crim, S.J
Cannon, L.A
Dogan, W.S
Dalrymple, T.E.J
Donald, T.P
Darnell, W.R
Davenport, W.R
Dobbins, J
Franklin, H.G
Franklin, J.N
Franklin, N
Feets, J
Fowler, P.O

Fuller, J.C
Fuller, J.N
Fuller, W
Furguson, J.W
Goodlett, S.P
Grant, M
Garlington, J.D
Hollingworth, J
Hitt, H
Hitt, B
Hitt, E
Jones, W
Johnson, H.S
Johnson, W.R
Johnson, Miller
Langey, B.P
Lindsay, J
Lindsay, A
Lowe, W.W
Lowe, P.W
Lake, J
Lake, Y
Madden, A
Madden, S.C
Madden, D.N
Madden, J.H
Madden, J
Martin, L
McGowan, J.S
McDowell, W
McGee, J
McCoy, A
McClure, D
McClure, W
McGowan, S
McWilliams, I
Mauldin, J
Monroe, W.E
Monroe, J.W
Morgan, J. C
Moore, H
Moore, E
Moore, G
Nabors, W.A.
Nichols, R.M
Nichols, T.D
Nichols, J

Nelson, A
Nelson, M
Neely, W
Nixon, W
O'Neal, J.B
Puckett, R
Pirvem, J.H
Pierce, C.E
Pills, J
Propes, M
Reid, M
Riddle, T.R
Riddle, J.S
Sadler, G.M
Shirley, J
Smith, T.M
Sincher, T
Sparks, S
Vance, W.A
Waldrop, T.M
Walker, J.P
Winn, J
Wilbur, J.Q
Waldrop, E
Wilson, C
Watson, S.

COMPANY "G."

Captain:
Todd, R.P.

Lieutenants:
Burnside, A.W
Barksdale, J.A
Watts, J.W.

Sergeants:
Wright, A.Y
Garlington, J.D
Winn, W.C
Sanford, B.W
Parley, H.L.

Corporals:
Owengs, A.S
Brownlee, D.J.G
McCarley, T.A

Patton, M.P
Thompson, A.G.H
Templeton, D.C.

Privates:
Avery, T.M
Avery, F.H
Adams, W.A
Ball, W.H
Ball, H.P
Barksdale, A
Barksdale, T.B
Barksdale, M.S
Branks, C.B
Brooks, L.R
Brooks, W.J
Bendle, R.T
Byrant, R.F
Blackaby J.L
Burns, B.F
Burns, J.H
Brownlee, J.R
Brumlett, C
Childress, D
Childress, W.A
Cook, Geo
Curry, J.A
Curry, T.R
Curry, W.L
Curry, J.P
Crisp. J
Coleman, J.D
Chisney, W
Chisney, J.N
Chisney, N
Chisney, R.J
Chisney, G
Craig, J
Chick, W
Coley, R.B
Dorroh, J.A
Dorroh, J.R
Dorroh, J.W
Dial, J
Edwards, L.L
Edwards, M
Evins, H.C
Fairbairn, E.J

Fairbairn, J.A
Fairbairn, J.D
Franks, B.T
Franks, S
Franklin, W
Fleming, M
Fuller J
Grumbles, R.P
Garrett, H.M
Harris, R.T
Hellams, J.T
Hellams, R.V
Hellams, W.R
Hellams, R.T.
Hellams, W.H
Henderson, T.Y
Henry, I.F
Henry, S.P
Hill, D.S
Higgins, R.J
Higgins, R.J
Higgins, J.B
Hunter, J.P
Hobby, J.A
Jones, E
Knight, J
Knight, R.S
Lamb, W
Lanford, J.M
Landford, P
Lindsey, E.E
Lanford, E.L
McNeely, A.Y
Martin, J.A
Martin, B.A
Martin, M.P
Martin, M.G
Martin, J
Martin, J.A
Morgan, W.B
Morris, W.H
McClentock, W.A
Maddox, J. A
Simpson, W.W
Simpson, A
Simpson, S
Stoddard, D.F

Stoddard, J.F
Stoddard, D.C
Stoddard, A.R
Stewart, J.C
Summers, W.W
Smith, R
Shockley, J.W
Stone, E
Shesly, E
Templeton, J.P
Thackston, E.R
Thackston, S.R
Thompson, I.G
Thompson, W
Thompson, A.Y
Thompson, W.F
Townsend, J
Vonodore, J
Wadell, A.J
Wadell, J.T
Wine, A.W
Wilson, T.C
Witte, J.B. H
White, J.K
Workman, J.M
Wofford, B.H.

COMPANY "H."

Captains:
Nunnamaker, D
Summer, J.C
Swygert, G.A
Dickert, D.A.

Lieutenants:
Epting, J.H
Nunnamaker, S
White, U.B
Fulmer, A.P
Huffman, J.

Sergeants:
Hipp, A.J
Derrick, F.W
Kesler, W.A
Swindler, W.C
Werts, A.A

Haltiwanger, J.S
Wheeler, S
Kempson, L.C.

Corporals:
Weed, T.C
Busby, W.A
Stoudemire, J.A.W
Mayer, J.A
Counts, W.J
Werts, W.W
Guise, A.

Privates:
Adams, M
Addy, J.M
Burrett, J
Burkett, H
Boozer, L
Boozer, B.F
Boozer, D.T
Bedenbaugh, L
Bundric, T.J
Busby, J.L
Busby, L
Busby, W
Cannon, J.J
Caughman, L
Chapman, H. H
Chapman, D
Chapman, B.F
Cook, J.S
Comerlander, M
Corley, F
Dawkins, J.D
Dickert, J.O
Dickert, B.F
Dickert, C.P
Dominick, H
Dreher, D.J
Dreher, T
Derrick, A
Ellisor, C.G
Ellisor, G.M
Ellisor, G.P
Ellisor, J.T
Enlow, B
Epting, J

Fulmer, H.J
Fulmer, G.W
Fulmer, J.E
Frost, E
Folk, S.H
Farr, J
Feugle, J.N
Fort, H.A
Green, W.T
Gibson, A
Guise, N.A
Geiger. W.D
George, J
Gortman, M
Hamiter, J.H
Haltiwanger, J.L
Haltiwanger, A.K
Hartman, S
Hobbs, L.P
Hipp, W.W
Hipp, J.M
Hipp, J.J
Hiller, G
Jacob, W.A
Kelly, B
Kinard, J.J
Kunkle, H.L
Koon, G.W
Long, H.M
Long, D.S
Long, D.P
Long, G.A
Long, J.H
Long, G
Long, J
Lake, T
Lake, E.J
Livingstone, J
Livingstone, S
Livingstone, M
Lester, G
Lever, C
Mayer, A.B
Miller, A.B
Miller, J
Miller, L
Monts, J.W

Monts, T
Monts, N
Monts, F
Monts. J
Martin, A
Metts, T
Nunnamaker, T.C
Rucker, W
Russell, L.F
Rikard, L
Riser. R.E
Summer, J.G
Summer, W
Summer, P
Summer, J.B
Summer, J.K
Summer, A.J
Stoudemire, G.W
Stoudemire, R.T
Smith, S.H
Smith, J.A
Shealy, P.H
Schwarts, G
Schwarts, H.C
Sease, A.M
Slice, G.N
Slice. R
Setzler, W
Setzler, J.T
Spillers, I
Stuck, G.M
Stuck, M.C
Swetingburg, D.R
Suber, A
Thompson, P
Wilson, H.C
Wilson, A.A
Werts, A
Werts, W.A
Werts, J
Werts, W.A
Werts, T
Weed, W
Wheeler, L.B
Youngener, G.W
Yonce, J
Yonce, W.

COMPANY "I."

Captains:
Jones, B.S
Langston, D.M.H
Pitts, T.H
Johnson, J.S.

Lieutenants:
Harris, N.S
West, S.L
Byrd, W.B
Belk, W. B
Duckett, T.J.

Sergeants:
Henry, D.L
Williams, E
McLangston, G
Byrd, A.B
Copeland, D.T
Berkley, T
Adair, J.W.

Corporals:
Maylan, P
Blakely, M
Goodwin, R
Butler, P.M
Blakely, W.

Privates:
Arnant, ——
Atrams, R
Anderson, J
Anderson, W
Anderson. M
Byrd, G
Byrd, J.D
Beasley, G
Bell, J.L
Bell, J.E
Blakely, E.T
Blakely, M.P
Richmond, ——
Boyce, C.B
Brown, J
Bearden. T
Compton, E

Canady, J.W
Craige, G
Cannon, H
Casey, C.C
Campbell, P
Dillard, G.W
Donnon, G.M
Donnon, W
Duval, C.W
Davis, W
Ferguson, J.G
Ferguson. C.C
Foster, J.F.M
Gordon, M
Graham, D
Hill, S
Holland, J.G
Holland, R. R
Hollingsworth, F
Hollingsworth, J
Hanby. J.W
Harris, F
Holland, W
Hewett, F.M
Hemkapeeler, C
Hipps, R
Hipps, C.M
Hirter, M
Huskey, W
Henry, J.E
Huckabee, J
Jones, A
Jones, R. F
James, Z
Johnson, R.C
Jacks, I
King, A.A
Langston, J.T
Lyles, P
McKelvy, J
Maddox, W.C
McInown, M.M
Meeks, T
Mars, N
McDowell, J.T.B
McMakin, G
Merton, G.

Newman T. D
Neal, S.H
Owens, T
Oxner, J.T
Prather, G
Prather, N.C
Powell, A
Powell, R.
Potter, M
Pearson. J.P
Philson, S.P
Philips, A.N
Ramage, J.W
Ray, W
Reynolds, M
Suber.M
Suber, M
Stokes, T
Stokes, W
Sneed, C
Simpson, J.M
Snook W. M
Smith, J.C
Taylor, W.J
Taylor.H.S
Templeton, A
Templeton, H
Templeton, J
Talleson, J
Talleson, J
Todd, N.C
Todd, S. A
Thaxton, Z.A
Willard, J
Young, G.R
Zeigler, ——

COMPANY "K."

Captains:
Kennedy, B
Lanford, S.M
Poster, L.P
Young, W. H
Cunningham, J.H
Roebuck, J.P.

Lieutenants:
Wofford, J.W
Wofford, J.Y
Bearden, W
Layton, A.B
Thomas, W
Smith, R.M.

Sergeants:
Bray, D.S
Wofford, W.B
Thomas, J.A
Varner, C.P
McArthur, J.N
Jentry, J.L.

Corporals:
Vise, James S
Nesbitt, W. A
Smith, W.A
Davis, A.F
James, G.W
Lanford, F.M
Pettitt, N. H
Roundtree, J.R
Smith, A.S
West, T.H
Bass, J.B.C.

Privates:
Bass, G.W
Beason, B.S
Beason, B
Bishop, J.W
Beard, J.C
Brewton, I
Brice, D
Birch, F.C
Bearden, W.S
Barnett, W.H
Bearden, G
Cook, N
Cunningham, H.W
Chunmey, G. W
Chunmey, J
Drummond, R.A
Elmore, J.H
Foster, J.A
Gwinn, C.T

Gwinn, D
Gwinn, M
Gwin, J
Harmon, T.P
Harmon, J
Harmon, W
Havener, J.P
Hyatt, G.T
Hyatt, J
Hamby, J.H
Hill, L
Johnson, J.A
Lanham S.W.T
Lawrence, W
Lancaster, W.H
Marco, J.J
Mattox, P
Mayes, S.S
Mayes, D.W
Mayes, W.J
Meadows, T.M
Meadows, T.S
McAbee, W
McAbee, J
McDonald, J.E
McArther, J
Pearson, J.W
Petty, T
Petty, P
Pettis, B.F
Pearson, H
Roundtree, J.S
Riddle, J.M
Riddle, T
Rogers, M
Rogers, J
Rogers, E
Rogers, W
Rogers, G
Roebuck, B.F
Roebuck, J
Roebuck, W
Sammonds, G
Shackleford, J.L
Stribblan, A.C
Stribland, S
Stribland, J

Shands, B.A
Shands, S
Stallions, J
Smith, B.M
Smith, S
Smith, E.F
Smith, Robt
Smith, W.P
Sherbutt, W.T
Sherbutt, S.Z
Sherbutt, A.T
Slater, Jno
Story, G.H
Storey, D.G
Story, J.S
Thomas, T.S
Thomas, L.P
Thomas, W
Thomas, M
Turner, J
Vehorn, W.J
Vaughan, L
Vaughan, J
Varner.R
Williams, R.M
Wofford, B
Wofford, W.T
Wofford, J.H
Wofford, W.A
West, T.J
West, G.W
West.E.M
West, H
Wingo, H.A
White, R.B
Westmoreland, S.B
Wright, W.M
Woodruff, R
Zimmerman, T.H.

Roll of Seventh South Carolina Volunteer Regiment

Colonels:
Bacon, T.G
Aiken, D.W
Bland, Elbert.

Lieutenant Colonel:
Fair, R.A.

Majors:
Seibles, E
Hard, J.S.

Adjutant:
Sill, T.M.

Quartermaster:
Lovelace, B.F.

Commissary Sergeant:
Smith, Fred.

Surgeons:
Dozier, ——
Spence, W.F
Horton, O.R.

Assistant Surgeons:
Carlisle, R.C
Stallworth, A.

Chaplain:
Carlisle, J.M

COMPANY "A."

Captains:
Bland, Elbert
Harrison, S.

Lieutenants:
Bland, J.A
Wenner, M.B.

Sergeants:
Addison, H.W
Bert, A.W
Smiles, N.G
Connels, J.R
Gregory, R.

Corporals:
Cogburn, R.M
Mathis, C.A
Regan, B.G
Fair, W.B
Hill, T.T
Butler, E.S.

Privates:
Aultman, Jno
Aultman, J
Burton, T
Boatwright, B
Boyce, W.G
Broadwets, T.A
Brown, J.J
Brown, J.C
Bryant, H.G
Barnett, W.H
Carpenter, J
Cogburn, B.J
Cogburn, W.H
Crawford, W
Courtney, J.G
Casar, E.H
Casar, C.G.D
Casar, J.L
Carson, H
Cushman, C.B
Daily, R.J
Day, J.S
Davis, E.G
Day, J.S
DeLoach, J
Dunagant, J
Easley, J
Edison, W.M
Elsman, J.E
Fair, J.E
Glover, A
Glover, R.J
Gomillian, L
Gray, H.C
Green, J
Green, M
Hagood, J.V
Walsenback, L
Horn, J.S
Johnson, L.S
Johnson, D.F
Johnson, D.W
Jones, S.A
Jones, F.A
Kirksey, W.H
Legg, E.W
Littleton, L.W
Libeschutts, M
Long. W.R
Lott, G.H
Lovelace. G.C
Miles, C.L

Miles, A
Miles, S
Mims, R.S
Minis, W.D
Mobley, G.S
Mobley, S.C
McDaniels, F.S
McGeires, Charley,
Nichholson, J.A
Perin, J.D
Powell, R
Prescott, H.H
Prescott, S.J
Radford, J.A
Radford, A
Raney, D.D
Randall. F.E
Riddle, S
Robertson, J.F
Rodgers, C.E
Ryon, S.D
Salter, G.P
Salter, J.R
Samuel, W
Smith, W.J
Smith, D.W
Smith, F.L
Sheppard. S
Stevenson, T
Sweringer, R
Swearinger, A.S
Snelgrove. J.F
Toney, Ed
Turner, H.R
Walker, P.E
Whitlock, W
Whitlock, G.W
Whitman, S.
Weathelsy, L
Williams, G.D
Williams, R.R
Williams, W.B.F
Williams. D.S
Willing. R
Willing, J
Woolsey, J.D
Wright, W.M

Wright, J.H.

COMPANY "B."

Captains:
Mattison, G.M
Hodges, W.L
Hudgens, T.A
Townsend, J.A.

Lieutenants:
Clinkscales, E.B
Townsend, I.F
Hodges, J.F
Klugh, P.D
Hodges, J.R
Callahan, S.W
Hodges, W.C.C.

Sergeants:
McGee, J.S
Riley, W
Agnew, J.A
Henderson, J.W
Franklin, T
Stevenson, F.A
Rolinson, C.

Corporals:
Norris. E.B
Sitton, J.Y
Mathis, J
McGee, A.C
Dolan, F
Tribble, D.A
Dunn, R.H
Brown, J.N
Pruitt, F.V.

Privates:
Armstrong, J.C
Armstrong, W.C
Austin, J.H
Ashley, J.S
Anderson, J.C
Alguny, II
Ashley, W.S
Allen, A
Bowles, I.W

Bowle, H.W
Bowle, E.B
Bowen, S.M
Bowen, J.O
Barmore, W.C
Bailey, J.M
Brownlee, J.R
Bramyon, T.M
Bell, F.M
Bryant, H
Coleman, T.J
Calvert, J.M
Cochran, R.M
Carpenter, T.J
Cromer, A.F
Callahan, M
Callahan, W.N
Coleman, J.T
Clark, H.B
Cowen, J.W
Davis, S.J
Davis, I.W
Davis, T
Davis, W.Y
Davis, J.A
Deal, M.L
Donald, J.L
Drennan, L.O
Duncan, W.P
Duncan, J.B
Duncan, D
Ellison, S
Graham, J.M
Graham, B.C
Graham, E.C
Griffen, J
Gilmore, J.W
Grimes, W.B
Hemphill, R.R
Hinton, A
Hughes, H.H
Hawthorn, H.B
Hawthorn, C.
Hawthorn, L
Hodges, C.R
Harris, J.N
Harris, W.M

Kay, W.A
Killingworth, W.P
Kirly, B
Latimer, S.N
Lindsay, A.B.C
Long, G.W.M
Long, H.J.S
Lovelace, R
Martin, J.R
McAdams, R.V
McAdams, W.N
McAdams, A.J
McDowell, W.N
McCown, J
McWhorter, J.R
McGee, J.M
Moore, T
Moore, R
Moseley, W.L
Nabors, A
Owens, S
Owens, V
Owens, W
Owens, D.B
Peeler, J.W
Pratt, T.W
Pratt, W.A
Pruitt. J.J
Pruitt, W.A
Robinson, R.A
Strickland, W.A
Sharp, M.C
Simpson, J.H
Stone, J.E
Stone, R.P
Seawright, J.B
Straborn, R
Shirley, G
Seawright, R.W
Smith, R.N
Taylor, J
Timms, J.T
Vandiver, E.W
Wakefield, J.A
Ware, W.A
Ware, R.A
Waddell, G.H

Webb, J
Weir, W.A
Whitelock, F
Wilson, J.S
Wilson, J.L
Wilson, John S
Williamson, J.A
Williams, J.F
Williams, G
Young, J.V
Young, L.J
Young, I.B
Young, J.C.

COMPANY "C."

Captains:
Bradley, P.H
Cothran, W.E
Palmer, N.H
Lyons, John.

Lieutenants:
Thayler, A.T
McClain, T.E
Childs, T.M
Calhoun, J.S
Rodgers, T.A.

Sergeants:
Hearst, J.W
Edmonds S.F
Corley, J.A
Gray, T.C
Bradley, T.C
Quarles, T.P
Robinson, J.P
Martin, J.C
Newby, E.G
Willis, J
Brown, J.S.

Corporals:
Pennal, C.D
Lyon, J.F
Joy, D.W
Weed, R
Walker, W.

Privates:
Adamson, J.L
Aiken, A.M
Ansley, J.A
Bosdell, I.S
Bosdell, S.E
Boisworth, J
Bouchilson, T.M
Baker, W
Benson, W
Bradley, W
Bradley, J.E
Bellot, J.E
Blackwell. J
Berdashaw, W.J
Butler, W
Belcher, J.C
Bond, I.C
Burns, M
Brugh, T.J
Barksdale, W
Barksdale, J
Barksdale, B.B
Barksdale, T.W
Banks, G.M
Banks, W.W
Banks, C.C
Barksdale, G.T
Belcher, H.C
Corroll, V
Chamberlain, W
Childs, T.W
Cook, W
Cook, F.L
Connor, A.P
Crose, W.M
Cook, T.W
Childs, T.C
Calhoun, E
Davis, P
Devlin, J.A
Devlin, W.P
Derracort, W.G
Drennan, D.H
Dowtin, D.W
Elkins, W
Eunis, G

Edmonds, W.F
Edwards, W.W
Edmonds, T.J
Finley, J.C
Gillebeau, J.C
Gillebeau, P.D
Hill, J.W
Harris, S.N
Holloway, J.L
Harrison, J
Knox, S
Kennedy, J.M
Kennedy, W.P
Link, J.J
Link, S.C
Link, W.T
Lyon, J.E
Lyon, L.W
Leak, T.N
Lyon, R.N
Lands, W
Ligon, T.C
Lamonds, J.F.A
LeRoy, J.N
Martin, G.W
Martin, P.C
McKettrick, J
McClinton, J
McQuerns, J.A
McKinney, W.W
McKinney, J
McKelvey, W.H
McCaslan, G.D
Morrow, W.B
Morrow, J.A
McClain, R
Noble, E.P
McGowan, O
New, F
Noble, J.S
O'Neill, P
Palmer, W.O
Pennal, J.E
Paris, H
Rodgers, M.J
Robinson, P.H
Russell, J.R

Reagan, Y.P
Seigler, J.A
Sibert, J.H
Shoemaker, A.M
Scott, C
Tennant, G.C
Tennant, P
Turnage, J
Traylor, A.A
Wells, W.H
Wideman, J.J
Wilson, J.L
Willis, W.W
Willis, J.P
Wideman, C.A
Zimmerman, D.R
Zimmerman, J.H.

COMPANY "D."

Captains:
Hester, S.J
Allen, T.W.

Lieutenants:
Owen, J.T
Carlisle, J.C
Power, E.P
Carlisle, R.H
Prince, H.M
Cunningham, J.R
McGee, M.M.

Sergeants:
Kennedy, J.T
Allen, J.B
Hester, J.J
Clark, A.D
Gibert, J.S
McCurne, W.L
Clinkscales, L.C.

Corporals:
Norwood, O.A
Bowen, L.M
Boyd, D
Barnes, A.J.

Privates:

Alewine, J.H
Allen, J.B
Allen, S
Burress, W
Bell, J.H
Bass, J
Black, J.P
Boyd, R.P
Brooks, R.H
Brooks, J.M
Bowen, L
Bowen, W
Burton, R.H
Barnes, J
Barnes, W
Basken, J.F
Beaty, W
Caldwell, E
Cowen, H.F
Cromer, H
Cunningham, J.D
Clark. A.D
Campbell, W.H
Campbell, M.B
Calhoun, J.C
Calhoun, W.N
Carmbe, J
Clinkscales, W.R
Davis, B.A
Danelly, J
Dunlop, W
Edwards, E.E
Edwards, F
Freeman. H
Freeman, R.V
Fleming, W
Frisk, J
Hogan, J
Hogan, W.A
Hall, Tuck
Hall, A
Hall, H
Harkness, W.B
Haddon, S.P
Hill, J.A
Huckabee, J.P
Hester, J.J

249

Hutchinson, B.F
Hodges, W.A
Hunter, T
Johnson, G.W
Jones, C.C
Kennedy, L.D
Kennedy, I
Kennedy, J.T
Kay, W.A
Longbridge, W.S
Longbridge, L.L
Latimer, W.A
McCurrie, M.C
McCurrie, W
Mauldin, A
Mauldin, H
McDaniel, ——
Morrow, W.R
Martin, H
Melford, C
Moore, T.A
McComb, J.F
McAdams, S.T
Newby, J.N
Norwood, O.H
Oliver, P.E
Presly, R.A
Powell, J.W
Russell, W.H
Ritchie, W
Ritchie, J.A
Starks, J.S.H
Sanders, J.W
Sanders, J
Shaw, J.A
Shaw, J.C
Shoemaker, A.M
Scott, J.E
Scott, J.J
Stevenson, J.E
Speers, E.H
Taylor, E.M
Taylor, M.T
Watts, A
Williams, B.W
Wilson, J.

COMPANY "E."

Captains:
Denny, D
Mitchell, J.

Lieutenants:
Rutland, W.A
Daniel, J.M
Pinson, J
Denny, J.W.

Sergeants:
Roach, J.C.H
Suddath, J.B
Denny, A.W
Coleman, M.W
Mitchel, E.

Corporals:
Powe, J
Smith, L.A
McGee, U.R
Padgett, E.

Privates:
Black, H
Black, J
Black, X
Crouch, W
Crouch, T.B
Crouch, H
Crouch, J.L
Crouch, R
Crouch, M
Crout, Q
Corley, J.M
Corley, J
Corley, F
Cooner, W.E
Chapman, J
Cash, R.F
Denny, G.W
Denny, J.O
Denny, J.M
Derrick, J
Dougalas, J
Douglass, W
Etheredge, W

Etheredge, W
Etheredge, N
Etheredge, H.C.
Etheredge, G.M
Edwards, J
Geiger, J
Geiger, D
Goodwin, W
Goff, J
Hughes, C.W
Inabinett, J
Little, W
Lott, L
Marony, A
Mitchell, P
Mitchell, W.A
Mitchell, J
Murich, J
Merchant, J.W
McCorty. D.D.W
McLendon, I
Parson, R
Penson, J.R
Powe, J.R
Padgett, E
Ridlehoover, W
Rodgers, F
Ramage, J.C
Ridgell, W
Ridgels, J
Ridgers, D
Story, ——
Smith, G.W
Smith, L.L
Smith, J.H
Smith, W.W
Shealy, J
Sheeley. A
Sheely, A
Samples, W.E
Saulter, J
Thompson, J
Thompson, J
Vansant, J.T
Vansant, H
Venters, W
Watson, M.B

Watson, J.L
Watson, N
Walker, R
Whittle, W
White, L
Yarbrough, J
Yarbrough, M.

COMPANY "F."

Captains:
Harde, J.S
Harden, J.E
Brooks, W.D
McKibbin, Mc.

Lieutenants:
Jennings, T.A
Greggs, J.B
Sentell, J.L
Baker, G.W
Wise, L.W
Hard, B.W.

Sergeants:
Matthensy, N.O
Gullege, T
Davis, J
Howard, H.H
Cobb, R.

Corporals:
Stevens, H.M
Rearden, W.E
Athenson, G.E
Odom, M
Readen, R.W.

Privates:
Athenson, J.L
Aulmond, J.R
Autmond, T
Arther, W.B
Baggate, E
Beck, W
Brown, J
Brown, J
Brown, M
Bagwell, L.B

Brewer, G.A
Brooks, G
Bland, L
Brooks, R
Cawall, W
Corten, J.A
Cashman, R
Cash, W
Cochran, G
Corley, J
Clark, H
Donold, R
Dickens, E
Davis, B
Duncan, J
Duncan, R
Davis, J
Duncan, B
Ellis, W
Friday, P.A
Faulklan, T
Faulkner, W.P
Franklan, A
Fagin P
German. W
Galledge, H
Galledge, Wm
Gissus, J
Henderson, C.R
Hall, J.C
Hamonett. W.P
Hatcher, W
Hawistow, S
Jackson, J
Jackson, J
Jackson, D.L
Johnson, E
Johnson, A.L
Kirksey, W.J
Key. J.A
Lacks, W
Lispard, W
Littleton. L
Lawrence. W
Lesoard, E
Maddox, J
Maddox, G

Maddox, J
Maddox, M
Medlock, B
Maddox, B
McKee. G.W
Myers, W
McGee, J.W
McKenzie, W
Mathews, M
Mathis, M
McKennie, M
McGee, J
New, J
New, E
New, J
Overstreet, J
Price, J.D
Platt, G.W
Parker, A
Prescott, L
Perden, G
Parker, J
Pruce, T
Radford, S
Ramsey, J.A
Ramsey, M
Rannold, E
Sharpton, B
Smith. W
Seigler, E
Stringfield, E
Seigler, A.S
Serger, W.B
Serger, B.F
Seitzes, J
Tarner, H
Tollison, T.P
Taylor, J.A
Taylor, B.F
Wade, H
West, W.A
Wicker, A
Walker, W.

COMPANY "G."

Captains:
Brooks, J.H
Clark, W.E
Kemp, J.W
Williams, J.C.

Lieutenants:
Edson, J.W
King, H.C
Strothers, G.J
Strothers, R.C.

Sergeants:
Youngblood, R.S
Calbreath, H.C
Griffen, J.W
Ouzts, M
Rambo, J.C
Clarey, R.C
Durst, T.W
Wrighlet, J.K
Calesman, D
Williams, C.T.

Privates:
Adams, S
Adams, H.W
Actoin, J.S
Actons, W.J
Atom, R
Attaway, S.C
Attaway, T
Bagwell, W
Boom, B.F
Boulware, J.S
Branson, T.N
Brooks, J.S
Brooks, L
Bryan, A.M
Bryan, R.C
Burkhalter, M.R
Burnett, J.L
Burnett, H
Clark, G
Clark, V
Clary, W.M
Coleman, J.S

Croach. D.H
Crawford, W.A
Dees, H.C
Dogen, H.C
Dogin, W
Dorn, D
Dorn, H
Duffy, J
Duffy, J
Edison, W.A
Edison, L
Foosher, B
Fell, J
Gasperson, J.B
Gentry, J.W
Grant, J.W.D.
Gragary, J
Griffeth, A.B
Griffeth, M.A
Haltiwanger, G
Hamilton, G.W
Hamilton, J.P
Hargrove, A
Hardy, M
Heard, Wm
Holloway, D.P
Holloway, R.C
Hollingsworth, J.A
Hudson, J.W
Jay, J
Jay, J
King, W.D
King, A.P
Koon, L
Lamb, B
May, J.A
Mannous, W.A
Neil J.W
Neil, M.W
Odum, W.L
Ouzts, F
Ouzts, W.H
Palmer, W.C
Procter, J.M
Quattlebaum, J.A
Reaves, G.E
Rhodes, J.B

Reley, J.M
Roton, J
Rushton, J.M
Rushton, W.M
Rushton, W.M
Rushton, D
Seatel, J.R
Smith, J.W
Smith, L.R
Smith, G
Stalworth, A.C
Steadman, J.C
Steadman, H
Steifle, H.C
Stevens, B.T
Stevens, R
Tompkins, J
Townsend, F.A
Turner, R.P
Turner, G.W
Turner, S
Turner, G
Turner, Wm
Walker, E.P
Walton, ——
Wallington, W.J
Wheeler, Wm
Whatley, J.P
Willingham, J
Williams, H.
Williams, P
William, T.H
William, M.P
Williams, W
Worter, L
Wright, J.H
Wright, W.H
Youngblood, D
Youngblood, Wm.

COMPANY "H."

Captains:
Goggans, J.E.

Lieutenants:
Bouknight, J.R

McCelvey, J.C
Bouknight, A.P
Huiet, H.

Sergeants:
McDaniel, J.C
Whittle, M.A
Watson, J.H
Ruston, W.

Corporals:
Huiet, J
Wyse, A.L
Sample, B.F
Jennings, G.

Privates:
Barnes, H
Bedenbaugh, J.T
Bedenbaugh, L
Bedenbaugh, J
Bouknight, A.S
Bouknight S.J
Bouknight, N
Buzzard, J.C
Charles, P
Duffie, J
Duffie, P
Duncan, A
Duncan, V
Faland, ----
Gunter, R
Goff, Z
Gibson, J
Gibson, W
Harris, W
Harris, S
Henson, D
Henson, J
Inabinet, I
Leppard, G
Leppard, J
Livingstone, P
Matthews, E
Miller, J.
Merchant, T
Mitchell, M
Martin, G
Padgett, E

Farmer, D.K
Rotten, J
Rushton, D
Rushton, H
Rushton, J
Sadler, J
Sadler, W
Smith, B
Spann, W
Spann, P
Shealy, M.W
Watson, W
Wise, J
Wise, W
Whittle, M
Wright, B.W.

COMPANY "I."

Captain:
Prescott, W.T.

Lieutenants:
Nixon, J.P
Roper, B
Blocker, S.B.

Sergeants:
Morgan, G.W
Holmes, W.J
Holmes, W.L
Brunson, R.V
Holson, Wm.

Corporals:
Crafton, T.M
Middleton, R.H
Mathis, J.A
Brunson, S.T
McKee, J.S
Griffis, J.N
Parkman, S
McDaniel, J.

Privates:
Anderson, E.J
Burt, A.H
Barkley, E.N
Bartley, J.W

Brigs, A.J
Brigs, H
Brigs, J
Bussey, W.N
Bussey, J.A
Broadwater, N.A
Broadwater, S
Brooks, R
Colloham, M
Garvett, W.A
Hammond, C
Holmes, S
Holmes, L.E
Jennings, W
Middleton, W.E
Matthis, W.H
Menerether, N
Morgan, E
McGee, T.W
Oham, R
Prince, J
Prince, D
Parkman, J.P
Parkman, S
Pressley, T.N
Patterson, T.H
Price, A.J
Parkman, N
Prescott, H.H
Shafton, J.S
Shafton, B.F
Shanall, J
Percy, J.H
Thernman, J.W
Thernman, T.B
Thomas, T.B
Bruse, J.W
Wood, H
Wood, J
Whitlock, ——
Whitaker, N
Wesman, C.L
Whitlock, W.

COMPANY "K."

Captain:
Burees, J.F.

Lieutenants:
Talbert, J.L
Berry, J.M
Chetham, J.W.

Sergeants:
Culbreath, O.T
Martin, W.N
Reynolds, W.M
Lamer, L.W
Burress, C.M.

Corporals:
Reynolds, J.W
Shibley, L.D
White, W.G
Williams, T.R.

Privates:
Adams, B.O
Blake, J.E
Carthledge, T.A
Crafton, T.M
Coleman, W.L
Coleman, G.R
Culbreth, J
Deal, A
Devore, C.L
Franks, J.A
Hammonds, C.T
Harrison, C.H
Henderson, J.T
Henderson, J.E
Holmes, W.L
Holmes, H.J
Howell, H
Lamer, T.B
Lamer, O.W
Limbecher, C.H
Lockridge, J.L
Mayson, J.H
Quarles, H.M
Reynolds, J.C
Reynolds, E.W

Rountree, T.J
Rush, T.P
Stalmaker, G.I
Stalmaker, J.R
Stalmaker, J.W
Timmerman, G.H
Williams, J.R
Wood, W.B
Yeldell, W.H.

COMPANY "L."

Captains:
White, W.C
Litchfield, J.L
Litchfield, G.S.

Lieutenants:
Beaty, T.W
Petman, S
Cooper, T.B
Newton, K.M
Grissett, J.D
Reves, J.W.

Sergeants:
Waid, G.W
Nercen, J.W
Floyd, A
Johnson, J.M
Anderson, ——
Gregary, T.H
Granger, J
Prince, J.L
Rabon, D
Johnson, C.L
Anderson, D.R.

Corporal:
Green, S.F.

Privates:
Barnhill, W.H
Barnhill. H
Cooper, L
Cooper, R
Creaven, W.H
Creach, C
Chesnut, D.M.W

Cork, M.C
Cox, P.V
Cox, G.W
Dussenberry, J.H
Dussenberry, N.G
Edge, D.M
Edge, W
Faulk, G
Floyd, W
Faulk, L
Faulk, J.L
Foreland, N
Fund, G
Grattely, J
Granger, J
Granger, W
Granger, F
Graddy, N
Graham, D
Graham, D.N
Gore, F
Grant, J.E
Hacks, ——
Harden, A.J
Harden, W.H
Hardwick, ——
Howell, ——
Harden, C.B
Hamilton, W.H
Hamilton, ——
Holland, W
Jenkins, Wm
Jewreth, ----
Jones, J
Jordan, J.T
Jordan, J
Johnson, T
Johnson, J.J
James, ——
Jenningham, D
King, J.J
King, J.D
King, G.W
Lilly, D
Murry, J.T
Murry, E.H
Misham, T.K

McKnot, Wm.R
Martin, B.W
Norris, J.K
Oliver, J.M
Powell, L
Perkins, ——
Parker, A.D
Parker, H.H

Powell, F.L
Powell, J.M
Roberts, J.T
Rhenark, J.C
Stalvey, C.M
Stalvey, J.J
Squers, J
Smith, Wm

Savris, A
Sessions, O
Sengleton, M.J
Vaught, S
Vereen, J.T
Watts, ——
Wade, K.

Roll of Eighth South Carolina Volunteer Regiment

Colonels:
Cash, E.B.C
Henagan, Jno. W
Stackhouse, E.T.

Lieutenant Colonels:
Hoole, A
McLeod, ——

Adjutants:
Lucas, Thomas E
Ingliss, Wm. C
Mullins, W.S
Weatherly, C.M.

Quartermasters:
McClenigan, Jno
Henagan, J.M
Hunagan, J.M.

Commissaries:
Cawley, J.H
Griffen, E.M.

Surgeons:
Wallace, W.D
David. W.J
Pearce, J.F
Coit, D.

Assistant Surgeons:
Dunlop, R.J
Dudley, T.E
Murdock, Byron
Henson, J.B
McIver, Hansford
Bristow, C.D.

Commissary Ser-geants:
McCown, R.A
Coker, C.W.

Orderly Sergeant:
Tyler, H.A.

COMPANY "A."

Captains:
Hoole, A.J
Muldrow, J.H
Odum, Wm
Odum, E
Rodgers, E
Rouse, J.J
Bryant, Jas. T
Goodson, J.T
Hudson, J.E.

Lieutenants:
Reynolds, W.C
Gardner, E.M
Bruce, C.A
Large, James F
Farmer, S.P
Branch. B
Morris, J.B.

Privates:
Reddick, W.H
Bryant, James, J
Boone, L.P
Blackburn, Wade
Bradshaw, J
Beck, W.D
Bass, Jesse
Blackman, John
Bradstraw, M
Beasley, O
Barns, Robt
Carter, W.R
Cox, B.F
Clemens, J
Dennis, Thomas A
Ervin, J.R
Flowers, C
Florence, T.D
Farmer, G.B
Garrison, J
Gorman, C
Goodson, J
Gudgen, J.I.B
Goodson, A
Gray, R
James, J.C
Gardner, C.D
Jordan, Wm. A
Gardner, P.T
Hill, W.M
Hill, B
Hill, E.T
Johnson, William
Johnson, Peter
Johnson, Robert
Langston, Jno. F
Langston, Ira D
Law, Frank
Large, N
Morrell, H
Morrell, W.E

Morrell, Isaac
Muller, J
Maye, R.F
Neal, Jno
Neal, J
Odom, J.S
Odom, S.J
Outlaw, James
Outlaw, John
Privett, E
Reynolds, E.J
Reddeck, W
Reddick, A
Stokes, J.F
Stokes, A.D
Sandesbery, J.H
Privett, W.B
Eligah, ——
Stakes, A.D
Stokes, J.H
Sandbarry, J.H
Severence, R.E
Stewart, A.C
Stewart, Hardey
Smith, S
Sexton, Thomas
Scott, W
Wingate, W.Z
Williams, W
Wadford, N
Woods, S.J.

COMPANY "B."

Captains:
Hough, M.J
Powell. R.T.

Lieutenants:
Parker. G.A
Thurman, M.T
Turnage, P.A
Sellers, D
Johnson, C.B
Hough, J.M
Moore, P.A
White, J.F

Chapman, H.C
Courtney, W.R.

Sergeants:
Jones. J
Rivers, W.F
Douglass, W
Rivers, W.F
Douglass, J.B
Sellers, R.C
Evans, B.F
Kite, B
Hammock. J.E.

Corporals:
Rivers, W.B
Rashing, J.P
Sellers, P.A
Herst, L
Campbell, J.A
Hancock, R.F.M.

Privates:
Anderson, B
Adams, B.P
Brown, V.F
Brown, D
Boon, E
Boon, C
Boon, A
Beaver, M
Brock, C
Boon, W.B
Cassadlay, A.J
Courtney, O
Courtney, J
Courtney, J.P
Cross. H
Cross, P
Chapman, A
Davis, F
Deas, T.A
Driggers, T
Dixon, R
Funderburk, H.W
Funderburk, J.B
Gaskins, J.B
Horn, J.D
Horn, J.W

Harp, W.C
Hancock, J.T
Hicks, J
Johnson, W.B
Johnson, T.B
Jordon, J.W
Lisenly, S
Lear, B.P
Lewis, T.H
McBride, J.A
McPriest, P
Massey, B.F
McKey, D.A
McCrany, D.A
Melton, J
Melton, A
Melton, W
Moore, H
McDuffie. J
McLean, J.W
McLean, D.A
McNair, ——
McManus, R
McNair. N.C
Nelson, M
Nelson, H
Price, H
Polson, J
Rivers, P
Rogers, P
Sellers, J.D
Sellers, W.B
Sellers, W.R
Sellers, H.J
Sillivan, T
Sillivan. S
Sweatt, W
Sweatt, S
Stricklen. H
Teed, T.B
Tarnage, D
Threatt, J.W
Threatt, W
Threatt, T
Threatt, H
Terry, J
Timmons, W

Tadlock, W
White, H
Whittaker, J.W
Wilkerson, J
West, J.S
McNair, N.

COMPANY "C."

Captains:
Coit, W.H
Powe. T.E
Malloy, S.G.

Lieutenants:
Gillespie, G.S
McIver, D.W
Evans, R.E
Hurst, L.

Sergeants:
Strother, J
Gayle, H.A
Crail, C.W
Crail, T.P
Stancel, J
Smith, W.P
McCallman, J.C
White, B.S
Coit, J.T
Grimsley, S.B
Sellers, J
McIver, H.

Corporals:
Malloy, C.A
Godfrey, W.R
Callens, J
Sellers, S.

Privates:
Adams, W
Adams, J
Bevil, J
Buchanan, J.A
Braddock, R
Clark, J
Cadien, B.F
Coker, H

Coker, M
Chapman, W.G
Chapman, A.G
Craig, J
Crawford, F.D
Campbell, D.A
DeLorne, T.W
Dickson, S.G
Douglas, A
Douglas, M.A
Ellerbe, A.W
Emanuel, E
Freeman, J
Freeman, W
Gardner, J.N
Gaskin, J.D
Goodwin, J
Grimsley, W
Grady, J.A
Goodwin, D
Grant. H.P
Grant, H
Grant, A
Graves, S
Hicks, W.H
Hayes, A.A
Haggins, A
Inglis, W.C
Inglas, L.S
Inglas, P
Knight, W.W
Lang, J
Link, J.A
Lisendy, W
Linton, J.H
Lee, H
McBride, F
McLean, J.K
McColl, W
Murphy, C.W
McIver, F.M
Mahon, J
McDuffie, F.J
McMillan, J.D
Malloy, J.H
Murray, J.C
McIntosh, J.W

Melton, H
Moore, H
Melton, E.H
McRa, D
Mash, ——
Melton, W
Nichols, W.P
Odom, D.P
Odom, J
Petter, L.L
Pinchman, H. C
Powell, A.H.C
Poston, H.C
Poston, W
Purvis, W
Purvis, L.D
Poston, J
Quick, B
Rainwaters, W.T
Richards, J.G
Roberson, G
Spencer, S.H
Sellers, H
Smith, S.S
Sweatt, T
Stacey, O
Spencer, T.D
Sellers W.B
Smith. T
Smith, J
Turnage, T.D
Turner, W.W
White, D
White, J
Wright, J
Wallace, J.C.

COMPANY "D."

Captains:
Miller, J.S
Miller. R.P
Spofferd, P.F.

Lieutenants:
Blakeney, H
Timmons, J.J

Baker, L.C
Kirkley, W.P
Lowry, J.H.

Sergeants:
Jackson, H.H
Baker, A.J
Gatlim, J.B
Jackson, A
Wesh, S.

Corporals:
Hendrick, J.H
King, E.T
Lee, J.C
Sowell, W.H.

Privates:
Adams, J.J
Carter, S.H
Carter, G.W
Calege, J
Crain, J.A
Crowley, B.D
Crowley, T.W
Dees, T.M
Dees, W
Foster, S
Griffith, J
Gandy, E
Gandy, W.H
Gibson, A
Handcock, J.P
Handcock, J.J
Handcock, J.J
Handcock, J.T
Handcock, R.F
Handcock, J.L
Hudrick, R
Hudrick, J.L
Horn, L
Horn, J
Horn, M
Horton. G.W
Horton, S
Holly, P.W
Hough, J.T
Hough, J.E
Jordan, H.S

Jordan, J
Jordan, A
Key, A
Key, J.A
Knight, J.H
Knight, J.R
Knight, J.A
Knight, W.H
Knight, T.J
Knighton, J.T
Kibbie, J
Lowery, J
Lowery, W
Love, J.J
Mangum, J.C
Mangum, W.P
Myers, J
Miller, J.T
McMillan, T.E
McMair, D.D
McManus, M.B
McLauchlin, D.A
Oliver, J.T
Ogburn, L
Philips, E
Philips. A
Philips, C
Plyler, A
Pate, Rollins, B.F
Rollins, G.W
Rollins, J
Rollins, J.C
Robinson, G
Robinson, S
Sinclair, J
Sinclair, J.A
Stricklin, J
Stricklin, M
Stricklin, M
Small, C
Threatt, J.S
Threatt, J
Threatt, R
Therrill, L
Terry J
Talbert, O.W
Talbert, W.S

Thratt, J.A
Watson, M
Watson, E
Watts, J.J
Williams, B.B.

COMPANY "E."

Captains:
Young, J.D
Joy, W.D.

Lieutenants:
Westhimes, H
Hewitt, T.M
Halford, J.J.

Sergeants:
Athenson, S.R
Ward, R.H
Hollyman, M.W
Miller, T.J.

Corporals:
Philips, J.R
Moody, E.T
Moon, W.W
Morris, T.E.

Privates:
Allen, R.M
Anderson, T.J
Anderson, W.D
Alford, R.H
Askin, J.A.J
Anderson, C
Anderson, J.F
Anderson, W.H
Anderson, W.T
Anderson, G
Anderson, J.M
Barfield, M
Bristow, C.C
Bristow, J.N
Barefoot, D.R
Brookington, E.S
Byrd, J.E
Carter, W.A
Carter, G

Carter, H.M
Carter, N.S.J
Carter, H
Carter, R.M
Carter, S.B
Coward, W
Cook, T.J
Courtney, S.J
Connor, E.J
Connor, G
Chandler, T.A
Cone, R
Danels, E
DaBase, A.E
Doralds, M.H
Evingston, G
Elliott, A.J
Graham, C.S
Gilchrist, J
Gee, S
Gardner, J.D
Gardner, C
Ganniginn, D
Hill, E.F
Hill, J.J
Hill, B
Hill, H
Hill, J
Hill, R.M
Hill, I.T
Howall. W.H
Hollan, J.S
Hollan, S.S
Hamphury, S.S
Hamphury, R.F
Hane, H.W
Hane, A.J
Hane, H.A.W
Hane, W
Hatchell, I
Hatchell, C.A
Hatchell, L
Hancock, H
Hollyman, A
Halford, J.M
Hix, T
Hase, G.N

Hickson, J.S
Jackson, T
Jones, R.M
Jordan, P.A
Kerth, J.H
Kirby, S.J
Kirby, H
Kent, J.L
Lockhart, J.C
Lockhart, R.C
Lockhart, G.R
Lockhart, W.J
McCoy, C.D
McCoy, T.G
McCoy, J.J
McCoy, S
McCoy, J
McGee, J.M
McGee, W
McKnight, W
Moore, J.G
Moore, J.D
McGill, J.F
McGill, J
Morris, M.E
Morris, H
Morris, J.L
Matthews, W.A
McKessick, W.J
Nettles, L.F
Nettles, G.T
Nettles. R.C
Norwood, J.E
Philips, J.R
Philips, L.A
Price, J.A
Price, G.P
Pool A.A
Pawley, J.H
Plummer, C.H
Powers, M.J
Powers, A.D
Powers, W
Rollins, R.D.F
Rice, D.H
Rogers, M.D
Singletary, C

Smoot, W.B
Smoot, W.L
Snipes, M
Timmons, W.H
Timmons, W.B
Truitt, J.E
Turner, J.C
Ward, J.W
Ward, R.H
Ward, C.E
Ward, J.J
Witherspoon, S.B
Windham, J.R
Windham, I
Windham, J.H
Wooten, S
Wittington, J.W
Wadford, N
Wadford, G.W
Winburn, S
Young, W.W.

COMPANY "F."

Captains:
Evans, W.H
Howle, T.E
McIver, J.K
Bass, J.E.

Lieutenants:
McIver, J.J
Kelly H
James, W.E
Ferguson, J.W
Griffin, P.E
Griffin, E.M
Rhodes, J.T
James, R.E
Coker, W.C
Smoot, J
Rhodes, W.B
Williams, J.A
Williams, A.L
Howle, J.F
Evans, C.D
Bearly, J.M

Wilson, I.D
Carter, W.P.

Corporals:
Parrott, A.W
Hearon, G.W
Bruce, C.A
Harroll, L.B
Parrott, B.M.

Privates:
Alexander, A
Atkinson, W.K
Bacot, T.W
Bass, J.C
Bass, B
Bass, J.B
Baswell, L.T
Bozeman, B.C
Bozeman, J.W
Bozeman, P.W
Bozeman, J
Bozeman, H
Bozeman, W
Brown, W
Byrd, D.M
Coltins, A
Colvin, J.R
Cook, D.B
Davis, J.M
Dixon, A.P
Dixon. J.E
Elliott, W.A
Ervin, E.M
Fraser, J.G
Fort, J.E
Flowers, J
Garland, W.H
Galloway, A
Galloway, W.M
Galloway, W.L
Galloway, M
Galloway, G.W
Gullege, A
Gullege, J.L
Gatlin, H
Hale, J.O
Halliburton, J.J

Halliburton, R.J
Harrall, J.M
Harris, D.J
Hazelton, J
Higgins, R.D
Hurst, S
Jenks, M
Jenks, G
Jordon, A
King, T.F
Kelly, T
Lawson, J.T
Lee, J.T
Lewis, W
McCown, R
McIntosh, J.H
McKenzie, W.W
Marco, M
Mazing, W.H
Mixon, J
Martin, W
Nettles, R.F
Outlaw, B
Outlaw, J
Parrott, J.R
Peoples, R.H
Price, A.J
Privett, J.H
Privett, J.H
Rhodes, J.D
Rhodes, F.E
Rhodes, R.B
Smith, A
Smith, J.S.M
Skinner, B
Shumaker, S
Stukey, A.F
Suggs, R.B
Stokes, R
Tallevasb, H.P
Thomas, J.M
Thomas, R.C
Tyler, H
Thomlinson, ——
Wallace, G
Wordham, A.E
Wilk, J

Wilson, P.

COMPANY "G."

Captain:
Harrington, J.W.

Lieutenants:
Townsend, C.F
Parker, John
Weatherly, C.M.

Sergeants:
Dudley, T.F
Lester, I.B
Murdock, John T
Odum, L
Crosland, W.A.

Corporals:
Easterling, Thomas,
Townsend, H.E
Cook, John A
Tatum, R.J
Gillespie, O.H
Douglas, H.J.

Privates:
Adams, E
Adams, H.A
Adams, J.T
Andrews, S.D
Briston, C.D
Briston, E.D
Bullard, Henry
Bundy, William
Butler, William
Butler, E
Campbell, J
Caulk, D
Cook, T.A.M
Cowen, L.M
Crosland, Samuel
Connor, R.D.T
Cooper, Wm.C
Cooper, V.H
David, E.C
David, R.J
David, J.H

Dudley, James
Drigger, Jesse
Drigger. J.G
David, A.I
Easterling, A.A
Easterling, R.C
Easterling, J.K
Easterling, W.T
Easterling, Elijah
Edens, T.W
Emanuel, C.L
Fletcher, J.D
Gibson, W.L
Grant, J.S
Graham, H.C
Gillespie, S.J
Harvel, John
Henagen, James M
Heyward, Isham
Hinson, J.B
Hinson, P.H
Huckabee, J.L
James, J.H
Hambrick, J
Irby, W.W
Jackson, I.A.L
Jackson, Enos
Johnson, N.D
Johnson, H.I
Johnson, D
Laviner, G.W
Laviner, D
Long, H.A
Lyles, J.R
Miller, J.M
Munnerlyn, C.T
Miller, Henry
McCollum, J.H
McIntosh, N.H
McIntosh, A
McQueen, J
McIrmis, S.J
McKenzie, A
Odum, Josiah
Odum, S.W
Odum, P.W
Parker, H

Prince, John T
Potter, Sol
Privatt, Evander
Pearson, R.C
Roscoe, John
Roscoe, G.W
Rowe, J.H
Roundtree, M
Skipper, J
Snead, Israel
Stanton, Noah
Stanton, J.A
Stanton, Milton
Thomas, C.J
Thomas, J.M
Thomas, R.D
Thornwell, C.A
Williams, David
Wright, D.G
Wright, F.E
Wright, G.W
Webster, H.D
Webster, T.M
Webster, H
Sutherland, T.A.

COMPANY "H."

Captains:
Singletary, B.L
McIntire, Duncan

Lieutenants:
Myers, M.G
Brunson, J.B
Culpepper, George,
McPherson, P.E
Gregg, Walter
Cooper, R.D.
Sergeants:
Gregg, Smith A
Gregg, McF
Moore, B
Gregg, John W
Mathews, Frank
Hughes, G.W
Godbold, D

Colston, G
Stone, W.C.P
Armfield, A.L
McWhite, E.

Privates:
Altman, J
Bartley, J.G
Barthy, Charles,
Barthy, E
Bellflower, H
Bragton, J.J
Balley, John
Broach, G.W
Cain, S.G
Cain, K.S
Cain, J.J
Cain, R.M
Cain, Church,
Cain, J. Coon
Cain, J.H
Cox, J.T
Cooper, Brunson,
Cooper, Witherspoon,
Christmas, Jarrett
Davis, J.G
Deas, Simeon
Eagerton, H
Finklen, John
Flowers, W.D
Guy, J.H
Graham, J.M
Hampton, Thomas,
Hampton, George,
Hutchinson, George,
Hutchinson, W.C
Hutchinson, Samuel,
Hunter, D
Harrall, E
Harrall, N.W
Harrall, W.T
Hyman, Benjamin,
Hughes, R.S
Holland, J.S
Holland, George
Hodges, Barney,
Kennedy, Alfred,
Kennedy, Andrew,

Kersey, E
Lewellyn, J.B
Leach, Julius
McKissick, A.G
McKissick, M
Myers, William,
McWhite, A.A
Myers, A.A
Pearce, R.H
Prosser, Michael
Rodgers, C
Rodgers, M
Roy, A
Stephenson, A
Stone, F.F
Williams, H
Williams, Thomas
Williams, R.L
Williams, S.B
Weatherford, W.S
Weatherford, Benjamin,
Gregg, S.J
Gregg, S.E
Howard, Tillman
Powers, Jonas.

COMPANY "I."

Captains:
Stackhouse, E.T
Harllee, A.T.

Lieutenants:
Cook, H. B
Ross, J.N
Rodgers, R.H
Carmichael, W.D
Stafford, D.C
Cusack, G.W.

Sergeants:
McClenagham, H.H
Harllee, Peter S
Pearce, J.F
Ayers, E.S
McDuffie, D.Q
Harllee, R.A
Gregg, A. Stuart

Jenkins, R.W.

Corporals:
Woodrow, J.E
Huggins. Geo. W
Harelson, Joel
Sparkman, Levi
Cusack, S.C
DeBarry, Edmond
Robbins, J.B
Fenaghan, James
Rodgers, E
Carmichael, Alex
Brigman, A
Butler, J.A
Butler, Silas W.

Privates:
Bigham, W.H
Bullock, Joel
Benton, Joel
Benton, G.W
Baker, John
Cox, G.B
Cribb, Levi
Collin, E.H
Crawford, H.W
Cottingham, Stewart
Cottingham, Thomas F
Cohen, David
Cohen, Isaac
Dove, J.W
Dove, H.G
Ellen, E.J
Elvington, Dennis
Fryer, A.J
Freeman, Joseph
Gaddy, R.M
Gaddy, W.D
Gregg, T.C
Harralson, M.J
Harralson, E.P
Herring, E.B
Hinton, J.W
Jones, J
James, Robert
Loyd, Henry
Llewellyn, B.F

Mace, James C
Meckins, P.B
Morgan, W.C
Miller, W.H
Myers, John E
Moody, John B
Murphy, J.C
McCall, L.A
McRae, James
Owens, D.R
Owens, S.S
Sparkman, G.R
Snipes, Michael
Smalley, Isaiah
Turner, John C
Watson, John R
Watson, Quinn,
Woodrow, W.J
Whitner, J.N
Woodberry, W.D.

COMPANY "K."

Captains:
McLeod, D.M.D
Manning. Frank
Rodgers, Ben. A.

Lieutenants:
McQueen, S.F
McLucas, John D
Hearsey, Geo. R
Rodgers, W.T
Peterkin, J.A
Alfred, J.M.I
McQuage, J.J
Smith, J.W
Alford, M.N
McCall, H.D
Willis, Eli
Smith, W.D
McRae, Frank
McLucas, Hugh
McKinnon, C
Gunter, John
Calhoun, J.C
McLaurin, L.A

Edens, J.A
McCall, C
Covington, J.T
Alford, N.A
Hargroves, David
Bruce, J.D.

Privates:
Allen, E
Barrington, H
Bruce, T.R
Bundy, W.R
Cottingham, C
Covington, E.T
Covington, J.T
Crowey, R.C
Crowley, William
Cape, Thomas
Curtin, ——
Clark, J
Drake, Ansel
Davis, C
Driggers, R.S
Dupre, Thomas J
Edens, Joseph
Edens, T. H
English, William,
Emanuel, J.M
Easterling, Lewis
Easterling, David
Freeman, L.D
Freeman, Benjamin,
Fletcher, W.R
Greggard, J.W
Graham, E
Groomes, F
Gunter, John
Hargrove, James
Hargrove, D.T
Harvel, Tristam
Hathcock, W
Hayes, J.J
Hayes, Robt. W
Hasken, John W
Huckabee, John
Huckabee, John W
Hodges, Thomas C
Ivey, H.W

Ivey, Levi
Jones, John C
Jones, Martin
Jacobs, Robert
Jacobs, J. Frost
Jackson, John C
John, Daniel C
Joy, W.H
Kirby, H
McCall, C
McCall, Alex
McCall, John T
McRae, A.D
McRae, John D
McRae, John C
McDaniel, J.R
McLucas, A.C
McLaurin, John F
McLeod, M
McPherson, Malcolm,
McPhearson, Angus,
Matherson, Hugh
Manship, John
Rodgers, C
Rodgers, F.A
Roscoe, Daniel
Smith, W.D
Stubbs, Lucius
Sparks, George
Sarvis, A.S
Staunton, A.A
Webster, Wm. R
Williams, Lazarus,
Woodley, Alex
Weatherly, A.W.

COMPANY "L."

Captains:
Stackhouse, E.T
Carmichael, W.D.

Lieutenants:
Higgins, W.D
Clark, G.W.

Sergeants:
Carmichael, D.D

Ayers, E.S
Rodgers, E
Manning, Eli
Murchison, Duncan

Corporals:
Carmichael, Alex
Page, J.N
Roberts, J.H
Barfield, Thompson.

Privates:
Alford, Robert H.
Alford, Artemus
Alford, W. McD
Ammonds, J.D
Ayers, D.D
Barfield, R. Tally
Barfield, M
Barfield, H
Bethea, J. Frank
Bethea, H.P
Bridgeman, A.P
Byrd, H.G
Carmichael, A
Carmichael, D.C
Cottingham, C
Candy, S
Clark, R. Knox
Crawley, W.C
Coward, H
Cook, John
Harper, J.M
Herring, Samuel
Huckabee, John
Hicks. John C
Huggens, W.E
Huggens, D
Hunt, J.E
Herring, E.B
Irwin, I.R
Jackson, Robert
Jackson, M
Jackson, N
Lane, Samuel
Lane, E
McPhane, D
McRae, Colin

McRae, N
McRae. Roderick,
McRae, Franklin,
McGill. Colin
McLaurin, D
Morgan, W.C
McGill, David
Owens, S.I
Page, D. N
Page, D.P
Rogers, Thompson,
Rogers, John F
Rogers, William D
Rogers, E.B
Rogers, L.B
Sarris, John
Turner, John C
Turberville, Calvin,
Waters, John W
Watson, John R
Watson, Quinn
Watson, Lindsay.

COMPANY "M."

Captains:
Howie, Thomas E
Coker, William C.

Lieutenants:
Howle, James F
Rhodes, W.B
Galloway, W.L
Smoot, J
Galloway, George.

Sergeants:
Brearly, James W
Halliburton, Robert,
Garland, W. H
Mixon, J.

Corporals:
Mozingo, W.H
Philips, J.C
McKenzie, W.W
Harrell, L.W
Mozingo, E

Howle, R.F.
Privates:
Alexander, H
Atkinson, Wiley
Byrd, D.M
Byrd, G.F
Bozeman, Peter
Beasley, Burton
Beasley, Ira
Bruce, C.A
Coker, C. W
Collins, E
Flowers, William
Galloway, Abram
Galloway, Nathan
Gainey, Isaiah
Gainey, Peter
Gulledge, Alex
Goodson, Robert
Halliburton, J.J
Harris, D.J
Hill, William T
Hill, William M
Hill, Nelson
Hudson, Jesse
Hall, David
Jenks, Mark
Jenks, Thomas
Jenks, G.W
Kirven, M.L
King, J.B
King, C.R
Lewis, Zach
McCown, J.M
McCown, J.J
McPherson, Robert
McKissick, ⎯⎯
Moore, William H
Mathews, William
Mozingo, William
Morrell. Peter
Northcoat, ⎯⎯
Norwood, James
Peebles, W.D
Peebles, Robert
Privett, J. Hamilton
Privett, J. Henry

Privett, John H
Parrott, Pinkney
Parrott, Benj. M
Plummer,. William
Rhodes, John J
Rhodes, John B
Skinner, Benj
Smith, J.S.M
Smith, Bryant
Suggs, A.T
Suggs, R. Rush
Thomas, J.M
Williams, David
Wright, Jonathan
Wright, Thomas L
Wright, J.B.C
Wilson, Peter
Wilson, Joseph
Woodman, A. Edward
Smith, Alex
Matuse, William
Colvin, John
Dixon, James
Bass, J.C.

Roll of Fifteenth South Carolina Volunteer Regiment

Colonels:
DeSaussure, W.D
Davis, J.B.

Lieutenant Colonels:
Gist, J.F
Lewie, S.F.

Major:
Gist, Wm. M.

Adjutant:
Davis, J.M.

Assistant Quartermaster:
Middleton, J.S.

Assistant Commissary Sergeant:
Kirkland, J.M.

Surgeon:
James, J.A.

Assistant Surgeons:
Wallace, A
McCullum, H.B.

Sergeant Major:
Giles, C.H.

Quartermaster Sergeant:
Price, J.R.

Ordnance Sergeant:
Boyd, R.W.

Hospital Steward:
Maurice, R.F.

COMPANY "A."

Captain:
Radcliffe, Thos. W.

Lieutenants:
Beard, Henry
Brown, Pressley
Shields, Wm.

Sergeants:
Black, J.E
Campbell, J.S
Cathcart, J.N
O'Neale, Richard,
Beard, T.A
Zealy, R.F.

Corporals:
Pollock, T.M
Long, S.S
Hutchison, J.H
Bruns, J. Henry.

Privates:
Anderson, W.C
Assman, W.J
Asbury, W.E
Anderson, Richard,
Brown, Ira B
Baum, M.H
Branham, R.T
Beckwith, Wm. H
Boscheen, Charley,
Blankenstine, Jacob,
Bedell, Allen
Bynum, Ben
Beckwith, L.R

Brown, Fred. J
Beck, Robt. C
Brown, J.H
Burrows, DeS
Beckham, W.M
Bass, Toland
Crawford, D.H
Capers, Geo. R
Clarkson, E. McC
Crawford, Daniel
Davis, John
Dougal, C.H
Dixon, S.W
Dreisden, Julius
DeSaussure, W.D
Ehelers, Geo
Emlyn, H.N
Edwards, J.G
Frazee, P.F
Fritz, J.A
Gibson. F.A
Gibenwrath, J.F
Grieshaber, Fritze
Gardener, C.H
Glaze, Wm
Green, M.B
Gandy, J.H
Graham, Wm
Geiger, J.G
Gunther, Jno
Gaither, J.W
Goodwin, G.W
Howel, D.B
Henrick, Lewis
Hardie, J.W

Howell, O.F
Johnson, C.P
Johnson, J.R
Isaacs, J.H
James, Joseph
Kaigler, I.A
Killian, Jno. II
Keenan, Roland A
Levin, G.W
Ledingham, W.J
Lesher, Wm
Lumsden, J.L
McCammon, G
McCammon, ----
Morgan, Isaac C
McGorvan, Jno
McKenzie, Frank L
McCoy, John M
Milling, James
Orchard, Henry
Pearson, A.W
Price, J.R
Puryear, R.T
Poppe, Julius
Parker, Wm. E
Perry, G.H
Pollock, B.C
Peixotto, S.C
Pope, F.M
Radcliffe, C.C
Reynolds, Jno. H
Roberts, W.H
Row, Louis
Rawley, Jno
Reed, R.C
Stark, A
Smith. J.C
Smith, Warren
Scott, John M
Stork, A
Stork, J.J
Stork, W.H
Schnider, Henry
Scott, W.H
Schultze, George
Stewart, Edmond
Starling, T.J

Tourney, Tim. J
Templeton, I.G
Templeton, Wm. A
Templeton, W.L
Townsend, J.V
Veal, J.M
Wells, Jacob H
Walker, T.P
Walsh, P.H
Wade, T.H
Wade, Geo. McD
Wallace, A
Yates, Joseph.

COMPANY "B."

Captains:
Gist, Wm. H
Sheldon, S.H.

Lieutenants:
Rogers, J. Rice
Barnett, Wm. R
Huckabee, ——
McWhirter, ——
Smith, W.M
Yarborough, P.P.

Sergeants:
Giles, C.H
West, John I
Haselwood, Hosea
Bailey, W.P.H
Bobo, Barham
Williams, J.H.

Corporals:
Hughes, J.A
Lowe, M.V
Lancaster, W.A
Young, I.H
Williams, Gordon.

Privates:
Abernathy, John
Anderson, Thomas
Barrett, T. Lyles
Barrett, Alonzo
Barnett, W. Franklin

Bethany, Jesse
Briggs, B. Franklin
Bogan, Isaac C
Bogan, P.P
Boram, W.H
Bobo, Jason
Canaday, C
Canaday, David, Sr
Canaday, David, Jr
Clefton, Wesley
Dillard, Wm
Eubanks, Shelton
Eubanks, Charner
Foster, W.A
Foster, I.F
Gee, P.M
Gossett, T.G
Goodlin, W.P
Gossett, Henry
Gist, D.C
Grass, J.C
Hembree, Ervin
Hollingsworth, Benj
Huckabee, W.P
Huckabee, James M
Huckabee, Philip
Huff, John
Huff, W.M
Haselwood, A
Haselwood, Thomas
Huges, Thomas H
Huges, E
Holcomb, Wallace
Jennings, Elias
Kelly, I.H
Lamb, Marion
Lamb, Robert
Lamb, John
Lamb, David
Lamb, Elijah
Lancaster. F.M
Lancaster, J.B
Lawson, Lemuel
Lawson, Munro
Lawson, J.H
Lawson, Elijah
Lawson, Charles

Lawson, Franklin
Lawson, Levi
Myers, G.W
Powell, James W
Prickett, H.P
Pool. Wm. M
Prince, Spencer
Prince, Franklin
Ray, Robt. F
Ray, Jeremiah
Ray, B.C
Rains, Wm
Rook, James
Rook, Franklin
Robinson, G.M
Sparks, William
Starns, W.A
Stone, H.C
Smith, Nimrod
Smith, Wm
Sumner, I.M
Sumner, F.S
Sumner, John
Sumner, Mattison
Templeton, Jno. A
Waldrip, W.M
West, B.E
West, W. McD
West, Jno. P
West, Isaac T
West, C.P
West, E.I
West, W.C
Whitton, John
Willard, Benj
Willard, William,
Wilbanks, F
Wilbanks, T
Whitmore, J.F
Whitmore, E.H
Whitmore, Thomas,
Whitehead, James,
Whitehead, Stephen,
Yarborough, Hiram,
Young, George
Young, Thomas
Young, Francis W.

COMPANY "C."

Captains:
Lewie, F.S
Lewie, J.H
Griffith, D.J.

Lieutenants:
Swygert, Y
Lewie, S.T
Fulmer, W.W
Spence, S
Jumper, J.B
Shealey, Lewis.

Sergeants:
Kyzer, S.W
Lewie, E.W
Derrick, H.F
Sanders, W.F
Lammack, J.S
Leaphart, F.E
Jumper, J.W
Butler, J.W
Derrick, D.S
Anderson, F.S
Hare, J.W
Heister, M.W.C
Price, H.L.

Corporals:
Sease, D.T
Earhart, C.B.W
Black, J.W
Oswalt, F. Wade
Huer, W.B.

Privates:
Adams, I.P
Alewine, Philip,
Alewine, W.W
Alewine, W.H
Alewine, J.L
Addy, M.W
Addy, S.L
Addy, E.I
Addy, J.W
Amick, E.R
Amick, H

Anderson, E
Anderson, J
Black, S.L
Blum, John
Busby, Tillman
Caughman, D.S
Craps, J.W
Craps. H.H
Crout, John
Crout, Ephraim
Crim, R.F
Derrick, A.E
Derrick, W.T
Derrick, Oliver
Fridell, J.M
Griffith, Allen
Hyler, N.W
Hare, D.T
Hare, L.P
Hallman, E
Hallman, W.B
Hartly, J.L
Hendrix, J.P
Hendrix, G.W
Hite, D.W
Kite, Noah W
Holeman, D.P
Jumper, D.A
Jumper, W.T
Jumper, H.F
Kelly, G.J
Kelly, Jasper
King, Luke
Hyzer, Henry L
Hyzer, J.T
Hyzer, J.S
Laurinack, Samuel
Laurinack, J.J
Laurinack, Noah
Laurinack, Paul
Long, L.W
Laurinack, E
Long, W.A
Long, J.W
Long, W.W
Long, Jacob
Long, I.A.

Mettze, J.E
Nichols, Levi.
Nichols. L.E
Nichols, Wesley
Oswold, Wilson
Oswold, James
Oswold, L.B
Oxner, N
Price, R.E
Price, Danl
Price, Jacob
Price, G.W Sr
Price, D.W
Price, R.I
Plymale, W.W
Rysinger, David
Rysinger, Noah
Rysinger, Geo. D
Rysinger, Wesley
Rawl, L
Rawl, Christian
Rawl, O.D
Rawl, Franklin
Sanford, Wade
Sanford, S
Salther, H
Snelgrove, M
Lybrand, Wm
Sease, M.T
Shull, John
Seay, Danl
Shirey, I.P
Snyder, John
Shealy, Albert
Shealy, E.H
Shealy, Littleton
Shealy, Wiley
Shealy, Henry
Shealy, A
Shealy, P.W
Smith, Henry A
Swygert, E
Taylor, Ruben
Taylor, I.L
Taylor, David
Vansant, Addison
Warren, T.I.

COMPANY "D."

Captain:
Warren, Thomas J.

Lieutenants:
Davis, James M
Lyles, James V
Schrock, I.A.

Sergeants:
Burns, O.B
Somers, Adolphus,
Huckabee, J.J
Davis, J.J
Fisher, C.A.

Corporals:
Springer, Rudolph,
Stewman, P.A.H
Wolf, Eugene
Young, Jno. W
Crosby, Geo.

Privates:
Ammons, H
Brannon, John
Brannon, Wm Sr
Brannon, Wm Jr
Brannon, David
Bradley, John
Brown, Wm
Corbitt, J.C
Corbitt, H.F
Copell, W.H
Copell, J.B
Copell, S.B
Creighton, E.E
Creighton, H.L.
Collier, F.J
Evins, John
Evain, Samuel
Fulghum, James
Falkuberry, John
Ford, E.J
Fletcher, David G
Gardner, Lewis
Gardner, James L
Graham, Wm

Griffin, Stephen
Gaymon, John B
Hays, Joseph
Hays, E
Hayes, James
Harrall, Jim
Harrall, John
Hornsby, Joseph
Hornsby, Samuel
Hornsby, S.W
Hough, Hollis
Hinson, John, Sr
Hinson, John, Jr
Hunter, A.A
Hall, Russell J
Johnson, Ben F
Johnson, W.B
Jackson, Douglas
Jordan, W.H
Jordan, D
Kirkley, D.C
Kemp, Tira
Kemp, Warren
Kelly, B.P
Kirby, A
Kirby, J.W
Munn, A.J
McInnis, N.M
Mattox, James
Mattox, Isaac S
Mattox, Sam
Mattox, Geo. W
McLeod, N.A
Moneyham, John
Marsh, Gates
Marsh, James
Marsh, John
McCullum, H.B
Minton, C
Minton, Jno. B
McGuire, Henry
Outlaw, Jno. E
Parker, Wm. E
Parker, Redding
Parker, B.B
Richburg, J.J
Ray, James

Scott, Hasting
Scott, Manning
Shedd, Jesse P
Smith, J.W
Spradley, W.J
Spradley, John
Shaylor, T.S
Shaylor, C.H
Shivey, Jos
Turner, Jno. F
Hassein, A. Von
Wilson, Joel
Wilson, Henry
Wilson, Paul H
Williams, A.W
Williams, B. Frank
Watson, W.W
Warren, Wm
Watts, C
Watts, Jno
Workman, W.H.R
Waddell, N.T
Ward, John
Watts, Frank
Young, Jno. W
Yates, Saml
Yates, Willis

COMPANY "E."

Captains:
Davis, J.B.
Dawkins, W.J
Kirkland, W.W.

Lieutenants:
Smart, Thomas H
Martin, Joseph B
Pearson, J.W
Hoy, J.B
Blair, C.B.

Sergeants:
Pettigrew, J.H
Blair, W. McD
Robinson, K.Y.

Corporals:
Gladney, J.D
Bridges, W.A
Gladney, Samuel.

Privates:
Aiken, W.B
Aiken, D.M
Bagley, J.S
Bagley, Lee
Barker, W.J
Barker, S.C
Butner, J.J
Barrmeau, J.J
Bridges, F.C
Barber, James
Cloxton, Wm
Cotton, W.J
Cotton, Joe
Crossland, Wm
Crossland, A.T
Camack, Samuel
Camack, A.F
Coleman, Robt.
Coleman, H.T
Crumpton, W.C
Crumpton, T.H
Crumpton, W.S
Clarke, J.S
Crawford, Robt
Carlisle, Jno
Dickerson, W.P
Davis, J.B.
Davis, Ross
Evans, J.W
Fenley, W.P
Fenley, D.D
Gladney, Amos
Gladney, John
Gladney, J.F
Gladden, W.A
Gibson, T.D
Gregg, C.D
Hamilton, D.G
Hodge, J.M
Hodge, R.B
Hodge, A.F
Hodge, J.C
Hutchinson, J.B
Hutchinson, J.P
Hunt, C.M
John, J.A
John, James
Kirkland, W.F
Kirkland, J.M
Lyles, I.B
Lyles, W.W
Lyles, A.C
Long, W.W
Long, J.J
Ligon, I.N
Morris, T.S
Martin, R.L
Murphy, W.E
Murphy, S.A
Murphy, E.E
Murphy, Jno. R
Moorehead, W.J
McCormack, Hugh
McConnell, W.H
McClure, John
McDowell, Alex
McCrorey. James
Neil, J.H
Pettigrew, W.T
Pettigrew. A.R
Pettigrew, D.H
Pettigrew. G.B
Poteet, Lafayette
Price, Fletcher
Price, J.W
Parrott, R.L
Pearson, G.B
Powell, R.M
Rabb, J.W
Richardson, J.D
Sprinkler, Hiram
Smith, D.A
Smith. J.W
Smith, W.E
Seymore, Jno
Tidewell, B.N
Veronee, C.B
Varnadoe, Henry
Wylie, J.T
Wylie. T.C

Wylie, Frank
Wylie, James
Walker, Danl
Walker, Alex
Williams, G.W
Yarborough, T.J
Yarborough, W.T
Yarborough, I.T.

COMPANY "F."

Captains:
Boyd, C.W
Jefferies, Jno R.

Lieutenants:
Norris, James
Walker, S.S
Steen, Geo
Jefferies, J.D
Hart, W.D
Wood, Moses

Sergeants:
Rowland, Jas. A
Boyd, R.W
Kendricks, M.S
Lipscomb, Smith
Shippey, Dexter
Wilkins, W.D
Jones, B.F
McKown, G.W.

Corporals:
Spears, G.S
Morgan, George
Balue, Thomas
Mays, Jno
Littlejohn, I.H
Reavs, Z
Vinson, Richard
Jones, N.C.

Privates:
Alston, M.K
Bailey, T.J
Berbage, D.B
Blanton, Ambrose
Blanton, D.D

Brown, Wm
Burgess, Thomas
Betenbough, Joseph,
Betenbough, Jno
Blanton, N.A
Burgess, L.I
Cellars, Wm
Clary, Herod,
Clary, G.B
Clary, Singleton
Clary, Wm
Carter, E.L
Dukes, I.C
Edge, Jno
Fowler, B.F
Fowler, Jno
Fowler, R.M
Fowler, Wm
Fowler, Richard
Fowler, W
Farr, F.M
Goudlock, T.D
Griffin, Thomas
Goforth, W.M
Hames, L.A
Horn, Asbury
Horn, Elias
Hughey, J.R
Horn, Wash
James, Wash
Jefferies, Hamlet
Jones, James
Jeter, S.A
Jones, S
Kirby, Wm. D
Knox, James
Kendrick, T.J
Knox, Morgan
Knox, Thomas
Lee, W.A
Leonard, Wm
Littlejohn, C.T
Littlejohn, Henry
Littlejohn, M.R
Lockhart, J.C
Lockhart, J.N
Lenoad, J.M

Lockhart, R.M
Maberry, Saml
McCafferty, G.A
Macornsor, D.R
Mayes, L.C
McKown, F.M
Millwood, J.C
Millwood, J.H
Millwood, Morgan,
Moorhead, J.T
Moorhead, W.G
Mosely, D.P
Moseley, W.D
Murphy, M
Murphy, S.M
Peeler, J.R
Page, J.L
Page, R
Peeler, A.J
Peeler, D.M
Perkinson, S
Phillips, S.G
Puckett, I.H
Pearson, I.A
Phillips, G.M
Phillips, J.T
Phillips, T.J
Rodgers, W.N
Scott, H.W
Scott, T.E
Scates, L
Spencer, D.N
Sprouse, W
Stroup, T.H
Sartor, T
Shippey, M
Spencer, J
Sanders, A.J
Thompson, M.D
Wakefield, L
Ward, I.L
Ward, I.N
Wilkins, R.S
Wilkins, T.T
Ward, W.

COMPANY "G."

Captains:
Chandler, J.B
McCutcheon, J.

Lieutenants:
Haselden, W.M
Barren, B.P
Timmons. F.M
Cooper, F.E.

Sergeants:
Fulton, T.M
Wilson, W.J
Eaddy, T
McClary, J
Gamble, H.D
Cox, W.G
Lenerieux, F.M.

Corporals:
Brown, J.J
Johnson, M.M
Burrows, J.T
Nesmith, J.

Privates:
Autman, J.A
Altman, L.C
Abrams, I.B
Abrams, W
Ard, R
Ard, J
Ard, F
Avant O.R
Barrimeau, B.T.L
Barrimeau, J.J
Baxley, O
Bratcher, A
Brown, J
Brown, A.W
Brown, D.L
Bowden, H
Buckles, H
Buckles, L
Buckles, J
Burns, J
Burrows, I.T

Burrow, W.S
Carter, E.W
Carter, A.W
Carter, A.B
Carter, J.D
Carter, T
Colyer, J
Cox, L
Cox, F
Cox, W.I
Cox, J.R
Cox, J.T
Cox, I.G
Cockfield, J.C
Christman, G.W
Cribb, C
Cribb. D.W
Donahoe, A.W
Eaddy, I.F
Eaddy, W.S
Eaddy, G.J
Eaddy, D
Ferrel, F
Flagler, A.P
Gaskin, J.J
Gaskin, E.V
Gaskin, J.C
Gaskin, C.A
Gaskin, A.M
Gist, G.G
Gordon, H
Graham, J. McC
Graham, W.L
Gurganus, J.E
Hanna, G.W
Hanna, R
Hanna, J.F
Haselden, S.B
Haselden, A.J
Haselden, J
Haselden, J.R
Haselden, W.B
Haselden, J
Hudson. J
Hughes, ——
James, J.A
June, T.G

June, A
Johnson, E.H
Kinder, H.H
Lambert, B.P
McDonald, ——
McAlister, W
Marsh, J
Matthews, J.J
Matthews, W.W
Matthews, J
Maurice, R.F
McConnell, W.S
McDaniel, J
McLellan, A.K
Miller, J
Owens, J.A
Perkins, W.G
Paston II, A
Ponncy, J.A
Ponncy, M
Scott, A.W
Scott, J.C
Scott, G.C
Spring, G.W
Spivey. H.E
Stone, P.T
Stone, T.B
Tanner. T.A
Tanner, J
Thompson. S.B
Thompson, J
Tomas. J
Tilton, H
Venters, L
Venters, J
Whitehead, N.M
Whitehead. J.

COMPANY "H."

Captains:
Sims, W.H
Farr, W.P
Briggs, W.R
Farr, F.M.

Lieutenants:

Barley, J.L
Porter, J
Parr, W
Howell, M.

Sergeants:
Savage, J
Greer, F
Barley, J
Smith, H.

Corporals:
Fair, G
Coleman, B.C
Morgan, D.V.

Privates:
Adams, A.R
Adams, B
Adis, J
Adis, Wm
Adis, R
Alverson, W.G
Bentley, John
Bentley, James
Burgess, F
Burgess, R
Bevell, W
Bevell, W.H.H
Bends, L
Barnes, M
Conner, W.F
Conner, W.E
Cadd, F.R
Cadd, W.F
Chapman, J
Davis, J
Davis, P.A
Dabbs, W
Dabbs, J
Edge, J
Farr, D
Farr, D.A.T
Farr, D
Farr, N
Fausett, K
Fowler, J.M
Fowler, T
Fowler, G

Fowler, M
Garner, G.W
Garner, W
Garner, C
Garner, L
Garner, J
Gault, H.C
Gregery, A
Gregery, F
Griffin, W
Griffin, D
Hawkins, W
Howell, W
Howell, S.J
Hames, E
Hames, J
Haney, J
Haney, F
Humphries, A
Inman, D
Ivey, Wm
Ivey, Wiley
Ivey, R
Milwood, Frank
Milwood, E.V
Milwood, James
Milwood, Wm
Mitchell, A
McKinney, G
Motte, Jno
Mott, Jeff
Nance, N
Palmer, J
Palmer, E
Parr, R.T
Parr, D
Parr, Richard
Savage, A
Sharp, C
Simpson, C
Smith, M
Smith, W
Smith, Jno
Stears, A.D
Stears, D
Sprouse, L
Sprouse, Jno

Sprouse, A
Tracy, J
Vaughn, K
Vaughn, A.L
Vinson, J.W
Vaudeford, H
Vaudeford, W.M
Vaudeford, J.W
Wishard, J
Wix, James
Wix, Joel
Worthy, C
Worthy, Richard
Leverett, J.

COMPANY "I."

Captains:
Koon, J.H
Derrick, J.A.

Lieutenants:
Frick, R.W
Derrick, F.W
Lake, J.T
Fulmer, H
Monts, F.W
Davis, R
Wessinger, H.J
Lybrand, J.N
Keisler, Wade
Shealy, W.C.

Sergeants:
Wiggers, H.J
Frick, A.J
Lindler, S.P
Eargle, J.A
Long, P.D
Derrick, J.F
Frick, S.J
Frick, L.A
Wessinger, W.F
Amick, H.L.

Coporals:
Fulmer, C.N.G
Wessinger, N.J

Ballentine, C
Bowers, A.J.

Privates:
Amick, J. Wesley
Amick, Joseph W
Amick, James J
Amick, S.D.W
Amick, E.L
Amick, V.E
Amick, G.H
Amick, D.I
Amick, L.J
Amick, J.L
Bickley, J.H
Bickley, D.W
Bickley, J.A
Bickley, J.I
Busby, W.T
Boland, S.B
Ballentine, W.P
Ballentine, J.W
Coogler, D
Crout, J
DeHart, D
DeHart, J
Derrick, D. I
Derrick, F
Derrick, J.A
Dreher, G.L
Epting, D.W
Eargle, G.E
Feagle, George
Fulmer, L.J
Fulmer, W.P
Fulmer, D.J
Frick, I.N
Griffith, A
Ham, D
Hodge, A
Holman, W.W
Jacobs, J.E
Keisler, J.J
Koon, G.E
Koon, J.B
Koon, H.M
Koon, S.D
Koon, S.W

Koon, W.F
Koon, J.F
Koon, John F
Koon, Walter W
Koon, Hamilton
Koon, J.D
Koon, J.F
Koon, H.W
Lindler, S. G
Lindler, Jacob
Lindler, John
Long G.J
Long, J.J
Long, J.W
Long, Jno. W
Lybrand, J
Monts, G.M
Mayer, A.G
Metz, O.P
Perkins, W.S
Risk, W.I
Risk, J.A
Sutton. J
Shealy, N.E
Shealy, M
Shealy, G.M
Shealy, G.W
Shealy, S
Shealy, J
Shealy, W.W
Smith, G.W
Talbert, J.W
Turner, C.B.
Wiley, E
Wheeler, J.W
Wheeler, L.G
Wessinger, H.J
Wessinger, J.A
Wyse, W.M
Wiggers, A
Wiggers, J.D.

COMPANY "K."

Captain:
Bird, H.J.

Lieutenants:
Rodgers, W.M
White, A
Taggert, W.H
Smith, W.A
McCaslan, W.M
Henderson, O.

Sergeants:
Dean, B.A
Smith, S.B
Jennings, J.C
Freeland, S.E
McBride, S.S
McBride, J.B
Calvin, A.P.

Coporals:
Deason, A
Ballard, F.S
McCaine, J.K
Hendrix, M.F
Berdeshaw, W.C
Dorn, J.J
Bird, M
Attaway, S.

Privates:
Adams, J.Q
Bearden. W
Bangham, W.W
Bell, E.B
Bouchillon, H.M
Bouchillon, J.S
Bull, W.W
Bussey, T.J
Bird, D
Bird, W
Brown, R
Brown, W.M
Brown, E
Brown, M
Brown, J
Bussey, D
Bodie, J.R
Carr, N
Caldwell, J.W
Corley, J.A
Corley, C

Collins, J.F
Crawford, J.R
Cothran, J.M
Crestian, J.T
Covin, O.W
Cook, S
Curry, W.L
Dean, F
Devore, S
Devore, J. S
Devore, J.W
Doollittle, J.E
Doollittle, S
Ennis, J.O
Ennis, G. W
Ennis, T.W
Elam, J
Evans, J
Freeland, J.P
Frith, T
Gardner, W.T
Gardner, A.H
Glansier, P
Griffin, E
Hamilton, W.M
Harrison, H.C
Harrison, J
Hasteing, J
Harris, A
Henderson, C
Henderson, J.E
Hendrix, H.H
Hughes, J.S
Hill, T
Horn, S
Hannon, W
Holsomback, H.H
Hill, J
Hemphill, ——
Hardy, J
Holloway, W.J
Ivy, T
Irvin, J
Johnson, E.C
Jeno, M
Jennings, C
King, W.M
King, T
King, S
Lawton, F.E
Lawton, J.W
Lawton, A
Lawton, L
Ludwick, W.C
Lukewire, H
Mathis, T.E
Mayson, R.C
Mayson, P.A
Mayson, J
Mayson, J.C
Martin, H.D
McCain, W.J
Miner, J
Miner, W
Merriweather, R
McKinney, J
McKelvin, G.T
Martin, A.M
McCannon, W.R
Moore, J.D
Medlock, A
Newby, G.W
Purdy, J.H
Price, W.C
Price, R
Price, H
Rich, J.S
Robertson, J.B
Robertson, H
Rearden, L.D
Rodgers, P.A
Rodgers, P
Sperry, E.C
Shadrack, T.N
Shannon, W.N
Scott, W.D
Shover, W
Steadman, J
Sheppard, L
Towles, E
Tompkins, S
Tompkins, W
Timmerman, F
Taggart, P
Vaughn, J
Vaughn, D
Weeks, C
Whitton, C
Walker, B.C
Walker, C
Whatley, E
Weeks, S
Weems, J.T
New, S
Smith, W.H
Robertson, J.S
Davis, W.M
Reynolds, J.M
Crawford, J.W
Vaughn, W.

Roll of Third Battalion (James)

Lieutenant Colonel:
James, G.S.

Major:
Rice, W.G.

Commissary:
Senn, R.D.

Adjutant:
Harris, W.C.

Quartermaster:
James, B.S.

Sergeant Major:
Ligon, G.A.

Quartermaster Sergeant:
Ligon, R.B.

COMPANY "A."

Captains:
Rice, W.G
Townsend, J.M.

Lieutenants:
Anderson, J.W
Anderson, D.W
Anderson, Jno. W
Murchison, B.K
King, A.A.

Sergeants:
Craig, J.D.
Wilcutt, B.F
Moore, G.W

Anderson, J.J
Calhoun, J.W
Hunter, W.S
Nickols, R.J
Anderson, J.S

Corporals:
Davenport, L.P
Elmore, L
Teague, L.

Privates:
Anderson, P.K
Anderson, A.W
Anderson, A.T
Anderson, J.B
Burns, W
Busby, J.S
Calhoun, J
Calhoun, J.W
Chaney, T
Chaney, J.R
Craddock, J.R
Cannon, B
Clardy, B.S
Connor, L.D
Davis, J
Davis, W.D
Davis, A
Davis, T
Davis, B.F
Dodson, W
Elmore, Massalome
Elmore, J
Elmore, Maston
Elmore, G

Fooshe, J.A
Fooshe, J.D
Foose, J.C
Finley, J.H
Goddard, J.E
Goddard, W.E
Graves, W
Golding, J.J
Griffin, W.H
Griffin, E.W
Hines, G.W
Hill, M.S
Hill, B.T
Hill, N
Hodges, M
Knight, J
King, R
King, J.J
Lomax, W
Lipford, A
McGee, L.H
Martin, L
McPherson, J.M
Martin, L
Nelson, J.M
Nelson, E
Nelson, W.A
Norman, J
Nichols, J.H
Nichols, J
Owens, B.L
Owens, J.T
Owens, E.N
Pinson, E.M
Pinsom, C.F

Puckett, W.H
Puckett, S.D
Puckett, K.C
Redden, Hazel
Rampy, J.M
Redden, Harry
Saxon, P.A
Shirly, D.A
Shirley, Tully
Sims, Thadeus
Sims, S.C
Taylor, J
Taylor, Jno
Taylor, G
Watts, W.D.

COMPANY "B."

Captains:
Williams, J.G
Ligon, R.B
Watson, O.A
Wells, W.A
Pitts, W.S.

Lieutenants:
Roberts, J.C
Fuller, A.A
Ligon, J.W
Miller, C.M
Dunlap, R.S.

Sergeants:
Davis, J.W
Watson, J.E
Starnes, R.C
Waldrop, R.G
Nance, W.G
Bryson, H
Wright, W.W
Dunlap, R.S
Griffin, R.S
Grant, G.W.

Corporals:
Milam, A.R
Cox, M
Sims, L.S

Fuller, J.C
Walker, F.M
Jones, J.A
Nance, R.G
Fuller, W.B.

Privates:
Austin, I.G
Austin, I.S
Boazman, W.M
Boazman, B.S
Brown, T.S
Bailey, J
Butler, R.P
Boozer, J.J
Butler, W.L
Brown, H.R
Benjamin, S.R
Bailey, M
Crawford, J.W
Coleman, T.T
Coleman, O.A
Calhoun, T.H
Cook, W.I
Cole, W.M
Daniel, T.D
Duncan, J.G
Dalrymple, J.H
Dendy, E.G
East, O.D
Fuller, A.S
Fuller, P.A
Fuller, E.P
Fuller, J
Fuller, E
Finley, S.J
Goodman, B
Goodman, B.B
Griffin, E
Harvey, J.H
Hitt, H.L
Hitt, P
Hitt, Robt
Hazel, G
Hazel, J
Hollingsworth, R.S
Hollingsworth, A
Hughes, J.H

Hand, W
Hacot, B.C
Irby, W.L
Kissick, F
Ligon, J.S
Ligon, G
Ligon, J
Lindsey, D.W
Lowe, I.G
Lake, R.S
Mates, W.M
Miller, W.P
Madden, W.C
Myres, Z.E
Milam, H.W
Milam, J.A
Milam, W
Nelson, M.L
Nelson, J.F
Nelson, A
Nelson, J.M
Nelson, W
Nance, F.W.N
O'Neal, J
Pitts, G.W
Pitts, F
Reed, J.Y
Reed, B
Roberts, J
Richardson, W
Smith, M
Snow, A.J
Thompson, W
Williams, R.E
Winnebrenner, G
Wells, W.J
Wheeler, M.A
Watts, E.C
Watts, J.G
Waldrop, W.E.

COMPANY "C."

Captains:
Shumate, J.J
Hudgens, W.L
Irby, G.M.

Lieutenants:
Woods, T.R.L
Henderson, M.W
Cooper, J.N
Fuller, H.Y
Wadkins, H.H
Baldwin, S.B
Fuller, A.C.

Sergeants:
Boyd, W.L
Hudgens, A.W
Donney, J
Bolt, W
Cooper, T.P.

Corporals:
Culbertson, Y.J
Anderson, D.S
Stone, W.W.

Privates:
Abereromble, J.C
Andrews, W.W
Avery, S.K
Avery, J
Adams, J.P
Boyd, J.Y
Burton, J.J
Bolt, S
Bolt, Saml
Bolt, Jno
Bolt, James
Bolt, Franklin
Brown, G.M
Brooks, J.P
Brooks, N.P
Baldwin, J.E
Baldwin, D.H
Baldwin, V
Burgess, E.R
Blackwell, J.H
Box, W.I
Cooper, H.H
Cooper, J.Y
Cooper, J.A
Cooper, D.M
Culbertson, Y.S
Culbertson, J.B

Culbertson, M.M
Culbertson, W.P
Culbertson, T.H
Culbertson, W.S
Culbertson, J.R
Culbertson, J.M
Culbertson, J.H
Cheshire, L.H
Cheshire, C
Cannon, W.N
Cannon, R
Duvall, J.H
Dugnall, W
Elledge, J.P
Fuller, I.M
Godfrey, J
Hudgens, R
Hudgens, C
Hellams, C.C
Henderson, L
Hill, W.T
Johnson, M
Johnson, B.F
Jenkins, J.A
Jenkins, R
Jones, B.F
Jones, J.B
Knight, W.D
Lindley, H
Lindsey, T
Lindley, W
Mitchell, M
Murff, M
Micham, A
Moore, L
Moore. M
Moore, Jackson
Moore, Frank
Moats, W.C
Morgan, W
Manley, B.T
Manley, P.J
Moats, T.A
McClellan, J.A
Malvey, P.W
Medlock, A
Nash, W.M

Nelson, W.Y
Nelson, J.W
Nelson, F
Pitts, J.W
Pitts, J.S
Puckitt, G.W
Puckitt, W.A
Robertson, J
Robertson, H.D
Ryley, J
Ross, A
Ross, T
Saxton, F
Shumate, R.Y
Shumate. L.J
Shumate, H
Sullivan, H
Stevens, J.P
Terry, B.F
Taylor, H.P
Taylor, B
Vaughn, B
Watkins, T.J
Watkins, L
Walker, J.A.

COMPANY "D."

Captain:
Gunnels, G.M.

Lieutenants:
James, B.S
Kirk, C.E
Allison, R.W.

Sergeants:
Harris, J
Potter, B.L
Dial, D.T
Armstrong, D

Corporals:
Shell, J.H
Allison, J
Ramage, F
Simmons, W.

Privates:

Adams, J
Adams, Robert
Armstrong, S
Atwood, M
Abrams, G.W
Babb, William
Babb, Doc
Babb, J
Belle, L.G
Barger, H.M
Boyd, E
Boyd, D.W
Bailey, A.P
Brownley, J.R
Burdette, G.W
Bishop, W
Bishop, J.W
Bailey, M.S
Bishop, J.C
Blalock, R
Chappell, W
Chambers, J.B
Cunningham, M.C
Cunningham, R.A
Curry, L
Cason, M.J
Crisp, A
Duncan, R
Epps, W
Eutrican, W.M
Evans, W.R
Garlington, C
Gunnels, W
Graham, A
Hollingsworth, J.I
Hollingsworth, A.C
Hellams, W
Hellams, Y
Harmond, F.F
Harris, S
Hatton, T.J
Hollingsworth, W
Joyce, J.C
Jones E.P
Jones, H.C
Johnson, Dr. J.P
Kelly, F

Knight, D
Langston, Henry
Loyd, T
Madden, D.C
Martin, J
Mason, A
May, J.P
Metts, M.B
McCawley, Martin
McCawley, James
McKnight, W.D
Milam, W.S
Munroe, W
Neal, A.T
Owens, J.H
Owens, L
Parks, A.R
Peas, Jno
Potter, Moses
Price, James
Ray, J.J
Rook, S
Rowland, A
Richardson, Jno
Shell, E.C
Shockley, J
Shockley, R
Simmonds, J
Starks, D
Spears, R.S
Spears, G.T
Speake, J.T
Speake, J.L
Stoddard, W
Taylor, A.S
Thomas, J.H
Tribble. E.E
Wesson, Thomas
West, S
Whitton, D.M
Winn, C
Wolff, W.Y
Harris, W.C.

COMPANY "E."

Captains:

Hunter, Melnott,
Fowler, W.H
Ware, H
Burnside, Alien

Lieutenants:
Riddle. A.J
Cooper, E
Cox, M.C
Henry, B.L
Moore, P

Sergeants:
Fowler, W.D
Farburn, N
Mills, J.A
Armstrong, D
Owens, M.

Corporals:
Riddle, M
Ball, S.P.

Privates:
Balle, L.G
Bramlett, C
Bramlett, H
Bramlett, J
Bramlett, R
Brown, J
Bryant. T.T
Bryant, W
Burdett. J
Burns, J
Burns, R
Cheek, J
Cook, W.C
Cox, S
Culbertson, B
Culbertson, M
Farrow, T
Fleming, P
Fowler. J.R
Frank, J
Fowler, W
Garner, J
Garrett. P
Garrett, W.A
Gillian. W

Gideons, J.L
Guinn, M
Gray, J
Grumble, W
Hand, W
Handback, M
Handback, W
Higgins, A.H
Holcomb, A
Holcomb, H
Holcomb, J
Holcomb, S
Holcomb, Wm
Hunt, ——
Hunt, ——
Kernell, Wm
Knight, J
Long, J
Long, T
Martin, J.R
McNeely, J
Miller, J.D
Moore, G
Newman, B
Newman, S
Osborn. W
Owens, A.Y
Owens, G
Owens, T
Owens, Y
Park, J.H
Park, T
Patton, W.P
Powers. B
Powers, P
Prior, L.
Riddle, D
Riddle, F
Riddle, G
Riddle, L
Riddle, M
Riddle. N
Riddle, W
Robertson, J.R
Ropp, H
Spelts, R
Stuart, B

Stuart, J
Stuart, John
Stuart, Joseph
Stuart, Robt
Sumerel, M
Sumerel, T
Sumerel, W
Switzer, L.O
Thompson, W
Todd, R.J
Garrett, J
Morgan, S.

COMPANY "F."

Captain:
Miller, D.B.

Lieutenants:
Percival, E.S
Morrison, R.S
Freidburg, Joseph.

Sergeants:
Percival, F.H
Kirkland, R.S
Diseker, J.H
Keough, P.H
DeLoria, A.

Corporals:
Friday, S.D
Montgomery, G.B.W
Scott, F.J
Cathcart, W.J.

Privates:
Altee, J.W
Barefoot, Sion
Bates, O.B
Baugn, Wm
Boyer, Moses
Bull, Thomas
Burroughs, W.D
Bellinger, Wm
Cloffy, P
Campbell, James,
Cooper, Jesse
Cooper, Thomas

Curlee, John
Dennis, H
Denkins, Saml
Flemming. A.H
Forbs, J.G
Friedman, B
Fulmer, W
Gardner, J.H
Glaze, Jno
Glaze, Allen
Gladden, L.T
Hickson, Sam
Howell, R.E
Jones, David
Legrand, W.W
Lever, Geo
Marsh, Edward
McCauley, J.B
Miles, E.H
Miot, C.H
Moye, J.E
Munson, W
Moore, Allen
Neely, Jno
Norman, Chas
North, S.R
Percival, G
Percival, N.N
Purse, T.P
Pollock, J.L
Reiley, James
Rembert, Jno
Reaves, Jno
Ross, Thos
Sill, T
Saunders, J.W
Senn, Dedrick
Schultz, W.C
Smith, T.N.C
Smith, Sol
Spriggs, H.V.L
Stokes, E.R Jr
Turner, W.T
Taylor, Wm
Taylor, Jno
Thrift, Robt
Tradewell, F.A

White, E.C
White, G.A
Williamson, T
Williamson, D.W
Wardlaw, W.H
Aughtry, Jno
Davis, Andrew
Elkins, James
Elkins, Spence
Hammond, E
Lee, John
Sealy, Wm
Wooten, Danl.

COMPANY "G."

Captains:
Irby, A.P
Whitner, B.M.

Lieutenants:
Gladney, Wash
Robinson, J.S
Shedd, J.P
DesPortes, R.S
Jennings, R.H.

Sergeants:
Martin, D
Ashford, J.W
Gibson, H.T
Trapp, Laban
Watt, B.F
Trapp, L.H
Mason, W.N.

Corporals:
Beard, J.M
Robinson, Wm
Blair, A.F
Craig, T.N.A
Craig, Wm.

Privates:
Aiken, Jim
Aiken, H.G
Aiken, H.N
Aiken, Robt
Brown, U

Brown, J.W
Brown, T.G
Brown, J.R
Blair, Thos
Blair, A.F
Boyd, John
Boney, Jesse
Bull, Thomas
Brown, Chas
Beard, James
Brown, Frank
Crawford, R.B
Crompton, Thomas,
Carman, Sam
Carman, Jesse
Crossland, H.J
Chandler, W
Craig, Wm
Crossland, Jasper
Carmack, Warren
Davis, T.C
DesPortes, J.A
Douglass, C.M
Douglass, W.T
Douglass, S.M
Flanigan, Z
Gladney, B
Gladney, W.R
Gradick, Jesse
Gibson, H.J
Gibson, Green
Hamilton, Wm
Hogan, Pink
Hawes, Tatum,
Haigwood, Jeff
Haigwood, R.M
Hook, W.T
Hopkins. Wm
Irby, W.F
Irby, Wm
Johns, Wm
Jennings, Robt
Lyles, B.F
McConnel, Butler
McClure, Jno
Millings, Rus
Mann, Thos

Martin, Jno
Morgan, Wm
Mason, W.N
Millings, J.N
Moore, Nathan
McKintry. T.B
McConnell, A.C
McCreight. S
McCrady. M.H
Milling, Hugh
Martin, Newton
Martin, Wm
Nelson, J.T
Paul, J.T
Porter, C
Pouge, W.C
Robinson, James
Robinson, W.W
Robinson, I.Y
Robinson, S.N
Robinson, W.I
Ragsdale, E.R
Rabb, Calvin
Russel, Jno
Shedd, W.H
Scott, Jesse
Tinkler, George
Tinkler, Wm
Turkett, T.W
Trapp, U.C
Wilson, Dave
Withers, James
Weldon, Wm
Veronce, C.B.

Roll of Twentieth South Carolina Volunteer Regiment.

Colonels:
Keitt, L.M
Boykin, S.M.

Lieutenant Colonels:
Dantzler, O.M
McMichael, P.A.

Majors:
Mimms, A
Partlow, J.M
Leaphart, G.

Adjutants:
Chisolm, R
Hane, W.C
Wilson, Jno. A.

Quartermasters:
Kinard, Jno. P
Woodward, T.W.

Commissary:
Heriot, Jno. O.

Surgeon:
Salley, A.S.

Assistant Surgeons:
Fripp, C.A
Barton, D.R.

Chaplains:
Meynardie, E.J
Duncan, Y.W.

Sergeant Majors:
Quattlebaum, T.A
Quattlebaum, E.R.

Quartermaster Sergeants:
Barton, T.F
Wannamaker, F.W.

Commissary Sergeant:
Solomons, J.T.

Ordnance Sergeant:
Phillips, T.H.

COMPANY "A."

Captains:
Partlow, Jno. M
Woodin, C.H.A
Lee, Jno.

Lieutenants:
Talley, Dyer
Williams, D.O
Norton, E.R
Siddall, Jno
Barr, S.A.

Sergeants:
Lusk, Newt
Wilcox, F.H
Knee, Hermon
Wilson, Mack.

Corporals:
Ansel, Harmon
Smith, C.M
Norrell, John
Fisher, James.

Privates:

Anderson, John
Appleton. Wm
Atkinson, Thomas
Burrell, Miles
Beiman, Henry
Bracke, Henry
Bramlett, Wm
Ballinger, Wm
Babb, ——
Brace, ——
Bowlin, Thos
Brown, Le
Butler, Levi
Craine, Wm
Craine, Isaac
Cannon, S.C
Carpenter, Wm
Crow, Isaac
Dawkins, ——
Darby, Thos
Ellenburg, Jno
Elrod, ——
Ellis, G
Fisher, Wm
Fisher, B.P
Heddin, J.P
Heddin, Isaac
Heddin, D.B
Holcomb, ——
Hembree, Wm
Handcock, Thos
Holly, James
Ivester, Anderson,
Knight, Jno
Kelly, Wm

Kelly, W.N
Lusk, Jno
Lyda, Jno
Owens, Riley
Partlow, Pickens
Patterson, Wesley
Powell, Ashley
Randolph, S.H
Reid, Samuel
Reid, Massey
Reid, James M
Rochester, W.T
Richie, D.L
Sanders, Elijah
Smith, Ezekiel
Smith, D.W.S
Teague, Wm
Teague, Isaac
Turner, Pickens
Vinson, D
Vinson, Jno
Ward, Nathaniel,
Woodsin, C.H.A
Wilson, Mack.

COMPANY "B."

Captain:
McMichael, P.A.

Lieutenants:
Barton, B.H
Whetstone, N.C
Cox, J.R.

Sergeants:
Inabinet, D.J
Way, A.H
Myers, D.D
McCorquodale, ——
Donald, J.A.

Corporals:
Shuler, J.W
Murphy, J.C
Grambling, A.M
Buyck, F.J.

Privates:
Arant, J.T

Bair, J.S
Bair, S.H
Barber, W.E
Bars, W
Baxter, D.F
Bolin, J.E.A
Bolin, J.S
Boltin, J.H
Boltin, E.A
Bonnet, J.D
Bonnet, W.R.E
Bozard, D.B
Bozard, J.D
Bozard, C.F
Brantley, E.W
Brodie, J.W
Brodie, John W
Brodie, Judson
Brodie, J.R
Buyck, J.W
Clayton, W
Collier, L.P
Cook, J.M
Cox, A.M
Crum, J.W
Crum, A.F
Culalasieur, N.W
Dantzler, G.M
DeWhit, M
Dixon, W
Dixon, Henry
Dukes, T.C
Elbrooks, H
Fair, G.S
Fair, J.W
Felkel, J.R
Felkel, J.A
Friday, P.D
Grambling, F.H
Grambling, J.H
Grey, A
Haigler, J.A
Heiner, H.W
Herron, R.R
Holman, A.C
Horger, J.F
Houck, J.J

Houser, J.D
Hutchins, J.C
Hutchins, J.A
Huff, G.W
Hunkerpieler, T.N
Hunkerpella, L
Jackson, J.F
Jackson. J.C
Joyner, D.P
Judy, H
Judy, H.I
Keiser, W.J
Keiser, F.D
Leaird, H.D
Lyles, T
Mack, J
Metts, D.G
Metts, G.W
Metts, W.J
Murphy, H.H
Murphy, L
Murphy, H.B
Murphy, P
Noble, S
Patrick, J
Patrick, D.W
Patrick, E
Patrick, S.P
Patrick, V.V
Pearson, J.H
Pooser, F.N
Pooser, E.H
Rast, J.A
Rast, J.C
Rast, J.L
Rast, T.F
Rast, J.S
Rast, G.D
McReady, E
Reay, M
Riley, H.W
Riley, O.B
Rutlin, W.W
Rutland, A.E
Rutland, H
Seagler, J.E
Sellars, G.D

Shuler, J.W
Smoak, R.F
Smoak. A.B
Smoak, M.T
Smoak, G.W
Stellinger, T.W
Stellinger, F
Till, H.F
Till, T.J
Walsh, J.J
Wannamaker, H.C
Wannamaker, F.M
Way, R.F
Way, J.D
Wolf, W.S
Zeigler, H.H
Zimmerman, D
Bonnett, J.D
McMichael, O
Smoak, G.W
Knights, J.D
Huff, D.W
Wethers, M.L
Kennerly, L.D.S.

COMPANY "C."

Captains:
Leaphart, G
Haltiwanger, G.T.

Lieutenants:
Huffman, J.E
Eleazer. W.S
Haltiwanger, H.W.

Sergeants:
Houseal, W.F
Metts, S.S
Eleazer, J.M
Haltiwanger, J.H
Burkett, T.

Corporals:
Hipps, I.A
Williamson, W
Addy, T.M.G
Ballentine, S

Haltiwanger, D.K
Smith, S.L.

Privates:
Arnick, T.W
Arnick, I.A
Arnick, W.R
Arnick, D.W
Addy, J.B
Addison, H.T
Archart, H.M
Baker, J
Black, N.L
Black, W.E
Bookman, S.W
Bouknight, W.J
Bouknight, J.W
Busby, L
Busby, W
Buff, H.J
Buff. J
Bickley, H.W
Bouknight, J.M
Bundrick, J.M
Bundrick, J.A
Bristow, J.M
Cumelander, W.N
Cumelander, A.W Sr
Cumelander, A.W Jr
Cumerlander, J.S
Cumerlander, S.C
Counts, H.A
Caughman, J.C
Coogler, J.P
Coogler, R.E
Clocus, H
Counts, H.A
Daly, J.T
Daly, W.A
Dean, J.A
Derrick, J.H
Derrick, J.S
Derrick, W.C
Derrick, J
Derrick, H.D
Derrick, J.D
Derrick, G.J
Derrick, S.W

Dreher, O.A
Dreher, E.J
Eleazer, R.J
Eleazer, G.B
Epting, D.J
Epting, J.H
Eargle, J.J
Eargle, A.D
Eargle, J.D
Eargle, J.W
Eargle, A.D
Fulmer, W.F
Fulmer, J.F
Farr, G
Farr, B
Freshley, G.W
Frick, E.D
Geiger, J
Geiger, D.W
Geiger, F.S
Geiger, J
Geiger, M
Geiger, E.W
Geiger, G.M
Geiger, J.A
Geiger, L.S
Haltiwonger, G.C
Haltiwonger, J.S
Haltiwonger, G.J
Haltiwonger, D.J
Haltiwonger, J.E
Haltiwonger, J.J
Hiller, P.J
Hiller, S.B
Hiller, S
Hiller, J.A
Hyler, J.B
Hunt, N
Hameter, G
Jacobs, W.A
Jacobs, J
Kibler A
Koon, W.W
Koon, J.F
Koon, J.L
Keitt, J.D
Lorick, J.D

Lowman, J.P
Lowman, S.G
Lowman, P.G
Lowman, J.S
Lowman, P.E
Lybrand, B.C
Long, D.E
Long, W.W
Mayer, G.W
Metts, G.S
Metts, G.S
Metts, J.F
Metts, M.S
Metts, E.C
Metts, J.C
Metts, R.A
Metts, J.T
Metts S.J
Metts, C
Metts, L
Metts, E.W
Mathias, L.S
Mathias, T.S.
McCartha, R
McCartha, J
Monts, J
Nates, J.T
Nates, J.A
Nunnamaker, A.S
Nunnamaker, J.H
Nunnamaker, D
Nunnamaker, W.A
Revel, J.W
Shuler, P.I
Shuler, J.L
Shuler, J.R
Stack, W
Stack, H
Sheeley, J.D
Sheeley, P.P
Sheeley, D
Sheeley, J.J
Sheeley, J.M
Suber, W.F
Slice, J.J
Slice, J.W
Slice, J.D

Summer, J.W Sr
Summer, J.W Jr
Seigler. J
Seigler, W
Schmitz, J.D
Stone, H
Swygert, J.W
Taylor, C
Williams, W.H
Williamson, W
Whites, E.M
Whites, A.E
Whites, S.H
Wessinger, G.S
Wessinger, J
Wessinger, J.D
Weed, C.A
Weed, J.C
Youngenener, J
Leaphart, L.

COMPANY "D."

Captain:
Donnelly, R.V.

Lieutenants:
Livingston, B
Jeffcoat, N.P
Inabenat, T.

Sergeants:
Jeffcoat, H.W
Jeffcoat, J
Redmorn, I
Livingston, J.S.

Privates:
Axson, W.A
Axson, F.D
Bailey, G
Brown, W.F
Bonnett, P
Cartin, E
Casson, J
Carson, R.A
Carton, W
Carton, E

Carson, W.H
Cain, W.P
Carson, T.J
Carton, W
Cook, J.A
Cook, J.Q
Cook, S
Crider, T.J
Crider, A
Crider, A
Crun, V.V
Crun, H
Culler, J
Chavis, P
Chavis, J
Cubsted, J
Davis, J
Evans, A
Fogle, P.S
Fogle, P
Fogle, J.W
Furtick, G
Furtick, W
Furtick, I
Gantt, C
Hughes, M.L
Hughes, E
Hughes, J.W
Hughes, A
Hughes, W
Hutts, J
Hutts, Jacob
Hooker, J.W
Hooker L.S
Hooker, J.L.G
Hooker. J.O.A
Hooker, G
Harley, J.M
Harley, J.H
Harley, G.W
Harley, J
Harley, T.W
Hoover, J
Inabinett, G
Jeffcoat, C.A
Jeffcoat, J.J
Jeffcoat, E.D.A

Jeffcoat, J.W
Jernegan, L
Johnson, P.P
Johnson, J.W
Johnson, J
Jorner, J
Jorner, H.W
King, W
Kneese, J
Kneese, W
Livingston, G.H
Livingston, W.B
Livingston, R
Livingston, M
Livingston, J.H
Livingston, F.D
Mennicken, J.A
Mack, J.B
Mack, W.C
Mack, F.H
McMichael, R.V
McMichael, W
Mixon, L
Murph, T.W
North, J.F
Ott, J.T
Oliver, T.W
Pou, J.A.R
Pou, W.G
Pou, B.F
Pound, J
Price, P
Porter, D.A
Porter, E
Porter, J
Porter, J.A
Phillips, J.F
Phillips, J.T
Phillips, G
Peil, W
Reed, J
Reid, J
Reid, R
Reid, W.H
Rucker, R
Rucker, W
Redman, A

Redmond, P
Robinson, L
Robinson, J.T
Starns, J
Searight, J
Stabler, M
Stabler, H
Tyler, L
Wacor, W.L
Williamson, W
Williamson, E
Williamson, T
Williamson, D.R
Williamson, G
Williamson, W
West, W
Wise, D
Wise, J
Wise, J
Witt, W.P
Zeigler, A
Donnely, O.

COMPANY "E."

Captain:
Cowan, N.A.

Lieutenants:
Shirley, J.J
Pruitt, W.C
King, J.A
Mattison, J.F.

Sergeants:
Copeland, J.J
Clinkscales, F
Parker, J.P
Hall, A.M
Broom, W.J.

Corporals:
Kay, C.M
Hanks, Luke
Shirley, N.A
Acker, W.H
Parker, R.E.

Privates:

Armstrong, J.A
Ashley, J.T
Adams, A.B
Armstrong, A.S
Ashley, John
Ashley, J.R
Ashley, J.T
Ashley, E.W
Arnold, Joel
Anderson, T.W
Brock, R.B
Brock, J.L
Bannister, M
Brock, J.H
Brock, W.C
Bancum, A
Bannister, Thomas
Bannister, W.L
Bannister, J.H Sr
Bannister, J.M
Bannister, J.H. Jr
Bannister, J.N
Broom, J.N
Broom, A
Bagwell, Baylis
Bigby, J.A
Coker, J.J
Cummings, C.C
Callahan, J.F
Cowan, W.M
Cummings, H.A
Callahan, J.R
Callahan, D.P
Coleman, Robert
Fox, F.J
Cobb, M.A
Crasberry, A
Cox, Mac
Diver, B.F
Dunlap, W.F
Drennan, S.A
Davis, A.M
Dalrymple, J
Drake, E.H
Elgin, H
Flower, J.Y
Fields, Stephen

Fields, T
Freeman, W.G
Gambrell, S.V
Gillespie, A
Gilkerson, W.D
Gilkerson, J.A
Gantt, E.S
Grubb, C.C
Gambrell, P.M
Gambrell, E.H
Greer, J.W
Greer, George
Hawkins, R.L
Hall, J.B
Haynie, S.P
Haynie, James
Haynie, J.C
Haynie, Pink
Holliday, J
Harris, E
Hall, W.C
Hanks, J.M
Hanks, Thomas
Harper, N
Johnson, W.G.W
King, D.P
Kay, W.R
Kay, M.V.S
Keaton, J.J
Kay, J.L
King, J.D
King, J.D Jr
Kay, M.H
Kay, J.B
Kay, W.S
Leopard, H.B
Lathan, J
Lusk. J.F
Mattison, James
Mulligan, W.H
Mann, S.H
McDavid, J.Q
Martin, Samuel
Mann, A.K
Martin, W.A
Morgan, David
Mattison. W.H

Massey, J.C
Massey, S.B
McLane, John
Murdock, J.T
Murdock, Stephen,
McCoy, E.W
Morrison, O.D
Mitchell, John
Mitchell, E.M
Martin, Welborn,
Neighbor, J.T
Owens, A.W
Pruitt, J.B
Pruitt, Joshua
Pruitt, E.O
Pruitt, E.D
Pruitt, T.C
Pruitt, J.P
Pearman, W.L
Pearman, W.C
Pearman, S.N
Pepper, E.K
Posey, R.L
Pack, J.B
Pitts, J.G
Pruitt, B.F
Robinson, Isaac
Robinson, Jesse
Robinson, R.B
Robinson, J.A
Robinson, J.H
Robinson, G.B
Robinson, J.M
Robinson, S.E
Robinson, R.B.A
Recketts, William
Ragsdale, F.A
Saylors, J.N
Saylors, Isaac
Shirley, S
Smith, William
Shaw, R.M
Shaw, C.M
Saylors, W.P
Saddler, Isaac
Saylor, J.W
Saylors, W.P

Saylors, W
Stone, A.H
Stone, J.B
Shaw, H.W
Shaw, J.C
Shirley. F.F
Shirley, J.J
Shirley, J.M
Smith, J.N
Smith, C
Saddler, William
Southerland, W.F
Simpson, J.D
Seawright, John
Seawright, J.S
Taylor, J.W
Tucker, L.P
Tucker, W.T
Tucker, Wm. L
Todd, I.A
Tribble, L.W
Tribble, S.M
Thurkill, ——
Vandiver, D.J
Williams, Ira
Woods, W.J
Wilson, J.J
Woods, Robert
Wilson, R.C
Wilson, J.M
Wilson, W.R
Wilson, W.N
Wilson, J.R
Wright, C.J
Wright, J.W
Wright, T.T
Williamson, M
Williamson, James,
Walden, J
Willingham, A.P
Willingham, J.N
Cowan, Andrew.

COMPANY "F."

Captains:
Kinard, John M
Kinard. Wm. M.

Lieutenants:
Sligh, Hilary
Kingsmore, E.R
Cannon, W.S.

Sergeants:
Reid, S.W
Buzzard, B.M
Epting, J.N
Graham, F.D
Goree, W.O.

Corporals:
Richie, C.M
Dickert, Jesse C
Rikard, Frank D.

Privates:
Abrams, Z.P
Abrams, S.S
Abrams, Daniel
Baker, M
Barrett, B
Brooks, H.J
Boozer, Tim
Boozer, Henry
Brown, M.L
Beard, S.P
Buzzard, O.H
Buzzard, Jeff
Buzzard, W.F
Buzzard, William
Bowles, W.H
Barre, S.C
Bedenbaugh, W.P
Cady, F.N
Calmes, C. Wash
Campell, Ed
Cannon, Geo. W
Chapman, D.N
Chapman, Henry
Counts, John C
Counts, Adam
Counts, A.B
Cromer, John R
Cromer, Jacob L
Cromer, Enoch
Cromer, R. Press
Collins, A.B
Crooks, John
Denson, John F
Denson, George
Dickert, Wm. T
Dickert, Marion
Dunwoody, S.H
Davis, John D
Dominick, L.F
Ducket, John
Epps, Wm. T
Epps, Micajah
Eady, Wm. H
Folk, Ham H
Farrow, Wood H
Glenn, Wm. H
Glenn, John D
Glenn, William
Glenn, Daniel
Glymph, B.J
Greer, R.P
Gary, I.N
Gaunt, Jeff
Henson, H.O
Hough, Andrew J
Houseal, John I
Hentz, Julius D
Hawkins, George
Herbert, Sullivan
Jones, J.E
Jones, Lewis
Kibler, Adam
Kibler, D.W.T
Kissick, J.W
Koon, W.F
Kinard, Miner
Kinard, N
Lane, J.C
Livingston, J.C
Livingston, Robert J
Livingston, Ham
Lindsay, James
Martin, Cline
McGill, Archie
McCullough, H.S
McCullough, W.P
Miller, J.F
Miller, Joseph T
Miller, J.D
Montgomery, William
Moody. J.P.
Nates, Jacob
Norris, John E
Nichols, Andrew
Rikard, A
Rhodes, J.W
Rook. J.T
Rook, S.J
Rook, J.W
Ropp, A.J
Rumbly, A.J
Reeder, William
Sanders, J.M
Setzler, W.A
Sloan, John P
Stone, J. William
Stone, Henry
Suber, D.F
Stewart, John C
Stewart, S.F
Singley, G.M
Singley, J.H
Bedenbaugh, Pink
Cook, C.J
Cowan, E
Sligh, Munroe
Spencer, M
Thomas, Ed
Thrift, John
Watts, W. Peck
Wedeman, J.D
Wedeman, Silas
Wheeler, J.F
Williams, Robert, H
Wilcox, W.P
Wicker, Lang
Wicker, D
Wicker, D.R
Wicker, T.V

Wicker, Belt
Willingham, P.W
Wilson, J.S
Wilson, J.C
Wilson, H.C
Wilson, G
Wright, M.J
Wilcox, W.P.

COMPANY "G."

Captains:
Boykin, S.M
Herriott, R.L
Mosely, A.

Lieutenants:
White, L.A
Rhame, G.S
McCaskill, K
Belvin, W.T
Herriott, J.V.

Sergeants:
Lafan, M.L
McLeod, William
McCaskill, F.D
Boykin, J.J
Boykin, S.B
Hancock, W.J
Jones, G.W
Madison, K
Mathis, J.R
McEachern, J.R.

Corporals:
McEachern, W.D
Allen, J.C
Andrews, O.T
Barfield, R.E
Mathis, J.V
Eachern, W.C
Smith, T.W.B.

Privates:
Atkinson, William
Atkinson, Wash
Andrews, E
Boykin, William

Boykin, Drewry
Boykin, S.L
Boykin, Elias
Boykin, M.H
Boykin, James
Boykin, C.M
Bounds, John
Brown, I.T
Brown Joshua
Button, C.S
Bradley, S.B
Bird, James
Baker, A
Brunson, J.I
Bradley, William
Croft, William
Croft, Wesly
Cannon, G
Corbitt, J.A
Collins, Alex
Caughman, Joe
Corbitt, J.N
Dorety, T.G
Dunlop, Samuel
Dorety, William
Dorety, Manning
Dorety, Henry
Dorety, Thomas
Dorety, Laton
Druggus, M.D
Dixon, Benj
Davis, G.P.W
Davis, Joel
Davis, J.D
Davis, Lucas
Davis, Offel
Davis, C.R
Deas, E
Duncan, George
Daniels, Wes
Daniels, Alf
Genobles, Rufus
Gaillard, Rufus
Gaillard, W.F
Hawkins, Wash
Harmon, James
Hatfield, Benj

Hatfield, William
Hatfield, Caleb
Hatfield, Charles
Hatfield, Wesly
Hancock, E.J
Hancock, T.D
Hancock, G.W
Hawkins, John
Huggins, Willie
Hutchens, ——
Hyott, James
Jeffers, Daniel
Jeffers, H.J
Jones, R.L
Jones, C.L
Jones, Henry
Jones, M
Jones, Francis
Jeffers, John
Kirby, ——
Lee, John
Lee, William
Lucas, T.B
Lucas, M.B
McCaskill, Robert
Mathis, William
Mathis, G.M
Mathis, E.B
Mathis, S
Mathis, Alex
Murph, Henry
Moseley, William
Moseley, George
Myers, T.S
Myers, P.A
McKensie, L.A
Moonyham, Stephen,
McCutcheon, John,
Marsh, J.
McCaswill, ——
Neighbors, H
Neighbors, David,
Neighbors, Isaac
Neighbors, Thomas,
Nichols, W.A
Otts, James
Partin, William

Partin, J.W
Rhame, Thomas
Rodgers, J.D
Rodgers, Latson
Rodgers, Manning,
Smith, J.M
Smith, Tally
Scott, Fleming
Scott, Benjamin
Syfan, C.E
Solomons, T.J
Solesby, ——
Stokes, J.L
Shiver, John
Sexious, ——
Tuninel, ——
Tensley, Thomas
Tidwell, Adison
Tidwell, William
Vassar, E.A
Vicks, William
Whites, Henry
Watson, J.T
White, John
Weldon, Benjamin
Weldon, Pake
Wacton, R.C
Watts, William
Boykin, M.S.

COMPANY "H."

Captains:
Kinsler, Edward
Roof, S.M.

Lieutenants:
Hook, E.E
Hook, R.T
Hook, J.S.
SERGEANTS:
Mills, Jack A
Sox, Jeff
Senn, J.E
Senn, A.D
Roof, Henry J
Hook, J.D.

Corporals:
Roof, D.J
Dooley, James L
Sox, H.E
Griffith, D.T
Hutto, Britton E
Hutto, Paul P
Sphraler, J.J.

Privates:
Bachman, C
Bachman, H.H
Bachman, R.H
Buff, M.W
Buff, T.J
Buff, M.B
Blackwell, C.B
Berry, Jacob
Berry, George
Berry, Treadway
Berry, John
Bell, John
Clark, P.P
Clark, J.D
Churchwell, Thomas
Cook, E.E
Cook, John C
Carter, Henry A
Chaney, J.T
Dooley, Jesse K
Dooley, Jacob E
Dooley, J.L
DeVore, Thomas
Fry, J.R
Fry, Tyler
Fry, Thomas A
Gable, Godfrey
Gable, E.E
Gregory, Franklin
Gregory, John G.A
Hook, M.M
Hook, Jacob
Hook, J.V
Hooks, J.G
Herron, E
Hutto, Murphy
Hutto, F.M
Hollman, J.H

Howard, Alex
Huckabee, Oliver
Joyner, William
Kirkland, E
Leach, R.P
Leach, Iseman
Lybrand, D.W
Lybrand, M.H
Lybrand, J.H
Lever, Jacob
Lecones, G.D
Miller, S.S
Miller, Thomas
Mathias, L.M
Mathias, J.B
Mack, J.F
Mack, H.L
Monts, George
Parr, Starkey
Pool, Isaac
Pool, Hiram
Reeves, J.C
Roof, Jesse M
Roof, Benjamin J
Roof, T.J
Roof, J.L
Roof, J.W
Roof, T.E
Roof, Martin
Roof, Jesse
Ramick, John
Rich, Michael
Roland, John
Sharp, Uriah
Sharp, P.M
Sharp, Lewie
Sharp, Barney
Sharp, J.D
Sharp, Jacob
Sharp, Reuben
Sharp, Calvin
Sharp, R
Sharp, D.J
Sharp, Emanuel
Sharp, Felix
Senn, R.N
Senn, W.B

Senn, Jacob
Stuart, Robert
Shull, H.W
Shull, D.E
Shull, R.W
Shull, H.M
Shull, John W
Roof, L
Shull, John
Shull, D.P
Shull, M.A
Shull, J.E
Smith, T.C
Sox, E.G
Sox, C.S
Sox, J.E
Sox, D.M
Sox, Jesse
Sightler, William A
Spraler, W.A
Spraler, E.C
Spraler, F
Spires, J.H
Spires, D
Spires, Amos
Spires, J.H
Spires, I.J
Spires, Andrew
Spires, Henry
Spires, W.A
Spires, James
Stuckey, C.R
Stuckey, D.C
Stuckey, Wesley
Schumpert, D.P
Schumpert, N.P
Taylor, J.F
Taylor, J.G
Taylor, James G
Taylor, B.J
Taylor, Andrew
Wilson, George A
Wilson, Henry
Wilson, William
Wilson, David
Williams, Sampson
Williams, T.J

Williams, T.D
Williams, F.E
Wise, James F
Wingard, Thomas A
Younce, George
Zenkee, William
Zenkee, John C.

COMPANY "I."

Captains:
Jones, J.M
Gunter, Elbert

Lieutenants:
Coleman, J.E
Gunter, M
Pitts, W.W
Gunter, Leroy
Gunter, D.B.

Sergeants:
Jones, N.T
Gunter, Zimri,
Gunter, Emanuel
Jones, John
Gunter, Levi
Gunter, Elliott
Gunter, W.C
Wise, John W.

Corporals:
Gunter, Mitchell
Abels, Pierce,
Garrin, Robert.

Privates:
Ables, Burk
Altman, James
Altman, Rufus
Altman, Ruben
Bennett, Tyler
Baggant, Freeman
Baggant, E.F
Brogdan, Jesse
Brogdan, M
Brogdan, William
Bryant, Mark
Burnett, Brazil

Burnett, D.P
Burnett, Willis
Burgess, Felix
Burgess, J.S
Braswell, George
Baltiziger, A
Blackwell, James
Burgess, N.J
Christmas, S.B
Creed, B.O
Cook, Chesley
Cook, Wyatt
Courtney, Young
Courtney, James
Fulmer, Adam
Fox, James H
Gunter, Drabel
Gunter, H.J
Gunter, Abel
Gunter, A.E
Gunter, Alfred
Gunter, Balaam
Gunter, Felix
Gunter, Joshua
Gunter, Lawson
Gunter, Macon
Gunter, Marshall,
Gunter, M.B
Gunter, Stancil
Gunter, V.A
Gunter, W.H
Gunter, William
Gunter, W.X
Gunter, Felix M
Gantt, E.M
Gantt, M.A
Gantt, William
Gantt, A.B
Garvin, C
Garvin, E.J
Garvin, J.C
Garvin, Larkin
Garvin, Wesly
Garvin, W.R
Gunter, Riely
Garvin, J.A
Gunter, Elridge

Hall, Jeremiah
Hall, Wayne
Heartly, Willis
Heartly, M
Heron, Abner
Heron, David
Huckabee, J.F
Huckabee, Joh
Hydrick, Emanuel
Hydrick, John
Hutto, W.B
Hall, J.C
Hall, J.T
Jernigan, L.W
Jones, L.C
Jones, Gideon
Jones, J.B
Jones, John P
Jones, Stanmore
Jones, W.B
Jones, N.B
Jones, Watson
Jackson, J.M
Jackson, J.P
Jones, Ezekiel
Kennedy, William,
Kennedy, Alex
Kirkling, E.S
Kirkling, G.W
Kirkling, Tillman
Kirkland, Hiram
Kneece, Jacob
Kennedy, Matthew
Kirkland, J.F
Mixon, D
Nobles, Ed
Pool, Elzy
Pool, J
Pool, Tillman
Pool, Elvin
Pool, John
Price, T
Rawls, Theodore
Rich, W.B
Richardson, Harrison
Richardson, W.B
Richardson, G.W

Rich, John
Sawyer, J.D
Sawyer, P.S
Sanders, John
Sanders, E
Starnes, Ezekiel
Starns, Wesly
Starns, Randy
Starns, John
Starns, Joshua
Storey, Wesly
Shelly, Melvin
Smith, I.B
Ward, A.G
Ward, John
Williams, G.W
Williams, Hiram
Williams, Rowland
Williams John
Williams, R.F
Williams, J.M
Wells, William
Wells, Thomas

COMPANY "K."

Captains:
Harman, W.D.M.

Lieutenants:
Haltiwonger, S.A
Harmon, T.S
Harmon, M.H
Seay, H
Harmon, F.J
Leaphart, J.E
Harmon, M.D.

Sergeants:
Sease, J.R.W
Quattlebaum, T.A.

Corporals:
Hendrix, J.E
Brown, S
Wingard, H
Earhart, J.W
Taylor, M.L

Rawl, E.A
Keisler, L
Wingard, J
Shealy, L.F.

Privates:
Alewine, J
Amick, J
Berry, J
Black, J.R
Blackwell, B
Boles, S.F
Bonenberger, P
Brown, J
Busby, P
Caughman, J.T
Caughman, L.W
Caughman, N.S
Caughman, H.J.W
Crout, L
Crout, J.T
Crout, W
Corley, E.L
Corley, L.W
Corley, S.A
Corley, W
Corley, W.A
Calk, W
Cook, W.L
Cook, W
Crapps, S
DeHart, A.H
Eargle, A.L
Eargle, F.P
Eargle, G.W
Fikes, J.A
Frey, J.W
Gross, A.H
Gregory, J
Gable, J.D
Gable, D.T
Gable, M.M
Hipps, W.S
Hite, J
Hicks, D
Hicks, R.J.A
Harmon, P.B
Harmon, G.W

Harmon, M.B
Harmon, G.M
Harmon, J.W
Harmon, J.A
Hartwell, J.J
Heyman, O
Hallman, M.L
Hallman, S.T
Hallman, E.R
Hallman, A.J
Hallman, E
Holeman, D
Hays, J.W.P
Hays, A.W.N
Hays, A.D.J
Hendrix, G.S
Hendrix, H.J
Hendrix, J.E
Hendrix, J.S
Hendrix, S.N
Hendrix, T.A
Hunt, J
Jackson, N.L
Jumper, H
Kyser, D
Kyser, J.I.B
Keisler, H
Keisler, S
Keisler, C.S
Keisler, D.F
Kaminer, W.P
Kaminer, J.M
Kaminer, J.A.W
King, E
Kistler, A.T
Kleckley, H.W
Kleckley, D.D
Kleckley, J.T
Kleckley, S
Kleckley, J.W
Lominack, D
Long, J.C
Long, J.A
Long, A.M
Long, J.H
Livingston, S
Lybrand, I.W

Lucas, M.H
Lewis, T.J
Harmon, L
Lewis, G.W
Leaphart, H.H
Miller, J
Mills, J.B
Meetze, G.A
Meetze, F.R
Mouts, S.P
Mouts, J.T
Mouts, J
Oswald, D
Price, W
Price, E.J
Price, I
Price, L
Quattlebaum, E.R
Rawl, B
Rawl, P.J
Rawl, J
Ranch, W.W
Ranch, C.S
Reeder, G.W
Reeder, J.W
Rich, ——
Roof, J.N
Roof, S.G
Roof, R
Satcher, S
Shealy, W.P
Shealy, U
Shealy, A
Shealy, J.J.B
Shealy, W.R
Shealy, N
Shealy, J.M
Shealy, P.W
Smith, J.W
Smith, A.J
See, J.B
See, D.E
Shirley, S.W
Snelgrove, C.P
Snelgrove, E.E
Steel, J
Steel, Z

Taylor, G.W
Taylor, J.W
Taylor, E
Taylor, W.C
Taylor, Z
Taylor, H
Taylor. H.W
Taylor, J.W
Taylor, J
Wingard, J.S
Wingard, T.J
Wingard, S
Wingard, G.W
Wingard, M
Wiggins, S.J.

COMPANY "L."

Captains:
Sparks, A.D
Bolton, C.P.

Lieutenants:
Peterkin, J.A
Kinney, W.F
Moore, A.E.

Sergeants:
Hodges, G
Emanuel, E.M
Walsh, W.W
Covington, J.T.

Corporals:
Manning, J
Rowe, A.J
Montgomery, J
Allen, E.

Privates:
Allen, J
Bridges, J.W
Bristow, J.D
Bristow, J.M
Bristow, R.N
Anderson, T.F
Bethea, J.W
Buzhart, J.T
Buchanan, J.A

Calder, W
Carter, W
Berry, D.F
Carrigan, W.A
Clark, R
Cope, E
Cottingham, J
Cowan, W.T
Coxe, R.A
Croley, D
Croley, R
Culler, C.W
David, A.L
DeBarry, E
Bridges, J.H
Bridges, S
Dunford, A.J
English, C
English, J
Evans, T.A
Fowler, W.D
Frasier, C
Frasier, W
Goss, H.L
Grice, E
Grice, J
Grice, T.S
Graham, W
Graham, Windsor
Graham, W
Havse, D
Hearsey, G.R
Holeman, E
Henegan, A.B
Henegan, S.A
Hubbard, J.G
Hodges, T.C
Hodges, W.L
Graham, J.J
Ivy, L
Jackson, J
Jackson, A
Jackson, O
Kendall, R.A
Lemaster, B.B
Lipscomb, E
Lipscomb, W.R

Manning, E
Manning, J.R
Moody, G.W
McCaskill, K
McCall, D
McCormie, A
McCall, C.S
McCall, J.D
McCall, L.H
McCall, P.R
McKee, J.A
McGee, A
McLeod, M
McAlister, J
McAlister, C
Mumford, W
Parham, I.H
Parham, H
Parham, H.A
Parham, W.H
Miles, G.W
Polson, C
Polson, J
Parish, J
Parish, H
Pearson, M
Pearson, P
Rascoe, W
McLane, G
McDaniel, J.R
McDaniel, W.W
Rodgers, H.J
Rowe, S.H
Cope, I.T
Byrd, J
Quick, A.W
Smith, H.B
Spears, H
Sports, G
Sports, J
Sturgis, J
Strickland, M
Stubbs, A.A
Stackhouse, W.R
Turner, I
Truwic, C.L
Ware, G

Wetherly, E
Wilkins, J
Willoughby, R
Willoughby, J.T
Woodle, J
Williams, S.V
Miller, P.A
Welch, H
Welch, T
Windham, R.E
Hinds, J
Hale, R.W
Wallace, G.T
Wallace, W
Webster, G.W
Webster, J
Wilson, M.R
Walsh, J.R
Wright, J.G
Watson, S
Watson, W
Wicker, J
Page, W.J
Lampley, J
Gay, J
Snead, L.P
Johns, P.M
Burlington, H
Stanton, J
Littlejohn, J
Murchison, R
Berry, F
Ivy, W.H
Hamer, J
Bethea, W.H
McLeod, B.F
McPearson, A
McPearson, M
Medling, J
Baggett, H
Conner, D
Conner, W
Covington, R
Covington, E
Covington, T
Proctor, C
Fletcher, J

Emanuel, J.M
Thomlinson, L
Thomlinson, J
Moore, B.P
Moore, T

Reese, J
Reese, John
Cottingham, A
Cottingham, J
Crabb, H.B

Leggett, A
Calhoun, J.C
Calhoun, H
Sparks, B.M.

ALSO FROM LEONAUR
AVAILABLE IN SOFTCOVER OR HARDCOVER WITH DUST JACKET

RGW1 RECOLLECTIONS OF THE GREAT WAR 1914 - 18
STEEL CHARIOTS IN THE DESERT *by S. C. Rolls*

The first world war experiences of a Rolls Royce armoured car driver with the Duke of Westminster in Libya and in Arabia with T.E. Lawrence.

SOFTCOVER : **ISBN 1-84677-005-X**
HARDCOVER : **ISBN 1-84677-019-X**

RGW2 RECOLLECTIONS OF THE GREAT WAR 1914 - 18
WITH THE IMPERIAL CAMEL CORPS IN THE GREAT WAR *by Geoffrey Inchbald*

The story of a serving officer with the British 2nd battalion against the Senussi and during the Palestine campaign.

SOFTCOVER : **ISBN 1-84677-007-6**
HARDCOVER : **ISBN 1-84677-012-2**

EW3 EYEWITNESS TO WAR SERIES
THE KHAKEE RESSALAH
by Robert Henry Wallace Dunlop

Service & adventure with the Meerut Volunteer Horse During the Indian Mutiny 1857-1858.

SOFTCOVER : **ISBN 1-84677-009-2**
HARDCOVER : **ISBN 1-84677-017-3**

WF1 THE WARFARE FICTION SERIES
NAPOLEONIC WAR STORIES
by Sir Arthur Quiller-Couch

Tales of soldiers, spies, battles & Sieges from the Peninsular & Waterloo campaigns

SOFTCOVER : **ISBN 1-84677-003-3**
HARDCOVER : **ISBN 1-84677-014-9**

AVAILABLE ONLINE AT
www.leonaur.com
AND OTHER GOOD BOOK STORES

ALSO FROM LEONAUR
AVAILABLE IN SOFTCOVER OR HARDCOVER WITH DUST JACKET

EW2 EYEWITNESS TO WAR SERIES
CAPTAIN OF THE 95th (Rifles) by Jonathan Leach

An officer of Wellington's Sharpshooters during the Peninsular, South of France and Waterloo Campaigns of the Napoleonic Wars.

SOFTCOVER : ISBN 1-84677-001-7
HARDCOVER : ISBN 1-84677-016-5

EW6 EYEWITNESS TO WAR SERIES
BUGLER & OFFICER OF THE RIFLES
by William Green & Harry Smith

With the 95th (Rifles) During the Peninsular & Waterloo Campaigns of the Napoleonic Wars.

SOFTCOVER : ISBN 1-84677-020-3
HARDCOVER : ISBN 1-84677-032-7

EW1 EYEWITNESS TO WAR SERIES
RIFLEMAN COSTELLO by Edward Costello

The adventures of a soldier of the 95th (Rifles) in the Peninsular & Waterloo Campaigns of the Napoleonic wars.

SOFTCOVER : ISBN 1-84677-000-9
HARDCOVER : ISBN 1-84677-018-1

MC1 THE MILITARY COMMANDERS SERIES
JOURNALS OF ROBERT ROGERS OF THE RANGERS by Robert Rogers

The exploits of Rogers & the Rangers in his own words during 1755-1761 in the French & Indian War.

SOFTCOVER : ISBN 1-84677-002-5
HARDCOVER : ISBN 1-84677-010-6

AVAILABLE ONLINE AT
www.leonaur.com
AND OTHER GOOD BOOK STORES

CLASSIC SF FROM LEONAUR
AVAILABLE IN SOFTCOVER OR HARDCOVER WITH DUST JACKET

SF1 CLASSIC SCIENCE FICTION SERIES
BEFORE ADAM & Other Stories
by Jack London

Volume 1 of The Collected Science Fiction & Fantasy of Jack London.
SOFTCOVER : **ISBN 1-84677-008-4**
HARDCOVER : **ISBN 1-84677-015-7**

Contains the complete novel Before Adam plus shorter works: The Scarlet Plague, A Relic of the Pliocene, When the World Was Young, The Red One, Planchette, A Thousand Deaths, Goliah, A Curious Fragment and The Rejuvenation of Major Rathbone

SF2 CLASSIC SCIENCE FICTION SERIES
THE IRON HEEL & Other Stories
by Jack London

Volume 2 of The Collected Science Fiction & Fantasy of Jack London.
SOFTCOVER : **ISBN 1-84677-004-1**
HARDCOVER : **ISBN 1-84677-011-4**

Contains the complete novel The Iron Heel plus shorter works: The Enemy of All the World, The Shadow and the Flash, The Strength of the Strong, The Unparalleled Invasion and The Dream of Debs

SF3 CLASSIC SCIENCE FICTION SERIES
THE STAR ROVER & Other Stories
by Jack London

Volume 3 of The Collected Science Fiction & Fantasy of Jack London.
SOFTCOVER : **ISBN 1-84677-006-8**
HARDCOVER : **ISBN 1-84677-013-0**

Contains the complete novel The Star Rover plus shorter works: The Minions of Midas, The Eternity of Forms and The Man With the Gash

AVAILABLE ONLINE AT
www.leonaur.com
AND OTHER GOOD BOOK STORES

www.ingramcontent.com/pod-product-compliance
Lightning Source LLC
Chambersburg PA
CBHW031618160426
43196CB00006B/190